INSIDER'S GUIDE

TO GRADUATE PROGRAMS
IN EDUCATION

INSIDER'S GUIDE

TO GRADUATE PROGRAMS IN EDUCATION

MARK J. DROZDOWSKI

PATRICK CULLEN

Allyn and Bacon
Boston • London • Toronto • Sydney • Tokyo • Singapore

Copyright © 1997 by Allyn & Bacon
A Viacom Company
160 Gould Street
Needham Heights, MA 02194

Internet: www.abacon.com
America Online: Keyword: College Online

ISBN: 0-205-19511-3

Printed in the United States of America

10 9 8 7 6 5 4 3 2 1   02 01 00 99 98 97

Data assembled 1995–1996.

CONTENTS

INTRODUCTION

Visit your local bookstore and examine the reference shelf. You will see a dozen or more guides to colleges and graduate schools, each, of course, claiming to be the definitive source. Many focus solely on the undergraduate level, while others target various graduate and professional disciplines: law, medicine and dentistry, engineering, business, architecture, film, and even culinary arts. Conspicuously absent from this list is education.

The exclusion of graduate schools of education (or "ed" schools, as they commonly are called) from this list is, indeed, a glaring omission. Judging by the numbers, education is the most popular graduate course of study in America. In a recent year, ed schools and departments enrolled 303,000 of the 1,851,000 students pursuing graduate degrees in the United States—by far the largest total among graduate disciplines. Yet for all this popularity and demand, there was no comprehensive guidebook to this field until now.

The *Insider's Guide to Graduate Programs in Education* was borne out of the authors' and their colleagues' experiences applying to and attending schools of education. Our friends in college who contemplated law or medical schools had a number of books to help them make informed decisions about where to apply and what to expect at each institution. Those of us interested in education, on the other hand, had to rely on more general guides to graduate schools and on materials distributed by the schools themselves. No singular comprehensive source existed. We knew it was time for ed schools and prospective students to have a guidebook of their own.

This book results from inquiries to more than one thousand deans and faculty members across the country. We aimed to be as inclusive as possible; we wanted to profile more than the top ten or twenty schools and departments, however defined. In many cases, we conducted follow-up calls for additional information. The colleges and universities in this book include some of the nation's most prestigious institutions as well as those education schools and departments enrolling the largest number of graduate students. Chances are, you'll find the schools you're looking for and choose the one most suited to your needs.

The *Insider's Guide to Graduate Programs in Education* has been designed in an easy-to-read format, allowing readers to find the information they desire quickly. We've included facts and figures on tuition and financial aid, courses and programs, faculty specialties, student demographics, technology resources, research units, and career paths of graduates. The last section of the book contains addresses of state boards of education; you should contact the appropriate agency to determine what you need to become certified or licensed.

IS GRADUATE SCHOOL FOR YOU?

Deciding to attend graduate school is among the most important career choices you'll make. Consider your options carefully. Graduate school can be the most challenging, rewarding and sometimes bewildering experience of your life. If you're lucky, your college will have prepared you well for the rigors you'll face in graduate school, but you will find that your undergraduate years have little in common with your graduate years. Certainly, both involve taking courses, writing papers, and interacting with peers. Yet the graduate experience is more intense. You'll have smaller classes and closer contact with professors. Above all, graduate school is self-directed. Students—especially doctoral candidates—do not merely plod through a number of sequential courses and amass a certain number of credits before graduating. They choose courses that fit their career aspirations, work with professors who share their interests, and complete master's theses, qualifying papers, proposals, oral exams, a dissertation and its defense. In short, a graduate student cannot simply float down the river with the current; he or she must power and steer the boat.

The profiles of ed schools in the next section will help you make an informed choice, but here we first offer some general guidelines.

1) *A smart student does not attend graduate school by default.* If you're graduating college and cannot think of a suitable career, you probably should not go on to graduate or professional school right away. Finishing the arduous and often lonely journey of graduate school requires an enormous amount of desire. You must love your field and know that it's what you want to pursue. Take a year or two to work, in any field, and explore your options. Some doctoral programs prefer their candidates to have worked and often will not consider an applicant who has not. Choosing to attend graduate school is as much a question of when as it is of where.

2) *Consider your financial resources and your impending investment.* Graduate schools offer a wide array of aid packages and options, from tuition remission to teaching assistantships to government and institutional loans. Talk with financial aid officers to find out what percentage of students receive scholarships and what is the average loan amount. Loans are easy to obtain, but may require serious sacrifice in the future. You might also consider attending school part-time while working part- or full-time. If you are interested in this option, determine if your prospective schools allow it.

3) *Make your choice based on the strength of the school or department, not the reputation of the college or university as a whole.* Many top universities have weak departments, while some institutions with regional reputations may excel in particular disciplines. Don't assume or rule out quality based on a name.

4) *Think about your ultimate goal.* Do you want, or need, a doctorate? If so, you should consider applying to schools offering doctoral programs, not just terminal master's programs. Universities often do not award scholarship aid to master's degree candidates.

5) *Be sure that an institution has a critical mass of faculty in your interest area, especially if you'll be a doctoral student.* Think twice about pinning your decision on one faculty member; if you do, be sure he or she is tenured and not near retirement. Nothing is more distressing than having your advisor depart halfway through your dissertation phase.

6) *Investigate whether or not a school offers the teacher certification or counseling licensure you desire.* If a school you're interested in doesn't offer the certification or licensure you seek, this should not preclude you from attending. Just keep in mind that you'll have to take an extra step following graduation.

7) *Remember that you'll be part of a college or university community.* Check out available extracurricular activities on campus, the town and neighboring areas where students live, off-campus employment and internship opportunities, sports facilities, museums and theaters, restaurants, malls and so on. Don't forget that graduate students, contrary to conventional wisdom, do have lives outside the classrooms and libraries.

If you've decided that it's time to attend graduate school, you'll have to do some homework about the schools in which you're interested. The *Insider's Guide* is an excellent source for starters, but you'll want to order catalogues from your prospective schools for more information about particular programs and faculty. Most colleges and universities also maintain home pages on the World Wide Web, often putting their catalogues online. Some even make applications available for downloading. If it is feasible, visit these institutions to talk with students and faculty and examine the physical facilities. A catalogue cannot give a true feeling for a school. While there, drop by the financial aid and placement offices as well as the admissions office.

Applying to graduate school is time-consuming, frustrating, and often expensive. These few tips should help. Once you have the application forms, check the submission deadlines. If the school operates on a rolling admissions basis and admits applicants one at time until all seats are filled, submit your application as early as possible; this increases your chances significantly. Be sure you've taken the required standardized tests and make arrangements to have your scores forwarded to the school(s). Most ed schools require the Graduate Record Exam (GRE) general test—which measures verbal, quantitative and analytic abilities—and/or the Miller Analogy Test (MAT), a series of verbal analogies designed to test reasoning abilities. Letters of recommendation (typically three) are required of applicants. Choose professors or supervisors most familiar with you and your work. Generic letters stating that you work hard and have a pleasant personality won't help your cause. After you have distributed recommendation forms, keep track of them. You don't want a professor's procrastination to result in your missing a deadline. Finally, when it comes to the personal statement, use the opportunity to convey something not otherwise evident in the application. Don't simply put your resume into prose; describe some interest or aspect of your life that demonstrates your individuality and evidences your suitability for graduate study in your chosen field.

THE PECULIAR NATURE OF ED SCHOOLS

If you're reading this book, then you are at least considering the study of education. Graduate schools and departments of education are among the most diversified, and therefore most confusing, academic units on campus.

What's more, their content and focus vary from one university to the next, so it's difficult to generalize. The students who attend this country's more than 1,200 ed schools and departments reflect this diversity, in terms of both interests and backgrounds. Are you a college senior contemplating a career in teaching? An experienced teacher thinking about moving into the administrative ranks? A mid-career professional looking for a change? A retired military officer seeking a second career? Or a social worker hoping to become a licensed counselor? Chances are ed school is for you; the task remains to find the right one.

The field of education includes a wide range of subject matter, focusing on the development of individuals from birth to adulthood. Comprehensive schools of education offer a wide array of courses in numerous subfields. The following list of these fields is not exhaustive but demonstrates this diversity:

Adult Education
Art Education
Bilingual Education
Computer Education
Counselor Education
Curriculum and Instruction
Early Childhood Education
English as a Second Language
Educational Administration
Educational Psychology
Education of the Gifted and Talented
Elementary Education
Higher Education
History of Education
Measurement and Evaluation
Multicultural Education
Music Education
Philosophy of Education
Reading
Secondary Education
Social Science Education
Sociology of Education
Special Education
Vocational and Technical Education

Along with these various subfields are numerous degree options. Master's degree programs come in many forms. The Master of Arts (M. A.) and Master of Science (M. S.) degrees, generally completed in one or two years, often have a research focus and might require a master's thesis. The Master of Education (M. Ed. and Ed.M), which also involves one or two years, is geared more for future administrators, although many teachers and researchers earn this degree. The Master of Arts in Teaching (M. A. T.) usually combines the study of teaching (pedagogy) with a specific content area (e.g. biology, mathematics, or history) and leads to certification or licensure at the elementary or secondary level. The Master of Science in Teaching (M. S. T.) has a similar purpose. Those with a master's degree can take additional courses toward a Certificate of Advanced Graduate Studies (C. A. G. S. or often just C. A. S.) to advance their career.

Doctoral students typically have two options: the Doctor of Philosophy (Ph.D. or D. Phil.) and the Doctor of Education (Ed.D. or D. Ed.) degrees. The differences here are open to much interpretation and are a source of continual debate. Essentially, the Ph.D. track prepares students to be college faculty and researchers, while the Ed.D. is geared more for school and college administrators, or practitioners. The Ph.D. always requires a dissertation, while the Ed.D. student can sometimes complete an internship, or practicum, and an analytic paper in place of the dissertation. When an ed school offers both options, this normally constitutes the difference. Some schools offer only one doctoral degree option. In such cases, the curriculum includes both research and practical courses to suit students' interests. Harvard, for example, offers only the Ed.D., but turns out university faculty as well as school superintendents.

As difficult as it is to generalize about ed school curricula and degree options, it is even harder to generalize about teacher certification or licensure. States differ widely as to particular requirements, so prospective students should inquire about their own state's guidelines. What's more, certification requirements change often, so be sure your information is current. Don't take word-of-mouth advice; request information from your state's department or board of education.

Certification is required to teach in public schools but not in private schools. In most cases, a state will offer two levels of certification: elementary (kindergarten through sixth grade) and secondary (seventh through twelfth grade). Any form of provisional certification allows an individual to teach in a probationary status for a specified number of years. Permanent certification enables a teacher to obtain tenure and teach indefinitely.

Counseling licensure also varies from one state to another. Again, examine your state's requirements. Students pursuing careers as counseling psychologists complete clinical internships while in graduate school and, upon completing their studies, sit for state-administered licensure examinations. Graduates practice in settings such as colleges, clinic, hospitals, and community agencies.

While investigating these degree options and certification or licensure requirements, look for programs that have been accredited by regional or national agencies. Accreditation helps to ensure quality, holding schools or programs to minimum standards of excellence. Individual programs within ed schools can be accredited even though the school itself is not. For various reasons not necessarily involving quality, however, some top programs are not accredited by the National Council for Accreditation of Teacher Education (NCATE), the largest such body. In fact, NCATE accredits only about 500 of the approximately 1,200 schools and departments of education nationwide.

Whatever school you choose, whatever discipline you study, and whatever degree option you pursue, you'll likely find your experience unlike any other. Ed schools, more than any other unit on campus, attract a student body diverse in age, backgrounds, interests and aspirations. In general, these students are among the oldest on campus. While ranging from their early twenties—straight out of college—to their fifties and sixties, the average age is in the mid-thirties. Many have been or are teachers, but not all. Others are studying to become licensed counselors, principals and superintendents, professors and administrators, consultants and executives. A significant number also will become nurses and other health professionals. At research universities, ed schools attract a large percentage of international students, adding new perspectives to how we view our educational system. In short, you'll meet and interact with a fascinating mix of peers and learn more about yourself in the process.

CURRENT ISSUES AND TRENDS

"Ed schools are in trouble. They are in a state of flux, looking for direction, and have less contact with practitioners than other professional schools. Too often they act as ivory towers."

Strong words from Arthur Levine, president of Teachers College at Columbia University, the nation's oldest, largest, and possibly best-known school of education. Yet his comments echo a common sentiment among education experts. Our nation's schools of education, they say, have not lived up to their potential to improve elementary and secondary education. What's more, ed schools too often shoulder the blame for the poor condition of America's schools. They are viewed as part of the problem, says Levine, not as a solution.

"The biggest challenge facing the teaching profession is coping with the multiple problems and issues of our society that affect children and youth," says James Cooper, former dean at the University of Virginia's Curry School of Education. According to Cooper, the effects of poverty, drugs and alcohol, violence in and around schools, teenage pregnancy, limited English proficiency, cultural diversity, single-parent households, the dominant influence of television, and part-time jobs that divert students' attention and efforts conspire to render the teacher's job of educating all but impossible.

"Today's teachers, administrators, counselors and school psychologists," Cooper told the *Insider's Guide*, "are challenged by many societal factors that impact children and make the teaching and learning process much more difficult than ever before."

Underlying these warnings, however, is a strong sense of optimism among these leading educators. They universally support the notion that ed schools can be, and in some cases are, powerful forces of change. "I truly believe that there are forces out there that will continue to improve schools of education," says Robert Peterkin, director of Harvard's Urban Superintendents Program.

"Schools of education are trying to . . . be aware of how these social factors affect children's learning," says Cooper, "and to provide safe and supportive school and classroom environments in which children can develop their minds and character."

"As a whole, ed schools have a bad reputation," admits Jerome Murphy, dean at Harvard's Graduate School of Education, "but they are better than that reputation. We create new ideas and put them into action, combining theory and practice to solve real-world problems."

This synergy of theory and practice, with one informing the other, is critical to effective reform. In this sense, ed school faculty and practicing teachers have much to learn from each other as they pursue a common goal: to improve teaching and learning at all levels.

"The melding of theory and practice," Cooper says, "coupled with reflection and analysis, are key characteristics of good schools of education."

The challenge, especially in research universities, is to encourage faculty to assume the dual role of researcher and practitioner, or "scholar–reformer," according to Murphy. As Cooper attests, education faculty are members of two cultures—that of the university and that of the schools. "This dual emphasis places challenges upon education faculty members that are not shared by many other faculties in the university," he says.

Under Levine's leadership and vision, Teachers College has undertaken ambitious restructuring that could hold implications for ed schools nationwide. Teachers College's articulated goals are to research critical issues; to educate the next generation of leaders; to educate current leaders such as school officials, legislators, the press and corporate and foundation officers; to help shape the national debate and form an agenda for educational reform; and to improve practice. In many ways, Levine's vision captures the essence of what schools of education hope to accomplish in the next century: widespread and systemic change.

"The next few years will see grassroots reform," Levine predicts, "changing education classroom by classroom. There are many different efforts, all competing to see what works."

LARGE-SCALE REFORM

While innovative reform initiatives abound, few have national impact. Three that command special attention are the Holmes Partnership, the National Network for Educational Renewal, and the Coalition of Essential Schools.

Holmes Partnership

Named for a former dean at Harvard, the Holmes Partnership began as the Holmes Group, based at Michigan State University. The Group was formed in 1986 as a consortium of leading schools of education across the nation. Its members have taken a critical view of teacher preparation, recommending changes in preservice and inservice training. One hallmark of these suggested reforms is the Professional Development School (PDS), along the lines of a teaching hospital affiliated with a medical school. There, education faculty, ed students, teachers, and their pupils, would continually reinvigorate teaching and learning, blending the theoretical with the practical in a classroom laboratory.

Ten years after its creation, the Holmes Group has metamorphosed into the Holmes Partnership and moved to the University of Delaware. Members now include research universities, public school districts and professional organization representing educators such as the National Education Association (NEA) and the American Federation of Teachers (AFT). Its philosophy still centers on the PDS, with education faculty acting as both researchers and clinical practitioners. The new charge of the Holmes Partnership also calls for reform measures aimed at the curriculum, the sci-

ence of pedagogy and student recruitment, and still stresses that teacher education be grounded in the liberal arts and include opportunities for internships in the schools.

Coalition of Essential Schools

At Brown University, Theodore Sizer leads the Coalition of Essential Schools, which also began its second decade in 1996. The network has grown to encompass 930 schools in 37 states. Like the Holmes Partnership, the Coalition stresses university-school collaboration to meld research with field-tested experience. While the Coalition focuses on implementation, the affiliated Annenberg Institute for School Reform, also at Brown, concentrates on research and professional development. The Institute—named for the benefactor, Walter Annenberg, whose $50 million grant sustains it—has been run by Sizer since its creation in 1993. It functions as a grant-making entity for reform projects with which it collaborates. The Coalition and the Institute obviously overlap in many respects but maintain autonomy.

Center for Educational Renewal

On the opposite coast resides another wide-spread and influential reform unit. The Center for Educational Renewal, based at the University of Washington and run by professor John Goodlad, a former UCLA dean, has created a National Network stretching from Maine to South Carolina to Hawaii. The consortium involves 25 universities, 93 school districts and 266 partner schools across fourteen states. Its philosophy is "the simultaneous renewal of schools and the education of educators," a key component of which is collaboration between education and arts and sciences faculty to provide future teachers with a solid general education curriculum. The Institute for Educational Inquiry, also run by Washington's Goodlad, works in concert with the Center, conducting research and training educational leaders. The Institute's impressive list of publications constitutes a blueprint for meaningful and effective reform.

Amidst all of these programs, one thing remains clear: nothing is sacred and inviolable. Everything about our classrooms is subject to modification. As a result, this is an especially exciting and rewarding time to embark on a career in education. Creative individuals will find numerous opportunities to help redefine and reshape what we know as the educational process. We at the *Insider's Guide* are confident that this and the next generation of educators are equal to the task.

ALABAMA

Auburn University College of Education

Graduate School, Hargis Hall, Auburn, AL 36849
Admissions: (PH)334 844-4470, (FAX)334 844-4348
Dean: (PH)334 844-4446, (FAX)334 844-5785,
(EMAIL)gorrett@mail.auburn.edu
Total Enrollment: 20,000
Grad Enrollment: FTM 50, PTM 200, FTD 42, PTD 297
Program Membership: Holmes Partnership
Academic Programs Available: MASTERS: Adult Ed.,
Counselor Ed., Early Childhood Ed., Ed. Admin, Ed. Psych.,
Ed. Tech., Elementary Ed., Foreign Lang. Ed., Higher Ed.,
Math Ed., Mid Level Ed., Music Ed., Physical Ed.,
Read/Lang Arts Ed., School Cons., Sci. Ed., Sec. Ed., Soc.
Ed., Spec. Ed. DOCTORATE: Adult Ed., Counselor Ed., Early
Childhood Ed., Ed. Admin, Ed. Psych., Ed. Tech.,
Elementary Ed., Foreign Lang. Ed., Higher Ed., Math Ed.,
Mid Level Ed., Music Ed., Physical Ed., Read/Lang Arts Ed.,
School Cons., Sci. Ed., Sec. Ed., Soc. Ed., Spec. Ed.
Library: Ralph B. Draughon Library, 2 million volumes
Computer Resources: Macintosh, Dual Platform, PCs,
CD-ROM, Videodisc

Research Areas	#Faculty
Adult Education	2
Art Education	
Bilingual Education	
Counselor Education	5
Early Childhood Ed.	3
Ed. Admin	4
Ed. Tech.	4
Elementary Ed.	8
Foreign Lang. Ed.	1
Higher Ed.	2
Math Ed.	2
Mid. Lev. Ed.	4
Multicultural Ed.	1
Music Ed.	2
Physical Ed.	8
Read/Lang. Arts Ed.	3
School Counseling	4
Science Ed.	3
Secondary Ed.	3
Soc. Studies Ed.	2
Special Ed.	5
Other	

Research Institutes/Centers: Truman Pierce Institute
Student Body Demographics: Average Age 28, 67% female,
33% male
Percent Ethnic Minorities: Hispanic-American 1%,
Asian-American 2%, African-American 11%,
Native-American 1%
Geographic Representation: New England 1%,
Midwest 2%, Mid Atlantic 1%, Southwest 2%, West 1%,
Southeast 90%, Northwest 1%
Graduate Career Paths: K-12 Teaching 44%, School
Counseling 4%, K-12 Special Ed 14%, School

Administration 10%, Higher Ed Administration 5%, Higher
Ed Counseling 1%, Community Counseling 2%
Tuition: 2,250 (in state), 6,750 (out of state)
Financial Aid Recipients: N/A
Average Annual Housing Cost: 2,700
Application Deadline: variable
Number of: applicants annually 411; applicants accepted
annually 236; students enrolled annually 153

Tests Required	Preferred/Min Score
Graduate Record Exam	800–1,100
National Teachers Exam	
Praxis II Exam	
TOEFL	550

Tuskegee University School of Education

Office of Admissions, Old Administration Building,
Tuskegee, AL 36088
Admissions: (PH)334 727-8500
Dean: (PH)334 727-8570, (FAX)334 727-8271
Total Enrollment: 1,000–5,000
Grad Enrollment: FTM 25, PTM 5, On campus 97%, Off
campus 3%
Program Membership: N/A
Academic Programs Available: MASTERS: Counselor Ed.,
Ed. Admin, DOCTORATE: Counselor Ed., Ed. Admin
Library: Hollis Burke Frissell Library, 300,000 volumes
Computer Resources: Macintosh, Dual Platform, PCs,
CD-ROM, Videodisc

Research Areas	#Faculty
Adult Education	
Art Education	
Bilingual Education	
Counselor Education	3
Early Childhood Ed.	
Ed. Admin	
Ed. Tech.	
Elementary Ed.	
Foreign Lang. Ed.	
Higher Ed.	
Math Ed.	
Mid. Lev. Ed.	
Multicultural Ed.	
Music Ed.	
Physical Ed.	
Read/Lang. Arts Ed.	
School Counseling	3
Science Ed.	
Secondary Ed.	
Soc. Studies Ed.	
Special Ed.	
Other	

Student Body Demographics: Average Age 25, 60% female,
40% male
Percent Ethnic Minorities: African-American 98%
Geographic Representation: N/A
Graduate Career Paths: K-12 School Counseling 2%, Higher
Ed Counseling 98%
Tuition: 6,000 (in state), 6,000 (out of state)
Financial Aid Recipients: 99%

Average Annual Housing Cost: 1,900
Application Deadline: rolling
Number of: applicants annually 25-30; applicants accepted annually 10-15; students enrolled annually N/A

Tests Required	Preferred/Min Score
Graduate Record Exam	
National Teachers Exam	
Praxis II Exam	

University of Alabama College of Education

Box 870108, Tuscaloosa, AL 35487-0108
Admissions: (PH)205 348-5666, (FAX)205 348-9046
Dean: (PH)205 348-6050, (FAX)205 348-6873
Total Enrollment: 10,000–20,000
Grad Enrollment: FTM 40, PTM 500, FTD 50, PTD 200, On campus 5%, Off campus 95%
Program Membership: Holmes Partnership
Academic Programs Available: MASTERS: Art Ed., Bilingual Ed., Counselor Ed., Early Childhood Ed., Ed. Admin, Ed. Psych., Elementary Ed., Foreign Lang. Ed., Higher Ed., Math Ed., Music Ed., Physical Ed., Read/Lang Arts Ed., School Cons., Sci. Ed., Sec. Ed., Soc. Ed., Spec. Ed. DOCTORATE: Art Ed., Bilingual Ed., Counselor Ed., Early Childhood Ed., Ed. Admin, Ed. Psych., Elementary Ed., Foreign Lang. Ed., Higher Ed., Math Ed., Music Ed., Physical Ed., Read/Lang Arts Ed., School Cons., Sci. Ed., Sec. Ed., Soc. Ed., Spec. Ed.
Library: N/A

Research Areas	#Faculty
Adult Education	
Art Education	
Bilingual Education	1
Counselor Education	5
Early Childhood Ed.	5
Ed. Admin	4
Ed. Tech.	4
Elementary Ed.	5
Foreign Lang. Ed.	1
Higher Ed.	2
Math Ed.	1
Mid. Lev. Ed.	
Multicultural Ed.	
Music Ed.	2
Physical Ed.	5
Read/Lang. Arts Ed.	3
School Counseling	5
Science Ed.	1
Secondary Ed.	1
Soc. Studies Ed.	2
Special Ed.	8
Other	

Student Body Demographics: Average Age 26, 70% female, 30% male
Percent Ethnic Minorities: Asian-American 1%, African-American 10%
Geographic Representation: Southeast 95%
Graduate Career Paths: K-12 Teaching 60%, Higher Ed Teaching 5%, School Counseling 5%, K-12 Special Ed 5%,

School Administration 15%, Higher Ed Administration 5%, Higher Ed Counseling 2%, Community Counseling 3%
Tuition: 1,130 (in state), 2,821 (out of state)
Financial Aid Recipients: 10%
Average Annual Housing Cost: 2,700
Application Deadline: N/A
Number of: applicants annually N/A; applicants accepted annually N/A; students enrolled annually N/A

Tests Required	Preferred/Min Score
Graduate Record Exam	1,000
National Teachers Exam	
Praxis II Exam	

University of Montevallo College of Education

Station 6350, Montevallo, AL 35115
Admissions: (PH)205 665-6350, (FAX)205 665-6353
Dean: (PH)205 665-6360, (FAX)205 665-6353
Total Enrollment: 1,000–5,000
Grad Enrollment: OTHER 387 CAS, On campus 1%, Off campus 99%
Program Membership: N/A
Academic Programs Available: MASTERS: Counselor Ed., Early Childhood Ed., Ed. Admin, Elementary Ed., Music Ed., Physical Ed., Sec. Ed., Soc. Ed., DOCTORATE: Counselor Ed., Early Childhood Ed., Ed. Admin, Elementary Ed., Music Ed., Physical Ed., Sec. Ed., Soc. Ed.
Library: Carmichael Library
Computer Resources: Macintosh, Dual Platform, PCs, CD-ROM, Videodisc

Research Areas	#Faculty
Adult Education	
Art Education	
Bilingual Education	
Counselor Education	5
Early Childhood Ed.	2
Ed. Admin	2
Ed. Tech.	2
Elementary Ed.	2
Foreign Lang. Ed.	
Higher Ed.	
Math Ed.	
Mid. Lev. Ed.	
Multicultural Ed.	
Music Ed.	2
Physical Ed.	
Read/Lang. Arts Ed.	
School Counseling	1
Science Ed.	
Secondary Ed.	
Soc. Studies Ed.	
Special Ed.	
Other	

Student Body Demographics: Average Age 30, 75% female, 25% male
Percent Ethnic Minorities: African-American 8%
Geographic Representation: N/A
Tuition: 84 (in state), 168 (out of state)
Financial Aid Recipients: 40%

Average Annual Housing Cost: 3,122
Application Deadline: 7/15; 11/15; 4/15
Number of: applicants annually 250; applicants accepted annually 235; students enrolled annually 200

Tests Required	Preferred/Min Score
Graduate Record Exam	
National Teachers Exam	850
Praxis II Exam	
TOEFL	550

University of North Alabama
School of Education
Florence, AL 35632
Admissions: (PH)205 760-4221
Grad Enrollment: 420 total
Program Membership: N/A
Academic Programs Available: MASTERS: Counselor Ed., Early Childhood Ed., Elementary Ed., Sec. Ed., Spec. Ed. DOCTORATE: Counselor Ed., Early Childhood Ed., Elementary Ed., Sec. Ed., Spec. Ed.
Library: N/A

Research Areas	#Faculty
Adult Education	
Art Education	
Bilingual Education	
Counselor Education	
Early Childhood Ed.	
Ed. Admin	
Ed. Tech.	
Elementary Ed.	
Foreign Lang. Ed.	
Higher Ed.	
Math Ed.	
Mid. Lev. Ed.	
Multicultural Ed.	
Music Ed.	
Physical Ed.	
Read/Lang. Arts Ed.	
School Counseling	
Science Ed.	
Secondary Ed.	
Soc. Studies Ed.	
Special Ed.	
Other	

Student Body Demographics: N/A
Percent Ethnic Minorities: N/A
Geographic Representation: N/A
Tuition: 1,896 (in state), 3,162 (out of state)
Financial Aid Recipients: N/A
Average Annual Housing Cost: N/A
Application Deadline: 4/1
Number of: applicants annually N/A; applicants accepted annually N/A; students enrolled annually N/A

Tests Required	Preferred/Min Score
Graduate Record Exam	
National Teachers Exam	
Praxis II Exam	

University of South Alabama
College of Education
AD 182, Mobile, AL 36695
Admissions: (PH)334 460-6141
Dean: (PH)334 460-6205, (FAX)334 460-7830
Total Enrollment: 10,000–20,000
Grad Enrollment: On campus 1%, Off campus 99%
Program Membership: Holmes Partnership
Academic Programs Available: MASTERS: Art Ed., Counselor Ed., Early Childhood Ed., Ed. Admin, Ed. Tech., Elementary Ed., Foreign Lang. Ed., Math Ed., Mid Level Ed., Music Ed., Physical Ed., Read/Lang Arts Ed., School Cons., Sci. Ed., Sec. Ed., Soc. Ed., Spec. Ed. DOCTORATE: Art Ed., Counselor Ed., Early Childhood Ed., Ed. Admin, Ed. Tech., Elementary Ed., Foreign Lang. Ed., Math Ed., Mid Level Ed., Music Ed., Physical Ed., Read/Lang Arts Ed., School Cons., Sci. Ed., Sec. Ed., Soc. Ed., Spec. Ed.
Library: 3 million volumes
Computer Resources: Macintosh, Dual Platform, PCs, CD-ROM, Videodisc

Research Areas	#Faculty
Adult Education	
Art Education	
Bilingual Education	
Counselor Education	
Early Childhood Ed.	
Ed. Admin	
Ed. Tech.	
Elementary Ed.	
Foreign Lang. Ed.	
Higher Ed.	
Math Ed.	
Mid. Lev. Ed.	
Multicultural Ed.	
Music Ed.	
Physical Ed.	
Read/Lang. Arts Ed.	
School Counseling	
Science Ed.	
Secondary Ed.	
Soc. Studies Ed.	
Special Ed.	
Other	

Student Body Demographics: N/A
Percent Ethnic Minorities: N/A
Geographic Representation: N/A
Tuition: 610 (in state), 935 (out of state)
Financial Aid Recipients: N/A
Average Annual Housing Cost: N/A
Application Deadline: varies
Number of: applicants annually N/A; applicants accepted annually N/A; students enrolled annually N/A

Tests Required	Preferred/Min Score
Graduate Record Exam	
National Teachers Exam	
Praxis II Exam	
TOEFL	525

ARIZONA

National Teachers Exam	1000
Praxis II Exam	
Spec. Ed. Spec. Ed.	

Arizona State University College of Education

Graduate College, P.O. Box 871003, Tempe, AZ 85287-1003
Admissions: (PH)602 965-6113,
(EMAIL)icfeb@asuvm.inre.asu.edu
Dean: (PH)602 965-1328, (FAX)602 965-9144
Grad Enrollment: FTM 522, PTM 565, FTD 265, PTD 245, On campus 2%, Off campus 98%
Program Membership: Holmes Partnership
Academic Programs Available: MASTERS: Counselor Ed., Ed. Admin, Ed. Psych., Ed. Tech., Elementary Ed., Higher Ed., Sec. Ed., DOCTORATE: Counselor Ed., Ed. Admin, Ed. Psych., Ed. Tech., Elementary Ed., Higher Ed., Sec. Ed.
Library: Hayden Library, 1.8 million volumes
Computer Resources: Macintosh, Dual Platform, PCs, CD-ROM, Videodisc

Research Areas	#Faculty
Adult Education	
Art Education	
Bilingual Education	
Counselor Education	5
Early Childhood Ed.	5
Ed. Admin	8
Ed. Tech.	12
Elementary Ed.	10
Foreign Lang. Ed.	
Higher Ed.	4
Math Ed.	
Mid. Lev. Ed.	
Multicultural Ed.	7
Music Ed.	
Physical Ed.	
Read/Lang. Arts Ed.	8
School Counseling	4
Science Ed.	
Secondary Ed.	
Soc. Studies Ed.	
Special Ed.	9
Other	11

Research Institutes/Centers: Center for Bilingual/Bicultural Education, Center for Indian Education
Student Body Demographics: Average Age 33, 73% female, 27% male
Percent Ethnic Minorities: Hispanic-American 12%, Asian-American 2%, African-American 2%, Native-American 1%
Geographic Representation: New England 1%, Midwest 4%, Southwest 85%, West 9%, Northwest 1%
Tuition: 975 (in state), 3989 (out of state)
Financial Aid Recipients: 60%
Average Annual Housing Cost: 3,100
Application Deadline: varies
Number of: applicants annually 900; applicants accepted annually 272; students enrolled annually 257

Tests Required	Preferred/Min Score
Graduate Record Exam	

Arizona State University West College of Education

P.O. Box 37100, Phoenix, AZ 85069-7100
Admissions: (PH)602 543-6378, (FAX)602 543-6350, (EMAIL)ihrxb@asuacad
Dean: (PH)602 543-6300, (FAX)602 543-6350, (EMAIL)ihrxb@asucad
Total Enrollment: 1,000–5,000
Grad Enrollment: PTM 150, Off campus 100%
Program Membership: N/A
Academic Programs Available: MASTERS: Bilingual Ed., Early Childhood Ed., Ed. Admin, Ed. Tech., Elementary Ed., Read/Lang Arts Ed., Sec. Ed., DOCTORATE: Bilingual Ed., Early Childhood Ed., Ed. Admin, Ed. Tech., Elementary Ed., Read/Lang Arts Ed., Sec. Ed.
Library: Fletcher Library, 150,000 volumes
Computer Resources: Macintosh, Dual Platform, PCs, CD-ROM, Videodisc

Research Areas	#Faculty
Adult Education	
Art Education	
Bilingual Education	3
Counselor Education	
Early Childhood Ed.	4
Ed. Admin	3
Ed. Tech.	2
Elementary Ed.	10
Foreign Lang. Ed.	
Higher Ed.	
Math Ed.	2
Mid. Lev. Ed.	1
Multicultural Ed.	1
Music Ed.	1
Physical Ed.	
Read/Lang. Arts Ed.	4
School Counseling	
Science Ed.	3
Secondary Ed.	3
Soc. Studies Ed.	1
Special Ed.	4
Other	3

Student Body Demographics: Average Age 29, 67% female, 33% male
Percent Ethnic Minorities: Hispanic-American 8%, Asian-American 2%, African-American 2%, Native-American 1%
Geographic Representation: Southwest 100%
Graduate Career Paths: K-12 Teaching 67%, K-12 School Administration 33%
Tuition: 99/hr (in state), 310/hr (out of state)
Financial Aid Recipients: 8%
Average Annual Housing Cost: 5,500
Application Deadline: none
Number of: applicants annually 200; applicants accepted annually 160; students enrolled annually 155

Tests Required	Preferred/Min Score
Graduate Record Exam	
National Teachers Exam	900
Praxis II Exam	

University of Arizona College of Education

Tucson, AZ 85721
Dean: (PH)520 621-1462, (FAX)520 621-9271
Program Membership: Holmes Partnership
Academic Programs Available: MASTERS: Bilingual Ed., Ed. Admin, Ed. Psych., Elementary Ed., Higher Ed., Math Ed., Read/Lang Arts Ed., Sci. Ed., Sec. Ed., Soc. Ed., Spec. Ed. DOCTORATE: Ed. Admin, Ed. Psych., Elementary Ed., Higher Ed., Math Ed., Sci. Ed., Sec. Ed., Soc. Ed., Spec. Ed.
Library: N/A
Computer Resources: Macintosh, Dual Platform, PCs, CD-ROM, Videodisc

Research Areas	#Faculty
Adult Education	
Art Education	
Bilingual Education	9
Counselor Education	
Early Childhood Ed.	4
Ed. Admin	1
Ed. Tech.	5
Elementary Ed.	15
Foreign Lang. Ed.	
Higher Ed.	5
Math Ed.	2
Mid. Lev. Ed.	3
Multicultural Ed.	18
Music Ed.	
Physical Ed.	
Read/Lang. Arts Ed.	5
School Counseling	
Science Ed.	2
Secondary Ed.	2
Soc. Studies Ed.	3
Special Ed.	25
Other	

Research Institutes/Centers: Center for the Study of Higher Education
Student Body Demographics: N/A
Percent Ethnic Minorities: N/A
Geographic Representation: N/A
Tuition: 975 (in state), 3,003 (out of state)
Financial Aid Recipients: N/A
Average Annual Housing Cost: 2,000
Number of: applicants annually N/A, applicants accepted annually N/A, students N/A

Tests Required	Preferred/Min Score
Graduate Record Exam	
National Teachers Exam	
Praxis II Exam	
TOEFL	550

ARKANSAS

Arkansas State University
College of Education

P.O. Box 1630, State University, AR 72467
Admissions: (PH)501 972-3024, (FAX)501 972-3843
Dean: (PH)501 972-3057, (FAX)501 972-3828
Total Enrollment: 5,000–10,000
Grad Enrollment: FTM 44, PTM 289, FTD 12, PTD 21, On campus 3%, Off campus 97%
Program Membership: N/A
Academic Programs Available: MASTERS: Counselor Ed., Early Childhood Ed., Ed. Admin, Elementary Ed., Math Ed., Music Ed., Physical Ed., Read/Lang Arts Ed., School Cons., Sci. Ed., Soc. Ed., Spec. Ed. DOCTORATE: Ed. Admin
Library: Dean B. Ellis Library, 1.3 million volumes
Computer Resources: PCs, CD-ROM

Research Areas	#Faculty
Adult Education	1
Art Education	
Bilingual Education	
Counselor Education	4
Early Childhood Ed.	3
Ed. Admin	10
Ed. Tech.	
Elementary Ed.	5
Foreign Lang. Ed.	
Higher Ed.	
Math Ed.	
Mid. Lev. Ed.	
Multicultural Ed.	
Music Ed.	
Physical Ed.	6
Read/Lang. Arts Ed.	2
School Counseling	
Science Ed.	
Secondary Ed.	
Soc. Studies Ed.	
Special Ed.	3
Other	

Student Body Demographics: Average Age 34, 63.9% female, 36.1% male
Percent Ethnic Minorities: Hispanic-American 0.4%, Asian-American 6.4%, African-American 6.7%, Native-American 0.3%
Geographic Representation: N/A
Tuition: 1,170 (in state), 1,990 (out of state)
Financial Aid Recipients: N/A
Average Annual Housing Cost: N/A
Number of: applicants annually N/A; applicants accepted annually N/A; students enrolled annually N/A

Tests Required	Preferred/Min Score
Graduate Record Exam	
National Teachers Exam	800
Praxis II Exam	
TOEFL	550

Henderson State University
School of Education

1,100 Henderson Street, Arkadelphia, AR 71999-0001
Admissions: (PH)501 230-5126, (FAX)501 230-5144
Dean: (PH)501 230-5367
Total Enrollment: 1,000–5,000
Grad Enrollment: On campus 1%, Off campus 99%
Program Membership: N/A
Academic Programs Available: MASTERS: Art Ed., Ed. Admin, Elementary Ed., Math Ed., Physical Ed., School Cons., Sci. Ed., Soc. Ed., Spec. Ed. DOCTORATE: Art Ed., Ed. Admin, Elementary Ed., Math Ed., Physical Ed., School Cons., Sci. Ed., Soc. Ed., Spec. Ed.
Library: Huie Library, 250,000 volumes
Computer Resources: Macintosh, Dual Platform, PCs, CD-ROM, Videodisc

Research Areas	#Faculty
Adult Education	
Art Education	4
Bilingual Education	
Counselor Education	
Early Childhood Ed.	
Ed. Admin	3
Ed. Tech.	
Elementary Ed.	7
Foreign Lang. Ed.	
Higher Ed.	
Math Ed.	6
Mid. Lev. Ed.	
Multicultural Ed.	
Music Ed.	
Physical Ed.	8
Read/Lang. Arts Ed.	
School Counseling	3
Science Ed.	8
Secondary Ed.	8
Soc. Studies Ed.	12
Special Ed.	3
Other	8

Student Body Demographics: Average Age 35, 70% female, 30% male
Percent Ethnic Minorities: African-American 8%
Geographic Representation: Southwest 100%
Graduate Career Paths: K-12 Teaching 45%, School Counseling 13%, K-12 Special Ed 16%, School Administration 26%
Tuition: 98/hr (in state), 196/hr (out of state)
Financial Aid Recipients: 35%
Average Annual Housing Cost: 3,000
Application Deadline: 6/15; 12/15; 5/15
Number of: applicants annually N/A; applicants accepted annually N/A; students enrolled annually 250

Tests Required	Preferred/Min Score
Graduate Record Exam	
National Teachers Exam	
Praxis II Exam	
TOEFL	550

University of Arkansas College of Education

119 Ozark Hall, Fayetteville, AR 72701
Admissions: (PH)501 575-5346, (FAX)501 575-7780
Dean: (PH)501 575-3208, (FAX)501 575-3119, (EMAIL)mfratzke@uafsysb.uark.edu
Total Enrollment: 10,000–20,000
Grad Enrollment: FTM 683, FTD 218, On campus 12%, Off campus 88%
Program Membership: Holmes Partnership
Academic Programs Available: MASTERS: Adult Ed., Counselor Ed., Early Childhood Ed., Ed. Admin, Ed. Tech., Elementary Ed., Higher Ed., Math Ed., Mid Level Ed., Music Ed., Physical Ed., Read/Lang Arts Ed., School Cons., Sci. Ed., Sec. Ed., Soc. Ed., Spec. Ed. DOCTORATE: Adult Ed., Counselor Ed., Early Childhood Ed., Ed. Admin, Ed. Tech., Elementary Ed., Higher Ed., Math Ed., Mid Level Ed., Music Ed., Physical Ed., School Cons., Sci. Ed., Sec. Ed., Soc.
Library: Mullins Library
Computer Resources: Macintosh, Dual Platform, PCs, CD-ROM, Videodisc

Research Areas	#Faculty
Adult Education	3
Art Education	
Bilingual Education	1
Counselor Education	5
Early Childhood Ed.	4
Ed. Admin	4
Ed. Tech.	3
Elementary Ed.	6
Foreign Lang. Ed.	1
Higher Ed.	2
Math Ed.	2
Mid. Lev. Ed.	3
Multicultural Ed.	2
Music Ed.	4
Physical Ed.	10
Read/Lang. Arts Ed.	3
School Counseling	5
Science Ed.	4
Secondary Ed.	4
Soc. Studies Ed.	2
Special Ed.	5
Other	

Research Institutes/Centers: Center for Middle Level Education, Center for Educational Technology
Student Body Demographics: Average Age 32, 67% female, 33% male
Percent Ethnic Minorities: Hispanic-American 2%, Asian-American 1%, African-American 5%, Native-American 2%
Geographic Representation: New England 10%, Midwest 20%, Southwest 40%, West 10%, Southeast 10%, Northwest 10%
Graduate Career Paths: K-12 Teaching 16%, Higher Ed Teaching 5%, School Counseling 6%, K-12 Special Ed 4%, School Administration 10%, Higher Ed Administration 2%, Higher Ed Counseling 4%, Community Counseling 3%
Tuition: 131/hr (in state), 300/hr (out of state)
Financial Aid Recipients: 4%

Average Annual Housing Cost: 4,800
Application Deadline: 3/15; 6/15; 9/15
Number of: applicants annually 375; applicants accepted annually 290; students enrolled annually N/A

Tests Required	Preferred/Min Score
Graduate Record Exam	1000
National Teachers Exam	
Praxis II Exam	
TOEFL	550

University of Central Arkansas
College of Education

Adm. 120, 201 Donaghey, Conway, AR 72035
Admissions: (PH)501 450-3124
Dean: (PH)501 450-3175, (FAX)501 450-5358
Total Enrollment: 5,000–10,000
Grad Enrollment: FTM 103, PTM 310
Program Membership: N/A
Academic Programs Available: MASTERS: Early Childhood Ed., Ed. Admin, Elementary Ed., Foreign Lang. Ed., Math Ed., Music Ed., Physical Ed., Read/Lang Arts Ed., School Cons., Sci. Ed., Spec. Ed. DOCTORATE: Early Childhood Ed., Ed. Admin, Elementary Ed., Foreign Lang. Ed., Math Ed., Music Ed., Physical Ed., Read/Lang Arts Ed., School Cons., Sci. Ed., Spec. Ed.
Library: Torreyson Library, 373,000 volumes
Computer Resources: Macintosh, Dual Platform, PCs, CD-ROM, Videodisc

Research Areas	#Faculty
Adult Education	
Art Education	
Bilingual Education	
Counselor Education	
Early Childhood Ed.	
Ed. Admin	
Ed. Tech.	
Elementary Ed.	
Foreign Lang. Ed.	
Higher Ed.	
Math Ed.	
Mid. Lev. Ed.	
Multicultural Ed.	
Music Ed.	
Physical Ed.	
Read/Lang. Arts Ed.	
School Counseling	
Science Ed.	
Secondary Ed.	
Soc. Studies Ed.	
Special Ed.	
Other	

Student Body Demographics: Average Age 32, 78% female, 22% male
Percent Ethnic Minorities: African-American 5%, Native-American 1%
Geographic Representation: N/A
Tuition: 96/hr (in state), 192/hr (out of state)
Financial Aid Recipients: N/A
Average Annual Housing Cost: N/A
Application Deadline: 3/1; 10/1

Number of: applicants annually N/A; applicants accepted annually N/A; students enrolled annually N/A

Tests Required	Preferred/Min Score
Graduate Record Exam	
National Teachers Exam	750
Praxis II Exam	

CALIFORNIA

California State University,
San Bernardino School of Education

San Bernardino, CA 92407
Admissions: (PH)909 880-5600, (FAX)909 880-7011
Grad Enrollment: 374 total
Program Membership: N/A
Academic Programs Available: MASTERS: Bilingual Ed., Counselor Ed., Ed. Admin, Elementary Ed., Read/Lang Arts Ed., Sec. Ed., DOCTORATE: Bilingual Ed., Counselor Ed., Ed. Admin, Elementary Ed., Read/Lang Arts Ed., Sec. Ed.
Library: N/A

Research Areas	#Faculty
Adult Education	
Art Education	
Bilingual Education	
Counselor Education	
Early Childhood Ed.	
Ed. Admin	
Ed. Tech.	
Elementary Ed.	
Foreign Lang. Ed.	
Higher Ed.	
Math Ed.	
Mid. Lev. Ed.	
Multicultural Ed.	
Music Ed.	
Physical Ed.	
Read/Lang. Arts Ed.	
School Counseling	
Science Ed.	
Secondary Ed.	
Soc. Studies Ed.	
Special Ed.	
Other	

Student Body Demographics: N/A
Percent Ethnic Minorities: N/A
Geographic Representation: N/A
Tuition: 1,896 (in state), N/A (out of state)
Financial Aid Recipients: N/A
Number of: applicants annually 125; applicants accepted annually 85; students enrolled annually N/A

Tests Required	Preferred/Min Score
Graduate Record Exam	
National Teachers Exam	
Praxis II Exam	

California State Polytechnic University, Pomona School of Education

3801 West Temple Avenue, Pomona, CA 91768
Admissions: (PH)909 869-2000, (FAX)909 869-4386
Dean: (PH)909 869-2307, (FAX)909 869-4747
Total Enrollment: 20,000
Grad Enrollment: PTM 200, On campus 5%, Off campus 95%
Program Membership: N/A
Academic Programs Available: MASTERS: Bilingual Ed., Ed. Tech., Read/Lang Arts Ed., Spec. Ed. DOCTORATE: Bilingual Ed., Ed. Tech., Read/Lang Arts Ed., Spec. Ed.
Library: Cal Poly Library, 600,000 volumes
Computer Resources: Macintosh, Dual Platform, PCs, CD-ROM, Videodisc

Research Areas	#Faculty
Adult Education	
Art Education	
Bilingual Education	2
Counselor Education	
Early Childhood Ed.	
Ed. Admin	
Ed. Tech.	
Elementary Ed.	5
Foreign Lang. Ed.	
Higher Ed.	
Math Ed.	2
Mid. Lev. Ed.	5
Multicultural Ed.	
Music Ed.	
Physical Ed.	
Read/Lang. Arts Ed.	4
School Counseling	
Science Ed.	2
Secondary Ed.	2
Soc. Studies Ed.	2
Special Ed.	2
Other	

Student Body Demographics: Average Age 24, 60% female, 40% male
Percent Ethnic Minorities: Hispanic-American 10%, Asian-American 10%, African-American 5%, Native-American 2%
Geographic Representation: West 100%
Graduate Career Paths: K-12 Teaching 80%, K-12 Special Ed 20%
Tuition: N/A (in state), N/A (out of state)
Financial Aid Recipients: 10%
Average Annual Housing Cost: N/A
Application Deadline: varies
Number of: applicants annually 150; applicants accepted annually 150; students enrolled annually N/A

Tests Required	Preferred/Min Score
Graduate Record Exam	800
National Teachers Exam	
Praxis II Exam	

California State University, Stanislaus School of Education

801 W. Monte Vista Avenue, Turlock, CA 95382
Admissions: (PH)209 667-3152
Dean: (PH)209 667-3145
Total Enrollment: 5,000–10,000
Grad Enrollment: PTM 149, On campus 4%, Off campus 96%
Program Membership: N/A
Academic Programs Available: MASTERS: Bilingual Ed., Ed. Admin, Elementary Ed., Physical Ed., Read/Lang Arts Ed., School Cons., Sec. Ed., Spec. Ed. DOCTORATE: Bilingual Ed., Ed. Admin, Elementary Ed., Physical Ed., Read/Lang Arts Ed., School Cons., Sec. Ed., Spec. Ed.
Library: N/A
Computer Resources: Macintosh, Dual Platform, PCs, CD-ROM, Videodisc

Research Areas	#Faculty
Adult Education	
Art Education	
Bilingual Education	3
Counselor Education	2
Early Childhood Ed.	
Ed. Admin	5
Ed. Tech.	
Elementary Ed.	7
Foreign Lang. Ed.	
Higher Ed.	
Math Ed.	
Mid. Lev. Ed.	
Multicultural Ed.	3
Music Ed.	
Physical Ed.	9
Read/Lang. Arts Ed.	2
School Counseling	2
Science Ed.	1
Secondary Ed.	1
Soc. Studies Ed.	
Special Ed.	2
Other	

Student Body Demographics: Average Age 35, 66% female, 34% male
Percent Ethnic Minorities: Hispanic-American 11%, Asian-American 7%, African-American 2%, Native-American 1%
Geographic Representation: West 97%
Tuition: N/A (in state), N/A (out of state)
Financial Aid Recipients: N/A
Average Annual Housing Cost: N/A
Application Deadline: N/A
Number of: applicants annually N/A; applicants accepted annually N/A; students enrolled annually N/A

Tests Required	Preferred/Min Score
Graduate Record Exam	
National Teachers Exam	
Praxis II Exam	

California State University, Sacramento School of Education

6000 J Street, Admission and Records, Sacramento, CA 95819-6048

Admissions: (PH)916 278-3901, (FAX)916 278-5603
Dean: (PH)916 278-6639, (FAX)916 278-5904
Total Enrollment: 20,000
Grad Enrollment: FTM 350, PTM 2400, On campus 5%, Off campus 95%
Program Membership: Holmes Partnership
Academic Programs Available: MASTERS: Bilingual Ed., Counselor Ed., Early Childhood Ed., Ed. Admin, Multicultural Ed., School Cons., Spec. Ed. DOCTORATE: Bilingual Ed., Counselor Ed., Early Childhood Ed., Ed. Admin, Multicultural Ed., School Cons., Spec. Ed.
Library: CSUS Library, 1 million volumes
Computer Resources: Macintosh, Dual Platform, PCs, CD-ROM, Videodisc

Research Areas	#Faculty
Adult Education	3
Art Education	
Bilingual Education	12
Counselor Education	30
Early Childhood Ed.	10
Ed. Admin	15
Ed. Tech.	10
Elementary Ed.	26
Foreign Lang. Ed.	
Higher Ed.	4
Math Ed.	5
Mid. Lev. Ed.	12
Multicultural Ed.	10
Music Ed.	
Physical Ed.	
Read/Lang. Arts Ed.	12
School Counseling	8
Science Ed.	4
Secondary Ed.	4
Soc. Studies Ed.	6
Special Ed.	23
Other	

Student Body Demographics: Average Age N/A, 80% female, 20% male
Percent Ethnic Minorities: Hispanic-American 15%, Asian-American 12%, African-American 5%, Native-American 0.1%
Geographic Representation: Midwest 2%, Southwest 4%, West 90%, Southeast 2%, Northwest 2%
Graduate Career Paths: K-12 Teaching 55%, Higher Ed Teaching 5%, School Counseling 5%, K-12 Special Ed 25%, School Administration 10%
Tuition: 936 (in state), 246 (out of state)
Financial Aid Recipients: 20%
Average Annual Housing Cost: 4,000
Application Deadline: 9/1; 7/1
Number of: applicants annually 900; applicants accepted annually 850; students enrolled annually N/A

Tests Required	Preferred/Min Score
Graduate Record Exam	
National Teachers Exam	
Praxis II Exam	

California State University, Dominguez Hills School of Education

1000 East Victoria Street, Carson, CA 90747

Admissions: (PH)310 516-3524
Dean: (PH)310 516-3524, (FAX)310 516-3518
Total Enrollment: 5,000–10,000
Grad Enrollment: FTM 120, PTM 470
Program Membership: N/A
Academic Programs Available: MASTERS: Bilingual Ed., Counselor Ed., Ed. Admin, Ed. Tech., Multicultural Ed., School Cons., Spec. DOCTORATE: Bilingual Ed., Counselor Ed., Ed. Admin, Ed. Tech., Multicultural Ed., School Cons., Spec.
Library: N/A
Computer Resources: Macintosh, Dual Platform, PCs, CD-ROM, Videodisc

Research Areas	#Faculty
Adult Education	
Art Education	
Bilingual Education	
Counselor Education	
Early Childhood Ed.	
Ed. Admin	3
Ed. Tech.	2
Elementary Ed.	
Foreign Lang. Ed.	
Higher Ed.	
Math Ed.	
Mid. Lev. Ed.	
Multicultural Ed.	2
Music Ed.	
Physical Ed.	
Read/Lang. Arts Ed.	
School Counseling	3
Science Ed.	
Secondary Ed.	
Soc. Studies Ed.	
Special Ed.	3
Other	3

Student Body Demographics: Average Age 27, 74% female, 26% male
Percent Ethnic Minorities: Hispanic-American 19.5%, Asian-American 6.4%, African-American 20.3%, Native-American 1%
Geographic Representation: N/A
Tuition: N/A (in state), N/A (out of state)
Financial Aid Recipients: N/A
Average Annual Housing Cost: N/A
Number of: applicants annually 204; applicants accepted annually 163; students enrolled annually 95

Tests Required	Preferred/Min Score
Graduate Record Exam	
National Teachers Exam	
Praxis II Exam	
Ed. Ed.	

College of Notre Dame Education Department

Graduate School, 1500 Ralston Ave., Belmont, CA 94010
Admissions: (PH)415 508-3527, (FAX)415 508-3736, (EMAIL)barbara@cnd.edu
Dean: (PH)415 508-3523, (FAX)415 508-3736, (EMAIL)ecohen@cnd.edu
Total Enrollment: 1,000–5,000
Grad Enrollment: FTM 5, PTM 45, CAS 1605, Off campus 100%
Program Membership: N/A
Academic Programs Available: MASTERS: Ed. Admin, Multicultural Ed., Sec. Ed., DOCTORATE: Ed. Admin, Multicultural Ed., Sec. Ed.
Library: College Library, 100,000 volumes
Computer Resources: Macintosh, Dual Platform, PCs, CD-ROM, Videodisc

Research Areas	#Faculty
Adult Education	
Art Education	
Bilingual Education	
Counselor Education	
Early Childhood Ed.	
Ed. Admin	4
Ed. Tech.	
Elementary Ed.	10
Foreign Lang. Ed.	
Higher Ed.	
Math Ed.	
Mid. Lev. Ed.	
Multicultural Ed.	4
Music Ed.	
Physical Ed.	
Read/Lang. Arts Ed.	
School Counseling	
Science Ed.	
Secondary Ed.	
Soc. Studies Ed.	
Special Ed.	
Other	

Student Body Demographics: Average Age 34, 70% female, 30% male
Percent Ethnic Minorities: Hispanic-American 7%, Asian-American 5%, African-American 3%, Native-American 1%
Geographic Representation: West 100%
Graduate Career Paths: K-12 Teaching 91%, K-12 School Administration 9%
Tuition: 12,000 (in state), 12000 (out of state)
Financial Aid Recipients: 34%
Average Annual Housing Cost: 5,000
Application Deadline: 8/1; 12/1; 4/1
Number of: applicants annually 770; applicants accepted annually 477; students enrolled annually 347

Tests Required	Preferred/Min Score
Graduate Record Exam	
National Teachers Exam	
Praxis II Exam	

Dominican College of San Rafael School of Education

50 Acacia Avenue, Bertrand #22, San Rafael, CA 94901
Admissions: (PH)415 485-3287, (FAX)415 485-3205
Dean: (PH)415 485-3287, (EMAIL)kaufman@dominican.edu
Total Enrollment: 1,000–5,000
Grad Enrollment: FTM 140, PTM 12, Off campus 100%
Program Membership: N/A
Academic Programs Available: MASTERS: Elementary Ed., Multicultural Ed., Sec. Ed., DOCTORATE: Elementary Ed., Multicultural Ed., Sec. Ed.
Library: Archbishop Alemany Library, 95,000 volumes
Computer Resources: Macintosh, Dual Platform, PCs, CD-ROM, Videodisc

Research Areas	#Faculty
Adult Education	
Art Education	
Bilingual Education	1
Counselor Education	
Early Childhood Ed.	
Ed. Admin	
Ed. Tech.	
Elementary Ed.	5
Foreign Lang. Ed.	
Higher Ed.	
Math Ed.	
Mid. Lev. Ed.	1
Multicultural Ed.	2
Music Ed.	
Physical Ed.	
Read/Lang. Arts Ed.	
School Counseling	
Science Ed.	1
Secondary Ed.	1
Soc. Studies Ed.	
Special Ed.	
Other	

Research Institutes/Centers: Institute for Global Education
Student Body Demographics: Average Age 32, 92% female, 8% male
Percent Ethnic Minorities: N/A
Geographic Representation: West 100%
Graduate Career Paths: K-12 Teaching 100%
Tuition: N/A (in state), N/A (out of state)
Financial Aid Recipients: 65%
Average Annual Housing Cost: N/A
Application Deadline: 5/30
Number of: applicants annually 180; applicants accepted annually 135; students enrolled annually 135

Tests Required	Preferred/Min Score
Graduate Record Exam	
National Teachers Exam	
Praxis II Exam	

John F. Kennedy University
Education Department

School of Liberal Arts, 12 Altarinda Road, Orinda, CA 94563
Admissions: (PH)510 253-2212
Dean: (PH)510 253-4352, (FAX)510 254-6964
Total Enrollment: 1,000–5,000
Grad Enrollment: FTM 20, PTM 10
Program Membership: N/A
Academic Programs Available: MASTERS: Ed. Psych.,
Multicultural Ed., DOCTORATE: Ed. Psych.,
Multicultural Ed.
Library: Robert M. Fisher Library
Computer Resources: PCs

Research Areas	#Faculty
Adult Education	
Art Education	
Bilingual Education	
Counselor Education	1
Early Childhood Ed.	1
Ed. Admin	
Ed. Tech.	
Elementary Ed.	
Foreign Lang. Ed.	
Higher Ed.	
Math Ed.	
Mid. Lev. Ed.	
Multicultural Ed.	1
Music Ed.	
Physical Ed.	1
Read/Lang. Arts Ed.	1
School Counseling	
Science Ed.	
Secondary Ed.	
Soc. Studies Ed.	1
Special Ed.	
Other	1

Research Institutes/Centers: Center for the Study of Parent
Involvement
Student Body Demographics: Average Age 35, 75% female,
25% male
Percent Ethnic Minorities: Hispanic-American 10%,
Asian-American 15%, African-American 15%
Geographic Representation: West 100%
Graduate Career Paths: K-12 Teaching 100%
Tuition: 237/unit (in state), 237/unit (out of state)
Financial Aid Recipients: 50%
Average Annual Housing Cost: N/A
Application Deadline: varies
Number of: applicants annually N/A; applicants accepted
annually N/A; students enrolled annually N/A

Tests Required	Preferred/Min Score
Graduate Record Exam	
National Teachers Exam	
Praxis II Exam	

Pepperdine University
Graduate School of Education

400 Corporate Pointe, Culver City, CA 90230
Admissions: (PH)310 568-5636, (FAX)310 568-5755
Dean: (PH)310 568-5615, (FAX)310 568-5755,
(EMAIL)nfagan@pepperdine.edu
Total Enrollment: 5,000–10,000
Grad Enrollment: FTM 200, PTM 100, FTD 200, PTD 30,
CAS 70, Off campus 100%
Program Membership: N/A
Academic Programs Available: MASTERS: Early
Childhood Ed., Ed. Admin, Ed. Psych., Ed. Tech.,
Elementary Ed., Higher Ed., Multicultural Ed., Sec. Ed.,
DOCTORATE: Early Childhood Ed., Ed. Admin, Ed. Psych.,
Ed. Tech., Elementary Ed., Higher Ed., Multicultural Ed.,
Sec. Ed.
Library: Pepperdine University Plaza Library
Computer Resources: Macintosh, Dual Platform, PCs,
CD-ROM, Videodisc

Research Areas	#Faculty
Adult Education	
Art Education	
Bilingual Education	
Counselor Education	
Early Childhood Ed.	
Ed. Admin	5
Ed. Tech.	
Elementary Ed.	
Foreign Lang. Ed.	
Higher Ed.	
Math Ed.	
Mid. Lev. Ed.	
Multicultural Ed.	
Music Ed.	
Physical Ed.	
Read/Lang. Arts Ed.	
School Counseling	
Science Ed.	
Secondary Ed.	
Soc. Studies Ed.	
Special Ed.	
Other	

Student Body Demographics: Average Age 28, 66% female,
34% male
Percent Ethnic Minorities: Hispanic-American 10%,
Asian-American 9%, African-American 9%
Geographic Representation: Southwest 5%, West 90%,
Northwest 5%
Graduate Career Paths: K-12 School Administration 20%
Tuition: N/A (in state), N/A (out of state)
Financial Aid Recipients: 90%
Average Annual Housing Cost: N/A
Application Deadline: 7/1; 11/1; 3/1
Number of: applicants annually N/A; applicants accepted
annually N/A; students enrolled annually N/A

Tests Required	Preferred/Min Score
Graduate Record Exam	
National Teachers Exam	
Praxis II Exam	
TOEFL	600

Point Loma Nazarene College Graduate Education Department

3900 Lomaland Drive, San Diego, CA 92106
Admissions: (PH)619 221-2418, (FAX)619 221-2647
Dean: (PH)619 221-2358, (FAX)619 221-2647
Total Enrollment: 1,000–5,000
Grad Enrollment: FTM 135, PTM 55, Off campus 100%
Program Membership: N/A
Academic Programs Available: MASTERS: Bilingual Ed., Counselor Ed., Ed. Admin, Elementary Ed., Multicultural Ed., School Cons., Sec. Ed., Spec. Ed. DOCTORATE: Bilingual Ed., Counselor Ed., Ed. Admin, Elementary Ed., Multicultural Ed., School Cons., Sec. Ed., Spec. Ed.
Library: Ryan Library
Computer Resources: Macintosh, Dual Platform, PCs, CD-ROM, Videodisc

Research Areas	#Faculty
Adult Education	
Art Education	
Bilingual Education	
Counselor Education	1
Early Childhood Ed.	
Ed. Admin	2
Ed. Tech.	1
Elementary Ed.	3
Foreign Lang. Ed.	
Higher Ed.	
Math Ed.	
Mid. Lev. Ed.	1
Multicultural Ed.	1
Music Ed.	
Physical Ed.	
Read/Lang. Arts Ed.	
School Counseling	1
Science Ed.	
Secondary Ed.	
Soc. Studies Ed.	
Special Ed.	1
Other	

Student Body Demographics: Average Age 40, 77% female, 23% male
Percent Ethnic Minorities: N/A
Geographic Representation: Southwest 99%
Tuition: 391 (in state), N/A (out of state)
Financial Aid Recipients: 50%
Average Annual Housing Cost: N/A
Application Deadline: 9/1; 1/2; 5/10
Number of: applicants annually 200; applicants accepted annually 140; students enrolled annually N/A

Tests Required	Preferred/Min Score
Graduate Record Exam	800–900
National Teachers Exam	
Praxis II Exam	
TOEFL	550

San Francisco State University
College of Education

San Francisco, CA 94132
Admissions: (PH)415 338-2051
Grad Enrollment: 622 total
Program Membership: Holmes Partnership
Academic Programs Available: MASTERS: Adult Ed., Early Childhood Ed., Ed. Admin, Ed. Tech., Elementary Ed., Sec. Ed., Spec. Ed. DOCTORATE: Adult Ed., Early Childhood Ed., Ed. Admin, Ed. Tech., Elementary Ed., Sec. Ed., Spec. Ed.
Library: N/A

Research Areas	#Faculty
Adult Education	
Art Education	
Bilingual Education	
Counselor Education	
Early Childhood Ed.	
Ed. Admin	
Ed. Tech.	
Elementary Ed.	
Foreign Lang. Ed.	
Higher Ed.	
Math Ed.	
Mid. Lev. Ed.	
Multicultural Ed.	
Music Ed.	
Physical Ed.	
Read/Lang. Arts Ed.	
School Counseling	
Science Ed.	
Secondary Ed.	
Soc. Studies Ed.	
Special Ed.	
Other	

Student Body Demographics: N/A
Percent Ethnic Minorities: N/A
Geographic Representation: N/A
Tuition: 1,982 (in state), 1,982 (out of state)
Financial Aid Recipients: N/A
Average Annual Housing Cost: N/A
Application Deadline: 11/30
Number of: applicants annually N/A; applicants accepted annually N/A; students enrolled annually N/A

Tests Required	Preferred/Min Score
Graduate Record Exam	
National Teachers Exam	
Praxis II Exam	

San Jose State University
College of Education

WC 168, San Jose, CA 95192
Admissions: (PH)408 924-2000
Dean: (PH)408 924-3600, (FAX)408 924-3713
Total Enrollment: 20,000
Grad Enrollment: FTM 2,704, PTM 3,017, Off campus 100%
Program Membership: Holmes Partnership
Academic Programs Available: MASTERS: Art Ed., Bilingual Ed., Counselor Ed., Early Childhood Ed., Ed.

Admin, Ed. Psych., Ed. Tech., Elementary Ed., Foreign Lang. Ed., Math Ed., Mid Level Ed., Music Ed., Physical Ed., Read/Lang Arts Ed., School Cons., Sci. Ed., Sec. Ed., Soc. Ed., Spec. Ed. DOCTORATE: Art Ed., Bilingual Ed., Counselor Ed., Early Childhood Ed., Ed. Admin, Ed. Psych., Ed. Tech., Elementary Ed., Foreign Lang. Ed., Math Ed., Mid Level Ed., Music Ed., Physical Ed., Read/Lang Arts Ed., School Cons., Sci. Ed., Sec. Ed., Soc. Ed., Spec. Ed.

Library: Clark Library, 55,000 volumes
Computer Resources: Macintosh, Dual Platform, PCs, CD-ROM, Videodisc

Research Areas	#Faculty
Adult Education	
Art Education	
Bilingual Education	11
Counselor Education	10
Early Childhood Ed.	7
Ed. Admin	6
Ed. Tech.	7
Elementary Ed.	37
Foreign Lang. Ed.	
Higher Ed.	
Math Ed.	2
Mid. Lev. Ed.	
Multicultural Ed.	
Music Ed.	
Physical Ed.	
Read/Lang. Arts Ed.	5
School Counseling	
Science Ed.	3
Secondary Ed.	3
Soc. Studies Ed.	
Special Ed.	29
Other	11

Research Institutes/Centers: Institute for Educational Research and Development, Center for Educational Research on Dyslexia
Student Body Demographics: Average Age N/A, 67% female, 33% male
Percent Ethnic Minorities: Hispanic-American 15%, Asian-American 20%, African-American 5%, Native-American 1%
Geographic Representation: N/A
Graduate Career Paths: K-12 Teaching 50%, School Counseling 5%, K-12 Special Ed 15%, School Administration 10%, Higher Ed Counseling 5%, Community Counseling 5%
Tuition: 998 (in state), 998 (out of state)
Financial Aid Recipients: 20%
Average Annual Housing Cost: 2,500
Application Deadline: varies
Number of: applicants annually 2,500; applicants accepted annually 2,000; students enrolled annually 1,800

Tests Required	Preferred/Min Score
Graduate Record Exam	
National Teachers Exam	
Praxis II Exam	

Stanford University
School of Education
Stanford, CA 94305-3096
Admissions: (PH)415 723-4066, (FAX)415 725-7412, (EMAIL)hf.pmh@forsythe.stanford.edu
Dean: (PH)415 723-2111, (FAX)415 725-7412
Total Enrollment: 10,000–20,000
Grad Enrollment: FTM 192, FTD 172
Program Membership: Holmes Partnership
Academic Programs Available: MASTERS: Art Ed., Bilingual Ed., Counselor Ed., Early Childhood Ed., Ed. Admin, Ed. Tech., Foreign Lang. Ed., Higher Ed., Math Ed., Mid Level Ed., Read/Lang Arts Ed., Sci. Ed., Sec. Ed., Soc. Ed., DOCTORATE: Art Ed., Bilingual Ed., Counselor Ed., Early Childhood Ed., Ed. Admin, Ed. Tech., Foreign Lang. Ed., Higher Ed., Math Ed., Mid Level Ed., Read/Lang Arts Ed., Sci. Ed., Sec. Ed., Soc. Ed.

Library: Cubberley Library, 147,000 volumes
Computer Resources: Macintosh, Dual Platform, PCs, CD-ROM, Videodisc

Research Areas	#Faculty
Adult Education	
Art Education	1
Bilingual Education	1
Counselor Education	1
Early Childhood Ed.	
Ed. Admin	
Ed. Tech.	
Elementary Ed.	
Foreign Lang. Ed.	
Higher Ed.	2
Math Ed.	2
Mid. Lev. Ed.	
Multicultural Ed.	2
Music Ed.	
Physical Ed.	
Read/Lang. Arts Ed.	2
School Counseling	
Science Ed.	4
Secondary Ed.	4
Soc. Studies Ed.	
Special Ed.	
Other	

Research Institutes/Centers: Accelerated Schools Project, Center for Policy Research in Education, National Center for Postsecondary Improvement, Project Read
Student Body Demographics: Average Age 30, 71% female, 29% male
Percent Ethnic Minorities: Hispanic-American 8%, Asian-American 13%, African-American 9%, Native-American 4%
Geographic Representation: N/A
Tuition: 19,695 (in state), 19,695 (out of state)
Financial Aid Recipients: 76%
Average Annual Housing Cost: 8,919
Application Deadline: 1/2; 2/1
Number of: applicants annually 929; applicants accepted annually 361; students enrolled annually 221

Tests Required	Preferred/Min Score
Graduate Record Exam	
National Teachers Exam	
Praxis II Exam	
TOEFL	600

UCLA Graduate School of Education & Information Studies

1009 Moore Hall, Box 951251, Los Angeles, CA 90095-1521
Admissions: (PH)310 825-8326, (FAX)310 206-6293, (EMAIL)whitcup@gse.ucla.edu
Dean: (PH)310 825-8308, (FAX)310 206-3076, (EMAIL)mitchell@gse.ucla.edu
Total Enrollment: 20,000
Grad Enrollment: FTM 280, PTM 36, FTD 541, On campus 5%, Off campus 95%
Program Membership: Holmes Partnership
Academic Programs Available: MASTERS: Bilingual Ed., Ed. Psych., Elementary Ed., Higher Ed., Math Ed., Mid Level Ed., Multicultural Ed., Music Ed., Soc. Ed., DOCTORATE: Bilingual Ed., Early Childhood Ed., Ed. Admin, Ed. Psych., Elementary Ed., Higher Ed., Math Ed., Mid Level Ed., Multicultural Ed., Soc. Ed., Spec. Ed.
Library: University Library, Over 6 million volumes
Computer Resources: Macintosh, Dual Platform, PCs, CD-ROM, Videodisc

Research Areas	#Faculty
Adult Education	2
Art Education	
Bilingual Education	3
Counselor Education	3
Early Childhood Ed.	3
Ed. Admin	10
Ed. Tech.	3
Elementary Ed.	10
Foreign Lang. Ed.	
Higher Ed.	5
Math Ed.	3
Mid. Lev. Ed.	3
Multicultural Ed.	3
Music Ed.	
Physical Ed.	
Read/Lang. Arts Ed.	4
School Counseling	
Science Ed.	2
Secondary Ed.	2
Soc. Studies Ed.	2
Special Ed.	3
Other	

Research Institutes/Centers: Higher Education Research Institute, Center for the Study of Evaluation, Urban Education Studies Center
Student Body Demographics: Average Age 30, 67% female, 33% male
Percent Ethnic Minorities: Hispanic-American 14%, Asian-American 12%, African-American 8%, Native-American 0.5%
Geographic Representation: West 90%

Tuition: 4,800 (in state), 12,500 (out of state)
Financial Aid Recipients: 25%
Average Annual Housing Cost: 10,000
Application Deadline: 1/5
Number of: applicants annually 990; applicants accepted annually 465; students enrolled annually 316

Tests Required	Preferred/Min Score
Graduate Record Exam	1000–1,300
National Teachers Exam	
Praxis II Exam	
TOEFL	560

United States International University Department of Education

10455 Pomerado Road, San Diego, CA 92131
Admissions: (PH)619 635-4772, (FAX)619 635-4739, (EMAIL)usiu_adm@sanac.usiu.edu
Dean: (PH)619 635-4505, (FAX)619 635-4711
Total Enrollment: 1,000–5,000
Grad Enrollment: FTM 138, PTM 56, FTD 17, PTD 43, On campus 10%, Off campus 90%
Program Membership: N/A
Academic Programs Available: MASTERS: Ed. Admin, Ed. Tech., Multicultural Ed., DOCTORATE: Ed. Admin, Ed. Tech., Multicultural Ed.
Library: Walter Library, 215,000 volumes
Computer Resources: Macintosh, Dual Platform, PCs, CD-ROM, Videodisc

Research Areas	#Faculty
Adult Education	
Art Education	
Bilingual Education	
Counselor Education	
Early Childhood Ed.	
Ed. Admin	1
Ed. Tech.	2
Elementary Ed.	3
Foreign Lang. Ed.	
Higher Ed.	
Math Ed.	
Mid. Lev. Ed.	
Multicultural Ed.	2
Music Ed.	
Physical Ed.	
Read/Lang. Arts Ed.	
School Counseling	
Science Ed.	
Secondary Ed.	
Soc. Studies Ed.	
Special Ed.	
Other	2

Student Body Demographics: Average Age 29, 52% female, 48% male
Percent Ethnic Minorities: Hispanic-American 8%, Asian-American 5.6%, African-American 6%, Native-American 1%
Geographic Representation: N/A
Tuition: 220-310/hr (in state), 220-310/hr (out of state)

Financial Aid Recipients: 65%
Average Annual Housing Cost: 4,350
Application Deadline: rolling
Number of: applicants annually 1,500; applicants accepted annually 900; students enrolled annually 360

Tests Required	Preferred/Min Score
Graduate Record Exam	
National Teachers Exam	
Praxis II Exam	
TOEFL	550–575

University of California-Berkeley
Graduate School of Education

Admissions Office, 1600 Tolman Hall, #1670, Berkeley, CA 94720
Admissions: (PH)510 642-0841, (FAX)510 642-4808
Dean: (PH)510 642-3726, (FAX)510 643-8904
Total Enrollment: 20,000
Grad Enrollment: FTM 88, FTD 276, CAS 13, On campus 5%, Off campus 95%
Program Membership: Holmes Partnership
Academic Programs Available: MASTERS: Ed. Admin, Ed. Psych., Elementary Ed., Higher Ed., Math Ed., Read/Lang Arts Ed., Sci. Ed., Spec. Ed. DOCTORATE: Ed. Admin, Ed. Psych., Elementary Ed., Higher Ed., Math Ed., Read/Lang Arts Ed., Sci. Ed., Spec. Ed.
Library: Education/Psychology Library, 110,000 volumes
Computer Resources: PCs, CD-ROM

Research Areas	#Faculty
Adult Education	
Art Education	
Bilingual Education	5
Counselor Education	
Early Childhood Ed.	1
Ed. Admin	10
Ed. Tech.	5
Elementary Ed.	10
Foreign Lang. Ed.	2
Higher Ed.	2
Math Ed.	7
Mid. Lev. Ed.	
Multicultural Ed.	6
Music Ed.	
Physical Ed.	
Read/Lang. Arts Ed.	14
School Counseling	5
Science Ed.	8
Secondary Ed.	8
Soc. Studies Ed.	
Special Ed.	5
Other	

Research Institutes/Centers: National Center for Research in Vocational Education, National Center for the Study of Writing and Literacy
Student Body Demographics: Average Age 31, 68% female, 32% male
Percent Ethnic Minorities: Hispanic-American 8.6%, Asian-American 9.9%, African-American 8.4%, Native-American 0.5%

Geographic Representation: New England 5%, Midwest 3%, Mid Atlantic 9%, Southwest 3%, West 72%, Southeast 3%, Northwest 4%
Tuition: 4,660 (in state), 12360 (out of state)
Financial Aid Recipients: 25%
Average Annual Housing Cost: 6,300
Application Deadline: 13/15
Number of: applicants annually 733; applicants accepted annually 222; students enrolled annually 121

Tests Required	Preferred/Min Score
Graduate Record Exam	
National Teachers Exam	
Praxis II Exam	155
TOEFL	570

University of California-Riverside
School of Education

University of California, Riverside, CA 92521
Admissions: (PH)909 787-5228, (FAX)909 787-3942, (EMAIL)dady.dewitt@ucr.edu
Dean: (PH)909 787-5228, (FAX)909 787-3942, (EMAIL)irving.hendrick@ucr.edu
Total Enrollment: 5,000–10,000
Grad Enrollment: FTM 30, PTM 10, FTD 85, On campus 20%, Off campus 80%
Program Membership: Holmes Partnership
Academic Programs Available: MASTERS: Bilingual Ed., Ed. Admin, Ed. Psych., School Cons., Spec. Ed. DOCTORATE: Bilingual Ed., Ed. Admin, Ed. Psych., School Cons., Spec. Ed.
Library: Rivera Library, 1.2 million volumes
Computer Resources: Macintosh, Dual Platform, PCs, CD-ROM, Videodisc

Research Areas	#Faculty
Adult Education	
Art Education	
Bilingual Education	1
Counselor Education	
Early Childhood Ed.	
Ed. Admin	5
Ed. Tech.	
Elementary Ed.	
Foreign Lang. Ed.	1
Higher Ed.	
Math Ed.	1
Mid. Lev. Ed.	1
Multicultural Ed.	1
Music Ed.	
Physical Ed.	
Read/Lang. Arts Ed.	
School Counseling	3
Science Ed.	
Secondary Ed.	
Soc. Studies Ed.	
Special Ed.	5
Other	

Research Institutes/Centers: California Educational Research Cooperative, Comprehensive Teacher Education Institute

Student Body Demographics: Average Age 35, 65% female, 35% male
Percent Ethnic Minorities: Hispanic-American 15%, Asian-American 3%, African-American 6%, Native-American 3%
Geographic Representation: New England 2%, Midwest 3%, Mid Atlantic 1%, Southwest 1%, West 90%, Southeast 1%, Northwest 2%
Graduate Career Paths: K-12 Teaching 55%, Higher Ed Teaching 20%, K-12 Special Ed 10%, School Administration 10%, Higher Ed Administration 5%
Tuition: 1,266 (in state), 3632 (out of state)
Financial Aid Recipients: 40%
Average Annual Housing Cost: 3,600
Application Deadline: 5/1
Number of: applicants annually 290; applicants accepted annually 150; students enrolled annually N/A

Tests Required	Preferred/Min Score
Graduate Record Exam	1100–1,200
National Teachers Exam	
Praxis II Exam	
TOEFL	550

University of California-Santa Barbara
Graduate School of Education

1175A Phelps Hall, Santa Barbara, CA 93106-9490
Admissions: (PH)805 893-2137
Dean: (PH)805 893-2185, (FAX)805 893-7264, (EMAIL)dixon@edstar.gse.ucsb.edu
Total Enrollment: 10,000–20,000
Grad Enrollment: FTM 114, FTD 192, CAS 14, On campus 25%, Off campus 75%
Program Membership: Holmes Partnership
Academic Programs Available: MASTERS: Counselor Ed., Early Childhood Ed., Ed. Admin, Ed. Psych., Elementary Ed., Math Ed., Read/Lang Arts Ed., School Cons., Sci. Ed., Sec. Ed., DOCTORATE: Counselor Ed., Early Childhood Ed., Ed. Admin, Ed. Psych., Elementary Ed., Math Ed., Read/Lang Arts Ed., School Cons., Sci. Ed., Sec. Ed.
Library: Davidson Library
Computer Resources: Macintosh, Dual Platform, PCs, CD-ROM, Videodisc

Research Areas	#Faculty
Adult Education	
Art Education	
Bilingual Education	2
Counselor Education	8
Early Childhood Ed.	3
Ed. Admin	7
Ed. Tech.	
Elementary Ed.	12
Foreign Lang. Ed.	
Higher Ed.	
Math Ed.	2
Mid. Lev. Ed.	
Multicultural Ed.	
Music Ed.	
Physical Ed.	
Read/Lang. Arts Ed.	2

School Counseling	2
Science Ed.	1
Secondary Ed.	1
Soc. Studies Ed.	1
Special Ed.	6
Other	

Research Institutes/Centers: Linguistic Minority Research Institute
Student Body Demographics: Average Age 41, 70% female, 30% male
Percent Ethnic Minorities: Hispanic-American 18%, Asian-American 8%, African-American 4%, Native-American 3%
Geographic Representation: New England 5%, Midwest 5%, Mid Atlantic 5%, Southwest 50%, West 30%, Southeast 5%, Northwest 10%
Graduate Career Paths: K-12 Teaching 35%, Higher Ed Teaching 50%
Tuition: 5,088 (in state), 8,469 (out of state)
Financial Aid Recipients: N/A
Average Annual Housing Cost: N/A
Application Deadline: varies
Number of: applicants annually 600; applicants accepted annually 200; students enrolled annually 140

Tests Required	Preferred/Min Score
Graduate Record Exam	1000–1,200
National Teachers Exam	
Praxis II Exam	
TOEFL	550

University of San Diego School of Education

5998 Alcala Park, San Diego, CA 92110-2492
Admissions: (PH)619 260-4524, (FAX)619 260-4158
Dean: (PH)619 260-4540
Total Enrollment: 5,000–10,000
Grad Enrollment: FTM 80, PTM 30, FTD 129, PTD 175, CAS 102
Program Membership: N/A
Academic Programs Available: MASTERS: Bilingual Ed., Counselor Ed., Ed. Admin, Spec. Ed. DOCTORATE: Bilingual Ed., Counselor Ed., Ed. Admin, Spec. Ed.
Library: Copley Library, 300,000 volumes
Computer Resources: Macintosh, Dual Platform, PCs, CD-ROM, Videodisc

Research Areas	#Faculty
Adult Education	
Art Education	
Bilingual Education	
Counselor Education	4
Early Childhood Ed.	
Ed. Admin	
Ed. Tech.	
Elementary Ed.	
Foreign Lang. Ed.	
Higher Ed.	
Math Ed.	
Mid. Lev. Ed.	
Multicultural Ed.	
Music Ed.	

Physical Ed.
Read/Lang. Arts Ed.
School Counseling
Science Ed.
Secondary Ed.
Soc. Studies Ed.
Special Ed.
Other
Research Institutes/Centers: Ahlers Center for
International Business
Student Body Demographics: Average Age 27, 62% female,
38% male
Percent Ethnic Minorities: Hispanic-American 8%,
Asian-American 5%, African-American 2.5%,
Native-American 1%
Geographic Representation: New England 1%,
Midwest 2%, Mid Atlantic 1.5%, Southwest 1.5%, West 83%,
Southeast 1%, Northwest 1%
Tuition: 505/unit (in state), 505/unit (out of state)
Financial Aid Recipients: N/A
Average Annual Housing Cost: 7,650
Application Deadline: 5/1; 11/15; 3/15
Number of: applicants annually 2016; applicants accepted
annually 1319; students enrolled annually 838

Tests Required	Preferred/Min Score
Graduate Record Exam	
National Teachers Exam	
Praxis II Exam	
TOEFL	600

University of Southern California
School of Education
WPH 803, Los Angeles, CA 90089-0031
Admissions: (PH)213 740-2606, (FAX)213 740-9433,
(EMAIL)montez@mizar.usc.edu
Dean: (PH)213 740-8313, (FAX)213 746-8142
Grad Enrollment: FTM 196, PTM 72, FTD 402, PTD 172
Program Membership: Holmes Partnership
Academic Programs Available: MASTERS: Counselor Ed.,
Early Childhood Ed., Ed. Admin, Ed. Psych., Ed. Tech.,
Elementary Ed., Foreign Lang. Ed., Higher Ed., Read/Lang
Arts Ed., Sci. Ed., Sec. Ed., Spec. Ed. DOCTORATE:
Counselor Ed., Early Childhood Ed., Ed. Admin, Ed. Psych.,
Ed. Tech., Elementary Ed., Foreign Lang. Ed., Higher Ed.,
Read/Lang Arts Ed., Sci. Ed., Sec. Ed., Spec. Ed.
Library: Stoops Education Library
Computer Resources: Macintosh, Dual Platform, PCs,
CD-ROM, Videodisc

Research Areas	#Faculty
Adult Education	
Art Education	
Bilingual Education	5
Counselor Education	6
Early Childhood Ed.	6
Ed. Admin	10
Ed. Tech.	5
Elementary Ed.	11
Foreign Lang. Ed.	2
Higher Ed.	6

Math Ed.	
Mid. Lev. Ed.	11
Multicultural Ed.	3
Music Ed.	
Physical Ed.	
Read/Lang. Arts Ed.	4
School Counseling	
Science Ed.	1
Secondary Ed.	1
Soc. Studies Ed.	
Special Ed.	
Other	

Research Institutes/Centers: California Writing Project,
Latino Teacher Project, Spanish Resource Center, Center for
Higher Education Policy Analysis
Student Body Demographics: Average Age N/A,
67% female, 33% male
Percent Ethnic Minorities: Hispanic-American 9%,
Asian-American 11%, African-American 8%,
Native-American 5%
Geographic Representation: N/A
Tuition: 614/unit (in state), 614/unit (out of state)
Financial Aid Recipients: N/A
Average Annual Housing Cost: N/A
Application Deadline: 7/1; 3/1; 1/1
Number of: applicants annually 535; applicants accepted
annually 315; students enrolled annually 181

Tests Required	Preferred/Min Score
Graduate Record Exam	1000
National Teachers Exam	
Praxis II Exam	

COLORADO

University of Colorado at Boulder
School of Education
Campus Box 249, Boulder, CO 80309
Admissions: (PH)303 492-8430, (FAX)303 492-7090
Dean: (PH)303 492-6937
Total Enrollment: 20,000
Grad Enrollment: FTM 246, PTM 87, FTD 78, PTD 26, On
campus 50%, Off campus 50%
Program Membership: Holmes Partnership
Academic Programs Available: MASTERS: Bilingual Ed.,
Ed. Psych., Elementary Ed., Math Ed., Mid Level Ed.,
Muticultrual Ed., Read/Lang Arts Ed., Sci. Ed., Sec. Ed., Soc.
Ed., Spec. Ed. DOCTORATE: Bilingual Ed., Ed. Psych.,
Elementary Ed., Math Ed., Mid Level Ed., Muticultrual Ed.,
Read/Lang Arts Ed., Sci. Ed., Sec. Ed., Soc. Ed., Spec. Ed.
Library: 2.6 million volumes
Computer Resources: Macintosh, Dual Platform, PCs,
CD-ROM, Videodisc

Research Areas	#Faculty
Adult Education	
Art Education	

Bilingual Education	6
Counselor Education	
Early Childhood Ed.	
Ed. Admin	
Ed. Tech.	2
Elementary Ed.	5
Foreign Lang. Ed.	
Higher Ed.	
Math Ed.	3
Mid. Lev. Ed.	
Multicultural Ed.	6
Music Ed.	
Physical Ed.	
Read/Lang. Arts Ed.	3
School Counseling	
Science Ed.	2
Secondary Ed.	2
Soc. Studies Ed.	2
Special Ed.	3
Other	8

Research Institutes/Centers: Laboratory for Educational Research, Bueno Center for Multicultural Education, Laboratory for Policy Studies
Student Body Demographics: Average Age 30, 80% female, 20% male
Percent Ethnic Minorities: Hispanic-American 8%, Asian-American 2%, African-American 1%, Native-American 1%
Geographic Representation: New England 6%, Midwest 10%, Mid Atlantic 3%, Southwest 65%, West 10%, Southeast 3%, Northwest 3%
Graduate Career Paths: K-12 Teaching 40%, Higher Ed Teaching 40%, K-12 Special Ed 10%
Tuition: 3,584 (in state), 13,710 (out of state)
Financial Aid Recipients: 18%
Average Annual Housing Cost: 4,162
Application Deadline: 2/1; 9/1
Number of: applicants annually 400; applicants accepted annually 250; students enrolled annually 150

Tests Required	Preferred/Min Score
Graduate Record Exam	1,000–1,250
National Teachers Exam	
Praxis II Exam	
TOEFL	550

University of Colorado at Denver School of Education

Campus Box 106, P.O. Box 173364, Denver, CO 80217-3364
Admissions: (PH)303 556-3287, (FAX)303 556-4838
Dean: (PH)303 556-2717, (FAX)303 556-4479
Total Enrollment: 10,000–20,000
Grad Enrollment: 2,000 total, Off campus 100%
Program Membership: Holmes Partnership
Academic Programs Available: MASTERS: Bilingual Ed., Counselor Ed., Early Childhood Ed., Ed. Admin, Ed. Psych., Ed. Tech., Elementary Ed., Foreign Lang. Ed., Math Ed., Read/Lang Arts Ed., School Cons., Sci. Ed., Soc. Ed., DOCTORATE: Bilingual Ed., Counselor Ed., Early

Childhood Ed., Ed. Admin, Ed. Psych., Ed. Tech., Elementary Ed., Foreign Lang. Ed., Math Ed., Read/Lang Arts Ed., School Cons., Sci. Ed., Soc. Ed.
Library: Auraria Library, 600,000 volumes
Computer Resources: Macintosh, Dual Platform, PCs, CD-ROM, Videodisc

Research Areas	#Faculty
Adult Education	1
Art Education	
Bilingual Education	5
Counselor Education	10
Early Childhood Ed.	2
Ed. Admin	8
Ed. Tech.	5
Elementary Ed.	8
Foreign Lang. Ed.	
Higher Ed.	
Math Ed.	2
Mid. Lev. Ed.	
Multicultural Ed.	1
Music Ed.	
Physical Ed.	
Read/Lang. Arts Ed.	4
School Counseling	3
Science Ed.	1
Secondary Ed.	1
Soc. Studies Ed.	1
Special Ed.	4
Other	26

Research Institutes/Centers: Colorado Principals Center
Student Body Demographics: Average Age 29, female % N/A, male % N/A
Percent Ethnic Minorities: Hispanic-American 7%, Asian-American 6%, African-American 1%, Native-American 1%
Geographic Representation: West 100%
Tuition: 188/hr (in state), 685/hr (out of state)
Financial Aid Recipients: N/A
Average Annual Housing Cost: N/A
Application Deadline: 2/15; 4/15; 9/15
Number of: applicants annually N/A; applicants accepted annually N/A; students enrolled annually N/A

Tests Required	Preferred/Min Score
Graduate Record Exam	1,000–1,100
National Teachers Exam	
Praxis II Exam	

University of Denver College of Education

Graduate Office, Ammi Hyde Building, 2450 S. Vine, Denver, CO 80208
Admissions: (PH)303 871-2509, (FAX)303 871-4456
Dean: (PH)303 871-3665
Total Enrollment: 5,000–10,000
Grad Enrollment: FTM 58, PTM 34, FTD 43, PTD 84, On campus 8%, Off campus 92%
Program Membership: N/A
Academic Programs Available: MASTERS: Counselor Ed., Ed. Admin, Ed. Psych., Higher Ed., School Cons.,

DOCTORATE: Counselor Ed., Ed. Admin, Ed. Psych., Higher Ed., School Cons.
Library: N/A

Research Areas	#Faculty
Adult Education	
Art Education	
Bilingual Education	
Counselor Education	
Early Childhood Ed.	
Ed. Admin	
Ed. Tech.	
Elementary Ed.	
Foreign Lang. Ed.	
Higher Ed.	
Math Ed.	
Mid. Lev. Ed.	
Multicultural Ed.	
Music Ed.	
Physical Ed.	
Read/Lang. Arts Ed.	
School Counseling	
Science Ed.	
Secondary Ed.	
Soc. Studies Ed.	
Special Ed.	
Other	

Student Body Demographics: Average Age 38, 70% female, 30% male
Percent Ethnic Minorities: Hispanic-American 3%, Asian-American 5%, African-American 1%
Geographic Representation: N/A
Tuition: N/A (in state), N/A (out of state)
Financial Aid Recipients: 75%
Average Annual Housing Cost: N/A
Application Deadline: N/A
Number of: applicants annually 250-300; applicants accepted annually 125; students enrolled annually N/A

Tests Required	Preferred/Min Score
Graduate Record Exam	870–930
National Teachers Exam	
Praxis II Exam	
TOEFL	550

University of Northern Colorado

Admissions Office, Greeley, CO 80639
Admissions: (PH)970 351-2831, (FAX)970 351-2371, (EMAIL)gradsch@sea.univnorthco.edu
Dean: (PH)970 351-2817, (FAX)970 351-2312
Total Enrollment: 10,000–20,000
Grad Enrollment: FTM 245, PTM 464, FTD 119, PTD 108, On campus 3%, Off campus 97%
Program Membership: Holmes Partnership
Academic Programs Available: MASTERS: Counselor Ed., Early Childhood Ed., Ed. Admin, Ed. Psych., Ed. Tech., Elementary Ed., Mid Level Ed., Read/Lang Arts Ed., School Cons., Spec. Ed.
DOCTORATE: Counselor Ed., Early Childhood Ed., Ed. Admin, Ed. Psych., Ed. Tech., Elementary Ed., Mid Level Ed., Read/Lang Arts Ed., School Cons., Spec. Ed.

Library: Michener Library
Computer Resources: Macintosh, Dual Platform, PCs, CD-ROM, Videodisc

Research Areas	#Faculty
Adult Education	
Art Education	
Bilingual Education	
Counselor Education	9
Early Childhood Ed.	3
Ed. Admin	6
Ed. Tech.	4
Elementary Ed.	6
Foreign Lang. Ed.	
Higher Ed.	
Math Ed.	
Mid. Lev. Ed.	2
Multicultural Ed.	
Music Ed.	
Physical Ed.	
Read/Lang. Arts Ed.	6
School Counseling	4
Science Ed.	
Secondary Ed.	
Soc. Studies Ed.	
Special Ed.	22
Other	

Student Body Demographics: Average Age 35, 72% female, 28% male
Percent Ethnic Minorities: Hispanic-American 6%, Asian-American 1%, African-American 2%, Native-American 1%
Geographic Representation: West 92%
Tuition: 2,822 (in state), 9,198 (out of state)
Financial Aid Recipients: 56%
Average Annual Housing Cost: 3,600
Application Deadline: varies
Number of: applicants annually 731; applicants accepted annually 486; students enrolled annually 311

Tests Required	Preferred/Min Score
Graduate Record Exam	
National Teachers Exam	
Praxis II Exam	
TOEFL	520

CONNECTICUT

Southern Connecticut State University School of Education

501 Crescent Street, New Haven, CT 06515
Admissions: (PH)203 392-5237, (FAX)203 392-5235, (EMAIL)diana@scsu.ctstateu.edu
Dean: (PH)203 392-5908, (FAX)203 392-5908, (EMAIL)lane@scsu.ctstateu.edu
Total Enrollment: 10,000–20,000

Grad Enrollment: FTM 179, PTM 1462
Program Membership: N/A
Academic Programs Available: MASTERS: Art Ed.,
Counselor Ed., Early Childhood Ed., Ed. Admin, Elementary
Ed., Foreign Lang. Ed., Math Ed., Mid Level Ed., Physical
Ed., Read/Lang Arts Ed., School Cons., Sci. Ed., Sec. Ed.,
Soc. DOCTORATE: Art Ed., Counselor Ed., Early Childhood
Ed., Ed. Admin, Elementary Ed., Foreign Lang. Ed., Math
Ed., Mid Level Ed., Physical Ed., Read/Lang Arts Ed.,
School Cons., Sci. Ed., Sec. Ed.
Library: Buley Library, 500,000 volumes
Computer Resources: Macintosh, Dual Platform, PCs,
CD-ROM, Videodisc

Research Areas	#Faculty
Adult Education	
Art Education	3
Bilingual Education	
Counselor Education	3
Early Childhood Ed.	
Ed. Admin	5
Ed. Tech.	
Elementary Ed.	8
Foreign Lang. Ed.	
Higher Ed.	
Math Ed.	3
Mid. Lev. Ed.	
Multicultural Ed.	
Music Ed.	
Physical Ed.	4
Read/Lang. Arts Ed.	2
School Counseling	3
Science Ed.	1
Secondary Ed.	1
Soc. Studies Ed.	
Special Ed.	10
Other	16

Student Body Demographics: Average Age 35, 79% female,
21% male
Percent Ethnic Minorities: Hispanic-American 1.3%,
African-American 3.7%
Geographic Representation: New England 98%
Tuition: 1,774 (in state), 4310 (out of state)
Financial Aid Recipients: 20%
Average Annual Housing Cost: 5,234
Application Deadline: varies
Number of: applicants annually 2,500–3,000; applicants
accepted annually 600; students enrolled annually N/A

Tests Required	Preferred/Min Score
Graduate Record Exam	
National Teachers Exam	
Praxis II Exam	

University of Connecticut School of Education

Storrs, CT 06269
Admissions: (PH)860 486-3815
Dean: (PH)860 486-3813
Total Enrollment: 20,000
Grad Enrollment: 1,259 total
Program Membership: Holmes Partnership, NNER

Academic Programs Available: MASTERS: Counselor Ed.,
Ed. Admin, Ed. Psych., Ed. Tech., Elementary Ed., Higher
Ed., School Cons., Sec. Ed., Spec. Ed. DOCTORATE:
Counselor Ed., Ed. Admin, Ed. Psych., Ed. Tech., Elementary
Ed., Higher Ed., School Cons., Sec. Ed., Spec. Ed.
Library: Homer Babbidge Library, 1.7 million volumes

Research Areas	#Faculty
Adult Education	
Art Education	
Bilingual Education	
Counselor Education	
Early Childhood Ed.	
Ed. Admin	
Ed. Tech.	
Elementary Ed.	
Foreign Lang. Ed.	
Higher Ed.	
Math Ed.	
Mid. Lev. Ed.	
Multicultural Ed.	
Music Ed.	
Physical Ed.	
Read/Lang. Arts Ed.	
School Counseling	
Science Ed.	
Secondary Ed.	
Soc. Studies Ed.	
Special Ed.	
Other	

Research Institutes/Centers: National Research Center on
the Gifted and Talented, A.J. Pappanikou Center for Special
Education and Rehabilitation
Student Body Demographics: N/A
Percent Ethnic Minorities: N/A
Geographic Representation: N/A
Tuition: 4,800 (in state), 12,474 (out of state)
Financial Aid Recipients: N/A
Average Annual Housing Cost: N/A
Application Deadline: 2/15
Number of: applicants annually 440; applicants accepted
annually 325; students enrolled annually N/A

Tests Required	Preferred/Min Score
Graduate Record Exam	
National Teachers Exam	
Praxis II Exam	

University of New Haven Program in Education

West Haven, CT 06516-1916
Admissions: (PH)203 932-7336
Grad Enrollment: 236 total
Program Membership: N/A
Academic Programs Available: MASTERS: Early
Childhood Ed., Ed. Admin, Ed. Tech., Elementary Ed., Math
Ed., Mid Level Ed., Sci. Ed., Sec. Ed., DOCTORATE: Early
Childhood Ed., Ed. Admin, Ed. Tech., Elementary Ed., Math
Ed., Mid Level Ed., Sci. Ed., Sec. Ed.
Library: N/A

Research Areas	#Faculty
Adult Education	
Art Education	

Bilingual Education
Counselor Education
Early Childhood Ed.
Ed. Admin
Ed. Tech.
Elementary Ed.
Foreign Lang. Ed.
Higher Ed.
Math Ed.
Mid. Lev. Ed.
Multicultural Ed.
Music Ed.
Physical Ed.
Read/Lang. Arts Ed.
School Counseling
Science Ed.
Secondary Ed.
Soc. Studies Ed.
Special Ed.
Other
Student Body Demographics: N/A
Percent Ethnic Minorities: N/A
Geographic Representation: N/A
Tuition: 1,020 (in state), 1,020 (out of state)
Financial Aid Recipients: N/A
Average Annual Housing Cost: N/A
Application Deadline: 5/1
Number of: applicants annually N/A; applicants accepted annually N/A; students enrolled annually N/A

Tests Required	Preferred/Min Score
Graduate Record Exam	
National Teachers Exam	
Praxis II Exam	

DELAWARE

University of Delaware College of Education
Newark, DE 19716
Admissions: (PH)302 831-2311
Grad Enrollment: 330 total
Program Membership: Holmes Partnership
Academic Programs Available: MASTERS: Counselor Ed., Ed. Psych., DOCTORATE: Counselor Ed., Ed. Psych.
Library: N/A

Research Areas	#Faculty
Adult Education	
Art Education	
Bilingual Education	
Counselor Education	
Early Childhood Ed.	
Ed. Admin	
Ed. Tech.	
Elementary Ed.	
Foreign Lang. Ed.	

Higher Ed.
Math Ed.
Mid. Lev. Ed.
Multicultural Ed.
Music Ed.
Physical Ed.
Read/Lang. Arts Ed.
School Counseling
Science Ed.
Secondary Ed.
Soc. Studies Ed.
Special Ed.
Other
Student Body Demographics: N/A
Percent Ethnic Minorities: N/A
Geographic Representation: N/A
Tuition: 3,860 (in state), 10,730 (out of state)
Financial Aid Recipients: N/A
Average Annual Housing Cost: N/A
Application Deadline: rolling
Number of: applicants annually N/A; applicants accepted annually N/A; students enrolled annually N/A

Tests Required	Preferred/Min Score
Graduate Record Exam	
National Teachers Exam	
Praxis II Exam	

WASHINGTON, DC

Catholic University of America
Department of Education
Cardinal Station, Washington, DC 20064
Admissions: (PH)202 319-5800, (FAX)202 319-5815, (EMAIL)stilwell@cua.edu
Dean: (PH)202 319-5800, (FAX)202 319-5815, (EMAIL)convey@cua.edu
Total Enrollment: 5,000–10,000
Grad Enrollment: On campus 5%, Off campus 95%
Program Membership: N/A
Academic Programs Available: MASTERS: Early Childhood Ed., Ed. Admin, Ed. Psych., Elementary Ed., School Cons., Sec. Ed., DOCTORATE: Early Childhood Ed., Ed. Admin, Ed. Psych., Elementary Ed., School Cons., Sec. Ed.
Library: Mullen Library, 1.25 million volumes
Computer Resources: Macintosh, Dual Platform, PCs, CD-ROM, Videodisc

Research Areas	#Faculty
Adult Education	
Art Education	
Bilingual Education	
Counselor Education	
Early Childhood Ed.	2
Ed. Admin	2

Ed. Tech.
Elementary Ed.   2
Foreign Lang. Ed.
Higher Ed.
Math Ed.
Mid. Lev. Ed.
Multicultural Ed.
Music Ed.
Physical Ed.
Read/Lang. Arts Ed.
School Counseling   2
Science Ed.
Secondary Ed.
Soc. Studies Ed.
Special Ed.
Other
Research Institutes/Centers: ERIC Center on Assessment and Evaluation
Student Body Demographics: Average Age 35, 80% female, 20% male
Percent Ethnic Minorities: Hispanic-American 1%, Asian-American 8%, African-American 16%
Geographic Representation: New England 10%, Midwest 5%, Mid Atlantic 80%, Southeast 5%
Graduate Career Paths: K-12 Teaching 30%, Higher Ed Teaching 10%, School Counseling 10%, K-12 School Administration 20%, Community Counseling 15%
Tuition: 14,612 (in state), 14,612 (out of state)
Financial Aid Recipients: 10%
Average Annual Housing Cost: N/A
Application Deadline: 2/1
Number of: applicants annually 100; applicants accepted annually 80; students enrolled annually 50

Tests Required	Preferred/Min Score
Graduate Record Exam	900–1,200
National Teachers Exam	
Praxis II Exam	
TOEFL	600

The George Washington University Graduate School of Education and Human Development

2134 G Street, NW, Suite 101, Washington, DC 20052
Admissions: (PH)202 994-6160, (FAX)202 994-7207, (EMAIL)gsehdapp@gwisz.circ.edu
Dean: (PH)202 994-6161, (FAX)202 994-7207
Total Enrollment: 10,000–20,000
Grad Enrollment: FTM 229, PTM 581, FTD 140, PTD 238
Program Membership: Holmes Partnership
Academic Programs Available: MASTERS: Ed. Admin, Ed. Tech., Elementary Ed., Higher Ed., School Cons., Sec. Ed., Spec. Ed. DOCTORATE: Ed. Admin, Ed. Tech., Elementary Ed., Higher Ed., School Cons., Sec. Ed., Spec. Ed.
Library: N/A

Research Areas	#Faculty
Adult Education	
Art Education	
Bilingual Education	
Counselor Education	

Early Childhood Ed.
Ed. Admin
Ed. Tech.
Elementary Ed.
Foreign Lang. Ed.
Higher Ed.
Math Ed.
Mid. Lev. Ed.
Multicultural Ed.
Music Ed.
Physical Ed.
Read/Lang. Arts Ed.
School Counseling
Science Ed.
Secondary Ed.
Soc. Studies Ed.
Special Ed.
Other
Student Body Demographics: Average Age 36, 70% female, 30% male
Percent Ethnic Minorities: Hispanic-American 3%, Asian-American 2%, African-American 16%, Native-American 1%
Geographic Representation: New England 2%, Midwest 5%, Mid Atlantic 42%, West 1%, Southeast 48%, Northwest 1%
Tuition: 600/hr (in state), 600/hr (out of state)
Financial Aid Recipients: 21%
Average Annual Housing Cost: 6,600
Application Deadline: 3/1; 10/1; 2/1
Number of: applicants annually 1,210; applicants accepted annually 762; students enrolled annually 244

Tests Required	Preferred/Min Score
Graduate Record Exam	
National Teachers Exam	
Praxis II Exam	
TOEFL	550

Trinity College School of Professional Studies

125 Michigan Ave., Washington, DC 20017
Admissions: (PH)202 939-5040, (FAX)202 839-5134
Dean: (PH)202 939-5462
Total Enrollment: 1,000–5,000
Grad Enrollment: FTM 52, PTM 368
Program Membership: N/A
Academic Programs Available: MASTERS: Counselor Ed., Early Childhood Ed., Ed. Admin, Elementary Ed., Higher Ed., Math Ed., Mid Level Ed., Read/Lang Arts Ed., School Cons., Sci. Ed., Sec. Ed., Soc. Ed., Spec. Ed. DOCTORATE: Counselor Ed., Early Childhood Ed., Ed. Admin, Elementary Ed., Higher Ed., Math Ed., Mid Level Ed., Read/Lang Arts Ed., School Cons., Sci. Ed., Sec. Ed., Soc. Ed., Spec. Ed.
Library: Helen Sheehan Library
Computer Resources: Macintosh, Dual Platform, PCs, CD-ROM, Videodisc

Research Areas	#Faculty
Adult Education	
Art Education	
Bilingual Education	

Counselor Education
Early Childhood Ed.   2
Ed. Admin   2
Ed. Tech.   3
Elementary Ed.   1
Foreign Lang. Ed.
Higher Ed.   1
Math Ed.
Mid. Lev. Ed.
Multicultural Ed.   2
Music Ed.
Physical Ed.
Read/Lang. Arts Ed.
School Counseling
Science Ed.
Secondary Ed.
Soc. Studies Ed.
Special Ed.   1
Other   1
Student Body Demographics: N/A
Percent Ethnic Minorities: N/A
Geographic Representation: N/A
Graduate Career Paths: K-12 Teaching 55%, School
Counseling 10%, K-12 Special Ed 5%, School
Administration 7%, Community Counseling 15%
Tuition: 390 (in state), 390 (out of state)
Financial Aid Recipients: 40%
Average Annual Housing Cost: 6,500
Application Deadline: rolling
Number of: applicants annually 300; applicants accepted
annually 200; students enrolled annually N/A
Tests Required   **Preferred/Min Score**
Graduate Record Exam
National Teachers Exam
Praxis II Exam
TOEFL   550-600

FLORIDA

Florida Atlantic University
College of Education
Boca Raton, FL 33431
Admissions: (PH)407 367-3564
Grad Enrollment: 635 total
Program Membership: N/A
Academic Programs Available: MASTERS: Adult Ed.,
Counselor Ed., Ed. Admin, Elementary Ed., Spec. Ed.
DOCTORATE: Adult Ed., Counselor Ed., Ed. Admin,
Elementary Ed., Spec. Ed.
Library: N/A
Research Areas   **#Faculty**
Adult Education
Art Education
Bilingual Education

Counselor Education
Early Childhood Ed.
Ed. Admin
Ed. Tech.
Elementary Ed.
Foreign Lang. Ed.
Higher Ed.
Math Ed.
Mid. Lev. Ed.
Multicultural Ed.
Music Ed.
Physical Ed.
Read/Lang. Arts Ed.
School Counseling
Science Ed.
Secondary Ed.
Soc. Studies Ed.
Special Ed.
Other
Student Body Demographics: N/A
Percent Ethnic Minorities: N/A
Geographic Representation: N/A
Tuition: 2,016 (in state), 6,570 (out of state)
Financial Aid Recipients: %
Application Deadline: rolling
Number of: applicants annually 535; applicants accepted
annually 318; students enrolled annually N/A
Tests Required   **Preferred/Min Score**
Graduate Record Exam
National Teachers Exam
Praxis II Exam

Florida State University College of Education
2249 UCA, Tallahassee, FL 32306-1009
Admissions: (PH)904 644-3420, (FAX)904 644-0197
Dean: (PH)904 644-6885, (FAX)904 644-2725
Total Enrollment: 20,000
Grad Enrollment: 1108 total
Program Membership: Holmes Partnership
Academic Programs Available: MASTERS: Adult Ed., Art
Ed., Counselor Ed., Early Childhood Ed., Ed. Admin, Ed.
Psych., Ed. Tech., Elementary Ed., Foreign Lang. Ed., Higher
Ed., Math Ed., Music Ed., Physical Ed., Read/Lang Arts Ed.,
School Cons., Sci. Ed., Sec. Ed., Soc. Ed., Spec. Ed.
DOCTORATE: Adult Ed., Art Ed., Counselor Ed., Early
Childhood Ed., Ed. Admin, Ed. Psych., Ed. Tech.,
Elementary Ed., Foreign Lang. Ed., Higher Ed., Math Ed.,
Music Ed., Physical Ed., Read/Lang Arts Ed., School Cons.,
Sci. Ed., Sec. Ed., Soc. Ed., Spec. Ed.
Library: Strozier Library, 2 million volumes
Computer Resources: Macintosh, Dual Platform, PCs,
CD-ROM, Videodisc
Research Areas   **#Faculty**
Adult Education   2
Art Education   6
Bilingual Education
Counselor Education   7
Early Childhood Ed.   2
Ed. Admin   6

Ed. Tech.	8
Elementary Ed.	7
Foreign Lang. Ed.	4
Higher Ed.	3
Math Ed.	5
Mid. Lev. Ed.	
Multicultural Ed.	
Music Ed.	11
Physical Ed.	8
Read/Lang. Arts Ed.	5
School Counseling	2
Science Ed.	4
Secondary Ed.	4
Soc. Studies Ed.	3
Special Ed.	11
Other	

Research Institutes/Centers: Center for Educational Technology, Center for Policy Studies in Education, Center for the Study of Teaching and Learning

Student Body Demographics: Average Age 31, 63% female, 37% male

Percent Ethnic Minorities: Hispanic-American 3%, Asian-American 4%, African-American 10%, Native-American 0.2%

Geographic Representation: New England 1%, Midwest 2%, Mid Atlantic 2%, Southwest 1%, West 1%, Southeast 90%, Europe 0.5%

Tuition: 112/hr (in state), 365/hr (out of state)

Financial Aid Recipients: 50%

Average Annual Housing Cost: N/A

Application Deadline: 7/15; 11/1; 4/1

Number of: applicants annually 1,247; applicants accepted annually 806; students enrolled annually N/A

Tests Required	Preferred/Min Score
Graduate Record Exam	1,000
National Teachers Exam	
Praxis II Exam	
TOEFL	550

University of Central Florida
College of Education

Orlando, FL 32816

Dean: (PH)407 823-2835, (FAX)407 823-5135

Total Enrollment: 20,000

Grad Enrollment: FTM 2, PTM 500, FTD 4, PTD 100

Program Membership: N/A

Academic Programs Available: MASTERS: Art Ed., Counselor Ed., Early Childhood Ed., Ed. Admin, Ed. Psych., Ed. Tech., Elementary Ed., Foreign Lang. Ed., Higher Ed., Math Ed., Music Ed., Physical Ed., Read/Lang Arts Ed., School Cons., Sci. Ed., Sec. Ed., Soc. Ed., Spec. Ed. DOCTORATE: Art Ed., Counselor Ed., Early Childhood Ed., Ed. Admin, Ed. Psych., Ed. Tech., Elementary Ed., Foreign Lang. Ed., Higher Ed., Math Ed., Music Ed., Physical Ed., Read/Lang Arts Ed., School Cons., Sci. Ed., Sec. Ed., Soc. Ed., Spec. Ed.

Library: N/A

Computer Resources: Macintosh, Dual Platform, PCs, CD-ROM, Videodisc

Research Areas	#Faculty
Adult Education	2
Art Education	1
Bilingual Education	
Counselor Education	3
Early Childhood Ed.	2
Ed. Admin	6
Ed. Tech.	4
Elementary Ed.	
Foreign Lang. Ed.	1
Higher Ed.	1
Math Ed.	2
Mid. Lev. Ed.	
Multicultural Ed.	1
Music Ed.	2
Physical Ed.	6
Read/Lang. Arts Ed.	4
School Counseling	4
Science Ed.	2
Secondary Ed.	2
Soc. Studies Ed.	2
Special Ed.	
Other	

Student Body Demographics: N/A

Percent Ethnic Minorities: N/A

Geographic Representation: N/A

Tuition: N/A (in state), N/A (out of state)

Financial Aid Recipients: N/A

Average Annual Housing Cost: N/A

Application Deadline: N/A

Number of: applicants annually 400; applicants accepted annually 200; students enrolled annually N/A

Tests Required	Preferred/Min Score
Graduate Record Exam	840–1,000
National Teachers Exam	
Praxis II Exam	

University of Florida College of Education

146 Norman Hall, Gainesville, FL 32611

Admissions: (PH)904 392-2315, (FAX)904 392-7159

Dean: (PH)904 392-2315, (FAX)904 392-7159

Total Enrollment: 20,000

Grad Enrollment: FTM 314, PTM 254, FTD 97, PTD 199

Program Membership: Holmes Partnership

Academic Programs Available: MASTERS: Counselor Ed., Early Childhood Ed., Ed. Admin, Ed. Psych., Ed. Tech., Elementary Ed., Foreign Lang. Ed., Higher Ed., Math Ed., Mid Level Ed., Read/Lang Arts Ed., School Cons., Sci. Ed., DOCTORATE: Counselor Ed., Early Childhood Ed., Ed. Admin, Ed. Psych., Ed. Tech., Elementary Ed., Foreign Lang. Ed., Higher Ed., Math Ed., Mid Level Ed., Read/Lang Arts Ed., School Cons., Sci. Ed.

Library: Education Library, 127,000 volumes

Computer Resources: Macintosh, Dual Platform, PCs, CD-ROM, Videodisc

Research Areas	#Faculty
Adult Education	2
Art Education	
Bilingual Education	1

Counselor Education	9
Early Childhood Ed.	3
Ed. Admin	6
Ed. Tech.	4
Elementary Ed.	6
Foreign Lang. Ed.	1
Higher Ed.	3
Math Ed.	4
Mid. Lev. Ed.	1
Multicultural Ed.	6
Music Ed.	
Physical Ed.	
Read/Lang. Arts Ed.	7
School Counseling	2
Science Ed.	2
Secondary Ed.	2
Soc. Studies Ed.	2
Special Ed.	15
Other	24

Research Institutes/Centers: Center for Educational Finance, Institute of Higher Education, Center for Community Education
Student Body Demographics: Average Age N/A, 73% female, 27% male
Percent Ethnic Minorities: Hispanic-American 6%, Asian-American 3%, African-American 10%, Native-American 1%
Geographic Representation: N/A
Tuition: 108/hr (in state), 361/hr (out of state)
Financial Aid Recipients: 13%
Average Annual Housing Cost: 300
Application Deadline: varies
Number of: applicants annually 532; applicants accepted annually 346; students enrolled annually N/A

Tests Required	Preferred/Min Score
Graduate Record Exam	1,000
National Teachers Exam	
Praxis II Exam	
TOEFL	550

University of Miami School of Education

P.O. Box 248065, Coral Gables, FL 33124
Admissions: (PH)305 284-2167, (FAX)305 284-3003
Dean: (PH)305 284-3505, (FAX)305 284-2003
Total Enrollment: 10,000–20,000
Grad Enrollment: FTM 245, FTD 129, CAS 177
Program Membership: Holmes Partnership
Academic Programs Available: MASTERS: Bilingual Ed., Early Childhood Ed., Elementary Ed., Higher Ed., Music Ed., Read/Lang Arts Ed., School Cons., Spec. Ed. DOCTORATE: Early Childhood Ed., Elementary Ed., Higher Ed., Music Ed., Read/Lang Arts Ed., School Cons., Spec. Ed.
Library: Richter Library, 2 million volumes
Computer Resources: PCs, CD-ROM

Research Areas	#Faculty
Adult Education	
Art Education	
Bilingual Education	2
Counselor Education	

Early Childhood Ed.	
Ed. Admin	
Ed. Tech.	
Elementary Ed.	
Foreign Lang. Ed.	
Higher Ed.	
Math Ed.	1
Mid. Lev. Ed.	
Multicultural Ed.	
Music Ed.	
Physical Ed.	
Read/Lang. Arts Ed.	
School Counseling	
Science Ed.	1
Secondary Ed.	1
Soc. Studies Ed.	
Special Ed.	5
Other	

Research Institutes/Centers: School-Based Research
Student Body Demographics: Average Age 34, 73.1% female, 26.9% male
Percent Ethnic Minorities: Hispanic-American 22.4%, Asian-American 1.5%, African-American 10.9%
Geographic Representation: Southeast 85%
Tuition: 706/cr (in state), 706/cr (out of state)
Financial Aid Recipients: 75%
Average Annual Housing Cost: N/A
Number of: applicants annually 600; applicants accepted annually 350; students enrolled annually 250

Tests Required	Preferred/Min Score
Graduate Record Exam	1,000
National Teachers Exam	
Praxis II Exam	
TOEFL	550

University of South Florida
College of Education

4202 East Fowler Ave., Tampa, FL 33620
Admissions: (PH)813 974-3350, (FAX)813 974-9689
Dean: (PH)813 974-3400, (FAX)813 974-3826
Total Enrollment: 20,000
Grad Enrollment: FTM 279, PTM 946, FTD 109, PTD 205, On campus 1%, Off campus 99%
Program Membership: Holmes Partnership
Academic Programs Available: MASTERS: Adult Ed., Art Ed., Counselor Ed., Early Childhood Ed., Ed. Admin, Ed. Psych., Ed. Tech., Elementary Ed., Foreign Lang. Ed., Higher Ed., Math Ed., Mid Level Ed., Music Ed., Physical Ed., Read/Lang Arts Ed., School Cons., Sci. Ed., Sec. Ed., Soc. Ed., Spec. Ed.
DOCTORATE: Adult Ed., Art Ed., Counselor Ed., Early Childhood Ed., Ed. Admin, Ed. Psych., Ed. Tech., Elementary Ed., Foreign Lang. Ed., Higher Ed., Math Ed., Mid Level Ed., Music Ed., Physical Ed., Read/Lang Arts Ed., School Cons., Sci. Ed., Sec. Ed., Soc. Ed., Spec. Ed.
Library: USF Library, 1.1 million volumes
Computer Resources: Macintosh, Dual Platform, PCs, CD-ROM, Videodisc

Research Areas	#Faculty
Adult Education	3
Art Education	2
Bilingual Education	
Counselor Education	5
Early Childhood Ed.	10
Ed. Admin	15
Ed. Tech.	5
Elementary Ed.	14
Foreign Lang. Ed.	2
Higher Ed.	
Math Ed.	5
Mid. Lev. Ed.	2
Multicultural Ed.	
Music Ed.	2
Physical Ed.	9
Read/Lang. Arts Ed.	16
School Counseling	
Science Ed.	4
Secondary Ed.	4
Soc. Studies Ed.	4
Special Ed.	24
Other	27

Research Institutes/Centers: Center for Arts and Community, Children's Center, Educational Research Center for Child Development, Institute for Instructional Research and Practice

Student Body Demographics: Average Age 36, 77% female, 23% male

Percent Ethnic Minorities: Hispanic-American 4.4%, African-American 5.4%

Geographic Representation: Southeast 99%

Graduate Career Paths: K-12 Teaching 28%, Higher Ed Teaching 1%, School Counseling 16%, K-12 Special Ed 11%, School Administration 15%

Tuition: 114/hr (in state), 367/hr (out of state)

Financial Aid Recipients: 40%

Average Annual Housing Cost: 2,500

Application Deadline: 10/22; 3/4; 6/3

Number of: applicants annually 1,325; applicants accepted annually 890; students enrolled annually 346

Tests Required	Preferred/Min Score
Graduate Record Exam	800–1,000
National Teachers Exam	
Praxis II Exam	
TOEFL	550

GEORGIA

Agnes Scott College

Office of Graduate Studies, Decatur, GA 30030
Admissions: (PH)404 638-6252, (FAX)404 638-6083
Total Enrollment: 1,000
Grad Enrollment: FTM 15, PTM 6, Off campus 100%

Program Membership: N/A
Academic Programs Available: MASTERS: Sec. Ed., DOCTORATE: Sec. Ed.
Library: McCain Library, 189,000 volumes
Computer Resources: Macintosh, Dual Platform, PCs, CD-ROM, Videodisc

Research Areas	#Faculty
Adult Education	
Art Education	
Bilingual Education	
Counselor Education	
Early Childhood Ed.	
Ed. Admin	
Ed. Tech.	
Elementary Ed.	
Foreign Lang. Ed.	
Higher Ed.	
Math Ed.	
Mid. Lev. Ed.	
Multicultural Ed.	
Music Ed.	
Physical Ed.	
Read/Lang. Arts Ed.	
School Counseling	
Science Ed.	1
Secondary Ed.	1
Soc. Studies Ed.	
Special Ed.	
Other	8

Student Body Demographics: Average Age 30, 95% female, 5% male

Percent Ethnic Minorities: Asian-American 1%, African-American 5%

Geographic Representation: Southeast 100%

Graduate Career Paths: K-12 Teaching 100%

Tuition: 3,620 (in state), 3,620 (out of state)

Financial Aid Recipients: 90%

Average Annual Housing Cost: N/A

Application Deadline: 5/1; 7/15

Number of: applicants annually 30; applicants accepted annually 20; students enrolled annually 20

Tests Required	Preferred/Min Score
Graduate Record Exam	
National Teachers Exam	
Praxis II Exam	

Berry College School of Education and Human Sciences

Box 159, Mount Berry Station, Mount Berry, GA 30149
Admissions: (PH)706 236-2215, (FAX)706 236-2248
Total Enrollment: 1,000–5,000
Grad Enrollment: FTM 30, PTM 170, Off campus 100%
Program Membership: N/A
Academic Programs Available: MASTERS: Art Ed., Early Childhood Ed., Foreign Lang. Ed., Math Ed., Mid Level Ed., Music Ed., Read/Lang Arts Ed., Sci. Ed., DOCTORATE: Art Ed., Early Childhood Ed., Foreign Lang. Ed., Math Ed., Mid Level Ed., Music Ed., Read/Lang Arts Ed., Sci. Ed.

Library: Berry Memorial Library, 557,000 volumes
Computer Resources: Macintosh, Dual Platform, PCs, CD-ROM, Videodisc

Research Areas	#Faculty
Adult Education	
Art Education	2
Bilingual Education	
Counselor Education	
Early Childhood Ed.	5
Ed. Admin	
Ed. Tech.	
Elementary Ed.	
Foreign Lang. Ed.	2
Higher Ed.	
Math Ed.	3
Mid. Lev. Ed.	5
Multicultural Ed.	
Music Ed.	
Physical Ed.	
Read/Lang. Arts Ed.	3
School Counseling	
Science Ed.	2
Secondary Ed.	2
Soc. Studies Ed.	2
Special Ed.	
Other	

Student Body Demographics: Average Age 25, 60% female, 40% male
Percent Ethnic Minorities: African-American 5%
Geographic Representation: N/A
Graduate Career Paths: K-12 Teaching 90%
Tuition: 4,100 (in state), 4,100 (out of state)
Financial Aid Recipients: 20%
Average Annual Housing Cost: N/A
Application Deadline: varies
Number of: applicants annually 219; applicants accepted annually 194; students enrolled annually 165

Tests Required	Preferred/Min Score
Graduate Record Exam	
National Teachers Exam	
Praxis II Exam	

Covenant College Master of Education Program

Scenic Highway, Lookout Mountain, GA 30750
Admissions: (PH)706 820-1560, (FAX)706 820-0672
Total Enrollment: 1,000
Grad Enrollment: On campus 60%, Off campus 40%
Program Membership: N/A
Academic Programs Available: MASTERS: Ed. Admin, DOCTORATE: Ed. Admin
Library: Dora MacLellan Brown Library
Computer Resources: Macintosh, Dual Platform, PCs, CD-ROM, Videodisc

Research Areas	#Faculty
Adult Education	
Art Education	
Bilingual Education	
Counselor Education	

Early Childhood Ed.
Ed. Admin
Ed. Tech.
Elementary Ed.
Foreign Lang. Ed.
Higher Ed.
Math Ed.
Mid. Lev. Ed.
Multicultural Ed.
Music Ed.
Physical Ed.
Read/Lang. Arts Ed.
School Counseling
Science Ed.
Secondary Ed.
Soc. Studies Ed.
Special Ed.
Other

Student Body Demographics: Average Age 33, N/A female, N/A male
Percent Ethnic Minorities: N/A
Geographic Representation: N/A
Tuition: 1,954 (in state), 1,954 (out of state)
Financial Aid Recipients: N/A
Average Annual Housing Cost: N/A
Application Deadline: 4/1
Number of: applicants annually 25; applicants accepted annually 23; students enrolled annually N/A

Tests Required	Preferred/Min Score
Graduate Record Exam	
National Teachers Exam	
Praxis II Exam	

Emory University Division of Educational Studies

Atlanta, GA 30322
Admissions: (PH)404 727-0606, (FAX)404 727-2799, (EMAIL)edusrjj@emory.edu
Total Enrollment: 5,000–10,000
Grad Enrollment: 86 total
Program Membership: Holmes Partnership
Academic Programs Available: N/A
Library: N/A

Research Areas	#Faculty
Adult Education	
Art Education	
Bilingual Education	
Counselor Education	1
Early Childhood Ed.	
Ed. Admin	1
Ed. Tech.	
Elementary Ed.	
Foreign Lang. Ed.	
Higher Ed.	
Math Ed.	1
Mid. Lev. Ed.	
Multicultural Ed.	1
Music Ed.	
Physical Ed.	

Read/Lang. Arts Ed.	2
School Counseling	
Science Ed.	1
Secondary Ed.	1
Soc. Studies Ed.	
Special Ed.	
Other	

Research Institutes/Centers: Center for Urban Learning/Teacher, Urban Research in Education
Student Body Demographics: N/A
Percent Ethnic Minorities: N/A
Geographic Representation: N/A
Tuition: 18,095 (in state), 18,095 (out of state)
Financial Aid Recipients: N/A
Average Annual Housing Cost: N/A
Application Deadline: 1/20
Number of: applicants annually 108; applicants accepted annually 43; students enrolled annually N/A

Tests Required	Preferred/Min Score
Graduate Record Exam	
National Teachers Exam	
Praxis II Exam	

Georgia Southern University College of Education

Landrum Box 8113, Statesboro, GA 30460
Admissions: (PH)912 681-5384, (FAX)912 681-0740, (EMAIL)jdiebolt@gasou.edu
Dean: (PH)912 681-3648, (FAX)912 681-5093
Total Enrollment: 10,000–20,000
Grad Enrollment: FTM 308, PTM 555, FTD 31, PTD 6, On campus 10%, Off campus 90%
Program Membership: N/A
Academic Programs Available: MASTERS: Adult Ed., Art Ed., Counselor Ed., Early Childhood Ed., Ed. Admin, Ed. Psych., Ed. Tech., Math Ed., Mid Level Ed., Muticultrual Ed., Music Ed., Physical Ed., Read/Lang Arts Ed., School Cons., Sci. Ed., Sec. Ed., Soc. Ed., Spec. Ed. DOCTORATE: Adult Ed., Art Ed., Counselor Ed., Early Childhood Ed., Ed. Admin, Ed. Psych., Ed. Tech., Math Ed., Mid Level Ed., Muticultrual Ed., Music Ed., Physical Ed., Read/Lang Arts Ed., School Cons., Sci. Ed., Sec. Ed., Soc. Ed., Spec. Ed.
Library: Henderson Library
Computer Resources: Macintosh, Dual Platform, PCs, CD-ROM, Videodisc

Research Areas	#Faculty
Adult Education	1
Art Education	1
Bilingual Education	
Counselor Education	5
Early Childhood Ed.	9
Ed. Admin	5
Ed. Tech.	3
Elementary Ed.	9
Foreign Lang. Ed.	4
Higher Ed.	1
Math Ed.	2
Mid. Lev. Ed.	5

Multicultural Ed.	2
Music Ed.	2
Physical Ed.	3
Read/Lang. Arts Ed.	4
School Counseling	4
Science Ed.	3
Secondary Ed.	3
Soc. Studies Ed.	2
Special Ed.	5
Other	

Research Institutes/Centers: Center for the Improvement of Science and Mathematics Education
Student Body Demographics: Average Age 34, 77% female, 23% male
Percent Ethnic Minorities: Hispanic-American 1%, Asian-American 1%, African-American 11%
Geographic Representation: Southeast 98%
Tuition: 1,965 (in state), 5,175 (out of state)
Financial Aid Recipients: N/A
Average Annual Housing Cost: 2,565
Application Deadline: N/A
Number of: applicants annually N/A; applicants accepted annually N/A; students enrolled annually N/A

Tests Required	Preferred/Min Score
Graduate Record Exam	800–1,000
National Teachers Exam	
Praxis II Exam	

Georgia State University College of Education

University Plaza, Atlanta, GA 30303
Admissions: (PH)404 651-2539
Dean: (PH)404 651-2525, (FAX)404 651-2555
Total Enrollment: 20,000
Grad Enrollment: FTM 877, PTM 838, FTD 151, PTD 198, Off campus 100%
Program Membership: Holmes Partnership
Academic Programs Available: MASTERS: Art Ed., Counselor Ed., Early Childhood Ed., Ed. Admin, Ed. Psych., Ed. Tech., Foreign Lang. Ed., Higher Ed., Math Ed., Mid Level Ed., Music Ed., Physical Ed., Read/Lang Arts Ed., School Cons., Sci. Ed., Soc. Ed., Spec. Ed. DOCTORATE: Art Ed., Counselor Ed., Early Childhood Ed., Ed. Admin, Ed. Psych., Ed. Tech., Foreign Lang. Ed., Higher Ed., Math Ed., Mid Level Ed., Music Ed., Physical Ed., Read/Lang Arts Ed., School Cons., Sci. Ed., Soc. Ed., Spec. Ed.
Library: William R. Pullen Library
Computer Resources: Macintosh, Dual Platform, PCs, CD-ROM, Videodisc

Research Areas	#Faculty
Adult Education	
Art Education	
Bilingual Education	
Counselor Education	
Early Childhood Ed.	
Ed. Admin	
Ed. Tech.	
Elementary Ed.	
Foreign Lang. Ed.	
Higher Ed.	

Math Ed.
Mid. Lev. Ed.
Multicultural Ed.
Music Ed.
Physical Ed.
Read/Lang. Arts Ed.
School Counseling
Science Ed.
Secondary Ed.
Soc. Studies Ed.
Special Ed.
Other
Student Body Demographics: Average Age 33, 79% female, 21% male
Percent Ethnic Minorities: Hispanic-American 1%, Asian-American 2%, African-American 19%
Geographic Representation: N/A
Graduate Career Paths: K-12 Teaching 58%, School Counseling 3%, K-12 Special Ed 12%, School Administration 8%, Higher Ed Administration 1%, Community Counseling 8%
Tuition: 522 (in state), 1,672 (out of state)
Financial Aid Recipients: N/A
Average Annual Housing Cost: 4,788
Application Deadline: varies
Number of: applicants annually 4,200; applicants accepted annually 2,270; students enrolled annually 1,120

Tests Required	Preferred/Min Score
Graduate Record Exam	800–1,000
National Teachers Exam	
Praxis II Exam	
TOEFL	550

Oglethorpe University Division of Education

4484 Peachtree Road, N.E., Atlanta, GA 30319
Admissions: (PH)404 364-8314, (FAX)404 364-8385, (EMAIL)ouadmis@aol.com
Dean: (PH)404 364-8387, (FAX)404 364-8387, (EMAIL)vvolante@aol.com
Total Enrollment: 1,000–5,000
Grad Enrollment: PTM 76
Program Membership: N/A
Academic Programs Available: MASTERS: Early Childhood Ed., Elementary Ed., Mid Level Ed., DOCTORATE: Early Childhood Ed., Elementary Ed., Mid Level Ed.
Library: Philip Weltner Library, 106,000 volumes
Computer Resources: Macintosh, Dual Platform, PCs, CD-ROM, Videodisc

Research Areas	#Faculty
Adult Education	
Art Education	
Bilingual Education	
Counselor Education	
Early Childhood Ed.	
Ed. Admin	
Ed. Tech.	
Elementary Ed.	
Foreign Lang. Ed.	

Higher Ed.	
Math Ed.	1
Mid. Lev. Ed.	1
Multicultural Ed.	
Music Ed.	
Physical Ed.	
Read/Lang. Arts Ed.	1
School Counseling	
Science Ed.	
Secondary Ed.	
Soc. Studies Ed.	
Special Ed.	
Other	1

Student Body Demographics: Average Age 32, 93% female, 7% male
Percent Ethnic Minorities: Asian-American 1%, African-American 5%, Native-American 1%
Geographic Representation: Southeast 99%
Graduate Career Paths: K-12 Teaching 96%, Higher Ed Teaching 2%, K-12 School Administration 2%
Tuition: 425/cse (in state), 425/cse (out of state)
Financial Aid Recipients: N/A
Average Annual Housing Cost: N/A
Application Deadline: 8/1; 12/1; 6/1
Number of: applicants annually 65-80; applicants accepted annually 58-73; students enrolled annually 45-50

Tests Required	Preferred/Min Score
Graduate Record Exam	1,960
National Teachers Exam	800
Praxis II Exam	
TOEFL	550

Piedmont College Graduate Education

P.O. Box 10, Demorest, GA 30535
Admissions: (PH)706 778-3000 x230, (FAX)706 778-2811
Dean: (PH)706 778-3000 x2
Total Enrollment: 1,000
Grad Enrollment: FTM 6, PTM 16, Off campus 100%
Program Membership: N/A
Academic Programs Available: MASTERS: Early Childhood Ed., DOCTORATE: Early Childhood Ed.
Library: Louise Patton Library, 90,000 volumes
Computer Resources: Macintosh, Dual Platform, PCs, CD-ROM, Videodisc

Research Areas	#Faculty
Adult Education	1
Art Education	
Bilingual Education	
Counselor Education	
Early Childhood Ed.	3
Ed. Admin	
Ed. Tech.	2
Elementary Ed.	
Foreign Lang. Ed.	
Higher Ed.	1
Math Ed.	
Mid. Lev. Ed.	
Multicultural Ed.	
Music Ed.	

Physical Ed.
Read/Lang. Arts Ed.
School Counseling
Science Ed.
Secondary Ed.
Soc. Studies Ed.
Special Ed.
Other
Student Body Demographics: Average Age 32, 85% female, 15% male
Percent Ethnic Minorities: N/A
Geographic Representation: Southeast 100%
Tuition: 265 (in state), 265 (out of state)
Financial Aid Recipients: 95%
Average Annual Housing Cost: N/A
Application Deadline: 8/1; 12/1; 4/1
Number of: applicants annually 40; applicants accepted annually 25-30; students enrolled annually 25-30

Tests Required	Preferred/Min Score
Graduate Record Exam	800–850
National Teachers Exam	
Praxis II Exam	
TOEFL	500

University of Georgia College of Education

Graduate School, Athens, GA 30602
Admissions: (PH)706 542-1739, (FAX)706 542-3219
Dean: (PH)706 542-3866, (FAX)706 542-0360, (EMAIL)junes@uga.cc.uga.edu
Total Enrollment: 20,000
Grad Enrollment: FTM 1,215, FTD 900, On campus 25%, Off campus 75%
Program Membership: Holmes Partnership
Academic Programs Available: MASTERS: Adult Ed., Art Ed., Early Childhood Ed., Ed. Admin, Ed. Psych., Ed. Tech., Elementary Ed., Foreign Lang. Ed., Higher Ed., Math Ed., Music Ed., Physical Ed., Read/Lang Arts Ed., School Cons., Sci. Ed., Soc. Ed., Spec. Ed. DOCTORATE: Adult Ed., Art Ed., Early Childhood Ed., Ed. Admin, Ed. Psych., Ed. Tech., Elementary Ed., Foreign Lang. Ed., Higher Ed., Math Ed., Music Ed., Physical Ed., Read/Lang Arts Ed., School Cons., Sci. Ed., Soc. Ed., Spec. Ed.
Library: University of Georgia Libraries, 3 million volumes
Computer Resources: Macintosh, Dual Platform, PCs, CD-ROM, Videodisc

Research Areas	#Faculty
Adult Education	8
Art Education	
Bilingual Education	
Counselor Education	18
Early Childhood Ed.	15
Ed. Admin	15
Ed. Tech.	10
Elementary Ed.	
Foreign Lang. Ed.	3
Higher Ed.	
Math Ed.	11
Mid. Lev. Ed.	6
Multicultural Ed.	

Music Ed.

Physical Ed.	38
Read/Lang. Arts Ed.	19
School Counseling	
Science Ed.	9
Secondary Ed.	9
Soc. Studies Ed.	9
Special Ed.	8
Other	27

Research Institutes/Centers: National Reading Research Center, National Research Center on the Gifted and Talented, Learning Disabilities Research and Training Center
Student Body Demographics: Average Age 35, 67% female, 33% male
Percent Ethnic Minorities: Hispanic-American 0.5%, Asian-American 0.5%, African-American 3%
Geographic Representation: New England 3%, Midwest 3%, Mid Atlantic 5%, Southwest 2%, West 1%, Southeast 85%, Northwest 1%
Graduate Career Paths: K-12 Teaching 75%, K-12 Special Ed 6%, School Administration 11%
Tuition: 836 (in state), 2,265 (out of state)
Financial Aid Recipients: N/A
Average Annual Housing Cost: 3,500
Application Deadline: rolling
Number of: applicants annually 1,300; applicants accepted annually 700; students enrolled annually 500

Tests Required	Preferred/Min Score
Graduate Record Exam	850-1000
National Teachers Exam	
Praxis II Exam	
TOEFL	550

IDAHO

Boise State University College of Education

1910 University Drive, Boise, ID 83725
Admissions: (PH)208 385-3903, (FAX)208 385-4061
Dean: (PH)208 385-1134, (FAX)208 385-4365, (EMAIL)rbarr@clavin.idbsu.edu
Total Enrollment: 10,000–20,000
Grad Enrollment: FTM 107, PTM 482, FTD 23, On campus 3%, Off campus 97%
Program Membership: Holmes Partnership
Academic Programs Available: MASTERS: Art Ed., Bilingual Ed., Early Childhood Ed., Ed. Tech., Math Ed., Music Ed., Physical Ed., Read/Lang Arts Ed., School Cons., Sci. Ed., Spec. Ed. DOCTORATE: Art Ed., Bilingual Ed., Early Childhood Ed., Ed. Tech., Math Ed., Music Ed., Physical Ed., Read/Lang Arts Ed., School Cons., Sci. Ed., Spec. Ed.
Library: Albertsons Library, 366,000 volumes
Computer Resources: Macintosh, Dual Platform, PCs, CD-ROM, Videodisc

Research Areas	#Faculty
Adult Education	

Art Education	
Bilingual Education	3
Counselor Education	2
Early Childhood Ed.	3
Ed. Admin	
Ed. Tech.	4
Elementary Ed.	6
Foreign Lang. Ed.	
Higher Ed.	
Math Ed.	1
Mid. Lev. Ed.	
Multicultural Ed.	
Music Ed.	
Physical Ed.	11
Read/Lang. Arts Ed.	6
School Counseling	2
Science Ed.	2
Secondary Ed.	2
Soc. Studies Ed.	5
Special Ed.	4
Other	6

Student Body Demographics: Average Age 28, 59% female, 41% male
Percent Ethnic Minorities: N/A
Geographic Representation: West 5%, Northwest 90%
Graduate Career Paths: K-12 Teaching 28%, Higher Ed Teaching 4%, K-12 Special Ed 2%
Tuition: 1,154 (in state), 3,247 (out of state)
Financial Aid Recipients: 3%
Average Annual Housing Cost: 3,730
Application Deadline: 7/26; 11/29; 5/1
Number of: applicants annually N/A; applicants accepted annually N/A; students enrolled annually N/A

Tests Required	Preferred/Min Score
Graduate Record Exam	800–1,000
National Teachers Exam	
Praxis II Exam	

Idaho State University College of Education

Office of Graduate Studies, Box 8075, Pocatello, ID 83209
Admissions: (PH)208 236-2150, (FAX)208 236-4697, (EMAIL)housedwi@isu.edu
Dean: (PH)208 236-2714, (FAX)208 236-4697
Total Enrollment: 10,000–20,000
Grad Enrollment: FTM 124, PTM 1,031, FTD 12, PTD 32, On campus 2%, Off campus 98%
Program Membership: Holmes Partnership
Academic Programs Available: MASTERS: Adult Ed., Early Childhood Ed., Ed. Admin, School Cons., Spec. Ed. DOCTORATE: Adult Ed., Early Childhood Ed., Ed. Admin, School Cons., Spec. Ed.
Library: Obelor Library, 400,000 volumes
Computer Resources: Macintosh, Dual Platform, PCs, CD-ROM, Videodisc

Research Areas	#Faculty
Adult Education	3
Art Education	
Bilingual Education	
Counselor Education	4

Early Childhood Ed.	2
Ed. Admin	3
Ed. Tech.	
Elementary Ed.	4
Foreign Lang. Ed.	
Higher Ed.	
Math Ed.	
Mid. Lev. Ed.	
Multicultural Ed.	
Music Ed.	
Physical Ed.	
Read/Lang. Arts Ed.	3
School Counseling	
Science Ed.	
Secondary Ed.	
Soc. Studies Ed.	
Special Ed.	3
Other	4

Student Body Demographics: Average Age 36, 50% female, 50% male
Percent Ethnic Minorities: Hispanic-American 1%, Asian-American 1%, African-American 1%, Native-American 1%
Geographic Representation: West 20%, Northwest 78%
Graduate Career Paths: K-12 Teaching 30%, School Counseling 20%, K-12 Special Ed 20%, School Administration 20%
Tuition: 101/cr (in state), 180/cr (out of state)
Financial Aid Recipients: 10%
Average Annual Housing Cost: 1,900
Application Deadline: 12/1; 5/1
Number of: applicants annually 1,500; applicants accepted annually 1,200; students enrolled annually 1,155

Tests Required	Preferred/Min Score
Graduate Record Exam	
National Teachers Exam	
Praxis II Exam	

ILLINOIS

Concordia University College of Education

Office of Graduate Admissions, 7400 Augusta, River Forest, IL 60305
Admissions: (PH)708 209-4093, (FAX)708 209-3176
Dean: (PH)708 209-3010
Total Enrollment: 1,000–5,000
Grad Enrollment: FTM 176, PTM 719, On campus 20%, Off campus 80%
Program Membership: N/A
Academic Programs Available: MASTERS: Bilingual Ed., Counselor Ed., Early Childhood Ed., Ed. Admin, Math Ed., Music Ed., Read/Lang Arts Ed., School Cons., DOCTORATE: Bilingual Ed., Counselor Ed., Early Childhood Ed., Ed. Admin, Math Ed., Music Ed., Read/Lang Arts Ed., School Cons.

Library: Klinck Memorial Library, 164,000 volumes
Computer Resources: Macintosh, Dual Platform

Research Areas	#Faculty
Adult Education	
Art Education	
Bilingual Education	
Counselor Education	9
Early Childhood Ed.	3
Ed. Admin	15
Ed. Tech.	
Elementary Ed.	33
Foreign Lang. Ed.	
Higher Ed.	
Math Ed.	2
Mid. Lev. Ed.	
Multicultural Ed.	2
Music Ed.	3
Physical Ed.	
Read/Lang. Arts Ed.	13
School Counseling	9
Science Ed.	1
Secondary Ed.	1
Soc. Studies Ed.	
Special Ed.	
Other	

Student Body Demographics: Average Age 32, 65% female, 35% male
Percent Ethnic Minorities: N/A
Geographic Representation: New England 2%, Midwest 85%, Mid Atlantic 1%, Southwest 3%, West 3%, Southeast 4%, Northwest 2%
Tuition: 219/hr (in state), 219/hr (out of state)
Financial Aid Recipients: 35%
Average Annual Housing Cost: 4,450
Application Deadline: rolling
Number of: applicants annually 475; applicants accepted annually N/A; students enrolled annually N/A

Tests Required	Preferred/Min Score
Graduate Record Exam	
National Teachers Exam	
Praxis II Exam	
TOEFL	550

Eastern Illinois University College of Education and Professional Studies

600 Lincoln Avenue, Charleston, IL 61920
Admissions: (PH)217 581-2223, (FAX)217 581-7060
Dean: (PH)217 581-2524, (FAX)217 581-2518
Total Enrollment: 10,000–20,000
Grad Enrollment: FTM 233, PTM 509
Program Membership: N/A
Academic Programs Available: MASTERS: Counselor Ed., Early Childhood Ed., Ed. Admin, Ed. Psych., Ed. Tech., Elementary Ed., Math Ed., Physical Ed., School Cons., Sci. Ed., Spec. Ed. DOCTORATE: Counselor Ed., Early Childhood Ed., Ed. Admin, Ed. Psych., Ed. Tech., Elementary Ed., Math Ed., Physical Ed., School Cons., Sci. Ed., Spec. Ed.
Library: Booth Library

Computer Resources: Macintosh, Dual Platform, PCs, CD-ROM, Videodisc

Research Areas	#Faculty
Adult Education	
Art Education	
Bilingual Education	
Counselor Education	4
Early Childhood Ed.	2
Ed. Admin	5
Ed. Tech.	
Elementary Ed.	5
Foreign Lang. Ed.	
Higher Ed.	
Math Ed.	
Mid. Lev. Ed.	
Multicultural Ed.	
Music Ed.	
Physical Ed.	6
Read/Lang. Arts Ed.	
School Counseling	4
Science Ed.	2
Secondary Ed.	2
Soc. Studies Ed.	2
Special Ed.	8
Other	

Research Institutes/Centers: Center for Educational Studies
Student Body Demographics: Average Age N/A, 67% female, 33% male
Percent Ethnic Minorities: Asian-American 3%, African-American 5%
Geographic Representation: Midwest 100%
Tuition: 1,429 (in state), 3505 (out of state)
Financial Aid Recipients: N/A
Average Annual Housing Cost: 2,286
Application Deadline: varies
Number of: applicants annually N/A; applicants accepted annually N/A; students enrolled annually N/A

Tests Required	Preferred/Min Score
Graduate Record Exam	
National Teachers Exam	
Praxis II Exam	

Governors State University College of Education

University Park, IL 60466
Admissions: (PH)708 534-4490, (FAX)708 534-8951
Dean: (PH)708 534-4050, (EMAIL)l-zalew@acs.gsu.bgu.edu
Total Enrollment: 5,000–10,000
Grad Enrollment: FTM 33, PTM 798, Off campus 100%
Program Membership: N/A
Academic Programs Available: MASTERS: Ed. Admin, Ed. Psych., School Cons., Spec. Ed. DOCTORATE: Ed. Admin, Ed. Psych., School Cons., Spec. Ed.
Library: University Library, 271,000 volumes
Computer Resources: PCs

Research Areas	#Faculty
Adult Education	
Art Education	
Bilingual Education	1
Counselor Education	

Early Childhood Ed.	1	Higher Ed.	
Ed. Admin	3	Math Ed.	
Ed. Tech.	1	Mid. Lev. Ed.	
Elementary Ed.	6	Multicultural Ed.	
Foreign Lang. Ed.		Music Ed.	
Higher Ed.		Physical Ed.	
Math Ed.	1	Read/Lang. Arts Ed.	
Mid. Lev. Ed.		School Counseling	
Multicultural Ed.		Science Ed.	
Music Ed.		Secondary Ed.	
Physical Ed.		Soc. Studies Ed.	
Read/Lang. Arts Ed.	1	Special Ed.	
School Counseling	2	Other	
Science Ed.	1		
Secondary Ed.	1		
Soc. Studies Ed.			
Special Ed.	2		
Other	5		

Student Body Demographics: Average Age 36, 80% female, 20% male
Percent Ethnic Minorities: Hispanic-American 2.6%, African-American 17%
Geographic Representation: Midwest 99%
Tuition: 1,103 (in state), 3179 (out of state)
Financial Aid Recipients: 33%
Average Annual Housing Cost: 3,200
Application Deadline: 7/14; 11/17; 4/12
Number of: applicants annually 970; applicants accepted annually 674; students enrolled annually 537

Tests Required	Preferred/Min Score
Graduate Record Exam	
National Teachers Exam	
Praxis II Exam	
TOEFL	550

Illinois State University College of Education
201 Hovey Hall, Normal, IL 61790-2200
Admissions: (PH)309 438-2181, (FAX)309 438-3932
Dean: (PH)309 438-5415, (FAX)309 438-3813, (EMAIL)sbpancra@rs6000.ilstu.edu
Total Enrollment: 10,000–20,000
Grad Enrollment: 580 total, On campus 94%, Off campus 6%
Program Membership: N/A
Academic Programs Available: MASTERS: Ed. Admin, Math Ed., Music Ed., Physical Ed., Read/Lang Arts Ed., Spec. Ed. DOCTORATE: Ed. Admin, Math Ed., Music Ed., Read/Lang Arts Ed., Spec. Ed.
Library: Milner Library, 1.3 million volumes

Research Areas	#Faculty
Adult Education	
Art Education	
Bilingual Education	
Counselor Education	
Early Childhood Ed.	
Ed. Admin	
Ed. Tech.	
Elementary Ed.	
Foreign Lang. Ed.	

Student Body Demographics: Average Age 27, 61% female, 39% male
Percent Ethnic Minorities: Hispanic-American 1.6%, Asian-American 2%, African-American 5%, Native-American 0.3%
Geographic Representation: New England 3%, Midwest 91%, Mid Atlantic 1.6%, Southwest 3%, West 1%, Southeast 4%, Northwest 1%
Tuition: 120/hr (in state), 301/hr (out of state)
Financial Aid Recipients: 23%
Average Annual Housing Cost: 2,983
Application Deadline: varies
Number of: applicants annually 1,422; applicants accepted annually 1,067; students enrolled annually 627

Tests Required	Preferred/Min Score
Graduate Record Exam	
National Teachers Exam	
Praxis II Exam	

Loyola University Chicago
School of Education
1041 Ridge Road, Wilmette, IL 60091
Admissions: (PH)708 853-3327, (FAX)708 853-3375, (EMAIL)mrosind@luc.edu
Dean: (PH)708 853-3338, (FAX)708 853-3375, (EMAIL)rroemer@luc.edu
Total Enrollment: 10,000–20,000
Grad Enrollment: FTM 425, PTM 219, FTD 245, PTD 96, On campus 1%, Off campus 99%
Program Membership: Holmes Partnership
Academic Programs Available: MASTERS: Adult Ed., Counselor Ed., Early Childhood Ed., Ed. Admin, Ed. Psych., Higher Ed., School Cons., Spec. Ed. DOCTORATE: Adult Ed., Counselor Ed., Early Childhood Ed., Ed. Admin, Ed. Psych., Higher Ed., School Cons., Spec. Ed.
Library: Loyola University Library
Computer Resources: Macintosh, Dual Platform, PCs, CD-ROM, Videodisc

Research Areas	#Faculty
Adult Education	2
Art Education	
Bilingual Education	
Counselor Education	6
Early Childhood Ed.	2
Ed. Admin	4

Ed. Tech.	
Elementary Ed.	8
Foreign Lang. Ed.	
Higher Ed.	3
Math Ed.	
Mid. Lev. Ed.	
Multicultural Ed.	
Music Ed.	
Physical Ed.	
Read/Lang. Arts Ed.	
School Counseling	4
Science Ed.	
Secondary Ed.	
Soc. Studies Ed.	
Special Ed.	3
Other	7

Student Body Demographics: Average Age 25, 60% female, 40% male

Percent Ethnic Minorities: Hispanic-American 10%, Asian-American 8%, African-American 12%, Native-American 1%

Geographic Representation: New England 1%, Midwest 89%, Mid Atlantic 3%, Southwest 1%, West 3%, Southeast 1%, Northwest 2%

Graduate Career Paths: K-12 Teaching 20%, Higher Ed Teaching 5%, School Counseling 10%, K-12 Special Ed 5%, School Administration 20%, Higher Ed Administration 20%, Higher Ed Counseling 5%, Community Counseling 15%

Tuition: 368/hr (in state), 368/hr (out of state)

Financial Aid Recipients: 5%

Average Annual Housing Cost: N/A

Application Deadline: 2/1; 5/1; 8/1; 12/1

Number of: applicants annually 840; applicants accepted annually 720; students enrolled annually N/A

Tests Required	Preferred/Min Score
Graduate Record Exam	1,000–1,200
National Teachers Exam	
Praxis II Exam	
TOEFL	650

National-Louis University
National College of Education

2840 Sheridan Road, Evanston, IL 60201

Admissions: (PH)847 475-1100 x2479, (FAX)847 256-7936, (EMAIL)whol@evan1.nl.edu

Dean: (PH)847 256-5150 x5201, (FAX)847 465-5629, (EMAIL)ltaf@wheelingl.nl.edu

Grad Enrollment: FTM 1280, PTM 1318, FTD 5, PTD 83, CAS 124, Off campus 100%

Program Membership: N/A

Academic Programs Available: MASTERS: Bilingual Ed., Early Childhood Ed., Ed. Admin, Ed. Psych., Ed. Tech., Elementary Ed., Math Ed., Read/Lang Arts Ed., Sci. Ed., Spec. Ed. DOCTORATE: Bilingual Ed., Early Childhood Ed., Ed. Admin, Ed. Psych., Ed. Tech., Elementary Ed., Math Ed., Read/Lang Arts Ed., Sci. Ed., Spec. Ed.

Library: 1 million volumes

Computer Resources: Macintosh, Dual Platform, PCs, CD-ROM, Videodisc

Research Areas	#Faculty
Adult Education	
Art Education	
Bilingual Education	
Counselor Education	
Early Childhood Ed.	
Ed. Admin	
Ed. Tech.	
Elementary Ed.	
Foreign Lang. Ed.	
Higher Ed.	
Math Ed.	
Mid. Lev. Ed.	
Multicultural Ed.	
Music Ed.	
Physical Ed.	
Read/Lang. Arts Ed.	
School Counseling	
Science Ed.	
Secondary Ed.	
Soc. Studies Ed.	
Special Ed.	
Other	

Research Institutes/Centers: The Reading Center, Center for City Schools, Teacher Leadership Center

Student Body Demographics: Average Age 38, 84% female, 16% male

Percent Ethnic Minorities: Hispanic-American 5%, Asian-American 2%, African-American 9%, Native-American 1%

Geographic Representation: New England 1%, Midwest 91%, Mid Atlantic 3%, Southwest 1%, West 1%, Southeast 5%, Northwest 1%

Graduate Career Paths: K-12 Teaching 69%, K-12 Special Ed 2%, School Administration 4%

Tuition: 344/hr (in state), 344/hr (out of state)

Financial Aid Recipients: N/A

Average Annual Housing Cost: N/A

Application Deadline: rolling

Number of: applicants annually 2178; applicants accepted annually 2149; students enrolled annually N/A

Tests Required	Preferred/Min Score
Graduate Record Exam	
National Teachers Exam	
Praxis II Exam	
TOEFL	550

Northern Illinois University
College of Education

DeKalb, IL 60115

Admissions: (PH)815 753-0446

Dean: (PH)815 753-1948, (FAX)815 753-2100

Total Enrollment: 20,000

Grad Enrollment: 1793 total, On campus 3%, Off campus 97%

Program Membership: N/A

Academic Programs Available: MASTERS: Adult Ed., Counselor Ed., Early Childhood Ed., Ed. Admin, Ed. Psych., Ed. Tech., Elementary Ed., Higher Ed., Math Ed., Music Ed., Physical Ed., Read/Lang Arts Ed., School Cons., Sci. Ed., DOCTORATE: Adult Ed., Counselor Ed., Early Childhood Ed., Ed. Admin, Ed. Psych., Ed. Tech., Elementary Ed., Higher Ed., Math Ed., Music Ed., Physical Ed., Read/Lang Arts Ed., School Cons.

Library: Founders Memorial Library, 1.3 million volumes

Computer Resources: Macintosh, Dual Platform, PCs, CD-ROM, Videodisc

Research Areas	#Faculty
Adult Education	12
Art Education	
Bilingual Education	
Counselor Education	9
Early Childhood Ed.	3
Ed. Admin	10
Ed. Tech.	7
Elementary Ed.	10
Foreign Lang. Ed.	
Higher Ed.	
Math Ed.	
Mid. Lev. Ed.	
Multicultural Ed.	
Music Ed.	
Physical Ed.	25
Read/Lang. Arts Ed.	5
School Counseling	9
Science Ed.	
Secondary Ed.	
Soc. Studies Ed.	
Special Ed.	13
Other	

Research Institutes/Centers: Office of Research, Evaluation and Policy Studies

Student Body Demographics: Average Age 34, 67% female, 33% male

Percent Ethnic Minorities: Hispanic-American 3%, Asian-American 1%, African-American 9%

Geographic Representation: Midwest 100%

Graduate Career Paths: K-12 Teaching 66%, Higher Ed Teaching 5%, School Counseling 5%, K-12 Special Ed 15%, School Administration 5%, Higher Ed Administration 1%, Higher Ed Counseling 1%, Community Counseling 2%

Tuition: 1,527 (in state), 3630 (out of state)

Financial Aid Recipients: 60%

Average Annual Housing Cost: 4,500

Application Deadline: 6/1; 11/1; 4/1

Number of: applicants annually N/A; applicants accepted annually N/A; students enrolled annually N/A

Tests Required	Preferred/Min Score
Graduate Record Exam	850–1000
National Teachers Exam	
Praxis II Exam	
TOEFL	550

Northwestern University
School of Education and Social Policy

2115 N. Campus Drive, Evanston, IL 60208

Admissions: (PH)708 491-3790, (FAX)708 467-2495

Dean: (PH)708 491-3790, (FAX)708 467-1418

Total Enrollment: 10,000–20,000

Program Membership: Holmes Partnership

Academic Programs Available: MASTERS: Adult Ed., Art Ed., Ed. Admin, Elementary Ed., Foreign Lang. Ed., Higher Ed., Math Ed., Mid Level Ed., Sci. Ed., Sec. Ed., Soc. Ed., DOCTORATE: Adult Ed., Art Ed., Ed. Admin, Elementary Ed., Foreign Lang. Ed., Higher Ed., Math Ed., Mid Level Ed., Sci. Ed., Sec. Ed., Soc. Ed.

Library: University Library, 3.6 million volumes

Computer Resources: Macintosh, Dual Platform, PCs, CD-ROM, Videodisc

Research Areas	#Faculty
Adult Education	
Art Education	
Bilingual Education	
Counselor Education	
Early Childhood Ed.	
Ed. Admin	
Ed. Tech.	
Elementary Ed.	
Foreign Lang. Ed.	
Higher Ed.	
Math Ed.	
Mid. Lev. Ed.	
Multicultural Ed.	
Music Ed.	
Physical Ed.	
Read/Lang. Arts Ed.	
School Counseling	
Science Ed.	
Secondary Ed.	
Soc. Studies Ed.	
Special Ed.	
Other	

Research Institutes/Centers: Institute for Learning Sciences, Family Institute, Center for Urban Affairs and Policy Research

Student Body Demographics: Average Age N/A, 75% female, 25% male

Percent Ethnic Minorities: Hispanic-American 1%, Asian-American 2%, African-American 3%

Geographic Representation: N/A

Tuition: 1,367 (in state), 1367 (out of state)

Financial Aid Recipients: N/A

Average Annual Housing Cost: N/A

Application Deadline: varies

Number of: applicants annually 108; applicants accepted annually 76; students enrolled annually 50

Tests Required	Preferred/Min Score
Graduate Record Exam	1246
National Teachers Exam	
Praxis II Exam	

Roosevelt University College of Education

430 South Michigan Avenue, Chicago, IL 60605
Admissions: (PH)312 341-2440, (FAX)312 341-3523
Dean: (PH)312 341-3700, (FAX)312 341-4326
Total Enrollment: 5,000–10,000
Grad Enrollment: FTM 25, PTM 500, PTD 100, Off campus 100%
Program Membership: N/A
Academic Programs Available: MASTERS: Counselor Ed., Early Childhood Ed., Ed. Admin, Elementary Ed., Foreign Lang. Ed., Math Ed., Music Ed., Read/Lang Arts Ed., School Cons., Sci. Ed., Sec. Ed., Soc. Ed., DOCTORATE: Counselor Ed., Early Childhood Ed., Ed. Admin, Elementary Ed., Foreign Lang. Ed., Math Ed., Music Ed., Read/Lang Arts Ed., School Cons., Sci. Ed., Sec. Ed., Soc. Ed.
Library: Roosevelt University Library
Computer Resources: Macintosh, Dual Platform

Research Areas	#Faculty
Adult Education	
Art Education	
Bilingual Education	
Counselor Education	3
Early Childhood Ed.	3
Ed. Admin	4
Ed. Tech.	
Elementary Ed.	4
Foreign Lang. Ed.	
Higher Ed.	1
Math Ed.	1
Mid. Lev. Ed.	
Multicultural Ed.	2
Music Ed.	4
Physical Ed.	
Read/Lang. Arts Ed.	1
School Counseling	3
Science Ed.	
Secondary Ed.	
Soc. Studies Ed.	1
Special Ed.	1
Other	

Research Institutes/Centers: Alliance for Educational Leadership
Student Body Demographics: Average Age 35, 65% female, 35% male
Percent Ethnic Minorities: N/A
Geographic Representation: Midwest 100%
Graduate Career Paths: K-12 Teaching 50%, School Counseling 10%, K-12 School Administration 30%, Community Counseling 10%
Tuition: 1,100 (in state), 1,100 (out of state)
Financial Aid Recipients: 50%
Average Annual Housing Cost: N/A
Application Deadline: rolling
Number of: applicants annually 517; applicants accepted annually 461; students enrolled annually 334

Tests Required	Preferred/Min Score
Graduate Record Exam	
National Teachers Exam	
Praxis II Exam	

University of Chicago Department of Education

5835 South Kimbark Avenue, Chicago, IL 60637
Admissions: (PH)312 702-9458, (FAX)312 702-0248
Dean: (PH)312 702-9456, (FAX)312 702-0248
Total Enrollment: 10,000–20,000
Grad Enrollment: FTM 21, PTM 5, FTD 106, PTD 3
Program Membership: Holmes Partnership
Academic Programs Available: MASTERS: Ed. Admin, Ed. Psych., Math Ed., Sec. Ed., DOCTORATE: Ed. Admin, Ed. Psych., Math Ed., Sec. Ed.
Library: Regenstein Library, 6 million volumes
Computer Resources: Macintosh, Dual Platform, PCs, CD-ROM, Videodisc

Research Areas	#Faculty
Adult Education	
Art Education	
Bilingual Education	
Counselor Education	
Early Childhood Ed.	
Ed. Admin	2
Ed. Tech.	
Elementary Ed.	
Foreign Lang. Ed.	
Higher Ed.	
Math Ed.	2
Mid. Lev. Ed.	
Multicultural Ed.	
Music Ed.	
Physical Ed.	
Read/Lang. Arts Ed.	
School Counseling	
Science Ed.	
Secondary Ed.	
Soc. Studies Ed.	
Special Ed.	
Other	

Research Institutes/Centers: Benton Center for the Improvement of Teaching and Learning, Center for School Improvement
Student Body Demographics: Average Age 30, 60% female, 40% male
Percent Ethnic Minorities: Hispanic-American 5%, Asian-American 7%, African-American 12%
Geographic Representation: New England 6%, Midwest 63%, Mid Atlantic 4%, Southwest 3%, West 4%, Southeast 4%, Northwest 1%
Tuition: 21,318 (in state), 21,318 (out of state)
Financial Aid Recipients: 50%
Average Annual Housing Cost: N/A
Application Deadline: 1/5
Number of: applicants annually 150; applicants accepted annually 80; students enrolled annually 40

Tests Required	Preferred/Min Score
Graduate Record Exam	
National Teachers Exam	
Praxis II Exam	
TOEFL	550

University of Illinois College of Education

1310 S. Sixth, Champaign, IL 61820
Admissions: (PH)217 333-0964, (FAX)217 333-5847
Dean: (PH)217 333-0960, (FAX)217 333-5847
Total Enrollment: 20,000
Grad Enrollment: FTM 255, PTM 106, FTD 413, PTD 22, On campus 60%, Off campus 40%
Program Membership: Holmes Partnership
Academic Programs Available: MASTERS: Adult Ed., Early Childhood Ed., Ed. Admin, Ed. Psych., Ed. Tech., Elementary Ed., Higher Ed., Math Ed., Mid Level Ed., Sci. Ed., Sec. Ed., Soc. Ed., DOCTORATE: Adult Ed., Early Childhood Ed., Ed. Admin, Ed. Psych., Ed. Tech., Elementary Ed., Higher Ed., Math Ed., Mid Level Ed., Sci. Ed., Sec. Ed., Soc. Ed.
Library: University Library, 8.6 million volumes
Computer Resources: Macintosh, Dual Platform, PCs, CD-ROM, Videodisc

Research Areas	#Faculty
Adult Education	2
Art Education	
Bilingual Education	
Counselor Education	3
Early Childhood Ed.	3
Ed. Admin	6
Ed. Tech.	6
Elementary Ed.	10
Foreign Lang. Ed.	
Higher Ed.	2
Math Ed.	3
Mid. Lev. Ed.	3
Multicultural Ed.	
Music Ed.	
Physical Ed.	
Read/Lang. Arts Ed.	2
School Counseling	
Science Ed.	3
Secondary Ed.	3
Soc. Studies Ed.	2
Special Ed.	12
Other	

Research Institutes/Centers: Center for Instructional Research and Curriculum Evaluation, Bureau of Educational Research, Center for Study of Reading
Student Body Demographics: Average Age 35, 67% female, 33% male
Percent Ethnic Minorities: Hispanic-American 3%, Asian-American 3%, African-American 14%
Geographic Representation: New England 4%, Midwest 67%, Mid Atlantic 2%, Southwest 2%, West 2%, Southeast 3%, Northwest 1%
Graduate Career Paths: K-12 Teaching 50%, K-12 Special Ed 10%, School Administration 10%, Higher Ed Administration 10%
Tuition: 4,406 (in state), 10460 (out of state)
Financial Aid Recipients: 40%
Average Annual Housing Cost: 5,168
Application Deadline: 1/15; 2/15
Number of: applicants annually 248; applicants accepted annually 112; students enrolled annually N/A

Tests Required	Preferred/Min Score
Graduate Record Exam	1200
National Teachers Exam	
Praxis II Exam	
TOEFL	560–590

INDIANA

Anderson University School of Education

1100 E. 5th Street, Anderson, IN 46012
Admissions: (PH)317 641-4084, (FAX)317 641-3851, (EMAIL)jking@anderson.edu
Dean: (PH)317 641-4400, (FAX)317 641-3851, (EMAIL)kenarm@anderson.edu
Total Enrollment: 1,000–5,000
Grad Enrollment: Off campus 100%
Program Membership: N/A
Academic Programs Available: MASTERS: Elementary Ed., Mid Level Ed., Sec. Ed., DOCTORATE: Elementary Ed., Mid Level Ed., Sec. Ed.
Library: Nicholson Library, 182,700 volumes
Computer Resources: Macintosh, Dual Platform, PCs, CD-ROM, Videodisc

Research Areas	#Faculty
Adult Education	
Art Education	
Bilingual Education	
Counselor Education	
Early Childhood Ed.	
Ed. Admin	
Ed. Tech.	2
Elementary Ed.	3
Foreign Lang. Ed.	
Higher Ed.	
Math Ed.	2
Mid. Lev. Ed.	2
Multicultural Ed.	1
Music Ed.	
Physical Ed.	
Read/Lang. Arts Ed.	
School Counseling	
Science Ed.	
Secondary Ed.	
Soc. Studies Ed.	
Special Ed.	
Other	

Tuition: 175/cr (in state), 175/cr (out of state)
Financial Aid Recipients: 60%
Average Annual Housing Cost: N/A
Application Deadline: 8/14; 12/11; 4/15
Number of: applicants annually N/A; applicants accepted annually N/A; students enrolled annually N/A

Tests Required	Preferred/Min Score
Graduate Record Exam	1,000–1,100
National Teachers Exam	
Praxis II Exam	
TOEFL	500

Ball State University Teachers College

2000 University Avenue, Muncie, IN 47306
Admissions: (PH)317 285-5251
Grad Enrollment: 613 total
Program Membership: N/A

Research Areas	#Faculty
Adult Education	
Art Education	
Bilingual Education	
Counselor Education	
Early Childhood Ed.	
Ed. Admin	
Ed. Tech.	
Elementary Ed.	
Foreign Lang. Ed.	
Higher Ed.	
Math Ed.	
Mid. Lev. Ed.	
Multicultural Ed.	
Music Ed.	
Physical Ed.	
Read/Lang. Arts Ed.	
School Counseling	
Science Ed.	
Secondary Ed.	
Soc. Studies Ed.	
Special Ed.	
Other	

Tuition: 3,048 (in state), 7,824 (out of state)

Tests Required	Preferred/Min Score
Graduate Record Exam	1,000
National Teachers Exam	
Praxis II Exam	

Butler University College of Education

4600 Sunset Avenue, Indianapolis, IN 46208
Admissions: (PH)317 283-9310, (FAX)317 921-6433, (EMAIL)jcollier@butler.edu
Dean: (PH)317 283-9752, (FAX)317 921-6481, (EMAIL)tracy@butler.edu
Total Enrollment: 1,000–5,000
Grad Enrollment: FTM 42, PTM 288, Off campus 100%
Program Membership: N/A
Academic Programs Available: MASTERS: Counselor Ed., Ed. Admin, Elementary Ed., Read/Lang Arts Ed., School Cons., Sec. Ed., Spec. DOCTORATE: Counselor Ed., Ed. Admin, Elementary Ed., Read/Lang Arts Ed., School Cons., Sec. Ed., Spec. Ed.
Library: Irwin Library and Ruth Lilly Science Library, 286,000 volumes
Computer Resources: Macintosh, Dual Platform, PCs, CD-ROM, Videodisc

Research Areas	#Faculty
Adult Education	
Art Education	
Bilingual Education	
Counselor Education	
Early Childhood Ed.	1

Ed. Admin	3
Ed. Tech.	1
Elementary Ed.	4
Foreign Lang. Ed.	
Higher Ed.	
Math Ed.	
Mid. Lev. Ed.	1
Multicultural Ed.	1
Music Ed.	
Physical Ed.	4
Read/Lang. Arts Ed.	1
School Counseling	3
Science Ed.	1
Secondary Ed.	1
Soc. Studies Ed.	
Special Ed.	3
Other	

Research Institutes/Centers: Indiana Middle Level Institute
Student Body Demographics: Average Age 35, 82% female, 18% male
Percent Ethnic Minorities: African-American 1%
Geographic Representation: Midwest 100%
Tuition: 200/hr (in state), 200/hr (out of state)
Financial Aid Recipients: 10%
Average Annual Housing Cost: N/A
Application Deadline: rolling
Number of: applicants annually 75; applicants accepted annually 75; students enrolled annually 75

Tests Required	Preferred/Min Score
Graduate Record Exam	875–1000
National Teachers Exam	
Praxis II Exam	

Indiana University School of Education

201 North Rose Avenue, Bloomington, IN 47405-1006
Admissions: (PH)812 856-8525, (FAX)812 856-8518
Dean: (PH)812 856-8001, (FAX)812 856-8088
Grad Enrollment: FTM 388, FTD 652
Program Membership: Holmes Partnership
Academic Programs Available: MASTERS: Art Ed., Counselor Ed., Early Childhood Ed., Ed. Admin, Ed. Psych., Elementary Ed., Higher Ed., Math Ed., Read/Lang Arts Ed., School Cons., Sci. Ed., Sec. Ed., Soc. Ed., Spec. Ed. DOCTORATE: Art Ed., Counselor Ed., Early Childhood Ed., Ed. Admin, Ed. Psych., Elementary Ed., Higher Ed., Math Ed., Read/Lang Arts Ed., School Cons., Sci. Ed., Sec. Ed., Soc. Ed., Spec. Ed.
Library: Education Library, 60,000 volumes
Computer Resources: Macintosh, Dual Platform, PCs, CD-ROM, Videodisc

Research Areas	#Faculty
Adult Education	2
Art Education	2
Bilingual Education	2
Counselor Education	8
Early Childhood Ed.	5
Ed. Admin	5
Ed. Tech.	13
Elementary Ed.	3

Foreign Lang. Ed.	2	Ed. Admin	
Higher Ed.	7	Ed. Tech.	2
Math Ed.	5	Elementary Ed.	3
Mid. Lev. Ed.	1	Foreign Lang. Ed.	
Multicultural Ed.	5	Higher Ed.	
Music Ed.		Math Ed.	
Physical Ed.		Mid. Lev. Ed.	
Read/Lang. Arts Ed.	11	Multicultural Ed.	3
School Counseling	6	Music Ed.	
Science Ed.	4	Physical Ed.	
Secondary Ed.	4	Read/Lang. Arts Ed.	2
Soc. Studies Ed.	8	School Counseling	
Special Ed.	10	Science Ed.	2
Other	17	Secondary Ed.	2
		Soc. Studies Ed.	
		Special Ed.	3
		Other	

Research Institutes/Centers: Family Literacy Center, Center for Reading and Language Studies, Indiana Education Policy Center, Social Studies Development Center
Student Body Demographics: Average Age 34, 65% female, 35% male
Percent Ethnic Minorities: Hispanic-American 2%, Asian-American 14%, African-American 6%
Geographic Representation: N/A
Tuition: 133/cr (in state), 388/cr (out of state)
Financial Aid Recipients: N/A
Average Annual Housing Cost: 5,000
Application Deadline: 6/1; 11/1; 3/1
Number of: applicants annually 1,127; applicants accepted annually 813; students enrolled annually N/A

Tests Required	Preferred/Min Score
Graduate Record Exam	1,000
National Teachers Exam	
Praxis II Exam	
TOEFL	550

Indiana University South Bend
Division of Education

1700 Mishawaka Ave., P.O. Box 7111, South Bend, IN 46634-7111
Admissions: (PH)219 237-4839, (FAX)219 237-4834, (EMAIL)eligon@vines.iusb.edu
Dean: (PH)219 237-4339, (FAX)219 237-4550, (EMAIL)emaher@vines.iusb.edu
Total Enrollment: 5,000–10,000
Grad Enrollment: FTM 50, PTM 800, Off campus 100%
Program Membership: N/A
Academic Programs Available: MASTERS: Counselor Ed., Ed. Admin, Elementary Ed., Music Ed., School Cons., Sec. Ed., Spec. Ed. DOCTORATE: Counselor Ed., Ed. Admin, Elementary Ed., Music Ed., School Cons., Sec. Ed., Spec. Ed.
Library: N/A
Computer Resources: Macintosh, Dual Platform, PCs, CD-ROM, Videodisc

Research Areas	#Faculty
Adult Education	
Art Education	
Bilingual Education	
Counselor Education	7
Early Childhood Ed.	5

Student Body Demographics: Average Age 36, 78% female, 22% male
Percent Ethnic Minorities: African-American 5%
Geographic Representation: Midwest 99%
Graduate Career Paths: K-12 Teaching 46%, K-12 Special Ed 18%, School Administration 5%, Community Counseling 14%
Tuition: 111/hr (in state), 269/hr (out of state)
Financial Aid Recipients: N/A
Average Annual Housing Cost: N/A
Application Deadline: rolling
Number of: applicants annually 1,000; applicants accepted annually 850; students enrolled annually 788

Tests Required	Preferred/Min Score
Graduate Record Exam	
National Teachers Exam	
Praxis II Exam	

Indiana University-Purdue University
Fort Wayne School of Education

2101 Coliseum Blvd. East, Fort Wayne, IN 46805-1499
Admissions: (PH)219 481-6812
Dean: (PH)219 481-6441, (FAX)219 481-6083
Total Enrollment: 10,000–20,000
Grad Enrollment: FTM 16, PTM 425, Off campus 100%
Program Membership: Holmes Partnership
Academic Programs Available: MASTERS: Counselor Ed., Ed. Admin, Elementary Ed., Read/Lang Arts Ed., School Cons., Sec. Ed., DOCTORATE: Counselor Ed., Ed. Admin, Elementary Ed., Read/Lang Arts Ed., School Cons., Sec. Ed.
Library: Helmke Library, 280,000 volumes
Computer Resources: Macintosh, Dual Platform, PCs, CD-ROM, Videodisc

Research Areas	#Faculty
Adult Education	
Art Education	
Bilingual Education	
Counselor Education	3
Early Childhood Ed.	1
Ed. Admin	5
Ed. Tech.	

Elementary Ed.	5
Foreign Lang. Ed.	
Higher Ed.	
Math Ed.	
Mid. Lev. Ed.	
Multicultural Ed.	
Music Ed.	
Physical Ed.	
Read/Lang. Arts Ed.	2
School Counseling	3
Science Ed.	
Secondary Ed.	
Soc. Studies Ed.	
Special Ed.	1
Other	

Student Body Demographics: N/A
Percent Ethnic Minorities: N/A
Geographic Representation: N/A
Tuition: 110 (in state), 247 (out of state)
Financial Aid Recipients: N/A
Average Annual Housing Cost: N/A
Application Deadline: varies
Number of: applicants annually N/A; applicants accepted annually N/A; students enrolled annually N/A

Tests Required	Preferred/Min Score
Graduate Record Exam	
National Teachers Exam	
Praxis II Exam	

Indiana University-Southeast Division of Education

Hillside Hall 0023, New Albany, IN 47150
Admissions: (PH)812 941-2388, (FAX)812 941-2667, (EMAIL)jrisico@ius.indiana.edu
Dean: (PH)812 941-2385, (FAX)812 941-2667, (EMAIL)cdegraaf@ius.indiana.edu
Grad Enrollment: FTM 4, PTM 280, Off campus 100%
Program Membership: N/A
Academic Programs Available: MASTERS: Counselor Ed., Elementary Ed., Sec. Ed., DOCTORATE: Counselor Ed., Elementary Ed., Sec. Ed.
Library: IU Southeast Library, 250,000 volumes
Computer Resources: Macintosh, Dual Platform, PCs, CD-ROM, Videodisc

Research Areas	#Faculty
Adult Education	
Art Education	
Bilingual Education	
Counselor Education	2
Early Childhood Ed.	2
Ed. Admin	1
Ed. Tech.	
Elementary Ed.	
Foreign Lang. Ed.	
Higher Ed.	
Math Ed.	1
Mid. Lev. Ed.	
Multicultural Ed.	

Music Ed.	
Physical Ed.	1
Read/Lang. Arts Ed.	1
School Counseling	
Science Ed.	1
Secondary Ed.	1
Soc. Studies Ed.	1
Special Ed.	2
Other	

Student Body Demographics: Average Age 26, 55% female, 45% male
Percent Ethnic Minorities: N/A
Geographic Representation: Midwest 98%
Graduate Career Paths: K-12 Teaching 90%, School Counseling 6%, K-12 School Administration 4%
Tuition: 104/hr (in state), 238/hr (out of state)
Financial Aid Recipients: N/A
Average Annual Housing Cost: N/A
Application Deadline: rolling
Number of: applicants annually 90; applicants accepted annually 90; students enrolled annually N/A

Tests Required	Preferred/Min Score
Graduate Record Exam	
National Teachers Exam	
Praxis II Exam	

Purdue University School of Education

1440 Liberal Arts & Education Building, Room 6104, Purdue University, West Lafayette, IN 47907-1440
Admissions: (PH)317 494-2345, (FAX)317 494-5832, (EMAIL)educgrad@vm.cc.purdue.edu
Dean: (PH)317 494-2336, (FAX)317 494-5832
Total Enrollment: 20,000
Grad Enrollment: FTM 120, PTM 106, FTD 58, PTD 154, CAS 7
Program Membership: Holmes Partnership
Academic Programs Available: MASTERS: Art Ed., Counselor Ed., Ed. Admin, Ed. Psych., Elementary Ed., Foreign Lang. Ed., Higher Ed., Math Ed., Read/Lang Arts Ed., School Cons., Sci. Ed., Sec. Ed., Soc. Ed., Spec. Ed. DOCTORATE: Art Ed., Counselor Ed., Ed. Admin, Ed. Psych., Elementary Ed., Foreign Lang. Ed., Higher Ed., Math Ed., Read/Lang Arts Ed., School Cons., Sci. Ed., Sec. Ed., Soc. Ed., Spec. Ed.
Library: Over 2 million volumes
Computer Resources: Macintosh, Dual Platform, PCs, CD-ROM, Videodisc

Research Areas	#Faculty
Adult Education	2
Art Education	
Bilingual Education	
Counselor Education	9
Early Childhood Ed.	3
Ed. Admin	8
Ed. Tech.	6
Elementary Ed.	
Foreign Lang. Ed.	2
Higher Ed.	2
Math Ed.	5

Mid. Lev. Ed.	
Multicultural Ed.	2
Music Ed.	
Physical Ed.	
Read/Lang. Arts Ed.	15
School Counseling	
Science Ed.	7
Secondary Ed.	7
Soc. Studies Ed.	2
Special Ed.	8
Other	2

Student Body Demographics: Average Age 27-30, 69.6% female, 30.4% male
Percent Ethnic Minorities: Hispanic-American 2%, Asian-American 2%, African-American 5%, Native-American 1%
Geographic Representation: N/A
Tuition: 109/hr (in state), 334/hr (out of state)
Financial Aid Recipients: 14%
Average Annual Housing Cost: 3,150
Application Deadline: 9/15; 1/15
Number of: applicants annually 900; applicants accepted annually 800; students enrolled annually 678

Tests Required	Preferred/Min Score
Graduate Record Exam	1,000
National Teachers Exam	
Praxis II Exam	
TOEFL	550

University of Indianapolis School of Education

1400 E. Hanna Drive, Indianapolis, IN 46227
Admissions: (PH)317 788-3285, (FAX)317 788-3300, (EMAIL)theobald@ganalf.unidy.edu
Dean: (PH)317 788-3285, (FAX)317 788-3300, (EMAIL)weisenbach@gandlf.uindy.edu
Total Enrollment: 1,000–5,000
Grad Enrollment: PTM 50, Off campus 100%
Program Membership: N/A
Academic Programs Available: MASTERS: Art Ed., Ed. Tech., Elementary Ed., Music Ed., Read/Lang Arts Ed., Spec. Ed. DOCTORATE: Art Ed., Ed. Tech., Elementary Ed., Music Ed., Read/Lang Arts Ed., Spec. Ed.
Library: Krannert Memorial Library
Computer Resources: Macintosh, Dual Platform, PCs, CD-ROM, Videodisc

Research Areas	#Faculty
Adult Education	
Art Education	
Bilingual Education	
Counselor Education	
Early Childhood Ed.	
Ed. Admin	
Ed. Tech.	1
Elementary Ed.	4
Foreign Lang. Ed.	
Higher Ed.	
Math Ed.	
Mid. Lev. Ed.	1
Multicultural Ed.	

Music Ed.	1
Physical Ed.	
Read/Lang. Arts Ed.	2
School Counseling	
Science Ed.	
Secondary Ed.	
Soc. Studies Ed.	
Special Ed.	2
Other	

Student Body Demographics: Average Age 30, 70% female, 30% male
Percent Ethnic Minorities: African-American 10%
Geographic Representation: Midwest 100%
Graduate Career Paths: K-12 Teaching 90%
Tuition: 192/hr (in state), 192/hr (out of state)
Financial Aid Recipients: 10%
Average Annual Housing Cost: N/A
Application Deadline: rolling
Number of: applicants annually N/A; applicants accepted annually N/A; students enrolled annually N/A

Tests Required	Preferred/Min Score
Graduate Record Exam	
National Teachers Exam	
Praxis II Exam	

IOWA

Coe College Master of Arts in Teaching

1220 First Ave. NE, Cedar Rapids, IA 52402
Admissions: (PH)800 332-8404, (FAX)319 399-8816, (EMAIL)admission@coe.edu
Dean: (PH)319 399-8575, (FAX)319 399-8667, (EMAIL)rjohanso@coe.edu
Total Enrollment: 1,000–5,000
Grad Enrollment: PTM 50, Off campus 100%
Program Membership: N/A
Academic Programs Available: MASTERS: Art Ed., Elementary Ed., Foreign Lang. Ed., Math Ed., Music Ed., Physical Ed., Sci. Ed., Sec. Ed., Soc. Ed., DOCTORATE: Art Ed., Elementary Ed., Foreign Lang. Ed., Math Ed., Music Ed., Physical Ed., Sci. Ed., Sec. Ed., Soc. Ed.
Library: Stewart Memorial Library, 188,000 volumes
Computer Resources: Macintosh, Dual Platform, PCs, CD-ROM, Videodisc

Research Areas	#Faculty
Adult Education	
Art Education	
Bilingual Education	
Counselor Education	
Early Childhood Ed.	
Ed. Admin	
Ed. Tech.	
Elementary Ed.	2
Foreign Lang. Ed.	

Research Areas	#Faculty
Higher Ed.	
Math Ed.	1
Mid. Lev. Ed.	
Multicultural Ed.	1
Music Ed.	
Physical Ed.	
Read/Lang. Arts Ed.	
School Counseling	
Science Ed.	
Secondary Ed.	
Soc. Studies Ed.	
Special Ed.	
Other	

Student Body Demographics: Average Age 38, 60% female, 40% male
Percent Ethnic Minorities: N/A
Geographic Representation: Midwest 100%
Graduate Career Paths: K-12 Teaching 100%
Tuition: 800/cse (in state), 800/cse (out of state)
Financial Aid Recipients: 100%
Average Annual Housing Cost: N/A
Application Deadline: rolling
Number of: applicants annually 25; applicants accepted annually 25; students enrolled annually 25

Tests Required	Preferred/Min Score
Graduate Record Exam	
National Teachers Exam	
Praxis II Exam	

Dordt College Education Department

498 4th Avenue, N.E., Sioux Center, IA 51250-1697
Admissions: (PH)712 722-6236, (FAX)712 72201198, (EMAIL)jfennema@dordt.edu
Total Enrollment: 1,000–5,000
Grad Enrollment: PTM 15
Program Membership: N/A
Academic Programs Available: N/A
Library: 143,000 volumes
Computer Resources: Macintosh, Dual Platform, PCs, CD-ROM, Videodisc

Research Areas	#Faculty
Adult Education	
Art Education	
Bilingual Education	
Counselor Education	
Early Childhood Ed.	
Ed. Admin	
Ed. Tech.	
Elementary Ed.	
Foreign Lang. Ed.	
Higher Ed.	
Math Ed.	
Mid. Lev. Ed.	
Multicultural Ed.	
Music Ed.	
Physical Ed.	
Read/Lang. Arts Ed.	
School Counseling	
Science Ed.	

Research Areas	#Faculty
Secondary Ed.	
Soc. Studies Ed.	
Special Ed.	
Other	

Research Institutes/Centers: Center for Educational Services
Student Body Demographics: Average Age N/A, 67% female, 33% male
Percent Ethnic Minorities: N/A
Geographic Representation: N/A
Tuition: 540/cse (in state), 540/cse (out of state)
Financial Aid Recipients: N/A
Average Annual Housing Cost: N/A
Application Deadline: N/A
Number of: applicants annually N/A; applicants accepted annually N/A; students enrolled annually N/A

Tests Required	Preferred/Min Score
Graduate Record Exam	
National Teachers Exam	
Praxis II Exam	
TOEFL	550

Drake University School of Education

Cole Hall, Des Moines, IA 50311
Admissions: (PH)515 271-3181, (FAX)515 271-2831, (EMAIL)admitinfo@acad.drake.edu
Dean: (PH)515 271-3726, (FAX)515 271-4140
Total Enrollment: 5,000–10,000
Grad Enrollment: FTM 24, PTM 598, PTD 18, On campus 10%, Off campus 90%
Program Membership: Holmes Partnership
Academic Programs Available: MASTERS: Adult Ed., Art Ed., Early Childhood Ed., Ed. Admin, Ed. Tech., Elementary Ed., Foreign Lang. Ed., Higher Ed., Math Ed., Mid Level Ed., Music Ed., Read/Lang Arts Ed., Sci. Ed., Sec. Ed., DOCTORATE: Adult Ed., Art Ed., Early Childhood Ed., Ed. Admin, Ed. Tech., Elementary Ed., Foreign Lang. Ed., Higher Ed., Math Ed., Mid Level Ed., Music Ed., Read/Lang Arts Ed., Sci. Ed., Sec. Ed.
Library: Cowles Library, 500,000 volumes
Computer Resources: Macintosh, Dual Platform, PCs, CD-ROM, Videodisc

Research Areas	#Faculty
Adult Education	2
Art Education	
Bilingual Education	
Counselor Education	4
Early Childhood Ed.	3
Ed. Admin	5
Ed. Tech.	10
Elementary Ed.	4
Foreign Lang. Ed.	
Higher Ed.	2
Math Ed.	2
Mid. Lev. Ed.	
Multicultural Ed.	
Music Ed.	
Physical Ed.	
Read/Lang. Arts Ed.	2

School Counseling	4	Mid. Lev. Ed.		
Science Ed.	1	Multicultural Ed.	2	
Secondary Ed.	1	Music Ed.	3	
Soc. Studies Ed.	1	Physical Ed.		
Special Ed.	4	Read/Lang. Arts Ed.		

Other

Research Institutes/Centers: Institute for Collaborative Leadership in Education

Student Body Demographics: Average Age 35, 68% female, 32% male

Percent Ethnic Minorities: Hispanic-American 1%, Asian-American 1%, African-American 3%, Native-American 1%

Geographic Representation: N/A

Graduate Career Paths: K-12 Teaching 30%, K-12 Special Ed 8%, School Administration 40%, Higher Ed Administration 7%

Tuition: 14,430 (in state), 14,430 (out of state)

Financial Aid Recipients: 43%

Average Annual Housing Cost: 4,750

Application Deadline: rolling

Number of: applicants annually 577; applicants accepted annually 395; students enrolled annually 353

Tests Required	Preferred/Min Score
Graduate Record Exam	1,000
National Teachers Exam	
Praxis II Exam	
TOEFL	550

School Counseling — 5
Science Ed. — 3
Secondary Ed. — 3
Soc. Studies Ed. — 2
Special Ed. — 5

Other

Research Institutes/Centers: Research Institute for Studies in Education, Instructional Resources Center, Center for Math and Science Teachers

Student Body Demographics: N/A

Percent Ethnic Minorities: N/A

Geographic Representation: N/A

Tuition: 1,417 (in state), 4,172 (out of state)

Financial Aid Recipients: N/A

Average Annual Housing Cost: 2,324

Application Deadline: 2/1; 9/1

Number of: applicants annually 387; applicants accepted annually 221; students enrolled annually 181

Tests Required	Preferred/Min Score
Graduate Record Exam	1,000
National Teachers Exam	
Praxis II Exam	
TOEFL	560

Iowa State University College of Education

100 Alumni Hall, Ames, IA 50011

Admissions: (PH)515 294-5836, (FAX)515 294-2592

Dean: (PH)515 294-7000, (FAX)515 294-9725, (EMAIL)krice@iastate.edu

Total Enrollment: 20,000

Grad Enrollment: FTM 472, FTD 177

Program Membership: Holmes Partnership

Academic Programs Available: MASTERS: Adult Ed., Counselor Ed., Early Childhood Ed., Ed. Admin, Ed. Tech., Elementary Ed., Higher Ed., Multicultural Ed., Physical Ed., School Cons., Sec. Ed., Spec. Ed. DOCTORATE: Adult Ed., Counselor Ed., Early Childhood Ed., Ed. Admin, Ed. Tech., Elementary Ed., Higher Ed., Multicultural Ed., Physical Ed., School Cons., Sec. Ed., Spec. Ed.

Library: Instruction Resources

Computer Resources: Macintosh, Dual Platform, PCs, CD-ROM, Videodisc

Research Areas	#Faculty
Adult Education	2
Art Education	1
Bilingual Education	
Counselor Education	5
Early Childhood Ed.	
Ed. Admin	6
Ed. Tech.	5
Elementary Ed.	5
Foreign Lang. Ed.	
Higher Ed.	7
Math Ed.	

University of Northern Iowa
College of Education

Cedar Falls, IA 50614

Admissions: (PH)319 273-2717

Grad Enrollment: 430 total

Program Membership: Holmes Partnership

Academic Programs Available: MASTERS: Counselor Ed., Early Childhood Ed., Ed. Admin, Ed. Psych., Ed. Tech., Elementary Ed., Mid Level Ed., Read/Lang Arts Ed., Sec. Ed., Spec. Ed. DOCTORATE: Counselor Ed., Early Childhood Ed., Ed. Admin, Ed. Psych., Ed. Tech., Elementary Ed., Mid Level Ed., Read/Lang Arts Ed., Sec. Ed., Spec. Ed.

Library: N/A

Research Areas	#Faculty
Adult Education	
Art Education	
Bilingual Education	
Counselor Education	
Early Childhood Ed.	
Ed. Admin	
Ed. Tech.	
Elementary Ed.	
Foreign Lang. Ed.	
Higher Ed.	
Math Ed.	
Mid. Lev. Ed.	
Multicultural Ed.	
Music Ed.	

Physical Ed.
Read/Lang. Arts Ed.
School Counseling
Science Ed.
Secondary Ed.
Soc. Studies Ed.
Special Ed.
Other
Student Body Demographics: N/A
Percent Ethnic Minorities: N/A
Geographic Representation: N/A
Tuition: 2,834 (in state), 6,986 (out of state)
Financial Aid Recipients: N/A
Average Annual Housing Cost: N/A
Application Deadline: rolling
Number of: applicants annually 205; applicants accepted annually 156; students enrolled annually N/A

Tests Required	Preferred/Min Score
Graduate Record Exam	
National Teachers Exam	
Praxis II Exam	

KANSAS

Benedictine College Education Department

Atchinson, KS 66002
Admissions: (PH)913 367-5340 x2475
Dean: (PH)913 367-5340 x2413
Total Enrollment: 1,000
Grad Enrollment: PTM 30, Off campus 100%
Program Membership: N/A
Academic Programs Available: MASTERS: Ed. Admin, DOCTORATE: Ed. Admin
Library: Benedictine Library
Computer Resources: Macintosh, Dual Platform, PCs, CD-ROM, Videodisc

Research Areas	#Faculty
Adult Education	
Art Education	
Bilingual Education	
Counselor Education	
Early Childhood Ed.	
Ed. Admin	1
Ed. Tech.	
Elementary Ed.	
Foreign Lang. Ed.	
Higher Ed.	
Math Ed.	
Mid. Lev. Ed.	
Multicultural Ed.	
Music Ed.	
Physical Ed.	
Read/Lang. Arts Ed.	
School Counseling	

Science Ed.
Secondary Ed.
Soc. Studies Ed.
Special Ed.
Other
Student Body Demographics: Average Age 34, 67% female, 33% male
Percent Ethnic Minorities: N/A
Geographic Representation: Midwest 50%, West 50%
Graduate Career Paths: K-12 Teaching 40%, K-12 School Administration 50%, Higher Ed Administration 10%
Tuition: 150/hr (in state), 150/hr (out of state)
Financial Aid Recipients: 25%
Average Annual Housing Cost: N/A
Application Deadline: N/A
Number of: applicants annually 15; applicants accepted annually 13; students enrolled annually N/A

Tests Required	Preferred/Min Score
Graduate Record Exam	960
National Teachers Exam	
Praxis II Exam	

Emporia State University Teachers College

Emporia, KS 66801
Admissions: (PH)316 341-5367
Grad Enrollment: 536 total
Program Membership: N/A
Academic Programs Available: MASTERS: Counselor Ed., Early Childhood Ed., Ed. Admin, Ed. Psych., Math Ed., Physical Ed., Soc. Ed., Spec. Ed. DOCTORATE: Counselor Ed., Early Childhood Ed., Ed. Admin, Ed. Psych., Math Ed., Physical Ed., Soc. Ed., Spec. Ed.
Library: N/A

Research Areas	#Faculty
Adult Education	
Art Education	
Bilingual Education	
Counselor Education	
Early Childhood Ed.	
Ed. Admin	
Ed. Tech.	
Elementary Ed.	
Foreign Lang. Ed.	
Higher Ed.	
Math Ed.	
Mid. Lev. Ed.	
Multicultural Ed.	
Music Ed.	
Physical Ed.	
Read/Lang. Arts Ed.	
School Counseling	
Science Ed.	
Secondary Ed.	
Soc. Studies Ed.	
Special Ed.	
Other	

Student Body Demographics: N/A
Percent Ethnic Minorities: N/A
Geographic Representation: N/A

Tuition: 1,670 (in state), 5,056 (out of state)
Financial Aid Recipients: N/A
Number of: applicants annually 209; applicants accepted annually 143; students enrolled annually N/A

Tests Required	Preferred/Min Score
Graduate Record Exam	
National Teachers Exam	
Praxis II Exam	
TOEFL	550

Fort Hays State University
College of Education

600 Park Street, Hays, KS 67601
Admissions: (PH)913 628-4222, (EMAIL)adjl@fhsuvm.fhsu.edu
Dean: (PH)913 628-5866, (FAX)913 628-4777, (EMAIL)edcl@fhsuvm.fhsu.edu
Total Enrollment: 5,000–10,000
Grad Enrollment: On campus 5%, Off campus 95%
Program Membership: N/A
Academic Programs Available: MASTERS: Art Ed., Counselor Ed., Ed. Admin, Ed. Tech., Elementary Ed., Math Ed., Music Ed., Physical Ed., Read/Lang Arts Ed., School Cons., Spec. Ed. DOCTORATE: Art Ed., Counselor Ed., Ed. Admin, Ed. Tech., Elementary Ed., Math Ed., Music Ed., Physical Ed., Read/Lang Arts Ed., School Cons., Spec. Ed.
Library: Forsyth Library, 3,000,000 volumes
Computer Resources: Macintosh, Dual Platform, PCs, CD-ROM, Videodisc

Research Areas	#Faculty
Adult Education	
Art Education	
Bilingual Education	
Counselor Education	4
Early Childhood Ed.	
Ed. Admin	4
Ed. Tech.	2
Elementary Ed.	
Foreign Lang. Ed.	
Higher Ed.	
Math Ed.	5
Mid. Lev. Ed.	
Multicultural Ed.	
Music Ed.	
Physical Ed.	
Read/Lang. Arts Ed.	1
School Counseling	2
Science Ed.	2
Secondary Ed.	2
Soc. Studies Ed.	
Special Ed.	3
Other	

Student Body Demographics: Average Age 30, 60% female, 40% male
Percent Ethnic Minorities: Hispanic-American 1%, Asian-American 1%, African-American 1%, Native-American 1%
Geographic Representation: Midwest 90%
Graduate Career Paths: K-12 Administration 30%, Community Counseling 10%

Tuition: 85/hr (in state), 226/hr (out of state)
Financial Aid Recipients: N/A
Average Annual Housing Cost: N/A
Application Deadline: N/A
Number of: applicants annually N/A; applicants accepted annually N/A; students enrolled annually N/A

Tests Required	Preferred/Min Score
Graduate Record Exam	
National Teachers Exam	
Praxis II Exam	

University of Kansas School of Education

102 Bailey Hall, Lawrence, KS 66045
Admissions: (PH)913 864-4510, (FAX)913 864-5076, (EMAIL)jpp@kuhub.cc.ukans.edu
Dean: (PH)913 864-4279, (FAX)913 864-5076
Total Enrollment: 20,000
Grad Enrollment: FTM 246, PTM 765, FTD 89, PTD 209, CAS 333, On campus 5%, Off campus 95%
Program Membership: Holmes Partnership
Academic Programs Available: MASTERS: Art Ed., Bilingual Ed., Counselor Ed., Early Childhood Ed., Ed. Admin, Ed. Psych., Ed. Tech., Elementary Ed., Foreign Lang. Ed., Higher Ed., Math Ed., Mid Level Ed., Multicultural Ed., Music Ed., Physical Ed., Read/Lang Arts Ed., School Cons., Sci. Ed., Sec. Ed., Soc. Ed., Spec. Ed. DOCTORATE: Art Ed., Bilingual Ed., Counselor Ed., Early Childhood Ed., Ed. Admin., Ed. Psych., Ed. Tech., Elementary Ed., Foreign Lang. Ed., Higher Ed., Math Ed., Mid Level Ed., Multicultural Ed., Music Ed., Physical Ed., Read/Lang Arts Ed., School Cons., Sci. Ed., Sec. Ed., Soc. Ed., Spec. Ed.
Library: Watson Library
Computer Resources: Macintosh, Dual Platform, PCs, CD-ROM, Videodisc

Research Areas	#Faculty
Adult Education	
Art Education	2
Bilingual Education	2
Counselor Education	6
Early Childhood Ed.	6
Ed. Admin	5
Ed. Tech.	3
Elementary Ed.	10
Foreign Lang. Ed.	2
Higher Ed.	4
Math Ed.	2
Mid. Lev. Ed.	2
Multicultural Ed.	2
Music Ed.	6
Physical Ed.	15
Read/Lang. Arts Ed.	5
School Counseling	9
Science Ed.	2
Secondary Ed.	2
Soc. Studies Ed.	3
Special Ed.	19
Other	

Research Institutes/Centers: Center for Educational Testing & Evaluation, Center for the Study of Research on Learning, Center for Economic Education
Student Body Demographics: Average Age 30, 74% female, 26% male
Percent Ethnic Minorities: Hispanic-American 3%, Asian-American 3%, African-American 6%, Native-American 3%
Geographic Representation: New England 4%, Midwest 80%, Mid Atlantic 2%, Southwest 4%, West 4%, Southeast 2%, Northwest 4%
Tuition: 1,256 (in state), 3,695 (out of state)
Financial Aid Recipients: N/A
Average Annual Housing Cost: 6,070
Application Deadline: 2/15; 6/15; 11/15
Number of: applicants annually 1,450; applicants accepted annually 1,180; students enrolled annually N/A

Tests Required	Preferred/Min Score
Graduate Record Exam	1,000
National Teachers Exam	
Praxis II Exam	
TOEFL	570

Washburn University Department of Education

1700 SW College Avenue, Topeka, KS 66621
Admissions: (PH)913 231-1010 x1437, (FAX)913 231-1089, (EMAIL)zzdunw@wuacc.acc.edu
Dean: (PH)913 231-1010 x1437, (FAX)913 231-1089
Total Enrollment: 5,000–10,000
Grad Enrollment: FTM 4, PTM 85, Off campus 100%
Program Membership: N/A
Academic Programs Available: MASTERS: Ed. Admin, Elementary Ed., Spec. Ed. DOCTORATE: Ed. Admin, Elementary Ed., Spec. Ed.
Library: Mabee Library
Computer Resources: Macintosh, Dual Platform, PCs, CD-ROM, Videodisc

Research Areas	#Faculty
Adult Education	
Art Education	
Bilingual Education	
Counselor Education	
Early Childhood Ed.	
Ed. Admin	2
Ed. Tech.	
Elementary Ed.	5
Foreign Lang. Ed.	
Higher Ed.	
Math Ed.	
Mid. Lev. Ed.	
Multicultural Ed.	
Music Ed.	
Physical Ed.	
Read/Lang. Arts Ed.	
School Counseling	
Science Ed.	
Secondary Ed.	
Soc. Studies Ed.	
Special Ed.	2
Other	

Student Body Demographics: Average Age 29, 70% female, 30% male
Percent Ethnic Minorities: Hispanic-American 3%, African-American 8%
Geographic Representation: Midwest 95%
Graduate Career Paths: K-12 Teaching 75%, K-12 Special Ed 15%, School Administration 10%
Tuition: 1,080 (in state), 2,061 (out of state)
Financial Aid Recipients: N/A
Average Annual Housing Cost: 1,350
Application Deadline: rolling
Number of: applicants annually 25; applicants accepted annually 25; students enrolled annually 25

Tests Required	Preferred/Min Score
Graduate Record Exam	
National Teachers Exam	
Praxis II Exam	

KENTUCKY

Morehead State University College of Education and Behavioral Sciences

Graduate Office, 701 Ginger Hall, Morehead, KY 40351
Admissions: (PH)606 783-2039, (FAX)606 783-2678, (EMAIL)d.demoss@moreheadst.edu
Dean: (PH)606 783-2040, (FAX)606 783-5029, (EMAIL)h.harty@moreheadst.edu
Total Enrollment: 5,000–10,000
Grad Enrollment: 390 total
Program Membership: N/A
Academic Programs Available: MASTERS: Adult Ed., Art Ed., Early Childhood Ed., Elementary Ed., Higher Ed., Mid Level Ed., Music Ed., Physical Ed., Read/Lang Arts Ed., School Cons., Soc. Ed., Spec. Ed. DOCTORATE: Adult Ed., Art Ed., Early Childhood Ed., Elementary Ed., Higher Ed., Mid Level Ed., Music Ed., Physical Ed., Read/Lang Arts Ed., School Cons., Soc. Ed., Spec. Ed.
Library: Camden Carroll Library, 6 million volumes
Computer Resources: Macintosh, Dual Platform, PCs, CD-ROM, Videodisc

Research Areas	#Faculty
Adult Education	2
Art Education	
Bilingual Education	
Counselor Education	4
Early Childhood Ed.	
Ed. Admin	2
Ed. Tech.	
Elementary Ed.	
Foreign Lang. Ed.	
Higher Ed.	1
Math Ed.	
Mid. Lev. Ed.	
Multicultural Ed.	
Music Ed.	
Physical Ed.	
Read/Lang. Arts Ed.	

School Counseling	2
Science Ed.	
Secondary Ed.	
Soc. Studies Ed.	
Special Ed.	
Other	

Research Institutes/Centers: Clearinghouse for School Services

Student Body Demographics: Average Age 25, 76% female, 24% male

Percent Ethnic Minorities: African-American 1%

Geographic Representation: N/A

Tuition: 1,080 (in state), 2,920 (out of state)

Financial Aid Recipients: 70%

Average Annual Housing Cost: 1,800

Application Deadline: rolling

Number of: applicants annually 1,300; applicants accepted annually 1,235; students enrolled annually 1,100

Tests Required	Preferred/Min Score
Graduate Record Exam	
National Teachers Exam	
Praxis II Exam	

University of Louisville School of Education

Houchens Building, Louisville, KY 40292

Admissions: (PH)502 852-6525, (FAX)502 852-4776, (EMAIL)admitme@ulkyvm.louisville.edu

Dean: (PH)502 852-6411, (FAX)502 852-0726, (EMAIL)ronyst01@ulkyvm.louisville.edu

Grad Enrollment: FTM 295, PTM 650, FTD 69, PTD 74, CAS 438

Program Membership: Holmes Partnership

Academic Programs Available: MASTERS: Art Ed., Counselor Ed., Early Childhood Ed., Ed. Admin, Ed. Psych., Ed. Tech., Elementary Ed., Higher Ed., Mid Level Ed., Physical Ed., Read/Lang Arts Ed., School Cons., Sec. Ed., Spec. Ed. DOCTORATE: Counselor Ed., Ed. Admin, Ed. Psych., Ed. Tech., Elementary Ed., Higher Ed., Mid Level Ed., Physical Ed., Read/Lang Arts Ed., School Cons., Sec. Ed., Spec. Ed.

Library: Educational Media Center

Computer Resources: Macintosh, Dual Platform, PCs, CD-ROM, Videodisc

Research Areas	#Faculty
Adult Education	9
Art Education	
Bilingual Education	
Counselor Education	10
Early Childhood Ed.	3
Ed. Admin	5
Ed. Tech.	1
Elementary Ed.	13
Foreign Lang. Ed.	
Higher Ed.	5
Math Ed.	3
Mid. Lev. Ed.	6
Multicultural Ed.	17
Music Ed.	
Physical Ed.	14

Read/Lang. Arts Ed.	10
School Counseling	10
Science Ed.	4
Secondary Ed.	4
Soc. Studies Ed.	6
Special Ed.	10
Other	

Research Institutes/Centers: Collaborative Advancement of the Teaching Profession, Center for Latin American Education

Student Body Demographics: Average Age 35, 76% female, 24% male

Percent Ethnic Minorities: Hispanic-American 0.7%, Asian-American 1%, African-American 9%, Native-American 0.2%

Geographic Representation: New England 0.3%, Midwest 2.4%, Southwest 0.5%, Southeast 95.6%, Northwest 0.1%, UK 0.1%

Tuition: 148/hr (in state), 424/hr (out of state)

Financial Aid Recipients: N/A

Average Annual Housing Cost: 5,628

Application Deadline: variable

Number of: applicants annually 700; applicants accepted annually 600; students enrolled annually N/A

Tests Required	Preferred/Min Score
Graduate Record Exam	800–1,000
National Teachers Exam	
Praxis II Exam	
TOEFL	535

LOUISIANA

Northeast Louisiana University
College of Education

ADM 1-109, 700 University Ave., Monroe, LA 71209

Admissions: (PH)318 342-1036

Dean: (PH)318 342-1235, (FAX)318 342-1240

Total Enrollment: 10,000–20,000

Grad Enrollment: On campus 2%, Off campus 98%

Program Membership: N/A

Academic Programs Available: MASTERS: Counselor Ed., Ed. Admin, Elementary Ed., Physical Ed., Read/Lang Arts Ed., School Cons., Sec. Ed., Spec. Ed. DOCTORATE: Counselor Ed., Ed. Admin, Elementary Ed., Physical Ed., Read/Lang Arts Ed., School Cons., Sec. Ed., Spec. Ed.

Library: Sandel Library, 1 million volumes

Computer Resources: Macintosh, Dual Platform, PCs, CD-ROM, Videodisc

Research Areas	#Faculty
Adult Education	
Art Education	
Bilingual Education	
Counselor Education	
Early Childhood Ed.	

Ed. Admin
Ed. Tech.
Elementary Ed.
Foreign Lang. Ed.
Higher Ed.
Math Ed.
Mid. Lev. Ed.
Multicultural Ed.
Music Ed.
Physical Ed.
Read/Lang. Arts Ed.
School Counseling
Science Ed.
Secondary Ed.
Soc. Studies Ed.
Special Ed.
Other
Student Body Demographics: Average Age 32, 66% female, 34% male
Percent Ethnic Minorities: Asian-American 1%, African-American 14%
Geographic Representation: N/A
Tuition: 966 (in state), 2,136 (out of state)
Financial Aid Recipients: 60%
Average Annual Housing Cost: 2,060
Application Deadline: 4/1; 11/1; 3/1
Number of: applicants annually 1,855; applicants accepted annually 1,683; students enrolled annually 590

Tests Required	Preferred/Min Score
Graduate Record Exam	900–1,000
National Teachers Exam	
Praxis II Exam	

Southeastern Louisiana University
College of Education

SLU Box 752, Hammond, LA 70402
Admissions: (PH)504 549-2066, (FAX)504 549-5632
Dean: (PH)504 549-3912, (FAX)504 549-2070
Total Enrollment: 10,000–20,000
Program Membership: N/A
Academic Programs Available: MASTERS: Counselor Ed., Ed. Admin, Elementary Ed., Physical Ed., Read/Lang Arts Ed., School Cons., Sec. Ed., Spec. Ed. DOCTORATE: Counselor Ed., Ed. Admin, Elementary Ed., Physical Ed., Read/Lang Arts Ed., School Cons., Sec. Ed., Spec. Ed.
Library: Linus A. Sims Memorial Library, 321,000 volumes
Computer Resources: Macintosh, Dual Platform, PCs, CD-ROM, Videodisc

Research Areas	#Faculty
Adult Education	
Art Education	
Bilingual Education	
Counselor Education	4
Early Childhood Ed.	
Ed. Admin	3
Ed. Tech.	
Elementary Ed.	8
Foreign Lang. Ed.	
Higher Ed.	

Math Ed.
Mid. Lev. Ed.
Multicultural Ed.
Music Ed.

Physical Ed..	8
Read/Lang. Arts Ed.	
School Counseling	4
Science Ed.	
Secondary Ed.	
Soc. Studies Ed.	
Special Ed.	6
Other	12

Student Body Demographics: Average Age 35, 76% female, 24% male
Percent Ethnic Minorities: Hispanic-American 1%, Asian-American 1%, African-American 9%, Native-American 1%
Geographic Representation: N/A
Tuition: N/A (in state), N/A (out of state)
Financial Aid Recipients: 36%
Average Annual Housing Cost: N/A
Application Deadline: 5/1; 7/15; 12/1
Number of: applicants annually 1,200; applicants accepted annually 1,190; students enrolled annually N/A

Tests Required	Preferred/Min Score
Graduate Record Exam	
National Teachers Exam	
Praxis II Exam	

MAINE

University of Maine College of Education

Graduate School, 5782 Winslow Hall, Orono, ME 04469-5782
Admissions: (PH)207 581-3218, (FAX)207 581-3232, (EMAIL)poisson@maine.maine.edu
Dean: (PH)207 581-2441, (FAX)207 581-2423, (EMAIL)WHarris@maine.maine.edu
Grad Enrollment: FTM 151, PTM 304, FTD 26, PTD 28, CAS 81
Program Membership: Holmes Partnership
Academic Programs Available: MASTERS: Adult Ed., Counselor Ed., Ed. Admin, Elementary Ed., Higher Ed., Mid Level Ed., Physical Ed., Read/Lang Arts Ed., Sci. Ed., Sec. Ed., Soc. Ed., Spec. Ed. DOCTORATE: Adult Ed., Counselor Ed., Ed. Admin, Elementary Ed., Higher Ed., Mid Level Ed., Physical Ed., Read/Lang Arts Ed., Sci. Ed., Sec. Ed., Soc. Ed., Spec. Ed.
Library: Raymond H. Fogler Library, 850,000 volumes
Computer Resources: Macintosh, Dual Platform, PCs, CD-ROM, Videodisc

Research Areas	#Faculty
Adult Education	
Art Education	
Bilingual Education	
Counselor Education	3

Early Childhood Ed.	
Ed. Admin	5
Ed. Tech.	1
Elementary Ed.	9
Foreign Lang. Ed.	
Higher Ed.	1
Math Ed.	1
Mid. Lev. Ed.	1
Multicultural Ed.	1
Music Ed.	
Physical Ed.	4
Read/Lang. Arts Ed.	5
School Counseling	
Science Ed.	2
Secondary Ed.	2
Soc. Studies Ed.	2
Special Ed.	3
Other	

Research Institutes/Centers: Center for Research and Evaluation, Institute for the Study of At-Risk Students, Center for Early Literacy
Student Body Demographics: Average Age 39, 74% female, 26% male
Percent Ethnic Minorities: Hispanic-American 3%, African-American 2%, Native-American 2%
Geographic Representation: New England 99%
Tuition: 168/hr (in state), 476/hr (out of state)
Financial Aid Recipients: N/A
Average Annual Housing Cost: N/A
Application Deadline: rolling
Number of: applicants annually 161; applicants accepted annually 115; students enrolled annually 69

Tests Required	Preferred/Min Score
Graduate Record Exam	1,250
National Teachers Exam	
Praxis II Exam	
TOEFL	550

University of Southern Maine College of Education and Human Development

Admissions and Advising Office, 118 Bailey Hall, Gorham, ME 04038
Admissions: (PH)207 780-5306, (FAX)207 780-5315, (EMAIL)belsan@maine.maine.edu
Dean: (PH)207 780-5371, (FAX)207 780-5315
Total Enrollment: 5,000–10,000
Grad Enrollment: FTM 274, PTM 304, Off campus 100%
Program Membership: Holmes Partnership, NNER
Academic Programs Available: MASTERS: Adult Ed., Counselor Ed., Ed. Admin, Ed. Psych., Elementary Ed., Mid Level Ed., Read/Lang Arts Ed., School Cons., Sec. Ed., Spec. Ed. DOCTORATE: Adult Ed., Counselor Ed., Ed. Admin, Ed. Psych., Elementary Ed., Mid Level Ed., Read/Lang Arts Ed., School Cons., Sec. Ed., Spec. Ed.
Library: USM Library, 1.4 million volumes
Computer Resources: Macintosh, Dual Platform, PCs, CD-ROM, Videodisc

Research Areas	#Faculty
Adult Education	2

Art Education	
Bilingual Education	
Counselor Education	12
Early Childhood Ed.	
Ed. Admin	10
Ed. Tech.	
Elementary Ed.	10
Foreign Lang. Ed.	
Higher Ed.	
Math Ed.	
Mid. Lev. Ed.	
Multicultural Ed.	
Music Ed.	
Physical Ed.	
Read/Lang. Arts Ed.	7
School Counseling	3
Science Ed.	
Secondary Ed.	
Soc. Studies Ed.	
Special Ed.	5
Other	

Research Institutes/Centers: Center for Educational Policy, Applied Research and Evaluation
Student Body Demographics: Average Age 34, 74% female, 26% male
Percent Ethnic Minorities: N/A
Geographic Representation: N/A
Graduate Career Paths: K-12 Teaching 35%, School Counseling 5%, K-12 Special Ed 10%, School Administration 17%, Community Counseling 10%
Tuition: 146/hr (in state), 412/hr (out of state)
Financial Aid Recipients: 8%
Average Annual Housing Cost: N/A
Application Deadline: 9/15; 2/1; 1/16
Number of: applicants annually 450; applicants accepted annually 320; students enrolled annually 290

Tests Required	Preferred/Min Score
Graduate Record Exam	900
National Teachers Exam	
Praxis II Exam	
TOEFL	550

MARYLAND

Loyola College in Maryland Education Department

4501 N. Charles Street, Baltimore, MD 21210
Admissions: (PH)410 617-5095, (FAX)410 617-5175
Dean: (PH)410 617-2480, (FAX)410 617-5175, (EMAIL)amoriell@loyola.edu
Total Enrollment: 5,000–10,000
Grad Enrollment: On campus 1%, Off campus 99%
Program Membership: N/A

Academic Programs Available: MASTERS: Art Ed., Counselor Ed., Ed. Admin, Elementary Ed., Read/Lang Arts Ed., School Cons., Sci. Ed., Sec. Ed., Soc. Ed., Spec. Ed. DOCTORATE: Art Ed., Counselor Ed., Ed. Admin, Elementary Ed., Read/Lang Arts Ed., School Cons., Sci. Ed., Sec. Ed., Soc. Ed., Spec. Ed.

Library: Loyola Notre Dame Library

Computer Resources: Macintosh, Dual Platform, PCs, CD-ROM, Videodisc

Research Areas	#Faculty
Adult Education	
Art Education	
Bilingual Education	
Counselor Education	2
Early Childhood Ed.	
Ed. Admin	1
Ed. Tech.	
Elementary Ed.	1
Foreign Lang. Ed.	
Higher Ed.	
Math Ed.	
Mid. Lev. Ed.	
Multicultural Ed.	
Music Ed.	
Physical Ed.	
Read/Lang. Arts Ed.	2
School Counseling	2
Science Ed.	1
Secondary Ed.	1
Soc. Studies Ed.	
Special Ed.	2
Other	2

Student Body Demographics: Average Age 34, 65% female, 35% male

Percent Ethnic Minorities: Hispanic-American 2%, Asian-American 4%, African-American 7%, Native-American 2%

Geographic Representation: N/A

Graduate Career Paths: K-12 Teaching 50%, School Counseling 10%, K-12 Special Ed 20%, School Administration 10%

Tuition: 187/hr (in state), 187/hr (out of state)

Financial Aid Recipients: N/A

Average Annual Housing Cost: N/A

Application Deadline: rolling

Number of: applicants annually 300; applicants accepted annually 250; students enrolled annually 230

Tests Required	Preferred/Min Score
Graduate Record Exam	
National Teachers Exam	
Praxis II Exam	

University of Maryland Baltimore County

5401 Wilkins Avenue, Baltimore, MD 21228
Admissions: (PH)410 455-2292, (FAX)410 455-1094
Dean: (PH)410 455-2465, (EMAIL)(410) 455-3986
Total Enrollment: 10,000–20,000

Grad Enrollment: PTM 550, PTD 3, On campus 2%, Off campus 98%

Program Membership: N/A

Academic Programs Available: MASTERS: Bilingual Ed., Early Childhood Ed., Ed. Tech., Elementary Ed., Foreign Lang. Ed., Math Ed., Mid Level Ed., Multicultural Ed., Read/Lang Arts Ed., Sci. Ed., Sec. Ed., Soc. Ed., DOCTORATE: Bilingual Ed., Early Childhood Ed., Ed. Tech., Elementary Ed., Foreign Lang. Ed., Math Ed., Mid Level Ed., Multicultural Ed., Read/Lang Arts Ed., Sci. Ed., Sec. Ed., Soc. Ed.

Library: Kuhn Library

Computer Resources: Macintosh, Dual Platform, PCs, CD-ROM, Videodisc

Research Areas	#Faculty
Adult Education	
Art Education	1
Bilingual Education	2
Counselor Education	
Early Childhood Ed.	3
Ed. Admin	1
Ed. Tech.	2
Elementary Ed.	6
Foreign Lang. Ed.	
Higher Ed.	
Math Ed.	2
Mid. Lev. Ed.	3
Multicultural Ed.	2
Music Ed.	
Physical Ed.	
Read/Lang. Arts Ed.	3
School Counseling	
Science Ed.	2
Secondary Ed.	2
Soc. Studies Ed.	1
Special Ed.	
Other	

Student Body Demographics: Average Age 34, 65% female, 35% male

Percent Ethnic Minorities: Hispanic-American 1%, Asian-American 1%, African-American 5%

Geographic Representation: New England 4%, Midwest 8%, Mid Atlantic 70%, Southwest 2%, West 4%, Southeast 10%, Northwest 2%

Graduate Career Paths: K-12 Teaching 70%, K-12 School Administration 5%

Tuition: 212/hr (in state), 212/hr (out of state)

Financial Aid Recipients: 6%

Average Annual Housing Cost: N/A

Application Deadline: rolling

Number of: applicants annually N/A; applicants accepted annually 75; students enrolled annually N/A

Tests Required	Preferred/Min Score
Graduate Record Exam	860–1060
National Teachers Exam	
Praxis II Exam	

University of Maryland College of Education

Graduate Studies and Research, College Park, MD 20742
Admissions: (PH)301 405-2344
Dean: (PH)301 405-5610, (FAX)301 314-9890,
(EMAIL)cb13@umar/umd.edu
Total Enrollment: 20,000
Grad Enrollment: FTM 163, PTM 358, FTD 217, PTD 417, 2
CAS, On campus 99%, Off campus 1%
Program Membership: Holmes Partnership
Academic Programs Available: MASTERS: Art Ed.,
Counselor Ed., Early Childhood Ed., Ed. Admin, Ed. Psych.,
Elementary Ed., Foreign Lang. Ed., Higher Ed., Math Ed.,
Music Ed., Read/Lang Arts Ed., School Cons., Sci. Ed., Sec.
Ed., DOCTORATE: Art Ed., Counselor Ed., Early Childhood
Ed., Ed. Admin, Ed. Psych., Elementary Ed., Foreign Lang.
Ed., Higher Ed., Math Ed., Music Ed., Read/Lang Arts Ed.,
School Cons., Sci. Ed., Sec. Ed., Soc. Ed., Spec. Ed.
Library: McKelden Library, 1.4 million volumes
Computer Resources: Macintosh, Dual Platform, PCs,
CD-ROM, Videodisc

Research Areas	#Faculty
Adult Education	
Art Education	2
Bilingual Education	2
Counselor Education	3
Early Childhood Ed.	5
Ed. Admin	3
Ed. Tech.	
Elementary Ed.	5
Foreign Lang. Ed.	2
Higher Ed.	2
Math Ed.	6
Mid. Lev. Ed.	
Multicultural Ed.	
Music Ed.	1
Physical Ed.	
Read/Lang. Arts Ed.	6
School Counseling	5
Science Ed.	3
Secondary Ed.	3
Soc. Studies Ed.	2
Special Ed.	15
Other	

Research Institutes/Centers: National Reading Center
Student Body Demographics: Average Age 36, 79% female,
21% male
Percent Ethnic Minorities: Hispanic-American 2.6%,
Asian-American 3.1%, African-American 13.9%,
Native-American 0.2%
Geographic Representation: New England 1.4%,
Midwest 8.9%, Mid Atlantic 83.4%, Southwest 0.6%,
West 2%, Southeast 2.5%, Northwest 1.2%
Graduate Career Paths: K-12 Teaching 10%, Higher Ed
Teaching 10%, School Counseling 5%, K-12 Special Ed 5%,
School Administration 5%, Higher Ed Administration 5%,
Higher Ed Counseling 10%, Community Counseling 10%
Tuition: 210/hr (in state), 365/hr (out of state)
Financial Aid Recipients: 52%
Average Annual Housing Cost: 1,498

Application Deadline: 9/1; 3/1
Number of: applicants annually 1,206; applicants accepted
annually 512; students enrolled annually 265
Tests Required   **Preferred/Min Score**
Graduate Record Exam
National Teachers Exam
Praxis II Exam

MASSACHUSETTS

American International College
School of Psychology & Education

1000 State Street, Box 16L, Springfield, MA 01109-3189
Admissions: (PH)413 747-6302, (FAX)413 737-2803
Total Enrollment: 1,000–5,000
Grad Enrollment: FTM 20, PTM 174, FTD 10, PTD 53
Program Membership: N/A
Academic Programs Available: MASTERS: Early
Childhood Ed., Ed. Admin, Ed. Psych., Elementary Ed., Mid
Level Ed., Read/Lang Arts Ed., School Cons., Sec. Ed., Spec.
Ed. DOCTORATE: Early Childhood Ed., Ed. Admin, Ed.
Psych., Elementary Ed., Mid Level Ed., Read/Lang Arts Ed.,
School Cons., Sec. Ed., Spec. Ed.
Library: Shea Library, 105,000 volumes
Computer Resources: Macintosh, Dual Platform, PCs,
CD-ROM, Videodisc

Research Areas	#Faculty
Adult Education	
Art Education	
Bilingual Education	
Counselor Education	
Early Childhood Ed.	
Ed. Admin	
Ed. Tech.	
Elementary Ed.	
Foreign Lang. Ed.	
Higher Ed.	
Math Ed.	
Mid. Lev. Ed.	
Multicultural Ed.	
Music Ed.	
Physical Ed.	
Read/Lang. Arts Ed.	
School Counseling	
Science Ed.	
Secondary Ed.	
Soc. Studies Ed.	
Special Ed.	
Other	

Student Body Demographics: Average Age 34, 65% female,
35% male
Percent Ethnic Minorities: Hispanic-American 3%,
Asian-American 1%, African-American 3%
Geographic Representation: New England 98%, Mid
Atlantic 2%

Graduate Career Paths: K-12 Teaching 77%, Higher Ed Teaching 1%, School Counseling 4%, K-12 Special Ed 5%, School Administration 1%, Community Counseling 2%
Tuition: 9,400 (in state), 9,400 (out of state)
Financial Aid Recipients: N/A
Average Annual Housing Cost: 1,000
Application Deadline: N/A
Number of: applicants annually 170; applicants accepted annually 160; students enrolled annually 110

Tests Required	Preferred/Min Score
Graduate Record Exam	1,000
National Teachers Exam	
Praxis II Exam	

Anna Maria College Education Department

50 Sunset Lane, Box 21, Paxton, MA 01612-1198
Admissions: (PH)508 849-3433, (FAX)508 849-3430
Dean: (PH)508 849-3335, (FAX)508 849-3339
Total Enrollment: 1,000
Grad Enrollment: PTM 50
Program Membership: N/A
Academic Programs Available: MASTERS: Elementary Ed., DOCTORATE: Elementary Ed.
Library: Mondor-Egan Library
Computer Resources: Macintosh, Dual Platform, PCs, CD-ROM, Videodisc

Research Areas	#Faculty
Adult Education	
Art Education	
Bilingual Education	
Counselor Education	
Early Childhood Ed.	1
Ed. Admin	
Ed. Tech.	1
Elementary Ed.	2
Foreign Lang. Ed.	
Higher Ed.	
Math Ed.	1
Mid. Lev. Ed.	
Multicultural Ed.	1
Music Ed.	
Physical Ed.	
Read/Lang. Arts Ed.	2
School Counseling	
Science Ed.	1
Secondary Ed.	1
Soc. Studies Ed.	
Special Ed.	
Other	

Student Body Demographics: Average Age N/A, 75% female, 25% male
Percent Ethnic Minorities: N/A
Geographic Representation: New England 100%
Tuition: N/A (in state), N/A (out of state)
Financial Aid Recipients: N/A
Average Annual Housing Cost: N/A
Application Deadline: rolling
Number of: applicants annually N/A; applicants accepted annually N/A; students enrolled annually N/A

Tests Required	Preferred/Min Score
Graduate Record Exam	
National Teachers Exam	
Praxis II Exam	

Boston College Graduate School of Education

Office of Graduate Admissions, Campion 103, Boston, MA 02167
Admissions: (PH)617 552-4214, (FAX)617 552-0812, (EMAIL)riordanA@hermes.bc.edu
Dean: (PH)617 552-4200, (FAX)617 552-0812
Total Enrollment: 10,000–20,000
Grad Enrollment: FTM 255, PTM 454, FTD 96, PTD 172, Off campus 100%
Program Membership: Holmes Partnership
Academic Programs Available: MASTERS: Counselor Ed., Early Childhood Ed., Ed. Admin, Ed. Psych., Elementary Ed., Higher Ed., Math Ed., Read/Lang Arts Ed., School Cons., Sci. Ed., Sec. Ed., Spec. Ed. DOCTORATE: Counselor Ed., Early Childhood Ed., Ed. Admin, Ed. Psych., Elementary Ed., Higher Ed., Math Ed., Read/Lang Arts Ed., School Cons., Sci. Ed., Sec. Ed., Spec. Ed.
Library: N/A
Computer Resources: Macintosh, Dual Platform, PCs, CD-ROM, Videodisc

Research Areas	#Faculty
Adult Education	1
Art Education	
Bilingual Education	
Counselor Education	
Early Childhood Ed.	1
Ed. Admin	6
Ed. Tech.	3
Elementary Ed.	
Foreign Lang. Ed.	
Higher Ed.	2
Math Ed.	1
Mid. Lev. Ed.	
Multicultural Ed.	3
Music Ed.	
Physical Ed.	
Read/Lang. Arts Ed.	3
School Counseling	
Science Ed.	1
Secondary Ed.	1
Soc. Studies Ed.	2
Special Ed.	4
Other	19

Research Institutes/Centers: Center for the Study of Testing, Evaluation and Educational Policy, Center for International Higher Education
Student Body Demographics: Average Age 25, 74% female, 26% male
Percent Ethnic Minorities: Hispanic-American 3%, Asian-American 3%, African-American 4%, Native-American 1%
Geographic Representation: New England 78%, Midwest 4%, Mid Atlantic 8%, Southwest 1%, West 3%, Southeast 1%, Northwest 1%

Graduate Career Paths: K-12 Teaching 30%, Higher Ed Teaching 10%, School Counseling 10%, K-12 Special Ed 10%, School Administration 10%, Higher Ed Administration 10%, Higher Ed Counseling 10%, Community Counseling 10%
Tuition: 536/hr (in state), 536/hr (out of state)
Financial Aid Recipients: 31%
Average Annual Housing Cost: N/A
Application Deadline: 3/15; 11/15; 7/15
Number of: applicants annually 1,500; applicants accepted annually 900; students enrolled annually N/A

Tests Required	Preferred/Min Score
Graduate Record Exam	
National Teachers Exam	
Praxis II Exam	
TOEFL	550

Boston University School of Education

605 Commonwealth Avenue, Boston, MA 02215
Admissions: (PH)617 353-4237, (FAX)617 353-8937
Dean: (PH)617 353-3212, (FAX)617 353-6156, (EMAIL)jdee@bu.edu
Total Enrollment: 20,000
Grad Enrollment: FTM 230, PTM 211, FTD 92, PTD 232, CAS 12
Program Membership: N/A
Academic Programs Available: MASTERS: Bilingual Ed., Counselor Ed., Early Childhood Ed., Ed. Admin., Ed. Tech., Elementary Ed., Foreign Lang. Ed., Higher Ed., Math Ed., Mid Level Ed., Physical Ed., Read/Lang Arts Ed., School Cons., Sci. Ed., Sec. Ed., Soc. Ed., Spec. Ed. DOCTORATE: Early Childhood Ed., Ed. Tech., Elementary Ed., Foreign Lang. Ed., Higher Ed., Math Ed., Read/Lang Arts Ed., Sci. Ed., Sec. Ed., Soc. Ed., Spec. Ed.
Library: Mugar Memorial Library, 1.9 million volumes
Computer Resources: Macintosh, Dual Platform, PCs, CD-ROM, Videodisc

Research Areas	#Faculty
Adult Education	
Art Education	
Bilingual Education	2
Counselor Education	3
Early Childhood Ed.	3
Ed. Admin	3
Ed. Tech.	1
Elementary Ed.	4
Foreign Lang. Ed.	1
Higher Ed.	3
Math Ed.	4
Mid. Lev. Ed.	12
Multicultural Ed.	
Music Ed.	
Physical Ed.	4
Read/Lang. Arts Ed.	1
School Counseling	1
Science Ed.	3
Secondary Ed.	3
Soc. Studies Ed.	2
Special Ed.	6
Other	15

Research Institutes/Centers: Center for the Advancement of Ethics & Character, Institute for Responsive Education, Center for Communication and Deafness
Student Body Demographics: Average Age 29.5, 70.4% female, 29.6% male
Percent Ethnic Minorities: Hispanic-American 4.5%, Asian-American 4.1%, African-American 2.4%, Native-American 0.4%
Geographic Representation: New England 74.8%, Midwest 0.9%, Mid Atlantic 7.2%, Southwest 0.5%, West 3%, Southeast 1.7%, Northwest 0.3%
Tuition: 19,420 (in state), 19,420 (out of state)
Financial Aid Recipients: 33%
Average Annual Housing Cost: 15,804
Application Deadline: 2/15
Number of: applicants annually 1,250; applicants accepted annually 996; students enrolled annually 500

Tests Required	Preferred/Min Score
Graduate Record Exam	1,108
National Teachers Exam	
Praxis II Exam	
TOEFL	550–600

Bridgewater State College School of Education

Graduate School, Bridgewater, MA 02325
Admissions: (PH)508 697-1300
Dean: (PH)508 697-1300, (FAX)508 697-1356
Total Enrollment: 5,000–10,000
Grad Enrollment: FTM 110, PTM 430, CAS 140, Off campus 100%
Program Membership: N/A
Academic Programs Available: MASTERS: Art Ed., Counselor Ed., Early Childhood Ed., Ed. Admin, Elementary Ed., Math Ed., Physical Ed., Read/Lang Arts Ed., School Cons., Sci. Ed., Soc. Ed., Spec. Ed. DOCTORATE: Art Ed., Counselor Ed., Early Childhood Ed., Ed. Admin, Elementary Ed., Math Ed., Physical Ed., Read/Lang Arts Ed., School Cons., Sci. Ed., Soc. Ed., Spec. Ed.
Library: Maxwell Library, 328,000 volumes
Computer Resources: Macintosh, Dual Platform, PCs, CD-ROM, Videodisc

Research Areas	#Faculty
Adult Education	
Art Education	
Bilingual Education	
Counselor Education	
Early Childhood Ed.	
Ed. Admin	
Ed. Tech.	
Elementary Ed.	
Foreign Lang. Ed.	
Higher Ed.	
Math Ed.	
Mid. Lev. Ed.	
Multicultural Ed.	
Music Ed.	
Physical Ed.	
Read/Lang. Arts Ed.	

School Counseling
Science Ed.
Secondary Ed.
Soc. Studies Ed.
Special Ed.
Other
Student Body Demographics: Average Age 35, 70% female, 30% male
Percent Ethnic Minorities: N/A
Geographic Representation: New England 99%
Tuition: 140/hr (in state), 300/hr (out of state)
Financial Aid Recipients: 5%
Average Annual Housing Cost: N/A
Application Deadline: varies
Number of: applicants annually 600–700; applicants accepted annually N/A; students enrolled annually N/A

Tests Required	Preferred/Min Score
Graduate Record Exam	900
National Teachers Exam	
Praxis II Exam	

Fitchburg State College

Division of Graduate and Continuing Education, 160 Pearl Street, Fitchburg, MA 01420-2697
Admissions: (PH)508 665-3146, (FAX)508 665-3658
Dean: (PH)508 665-3183, (FAX)508 665-3658
Total Enrollment: 5,000–10,000
Grad Enrollment: PTM 491, CAS 75, Off campus 100%
Program Membership: N/A
Academic Programs Available: MASTERS: Art Ed., Early Childhood Ed., Ed. Tech., Elementary Ed., Mid Level Ed., School Cons., Sci. Ed., Sec. Ed., Spec. Ed. DOCTORATE: Art Ed., Early Childhood Ed., Ed. Tech., Elementary Ed., Mid Level Ed., School Cons., Sci. Ed., Sec. Ed., Spec. Ed.
Library: FSC Library, 229,000 volumes
Computer Resources: Macintosh, Dual Platform, PCs, CD-ROM, Videodisc

Research Areas	#Faculty
Adult Education	
Art Education	
Bilingual Education	
Counselor Education	
Early Childhood Ed.	
Ed. Admin	
Ed. Tech.	
Elementary Ed.	
Foreign Lang. Ed.	
Higher Ed.	
Math Ed.	
Mid. Lev. Ed.	
Multicultural Ed.	
Music Ed.	
Physical Ed.	
Read/Lang. Arts Ed.	
School Counseling	
Science Ed.	
Secondary Ed.	
Soc. Studies Ed.	
Special Ed.	

Other
Student Body Demographics: Average Age 35, 64% female, 36% male
Percent Ethnic Minorities: Hispanic-American 2%, Asian-American 2%, African-American 2.5%, Native-American 0.2%
Geographic Representation: New England 99%
Graduate Career Paths: K-12 Teaching 29%, School Counseling 3%, K-12 Special Ed 37%, School Administration 3%, Community Counseling 4%
Tuition: 140/hr (in state), N/A (out of state)
Financial Aid Recipients: N/A
Average Annual Housing Cost: 2,330
Application Deadline: rolling
Number of: applicants annually 518; applicants accepted annually 258; students enrolled annually 102

Tests Required	Preferred/Min Score
Graduate Record Exam	
National Teachers Exam	
Praxis II Exam	

Harvard University Graduate School of Education

111 Longfellow Hall, Appian Way, Cambridge, MA 02138
Admissions: (PH)617 495-3414, (FAX)617 496-3577, (EMAIL)admit@hugse2.harvard.edu
Dean: (PH)617 495-3401, (FAX)617 495-8510
Total Enrollment: 20,000
Grad Enrollment: FTM 440, PTM 131, FTD 446, PTD 130, CAS 35, On campus 6%, Off campus 94%
Program Membership: Holmes Partnership
Academic Programs Available: MASTERS: Ed. Admin, Ed. Tech., Foreign Lang. Ed., Higher Ed., Math Ed., Mid Level Ed., Multicultural Ed., Read/Lang Arts Ed., Sci. Ed., Sec. Ed., Soc. Ed., DOCTORATE: Ed. Admin, Ed. Tech., Foreign Lang. Ed., Higher Ed., Math Ed., Multicultural Ed., Read/Lang Arts Ed.
Library: Gutman Library, 180,000 volumes
Computer Resources: Macintosh, Dual Platform, PCs, CD-ROM, Videodisc

Research Areas	#Faculty
Adult Education	3
Art Education	3
Bilingual Education	3
Counselor Education	2
Early Childhood Ed.	
Ed. Admin	20
Ed. Tech.	7
Elementary Ed.	
Foreign Lang. Ed.	
Higher Ed.	12
Math Ed.	6
Mid. Lev. Ed.	6
Multicultural Ed.	2
Music Ed.	
Physical Ed.	
Read/Lang. Arts Ed.	4
School Counseling	2
Science Ed.	7

Secondary Ed.	7
Soc. Studies Ed.	2
Special Ed.	2
Other	

Research Institutes/Centers: Harvard Family Research Project, Harvard Literacy Laboratory, Project Zero, Philosophy of Education Research Center

Student Body Demographics: Average Age 30, 74% female, 26% male

Percent Ethnic Minorities: Hispanic-American 7%, Asian-American 5%, African-American 10%, Native-American 1%

Geographic Representation: New England 55%, Midwest 4%, Mid Atlantic 10%, Southwest 2%, West 9%, Southeast 4%, Northwest 1%

Graduate Career Paths: K-12 Teaching 31%, Higher Ed Teaching 5%, School Counseling 5%, K-12 School Administration 4%, Higher Ed Administration 10%, Community Counseling 5%

Tuition: 17,498 (in state), 17,498 (out of state)

Financial Aid Recipients: 63-89%

Average Annual Housing Cost: 9,000

Application Deadline: 1/2

Number of: applicants annually 1,637; applicants accepted annually 770; students enrolled annually N/A

Tests Required	Preferred/Min Score
Graduate Record Exam	
National Teachers Exam	
Praxis II Exam	
TOEFL	600

Lesley College School of Education

29 Everett Street, Cambridge, MA 02138

Admissions: (PH)617 349-8300, (FAX)617 349-8313

Dean: (PH)617 349-8375, (FAX)617 349-8607

Total Enrollment: 5,000–10,000

Grad Enrollment: FTM 100, PTM 2,261, FTD 10, PTD 24, CAS 12

Program Membership: N/A

Academic Programs Available: MASTERS: Counselor Ed., Ed. Admin, Ed. Tech., Elementary Ed., Mid Level Ed., School Cons., Spec. Ed. DOCTORATE: Counselor Ed., Ed. Admin, Ed. Tech., Elementary Ed., Mid Level Ed., School Cons., Spec.

Library: Ludcke Library

Computer Resources: Macintosh, Dual Platform, PCs, CD-ROM, Videodisc

Research Areas	#Faculty
Adult Education	1
Art Education	1
Bilingual Education	1
Counselor Education	2
Early Childhood Ed.	4
Ed. Admin	1
Ed. Tech.	4
Elementary Ed.	1
Foreign Lang. Ed.	
Higher Ed.	
Math Ed.	3

Mid. Lev. Ed.	
Multicultural Ed.	5
Music Ed.	
Physical Ed.	
Read/Lang. Arts Ed.	6
School Counseling	
Science Ed.	1
Secondary Ed.	1
Soc. Studies Ed.	
Special Ed.	7
Other	

Research Institutes/Centers: Center for Adult Learning, Center for Children, Families and Public Policy, Center for Mathematics, Science and Technology in Education

Student Body Demographics: Average Age 34, 83% female, 17% male

Percent Ethnic Minorities: Hispanic-American 2%, Asian-American 1%, African-American 2%

Geographic Representation: New England 49%, Midwest 7%, Mid Atlantic 6%, Southwest 1%, West 16%, Southeast 1%, Northwest 9%

Tuition: N/A(in state), N/A(out of state)

Financial Aid Recipients: 36%

Average Annual Housing Cost: N/A

Application Deadline: varies

Number of: applicants annually 1,257; applicants accepted annually 998; students enrolled annually N/A

Tests Required	Preferred/Min Score
Graduate Record Exam	
National Teachers Exam	
Praxis II Exam	
TOEFL	550

Northeastern University
Education Department

54 Lake Hall, 360 Huntington Avenue, Boston, MA 02115

Admissions: (PH)617 373-5908

Total Enrollment: 20,000

Grad Enrollment: FTM 21, PTM 10

Program Membership: N/A

Academic Programs Available: MASTERS: Elementary Ed., Math Ed., Read/Lang Arts Ed., Sci. Ed., Sec. Ed., Soc. Ed., DOCTORATE: Elementary Ed., Math Ed., Read/Lang Arts Ed., Sci. Ed., Sec. Ed., Soc. Ed.

Library: N/A

Computer Resources: Macintosh, PCs

Research Areas	#Faculty
Adult Education	
Art Education	
Bilingual Education	
Counselor Education	
Early Childhood Ed.	1
Ed. Admin	
Ed. Tech.	2
Elementary Ed.	7
Foreign Lang. Ed.	
Higher Ed.	
Math Ed.	1
Mid. Lev. Ed.	8

Multicultural Ed.
Music Ed.
Physical Ed.

Read/Lang. Arts Ed.	3
School Counseling	
Science Ed.	1
Secondary Ed.	1
Soc. Studies Ed.	2
Special Ed.	
Other	2

Research Institutes/Centers: Center for Innovation in Urban Education
Student Body Demographics: Average Age 31, 61% female, 39% male
Percent Ethnic Minorities: Hispanic-American 3%, Asian-American 15%, African-American 3%
Geographic Representation: New England 77%, Southeast 6%, UK 3%
Graduate Career Paths: K-12 Teaching 70%, K-12
Tuition: N/A (in state), N/A (out of state)
Financial Aid Recipients: N/A
Average Annual Housing Cost: N/A
Application Deadline: 5/1; 11/1; 2/1
Number of: applicants annually 50; applicants accepted annually 40; students enrolled annually 25

Tests Required	Preferred/Min Score
Graduate Record Exam	960
National Teachers Exam	
Praxis II Exam	
TOEFL	550

Simmons College Graduate Programs in Education

Graduate Studies Admissions, 300 The Fenway, Boston, MA 02115-5898
Admissions: (PH)617 521-2910, (FAX)617 521-3199, (EMAIL)gsa@vmsvax
Dean: (PH)617 521-2089, (FAX)617 521-3199
Total Enrollment: 1,000–5,000
Grad Enrollment: FTM 115, PTM 171, On campus 10%, Off campus 90%
Program Membership: N/A
Academic Programs Available: MASTERS: Elementary Ed., Foreign Lang. Ed., Math Ed., Mid Level Ed., Sci. Ed., Sec. Ed., Soc. Ed., DOCTORATE: Elementary Ed., Foreign Lang. Ed., Math Ed., Mid Level Ed., Sci. Ed., Sec. Ed., Soc. Ed., Spec. Ed.
Library: Beatley Library, 262,000 volumes
Computer Resources: Macintosh, Dual Platform, PCs, CD-ROM, Videodisc

Research Areas	#Faculty
Adult Education	
Art Education	
Bilingual Education	
Counselor Education	
Early Childhood Ed.	
Ed. Admin	
Ed. Tech.	
Elementary Ed.	2

Foreign Lang. Ed.	1
Higher Ed.	
Math Ed.	1
Mid. Lev. Ed.	2
Multicultural Ed.	1
Music Ed.	
Physical Ed.	
Read/Lang. Arts Ed.	2
School Counseling	
Science Ed.	
Secondary Ed.	
Soc. Studies Ed.	2
Special Ed.	4
Other	4

Student Body Demographics: Average Age 30, 72% female, 28% male
Percent Ethnic Minorities: Hispanic-American 2%, Asian-American 2%, African-American 6%, Native-American 1%
Geographic Representation: New England 85%, Midwest 1%, Mid Atlantic 10%, Southwest 1%, West 1%, Southeast 1%, Northwest 1%
Graduate Career Paths: K-12 Teaching 37%, K-12 Special Ed 52%
Tuition: 530/hr (in state), 530/hr (out of state)
Financial Aid Recipients: 100%
Average Annual Housing Cost: 11,600
Application Deadline: 8/1; 11/15; 4/1
Number of: applicants annually 266; applicants accepted annually 260; students enrolled annually 195

Tests Required	Preferred/Min Score
Graduate Record Exam	1,000
National Teachers Exam	
Praxis II Exam	
TOEFL	550–600

Springfield College Education Department

Graduate Admissions, 263 Alden Street, Springfield, MA 01109
Admissions: (PH)413 748-3225, (FAX)(413) 748-3649, (EMAIL) graduate@spfldcol.edu
Dean: (PH)413 748-3295
Total Enrollment: 1,000–5,000
Grad Enrollment: FTM 26, PTM 45, CAS 11, On campus 20%, Off campus 80%
Program Membership: N/A
Academic Programs Available: MASTERS: Early Childhood Ed., Ed. Admin, Elementary Ed., Physical Ed., DOCTORATE: Early Childhood Ed., Ed. Admin, Elementary Ed., Physical Ed.
Library: Babson Library, 132,000 volumes
Computer Resources: Macintosh, Dual Platform, PCs, CD-ROM, Videodisc

Research Areas	#Faculty
Adult Education	
Art Education	
Bilingual Education	
Counselor Education	
Early Childhood Ed.	

Ed. Admin
Ed. Tech.
Elementary Ed.
Foreign Lang. Ed.
Higher Ed.
Math Ed.
Mid. Lev. Ed.
Multicultural Ed.
Music Ed.
Physical Ed.   10
Read/Lang. Arts Ed.
School Counseling
Science Ed.
Secondary Ed.
Soc. Studies Ed.
Special Ed.
Other

Student Body Demographics: Average Age 28, 67% female, 33% male
Percent Ethnic Minorities: Hispanic-American 3%, Asian-American 2%, African-American 5%
Geographic Representation: New England 77%, Midwest 1%, Mid Atlantic 10%, Southwest 1%, West 5%, Southeast 5%, Northwest 1%
Graduate Career Paths: K-12 Teaching 52%, K-12 School Administration 48%
Tuition: 386/hr (in state), 386/hr (out of state)
Financial Aid Recipients: N/A
Average Annual Housing Cost: 3,800
Application Deadline: 2/1; 11/1
Number of: applicants annually 77; applicants accepted annually 66; students enrolled annually N/A

Tests Required	Preferred/Min Score
Graduate Record Exam	1,000–1,200
National Teachers Exam	
Praxis II Exam	
TOEFL	550

Suffolk University Department of Education and Human Services

8 Ashburton Place, Boston, MA 02108
Admissions: (PH)617 573-8302, (FAX)617 523-0116, (EMAIL)grad.admission@admin.suffolk.edu
Total Enrollment: 5,000–10,000
Grad Enrollment: Off campus 100%
Program Membership: N/A
Academic Programs Available: MASTERS: Adult Ed., Counselor Ed., Ed. Admin, Higher Ed., School Cons., Sec. Ed., DOCTORATE: Adult Ed., Counselor Ed., Ed. Admin, Higher Ed., School Cons., Sec. Ed.
Library: Sawyer Library, 100,000 volumes
Computer Resources: Macintosh, Dual Platform, PCs, CD-ROM, Videodisc

Research Areas	#Faculty
Adult Education	
Art Education	
Bilingual Education	
Counselor Education	

Early Childhood Ed.
Ed. Admin
Ed. Tech.
Elementary Ed.
Foreign Lang. Ed.
Higher Ed.
Math Ed.
Mid. Lev. Ed.
Multicultural Ed.
Music Ed.
Physical Ed.
Read/Lang. Arts Ed.
School Counseling
Science Ed.
Secondary Ed.
Soc. Studies Ed.
Special Ed.
Other

Student Body Demographics: Average Age 27, 80% female, 20% male
Percent Ethnic Minorities: N/A
Geographic Representation: N/A
Tuition: 12,000 (in state), 12,000 (out of state)
Financial Aid Recipients: N/A
Average Annual Housing Cost: 6,000
Application Deadline: 6/15; 11/15; 4/15
Number of: applicants annually 150-200; applicants accepted annually N/A; students enrolled annually N/A

Tests Required	Preferred/Min Score
Graduate Record Exam	
National Teachers Exam	
Praxis II Exam	
TOEFL	550

Tufts University Department of Education

Lincoln Filene Center, Medford, MA 02115
Admissions: (PH)617 627-3244
Total Enrollment: 5,000–10,000
Grad Enrollment: 110 total
Program Membership: N/A
Academic Programs Available: MASTERS: Elementary Ed., Math Ed., Mid Level Ed., School Cons., Sci. Ed., Sec. Ed., Soc. Ed., DOCTORATE: Elementary Ed., Math Ed., Mid Level Ed., School Cons., Sci. Ed., Sec. Ed., Soc. Ed.
Library: N/A

Research Areas	#Faculty
Adult Education	
Art Education	1
Bilingual Education	
Counselor Education	
Early Childhood Ed.	
Ed. Admin	
Ed. Tech.	2
Elementary Ed.	
Foreign Lang. Ed.	1
Higher Ed.	1
Math Ed.	2
Mid. Lev. Ed.	2
Multicultural Ed.	1

Music Ed.
Physical Ed.
Read/Lang. Arts Ed.

School Counseling	2
Science Ed.	1
Secondary Ed.	1

Soc. Studies Ed.

Special Ed.	3

Other

Research Institutes/Centers: Center for Science and Mathematics Teaching, H. Dudley Wright Center for Innovations in Science Education
Student Body Demographics: Average Age N/A, 80% female, 20% male
Percent Ethnic Minorities: N/A
Geographic Representation: N/A
Tuition: 18,340 (in state), 18,340 (out of state)
Financial Aid Recipients: N/A
Average Annual Housing Cost: N/A
Application Deadline: rolling
Number of: applicants annually 146; applicants accepted annually 121; students enrolled annually N/A

Tests Required	Preferred/Min Score
Graduate Record Exam	
National Teachers Exam	
Praxis II Exam	
TOEFL	550

University of Massachusetts at Amherst School of Education

Box 33291, Amherst, MA 01003
Admissions: (PH)413 545-0223, (FAX)413 577-0010
Dean: (PH)413 545-0236, (FAX)413 545-6130
Total Enrollment: 20,000
Grad Enrollment: FTM 264, PTM 208, FTD 766, PTD 370
Program Membership: Holmes Partnership
Academic Programs Available: MASTERS: Early Childhood Ed., Ed. Admin, Ed. Tech., Elementary Ed., Higher Ed., Math Ed., Mid Level Ed., Multicultural Ed., Read/Lang Arts Ed., School Cons., Sci. Ed., Sec. Ed., Soc. Ed., Spec. Ed. DOCTORATE: Early Childhood Ed., Ed. Admin, Ed. Tech., Elementary Ed., Higher Ed., Math Ed., Mid Level Ed., Multicultural Ed., Read/Lang Arts Ed., School Cons., Sci. Ed., Sec. Ed., Soc. Ed., Spec.
Library: University Library, 2 million volumes
Computer Resources: Macintosh, Dual Platform, PCs, CD-ROM, Videodisc

Research Areas	#Faculty
Adult Education	
Art Education	
Bilingual Education	2
Counselor Education	4
Early Childhood Ed.	4
Ed. Admin	4
Ed. Tech.	5
Elementary Ed.	3
Foreign Lang. Ed.	
Higher Ed.	4
Math Ed.	2

Mid. Lev. Ed.	1
Multicultural Ed.	5
Music Ed.	
Physical Ed.	3
Read/Lang. Arts Ed.	2
School Counseling	2
Science Ed.	3
Secondary Ed.	3
Soc. Studies Ed.	1
Special Ed.	3

Other

Student Body Demographics: Average Age N/A, 68% female, 32% male
Percent Ethnic Minorities: Hispanic-American 5%, Asian-American 2%, African-American 5%
Geographic Representation: New England 70%
Graduate Career Paths: K-12 Teaching 29%, Higher Ed Teaching 20%, School Counseling 9%, K-12 Special Ed 4%, School Administration 2%, Higher Ed Administration 4%, Community Counseling 9%
Tuition: 1,389 (in state), 4,421 (out of state)
Financial Aid Recipients: 80%
Average Annual Housing Cost: 2,876
Application Deadline: varies
Number of: applicants annually 888; applicants accepted annually 395; students enrolled annually 235

Tests Required	Preferred/Min Score
Graduate Record Exam	
National Teachers Exam	
Praxis II Exam	
TOEFL	550

MICHIGAN

Andrews University School of Education

Graduate Admissions, Berrien Springs, MI 49104
Admissions: (PH)616 471-3490, (FAX)616 471-9751, (EMAIL)verna@andrews.edu
Dean: (PH)616 471-3109, (FAX)616 471-6374, (EMAIL)piskozub@andrews.edu
Total Enrollment: 1,000–5,000
Program Membership: N/A
Academic Programs Available: MASTERS: Counselor Ed., Ed. Admin, Ed. Psych., Elementary Ed., Foreign Lang. Ed., Higher Ed., Mid Level Ed., Read/Lang Arts Ed., School Cons., Sec. Ed., DOCTORATE: Counselor Ed., Ed. Admin, Ed. Psych., Elementary Ed., Foreign Lang. Ed., Higher Ed., Mid Level Ed., Read/Lang Arts Ed., School Cons., Sec. Ed.
Library: James White Library, 1 million volumes
Computer Resources: Macintosh, Dual Platform, PCs, CD-ROM, Videodisc

Research Areas	#Faculty
Adult Education	
Art Education	
Bilingual Education	

Counselor Education	5
Early Childhood Ed.	
Ed. Admin	4
Ed. Tech.	
Elementary Ed.	6
Foreign Lang. Ed.	
Higher Ed.	2
Math Ed.	
Mid. Lev. Ed.	2
Multicultural Ed.	
Music Ed.	
Physical Ed.	
Read/Lang. Arts Ed.	2
School Counseling	2
Science Ed.	
Secondary Ed.	
Soc. Studies Ed.	
Special Ed.	
Other	4

Student Body Demographics: Average Age N/A, 56% female, 44% male
Percent Ethnic Minorities: Hispanic-American 4%, Asian-American 11%, African-American 23%, Native-American 1%
Geographic Representation: New England 5%, Midwest 52%, Mid Atlantic 5%, Southwest 1%, West 3%, Southeast 5%, Northwest 1%
Tuition: 290/hr (in state), 290/hr (out of state)
Financial Aid Recipients: N/A
Average Annual Housing Cost: 4,890
Application Deadline: 6/1; 10/1; 1/1; 3/1
Number of: applicants annually 200; applicants accepted annually 180; students enrolled annually N/A

Tests Required	Preferred/Min Score
Graduate Record Exam	
National Teachers Exam	
Praxis II Exam	
TOEFL	500

Central Michigan University College of Education, Health and Human Services

200 IET Building, Mt. Pleasant, MI 48859
Admissions: (PH)517 774-4723, (FAX)517 774-3439, (EMAIL)grad@mich.edu
Dean: (PH)517 774-6995, (FAX)517 774-4374, (EMAIL)kelvie.c.comer@mich.edu
Total Enrollment: 10,000–20,000
Grad Enrollment: FTM 105, PTM 400, FTD 20, On campus 10%, Off campus 90%
Program Membership: Holmes Partnership
Academic Programs Available: MASTERS: Art Ed., Counselor Ed., Early Childhood Ed., Ed. Admin, Ed. Psych., Ed. Tech., Elementary Ed., Math Ed., Mid Level Ed., Music Ed., Read/Lang Arts Ed., School Cons., Sec. Ed., Spec. Ed. DOCTORATE: Art Ed., Counselor Ed., Early Childhood Ed., Ed. Admin, Ed. Psych., Ed. Tech., Elementary Ed., Math Ed., Mid Level Ed., Music Ed., Read/Lang Arts Ed., School Cons., Sec. Ed., Spec. Ed.
Library: Park Library

Computer Resources: Macintosh, Dual Platform, PCs, CD-ROM, Videodisc

Research Areas	#Faculty
Adult Education	
Art Education	
Bilingual Education	
Counselor Education	
Early Childhood Ed.	
Ed. Admin	
Ed. Tech.	
Elementary Ed.	
Foreign Lang. Ed.	
Higher Ed.	
Math Ed.	
Mid. Lev. Ed.	
Multicultural Ed.	
Music Ed.	
Physical Ed.	
Read/Lang. Arts Ed.	
School Counseling	
Science Ed.	
Secondary Ed.	
Soc. Studies Ed.	
Special Ed.	
Other	

Student Body Demographics: Average Age 31, 61% female, 39% male
Percent Ethnic Minorities: Hispanic-American 1%, Asian-American 1%, African-American 3%, Native-American 1%
Geographic Representation: Midwest 92%
Tuition: 126/hr (in state), 251/hr (out of state)
Financial Aid Recipients: 29%
Average Annual Housing Cost: 4,332
Application Deadline: varies
Number of: applicants annually 2,529; applicants accepted annually 1,611; students enrolled annually N/A

Tests Required	Preferred/Min Score
Graduate Record Exam	
National Teachers Exam	
Praxis II Exam	
TOEFL	500–550

Eastern Michigan University College of Education

Graduate Admissions, Starkweather Hall, Ypsilanti, MI 48197
Admissions: (PH)313 487-3400, (FAX)313 487-0050, (EMAIL)aiko.nakatani@emich.edu
Dean: (PH)313 487-1414, (FAX)313 484-6471, (EMAIL)jerry.robbins@emich.edu
Total Enrollment: 20,000
Grad Enrollment: FTM 130, PTM 1010, FTD 4, PTD 28, On campus 1%, Off campus 99%
Program Membership: Holmes Partnership
Academic Programs Available: MASTERS: Counselor Ed., Early Childhood Ed., Ed. Admin, Ed. Psych., Elementary Ed., Mid Level Ed., Physical Ed., Read/Lang Arts Ed., School Cons., Sec. Ed., Spec. Ed. DOCTORATE: Counselor

Ed., Early Childhood Ed., Ed. Admin, Ed. Psych., Elementary Ed., Mid Level Ed., Physical Ed., Read/Lang Arts Ed., School Cons., Sec. Ed., Spec. Ed.
Library: University Library, 625,000 volumes
Computer Resources: Macintosh, Dual Platform, PCs, CD-ROM, Videodisc

Research Areas	#Faculty
Adult Education	2
Art Education	2
Bilingual Education	2
Counselor Education	8
Early Childhood Ed.	4
Ed. Admin	8
Ed. Tech.	2
Elementary Ed.	6
Foreign Lang. Ed.	3
Higher Ed.	2
Math Ed.	2
Mid. Lev. Ed.	2
Multicultural Ed.	5
Music Ed.	2
Physical Ed.	18
Read/Lang. Arts Ed.	8
School Counseling	3
Science Ed.	2
Secondary Ed.	2
Soc. Studies Ed.	2
Special Ed.	29
Other	40

Student Body Demographics: Average Age 44, 77% female, 23% male
Percent Ethnic Minorities: Hispanic-American 1%, Asian-American 1%, African-American 4%, Native-American 1%
Geographic Representation: Midwest 95%
Graduate Career Paths: K-12 Teaching 33%, School Counseling 11%, K-12 Special Ed 24%, School Administration 22%, Higher Ed Administration 3%, Higher Ed Counseling 6%, Community Counseling 5%
Tuition: 130/hr (in state), 300/hr (out of state)
Financial Aid Recipients: 4%
Average Annual Housing Cost: N/A
Application Deadline: 3/15
Number of: applicants annually N/A; applicants accepted annually N/A; students enrolled annually N/A

Tests Required	Preferred/Min Score
Graduate Record Exam	1000
National Teachers Exam	
Praxis II Exam	

Michigan State University
College of Education

134 Erickson Hall, East Lansing, MI 48824
Admissions: (PH)517 353-9683, (FAX)517 432-2718, (EMAIL)edulo@msu.edu
Dean: (PH)517 355-1787, (FAX)517 353-6393, (EMAIL)cassbook@msu.edu
Total Enrollment: 20,000

Grad Enrollment: FTM 145, PTM 406, FTD 318, PTD 156, On campus 10%, Off campus 90%
Program Membership: Holmes Partnership
Academic Programs Available: MASTERS: Adult Ed., Counselor Ed., Ed. Admin, Ed. Psych., Higher Ed., Physical Ed., Read/Lang Arts Ed., School Cons., Spec. Ed. DOCTORATE: Adult Ed., Counselor Ed., Ed. Admin, Ed. Psych., Higher Ed., Physical Ed., Read/Lang Arts Ed., School Cons., Spec. Ed.
Library: MSU Library, 4 million volumes
Computer Resources: Macintosh, Dual Platform, PCs, CD-ROM, Videodisc

Research Areas	#Faculty
Adult Education	15
Art Education	
Bilingual Education	
Counselor Education	3
Early Childhood Ed.	
Ed. Admin	12
Ed. Tech.	20
Elementary Ed.	40
Foreign Lang. Ed.	
Higher Ed.	12
Math Ed.	13
Mid. Lev. Ed.	2
Multicultural Ed.	12
Music Ed.	
Physical Ed.	11
Read/Lang. Arts Ed.	16
School Counseling	3
Science Ed.	8
Secondary Ed.	8
Soc. Studies Ed.	5
Special Ed.	10
Other	

Research Institutes/Centers: Institute for Research on Teaching and Learning Across the Life Span, Institute for Research on Teaching Adults, National Center for Research on Teacher Learning
Student Body Demographics: Average Age 35, 65% female, 35% male
Percent Ethnic Minorities: N/A
Geographic Representation: New England 5%, Midwest 71%, Mid Atlantic 3%, West 5%, Northwest 3%
Graduate Career Paths: K-12 Teaching 28%, Higher Ed Teaching 26%, School Counseling 12%, K-12 Special Ed 5%, School Administration 15%, Higher Ed Administration 12%, Community Counseling 2%
Tuition: 203/cr (in state), 411/cr (out of state)
Financial Aid Recipients: 75%
Average Annual Housing Cost: N/A
Application Deadline: 1/31; 3/15
Number of: applicants annually 800; applicants accepted annually 380; students enrolled annually 200-225

Tests Required	Preferred/Min Score
Graduate Record Exam	
National Teachers Exam	
Praxis II Exam	
TOEFL	520–550

Oakland University School of Education and Human Resources

Graduate Admissions, Rochester, MI 48309-4401
Admissions: (PH)810 370-3168, (FAX)810 370-4119, (EMAIL)rammel@vela.acs.oakland.edu
Dean: (PH)810 370-3050, (FAX)810 370-4202, (EMAIL)oho@vela.acs.oakland.edu
Total Enrollment: 10,000–20,000
Grad Enrollment: FTM 249, PTM 891, FTD 18, PTD 16, On campus 1%, Off campus 99%
Program Membership: N/A
Academic Programs Available: MASTERS: Early Childhood Ed., Ed. Admin, Elementary Ed., Foreign Lang. Ed., Math Ed., Read/Lang Arts Ed., School Cons., Spec. Ed. DOCTORATE: Early Childhood Ed., Ed. Admin, Elementary Ed., Foreign Lang. Ed., Math Ed., Read/Lang Arts Ed., School Cons., Spec. Ed.
Library: Kresge Library
Computer Resources: Macintosh, Dual Platform, PCs, CD-ROM, Videodisc

Research Areas	#Faculty
Adult Education	
Art Education	1
Bilingual Education	
Counselor Education	
Early Childhood Ed.	4
Ed. Admin	3
Ed. Tech.	5
Elementary Ed.	10
Foreign Lang. Ed.	
Higher Ed.	
Math Ed.	
Mid. Lev. Ed.	
Multicultural Ed.	
Music Ed.	2
Physical Ed.	
Read/Lang. Arts Ed.	12
School Counseling	6
Science Ed.	3
Secondary Ed.	3
Soc. Studies Ed.	2
Special Ed.	3
Other	

Research Institutes/Centers: Institute for Action Research, Reading Recovery Program
Student Body Demographics: Average Age 34, 92% female, 8% male
Percent Ethnic Minorities: Hispanic-American 1%, Asian-American 0.5%, African-American 5%, Native-American 0.3%
Geographic Representation: Midwest 98%, Mid Atlantic 1%, Southeast 1%
Graduate Career Paths: K-12 Teaching 95%, K-12 Special Ed 1%, Community Counseling 1%
Tuition: 189/hr (in state), 418/hr (out of state)
Financial Aid Recipients: N/A
Average Annual Housing Cost: 2,350
Application Deadline: 6/15; 11/1; 3/1
Number of: applicants annually 3,000; applicants accepted annually 2,700; students enrolled annually 2,500

Tests Required	Preferred/Min Score
Graduate Record Exam	
National Teachers Exam	
Praxis II Exam	

University of Detroit Mercy College of Education and Human Services

P.O. Box 19900, Detroit, MI 48219-0900
Admissions: (PH)313 993-3305, (FAX)313 993-6303
Dean: (PH)313 993-6301, (FAX)313 993-6303
Total Enrollment: 5,000–10,000
Grad Enrollment: FTM 70, PTM 200, Off campus 100%
Program Membership: N/A
Academic Programs Available: MASTERS: Counselor Ed., Early Childhood Ed., Ed. Admin, Elementary Ed., Math Ed., School Cons., Sec. Ed., Spec. Ed. DOCTORATE: Counselor Ed., Early Childhood Ed., Ed. Admin, Elementary Ed., Math Ed., School Cons., Sec. Ed., Spec. Ed.
Library: N/A

Research Areas	#Faculty
Adult Education	
Art Education	
Bilingual Education	
Counselor Education	2
Early Childhood Ed.	
Ed. Admin	1
Ed. Tech.	
Elementary Ed.	
Foreign Lang. Ed.	
Higher Ed.	
Math Ed.	
Mid. Lev. Ed.	
Multicultural Ed.	
Music Ed.	
Physical Ed.	
Read/Lang. Arts Ed.	
School Counseling	
Science Ed.	
Secondary Ed.	
Soc. Studies Ed.	
Special Ed.	1
Other	

Student Body Demographics: Average Age 28, 70% female, 30% male
Percent Ethnic Minorities: N/A
Geographic Representation: Midwest 100%
Graduate Career Paths: K-12 Teaching 60%, School Counseling 3%, K-12 Special Ed 20%, School Administration 3%, Higher Ed Counseling 1%, Community Counseling 20%
Tuition: 400 (in state), 400 (out of state)
Financial Aid Recipients: 50%
Average Annual Housing Cost: N/A
Application Deadline: rolling
Number of: applicants annually 200; applicants accepted annually 100; students enrolled annually N/A

Tests Required	Preferred/Min Score
Graduate Record Exam	
National Teachers Exam	
Praxis II Exam	

University of Michigan School of Education

Office of Student Services, Room 1033, Ann Arbor,
MI 48109-1259
Admissions: (PH)313 764-7563, (FAX)313 763-1229
Dean: (PH)313 764-9470, (FAX)313 763-1229
Total Enrollment: 20,000
Grad Enrollment: FTM 95, PTM 33, FTD 167, PTD 61, On
campus 80%, Off campus 20%
Program Membership: Holmes Partnership
Academic Programs Available: MASTERS: Adult Ed., Early
Childhood Ed., Ed. Admin., Ed. Psych., Ed. Tech.,
Elementary Ed., Higher Ed., Math Ed., Read/Lang Arts Ed.,
Sci. Ed., Sec. Ed., Soc. Ed., Spec. Ed. DOCTORATE: Early
Childhood Ed., Ed. Admin., Ed. Psych., Ed. Tech.,
Elementary Ed., Higher Ed., Math Ed., Read/Lang Arts Ed.,
Sci. Ed., Sec. Ed., Soc. Ed., Spec. Ed.
Library: 6.6 million volumes
Computer Resources: Macintosh, Dual Platform, PCs,
CD-ROM, Videodisc

Research Areas	#Faculty
Adult Education	1
Art Education	
Bilingual Education	
Counselor Education	
Early Childhood Ed.	4
Ed. Admin	4
Ed. Tech.	13
Elementary Ed.	5
Foreign Lang. Ed.	
Higher Ed.	10
Math Ed.	3
Mid. Lev. Ed.	5
Multicultural Ed.	11
Music Ed.	
Physical Ed.	
Read/Lang. Arts Ed.	3
School Counseling	
Science Ed.	3
Secondary Ed.	3
Soc. Studies Ed.	2
Special Ed.	4
Other	

Research Institutes/Centers: Institute for Social Research,
Center for Human Growth and Development
Student Body Demographics: Average Age 28, 68% female,
32% male
Percent Ethnic Minorities: Hispanic-American 4%,
Asian-American 6%, African-American 9%,
Native-American 1%
Geographic Representation: New England 18%,
Midwest 45%, Mid Atlantic 1%, Southwest 4%, West 9%,
Southeast 5%, Northwest 1%

Graduate Career Paths: K-12 Teaching 30%, Higher Ed
Teaching 35%, K-12 Special Ed 2%, School
Administration 4%, Higher Ed Administration 20%
Tuition: 4,150 (in state), 8,437 (out of state)
Financial Aid Recipients: 50%
Average Annual Housing Cost: 7,000
Application Deadline: varies
Number of: applicants annually 514; applicants accepted
annually 281; students enrolled annually 150

Tests Required	Preferred/Min Score
Graduate Record Exam	1,800
National Teachers Exam	
Praxis II Exam	
TOEFL	600

University of Michigan/Dearborn School of Education

4901 Evergreen Road, Dearborn, MI 48128
Admissions: (PH)313 593-5090, (FAX)313 593-9961,
(EMAIL)rkapelan@fob.f1.umd.umich.edu
Dean: (PH)313 593-5435, (FAX)313 593-9961,
(EMAIL)jposter@fob.f1.umd.umich.edu
Total Enrollment: 5,000–10,000
Grad Enrollment: FTM 240, Off campus 100%
Program Membership: N/A
Academic Programs Available: MASTERS: Adult Ed., Early
Childhood Ed., Ed. Admin, Elementary Ed., Mid Level Ed.,
Spec. Ed. DOCTORATE: Adult Ed., Early Childhood Ed., Ed.
Admin, Elementary Ed., Mid Level Ed., Spec. Ed.
Library: Mardigian Library, 500,000 volumes
Computer Resources: Macintosh, CD-ROM

Research Areas	#Faculty
Adult Education	2
Art Education	
Bilingual Education	
Counselor Education	
Early Childhood Ed.	3
Ed. Admin	4
Ed. Tech.	1
Elementary Ed.	5
Foreign Lang. Ed.	2
Higher Ed.	
Math Ed.	4
Mid. Lev. Ed.	1
Multicultural Ed.	2
Music Ed.	
Physical Ed.	1
Read/Lang. Arts Ed.	2
School Counseling	
Science Ed.	1
Secondary Ed.	1
Soc. Studies Ed.	1
Special Ed.	1
Other	

Student Body Demographics: Average Age 26, 75% female,
25% male

Percent Ethnic Minorities: Hispanic-American 2%, Asian-American 4%, African-American 8%, Native-American 1%
Geographic Representation: Midwest 100%
Graduate Career Paths: K-12 Teaching 80%, K-12 Special Ed 10%, School Administration 5%
Tuition: 216/hr (in state), 694/hr (out of state)
Financial Aid Recipients: N/A
Average Annual Housing Cost: N/A
Application Deadline: rolling
Number of: applicants annually 400; applicants accepted annually 300; students enrolled annually 200

Tests Required	Preferred/Min Score
Graduate Record Exam	
National Teachers Exam	
Praxis II Exam	

Wayne State University College of Education

489 Education Building, Detroit, MI 48202
Admissions: (PH)313 577-1605, (FAX)313 577-4944, (EMAIL)sitzkow@cms.cc.wayne.edu
Dean: (PH)313 577-1620
Total Enrollment: 20,000
Grad Enrollment: FTM 588, PTM 1763, FTD 95, PTD 313, On campus 1%, Off campus 99%
Program Membership: Holmes Partnership
Academic Programs Available: MASTERS: Art Ed., Bilingual Ed., Counselor Ed., Early Childhood Ed., Ed. Admin, Ed. Psych., Ed. Tech., Elementary Ed., Foreign Lang. Ed., Math Ed., Music Ed., DOCTORATE: Art Ed., Bilingual Ed., Counselor Ed., Early Childhood Ed., Ed. Admin, Ed. Psych., Ed. Tech., Elementary Ed., Foreign Lang. Ed., Math Ed., Music Ed.
Library: Wayne State University Libraries, 2.8 million volumes
Computer Resources: Macintosh, Dual Platform, PCs, CD-ROM, Videodisc

Research Areas	#Faculty
Adult Education	
Art Education	2
Bilingual Education	1
Counselor Education	4
Early Childhood Ed.	3
Ed. Admin	6
Ed. Tech.	5
Elementary Ed.	4
Foreign Lang. Ed.	1
Higher Ed.	
Math Ed.	2
Mid. Lev. Ed.	
Multicultural Ed.	2
Music Ed.	
Physical Ed.	8
Read/Lang. Arts Ed.	1
School Counseling	3
Science Ed.	3
Secondary Ed.	3
Soc. Studies Ed.	1
Special Ed.	4

Other
Student Body Demographics: Average Age 29, N/A female, N/A male
Percent Ethnic Minorities: Hispanic-American 2%, Asian-American 0.5%, African-American 26%, Native-American 0.5%
Geographic Representation: Midwest 99%
Graduate Career Paths: K-12 Teaching 74%, School Counseling 5%, K-12 Special Ed 2%, School Administration 18%
Tuition: 148/hr (in state), 319/hr (out of state)
Financial Aid Recipients: 1%
Average Annual Housing Cost: 4,500
Application Deadline: 7/1; 11/1; 3/15
Number of: applicants annually 1,800; applicants accepted annually 1,200; students enrolled annually 900

Tests Required	Preferred/Min Score
Graduate Record Exam	
National Teachers Exam	
Praxis II Exam	
TOEFL	550

MINNESOTA

Southwest State University Education Department

State Street, Marshall, MN 56258
Admissions: (PH)507 537-6286, (FAX)507 537-7154
Dean: (PH)507 537-6108, (FAX)507 537-7154
Total Enrollment: 1,000–5,000
Grad Enrollment: PTM 17, Off campus 100%
Program Membership: N/A
Academic Programs Available: MASTERS: Elementary Ed., Sec. Ed., DOCTORATE: Elementary Ed., Sec. Ed.
Library: University Library, 160,000 volumes
Computer Resources: Macintosh, Dual Platform, PCs, CD-ROM, Videodisc

Research Areas	#Faculty
Adult Education	
Art Education	
Bilingual Education	
Counselor Education	
Early Childhood Ed.	
Ed. Admin	
Ed. Tech.	
Elementary Ed.	
Foreign Lang. Ed.	
Higher Ed.	1
Math Ed.	1
Mid. Lev. Ed.	
Multicultural Ed.	
Music Ed.	
Physical Ed.	

Read/Lang. Arts Ed.	1
School Counseling	
Science Ed.	1
Secondary Ed.	1
Soc. Studies Ed.	1
Special Ed.	
Other	1

Student Body Demographics: Average Age 35, 94% female, 6% male
Percent Ethnic Minorities: N/A
Geographic Representation: Midwest 100%
Graduate Career Paths: K-12 Teaching 100%
Tuition: 80/hr (in state), 120/hr (out of state)
Financial Aid Recipients: N/A
Average Annual Housing Cost: N/A
Application Deadline: varies
Number of: applicants annually 17; applicants accepted annually N/A; students enrolled annually N/A

Tests Required	Preferred/Min Score
Graduate Record Exam	
National Teachers Exam	
Praxis II Exam	

St. Cloud State University
College of Education

720 Fourth Avenue South, St. Cloud, MN 56301-4498
Admissions: (PH)612 255-2113, (FAX)612 654-5371
Dean: (PH)612 255-3023, (FAX)212 255-4237, (EMAIL)dklitsch@tiger.stcloud.msus.edu
Total Enrollment: 10,000–20,000
Grad Enrollment: FTM 90, PTM 500, On campus 17%, Off campus 83%
Program Membership: N/A
Academic Programs Available: MASTERS: Art Ed., Bilingual Ed., Counselor Ed., Early Childhood Ed., Ed. Admin, Ed. Tech., Elementary Ed., Math Ed., Mid Level Ed., Music Ed., Read/Lang Arts Ed., School Cons., Sci. Ed., Sec. DOCTORATE: Art Ed., Bilingual Ed., Counselor Ed., Early Childhood Ed., Ed. Admin, Ed. Tech., Elementary Ed., Math Ed., Mid Level Ed., Music Ed., Read/Lang Arts Ed., School Cons., Sci. Ed., Sec.
Library: Learning Resources Services, 580,000 volumes
Computer Resources: Macintosh, Dual Platform, PCs, CD-ROM, Videodisc

Research Areas	#Faculty
Adult Education	
Art Education	1
Bilingual Education	1
Counselor Education	6
Early Childhood Ed.	5
Ed. Admin	5
Ed. Tech.	11
Elementary Ed.	12
Foreign Lang. Ed.	
Higher Ed.	
Math Ed.	2
Mid. Lev. Ed.	4
Multicultural Ed.	
Music Ed.	5

Physical Ed.	
Read/Lang. Arts Ed.	5
School Counseling	2
Science Ed.	2
Secondary Ed.	2
Soc. Studies Ed.	2
Special Ed.	9
Other	31

Research Institutes/Centers: Curriculum and Technology Center
Student Body Demographics: Average Age 34, 67% female, 33% male
Percent Ethnic Minorities: Hispanic-American 0.5%, Asian-American 1%, African-American 1%
Geographic Representation: Midwest 80%, Southwest 1%, West 1%, Southeast 1%, Northwest 1%
Graduate Career Paths: K-12 Teaching 37%, School Counseling 4%, K-12 Special Ed 14%, School Administration 11%, Community Counseling 13%
Tuition: 69/hr (in state), 109/hr (out of state)
Financial Aid Recipients: 45%
Average Annual Housing Cost: 2,400
Application Deadline: varies
Number of: applicants annually 340; applicants accepted annually 145; students enrolled annually N/A

Tests Required	Preferred/Min Score
Graduate Record Exam	1,000
National Teachers Exam	
Praxis II Exam	
TOEFL	550

University of Minnesota, Twin Cities
College of Education

Minneapolis, MN 55455
Dean: (PH)612 625-3394, (FAX)612 626-7431
Total Enrollment: 20,000
Program Membership: Holmes Partnership
Academic Programs Available: MASTERS: Adult Ed., Art Ed., Early Childhood Ed., Ed. Admin, Ed. Psych., Elementary Ed., Math Ed., Music Ed., Physical Ed., Read/Lang Arts Ed., Sci. Ed., Spec. Ed. DOCTORATE: Adult Ed., Art Ed., Early Childhood Ed., Ed. Admin, Ed. Psych., Elementary Ed., Math Ed., Music Ed., Physical Ed., Read/Lang Arts Ed., Sci. Ed., Spec. Ed.
Library: N/A

Research Areas	#Faculty
Adult Education	
Art Education	
Bilingual Education	
Counselor Education	
Early Childhood Ed.	
Ed. Admin	
Ed. Tech.	
Elementary Ed.	
Foreign Lang. Ed.	
Higher Ed.	
Math Ed.	
Mid. Lev. Ed.	
Multicultural Ed.	

Music Ed.
Physical Ed.
Read/Lang. Arts Ed.
School Counseling
Science Ed.
Secondary Ed.
Soc. Studies Ed.
Special Ed.
Other
Student Body Demographics: N/A
Percent Ethnic Minorities: N/A
Geographic Representation: N/A
Tuition: 4,350 (in state), 9,390 (out of state)
Financial Aid Recipients: N/A
Average Annual Housing Cost: N/A
Number of: applicants annually N/A; applicants accepted annually N/A; students enrolled annually N/A

Tests Required	Preferred/Min Score
Graduate Record Exam	
National Teachers Exam	
Praxis II Exam	

MISSISSIPPI

Jackson State University School of Education

P.O. Box 17095, Jackson, MS 39217
Admissions: (PH)601 968-2455, (FAX)601 973-3664
Dean: (PH)601 968-2455, (FAX)601 973-3664
Total Enrollment: 5,000–10,000
Grad Enrollment: FTM 73, PTM 155, FTD 16, PTD 37
Program Membership: N/A
Academic Programs Available: MASTERS: Counselor Ed., Early Childhood Ed., Ed. Admin, Elementary Ed., Math Ed., Music Ed., DOCTORATE: Counselor Ed., Early Childhood Ed., Ed. Admin, Elementary Ed., Math Ed., Music Ed.
Library: N/A

Research Areas	#Faculty
Adult Education	
Art Education	
Bilingual Education	
Counselor Education	
Early Childhood Ed.	
Ed. Admin	
Ed. Tech.	
Elementary Ed.	
Foreign Lang. Ed.	
Higher Ed.	
Math Ed.	
Mid. Lev. Ed.	
Multicultural Ed.	
Music Ed.	
Physical Ed.	
Read/Lang. Arts Ed.	
School Counseling	
Science Ed.	

Secondary Ed.
Soc. Studies Ed.
Special Ed.
Other
Student Body Demographics: Average Age N/A, 67% female, 33% male
Percent Ethnic Minorities: Hispanic-American 0.5%, Asian-American 2%, African-American 80%
Geographic Representation: Midwest 4%, Mid Atlantic 1%, West 1%, Southeast 74%, Northwest 1%
Graduate Career Paths: K-12 Teaching 40%, Higher Ed Teaching 5%, School Counseling 5%, K-12 Special Ed 15%, School Administration 15%, Higher Ed Administration 3%, Higher Ed Counseling 2%, Community Counseling 5%
Tuition: 132/hr (in state), 276/hr (out of state)
Financial Aid Recipients: N/A
Average Annual Housing Cost: N/A
Application Deadline: 3/1; 3/15; 10/1
Number of: applicants annually 300; applicants accepted annually ; students enrolled annually 281

Tests Required	Preferred/Min Score
Graduate Record Exam	
National Teachers Exam	
Praxis II Exam	

Mississippi State University
College of Education

Box 9700, Mississippi State, MS 39762-9700
Admissions: (PH)601 325-2224, (FAX)601 325-7360, (EMAIL)sharron@admissions.msstate.edu
Dean: (PH)601 325-3717, (FAX)whgl@ra.msstate.edu, (EMAIL)(601) 325-8784
Total Enrollment: 10,000–20,000
Grad Enrollment: FTM 164, PTM 175, FTD 88, PTD 140, CAS 49, On campus 5%, Off campus 95%
Program Membership: Holmes Partnership
Academic Programs Available: MASTERS: Counselor Ed., Ed. Admin, Ed. Psych., Ed. Tech., Elementary Ed., Foreign Lang. Ed., Higher Ed., Math Ed., Music Ed., Physical Ed., School Cons., Sci. Ed., Soc. Ed., Spec. Ed.
DOCTORATE: Counselor Ed., Ed. Admin, Ed. Psych., Ed. Tech., Elementary Ed., Foreign Lang. Ed., Higher Ed., Math Ed., Music Ed., Physical Ed., School Cons., Sci. Ed., Soc. Ed., Spec. Ed.
Library: Mitchell Memorial, 1.3 million volumes
Computer Resources: Macintosh, Dual Platform, PCs, CD-ROM, Videodisc

Research Areas	#Faculty
Adult Education	
Art Education	
Bilingual Education	
Counselor Education	9
Early Childhood Ed.	2
Ed. Admin	5
Ed. Tech.	13
Elementary Ed.	12
Foreign Lang. Ed.	
Higher Ed.	2
Math Ed.	2

Mid. Lev. Ed.

Multicultural Ed.	1
Music Ed.	17
Physical Ed.	9
Read/Lang. Arts Ed.	3
School Counseling	4
Science Ed.	1
Secondary Ed.	1
Soc. Studies Ed.	2
Special Ed.	4

Other

Research Institutes/Centers: Research and Curriculum Unit for Vocational/Technical Education, Writing/Thinking Institute, Program of Research and Evaluation with Public Schools

Student Body Demographics: Average Age 33, 70% female, 30% male

Percent Ethnic Minorities: African-American 22%

Geographic Representation: New England 1%, Midwest 2%, Southwest 1%, West 1%, Southeast 89%, Northwest 1%

Graduate Career Paths: K-12 Teaching 45%, Higher Ed Teaching 3%, School Counseling 23%, K-12 Special Ed 4%, School Administration 11%, Higher Ed Administration 1%, Higher Ed Counseling 1%, Community Counseling 3%

Tuition: 998 (in state), 1,410 (out of state)

Financial Aid Recipients: 10%

Average Annual Housing Cost: 2,115

Application Deadline: 11/1; 7/1; 4/1

Number of: applicants annually 364; applicants accepted annually 282; students enrolled annually 221

Tests Required	Preferred/Min Score
Graduate Record Exam	1,000
National Teachers Exam	
Praxis II Exam	
TOEFL	550

University of Mississippi School of Education

Office of the Registrar, University, MS 38677

Admissions: (PH)601 232-7226, (FAX)601 232-5869, (EMAIL)admbh@vm.cc.edu

Dean: (PH)601 232-7063, (FAX)601 232-7249, (EMAIL)edjp@vm.cc.edu

Total Enrollment: 10,000–20,000

Grad Enrollment: FTM 88, PTM 100, FTD 47, PTD 87, CAS 28

Program Membership: Holmes Partnership

Academic Programs Available: MASTERS: Art Ed., Bilingual Ed., Counselor Ed., Early Childhood Ed., Ed. Admin, Ed. Psych., Ed. Tech., Elementary Ed., Music Ed., Sec. Ed., Spec. Ed. DOCTORATE: Art Ed., Bilingual Ed., Counselor Ed., Early Childhood Ed., Ed. Admin, Ed. Psych., Ed. Tech., Elementary Ed., Music Ed., Sec. Ed., Spec. Ed.

Library: J.D. Williams Library, 1.7 million volumes

Computer Resources: Macintosh, Dual Platform, PCs, CD-ROM, Videodisc

Research Areas	#Faculty
Adult Education	
Art Education	1

Bilingual Education

Counselor Education	4
Early Childhood Ed.	
Ed. Admin	3
Ed. Tech.	1
Elementary Ed.	7
Foreign Lang. Ed.	1
Higher Ed.	2
Math Ed.	1
Mid. Lev. Ed.	
Multicultural Ed.	
Music Ed.	
Physical Ed.	
Read/Lang. Arts Ed.	
School Counseling	4
Science Ed.	1
Secondary Ed.	1
Soc. Studies Ed.	1
Special Ed.	4

Other

Student Body Demographics: Average Age N/A, 69% female, 31% male

Percent Ethnic Minorities: Hispanic-American 1%, Asian-American 1%, African-American 25%, Native-American 1%

Geographic Representation: N/A

Tuition: 2,456 (in state), 5,866 (out of state)

Financial Aid Recipients: 90%

Average Annual Housing Cost: 2,580

Application Deadline: 4/1; 10/1

Number of: applicants annually N/A; applicants accepted annually N/A; students enrolled annually N/A

Tests Required	Preferred/Min Score
Graduate Record Exam	800–1,000
National Teachers Exam	
Praxis II Exam	

University of Southern Mississippi College of Education and Psychology

Box 5098, Hattiesburg, MS 39406

Admissions: (PH)601 266-5139, (FAX)601 266-5138

Dean: (PH)601 266-4373, (FAX)601 266-5138

Total Enrollment: 10,000–20,000

Grad Enrollment: FTM 143, PTM 189, FTD 96, PTD 109, On campus 51%, Off campus 49%

Program Membership: N/A

Academic Programs Available: MASTERS: Adult Ed., Art Ed., Bilingual Ed., Counselor Ed., Early Childhood Ed., Ed. Admin, Ed. Tech., Elementary Ed., Foreign Lang. Ed., Higher Ed., Math Ed., Music Ed., Physical Ed., Read/Lang Arts Ed., School Cons., Sci. Ed., Spec. Ed.

DOCTORATE: Adult Ed., Art Ed., Bilingual Ed., Counselor Ed., Early Childhood Ed., Ed. Admin, Ed. Tech., Elementary Ed., Foreign Lang. Ed., Higher Ed., Math Ed., Music Ed., Physical Ed., Read/Lang Arts Ed., School Cons., Sci. Ed., Spec. Ed.

Library: Cook Library

Computer Resources: Macintosh, Dual Platform, PCs, CD-ROM, Videodisc

Research Areas	#Faculty
Adult Education	
Art Education	
Bilingual Education	
Counselor Education	
Early Childhood Ed.	2
Ed. Admin	
Ed. Tech.	3
Elementary Ed.	
Foreign Lang. Ed.	
Higher Ed.	2
Math Ed.	2
Mid. Lev. Ed.	
Multicultural Ed.	1
Music Ed.	
Physical Ed.	
Read/Lang. Arts Ed.	4
School Counseling	4
Science Ed.	1
Secondary Ed.	1
Soc. Studies Ed.	1
Special Ed.	5
Other	5

Student Body Demographics: Average Age 33, 67% female, 33% male

Percent Ethnic Minorities: Asian-American 1%, African-American 11%, Native-American 1%

Geographic Representation: New England 6%, Midwest 10%, Mid Atlantic 4%, Southwest 7%, West 5%, Southeast 45%, Northwest 3%

Graduate Career Paths: K-12 Teaching 32%, Higher Ed Teaching 8%, School Counseling 5%, K-12 Special Ed 5%, School Administration 33%, Higher Ed Administration 5%, Higher Ed Counseling 2%, Community Counseling 2%

Tuition: 1,146 (in state), 1,230 (out of state)

Financial Aid Recipients: 52%

Average Annual Housing Cost: 1,300

Application Deadline: 5/1

Number of: applicants annually 625; applicants accepted annually 300; students enrolled annually 250

Tests Required	Preferred/Min Score
Graduate Record Exam	850–1000
National Teachers Exam	1965–1975
Praxis II Exam	

MISSOURI

Avila College Department of Education

700 Hodes, 11901 Wornall Road, Kansas City, MO 64145-1698
Admissions: (PH)816 942-8400, (FAX)816 942-3362
Dean: (PH)816 942-8400,
(EMAIL)eschbacher.m.g.@mail.avila.edu

Total Enrollment: 1,000–5,000
Grad Enrollment: PTM 35, Off campus 100%
Program Membership: N/A
Academic Programs Available: N/A
Library: Hooley-Bundschuh, 70,000 volumes
Computer Resources: Macintosh, CD-ROM

Research Areas	#Faculty
Adult Education	
Art Education	
Bilingual Education	
Counselor Education	
Early Childhood Ed.	
Ed. Admin	
Ed. Tech.	
Elementary Ed.	1
Foreign Lang. Ed.	
Higher Ed.	
Math Ed.	
Mid. Lev. Ed.	
Multicultural Ed.	1
Music Ed.	
Physical Ed.	
Read/Lang. Arts Ed.	1
School Counseling	
Science Ed.	1
Secondary Ed.	1
Soc. Studies Ed.	1
Special Ed.	1
Other	

Student Body Demographics: Average Age 35, 65% female, 35% male

Percent Ethnic Minorities: African-American 1%

Geographic Representation: N/A

Graduate Career Paths: K-12 Teaching 70%, K-12 Special Ed 30%

Tuition: 245 (in state), 245 (out of state)

Financial Aid Recipients: 70%

Average Annual Housing Cost: 1,900

Application Deadline: 7/30

Number of: applicants annually 50; applicants accepted annually N/A; students enrolled annually 25

Tests Required	Preferred/Min Score
Graduate Record Exam	
National Teachers Exam	
Praxis II Exam	

Central Missouri State University

Curriculum and Instruction, HUM 410, Warrensburg, MO 64093
Admissions: (PH)816 543-4621, (FAX)816 543-8333
Dean: (PH)816 543-4092, (FAX)816 543-8333
Total Enrollment: 10,000–20,000
Grad Enrollment: FTM 474, PTM 1,238
Program Membership: N/A
Academic Programs Available: MASTERS: Adult Ed., Art Ed., Counselor Ed., Early Childhood Ed., Ed. Admin, Ed. Psych., Ed. Tech., Elementary Ed., Higher Ed., Math Ed., Mid Level Ed., Music Ed., Physical Ed., Read/Lang Arts Ed., School Cons., Sci. Ed., Sec. Ed., Soc. Ed., Spec. Ed.

DOCTORATE: Adult Ed., Art Ed., Counselor Ed., Early Childhood Ed., Ed. Admin, Ed. Psych., Ed. Tech., Elementary Ed., Higher Ed., Math Ed., Mid Level Ed., Music Ed., Physical Ed., Read/Lang Arts Ed., School Cons., Sci. Ed., Sec. Ed., Soc. Ed., Spec. Ed.
Library: Ward Edwards Library, 2.1 million volumes
Computer Resources: Macintosh, Dual Platform, PCs, CD-ROM, Videodisc

Research Areas	#Faculty
Adult Education	
Art Education	
Bilingual Education	
Counselor Education	
Early Childhood Ed.	1
Ed. Admin	2
Ed. Tech.	
Elementary Ed.	3
Foreign Lang. Ed.	
Higher Ed.	1
Math Ed.	1
Mid. Lev. Ed.	
Multicultural Ed.	1
Music Ed.	1
Physical Ed.	2
Read/Lang. Arts Ed.	2
School Counseling	
Science Ed.	1
Secondary Ed.	1
Soc. Studies Ed.	
Special Ed.	1
Other	

Student Body Demographics: Average Age 34, 61% female, 39% male
Percent Ethnic Minorities: African-American 4%
Geographic Representation: Midwest 84%
Graduate Career Paths: K-12 Teaching 60%, School Counseling 5%, K-12 Special Ed 4%, School Administration 10%
Tuition: 123/hr (in state), 246/hr (out of state)
Financial Aid Recipients: 56%
Average Annual Housing Cost: 3,578
Application Deadline: N/A
Number of: applicants annually 1,600; applicants accepted annually N/A; students enrolled annually N/A

Tests Required	Preferred/Min Score
Graduate Record Exam	
National Teachers Exam	
Praxis II Exam	

Lindenwood College Education Division

209 Kings Highway, St. Charles, MO 63376
Admissions: (PH)314 949-2000
Dean: (PH)314 949-4905, (FAX)314 949-4992
Total Enrollment: 5,000–10,000
Grad Enrollment: FTM 25, PTM 275, On campus 10%, Off campus 90%
Program Membership: N/A
Academic Programs Available: MASTERS: Art Ed., Counselor Ed., Early Childhood Ed., Ed. Admin, Elementary

Ed., Mid Level Ed., School Cons., Sec. Ed., Spec. Ed.
DOCTORATE: Art Ed., Counselor Ed., Early Childhood Ed., Ed. Admin, Elementary Ed., Mid Level Ed., School Cons., Sec. Ed., Spec. Ed.
Library: Butler Library, 425,000 volumes
Computer Resources: Macintosh, Dual Platform, PCs, CD-ROM, Videodisc

Research Areas	#Faculty
Adult Education	
Art Education	
Bilingual Education	
Counselor Education	
Early Childhood Ed.	
Ed. Admin	2
Ed. Tech.	
Elementary Ed.	3
Foreign Lang. Ed.	
Higher Ed.	
Math Ed.	
Mid. Lev. Ed.	
Multicultural Ed.	
Music Ed.	
Physical Ed.	
Read/Lang. Arts Ed.	
School Counseling	
Science Ed.	
Secondary Ed.	
Soc. Studies Ed.	
Special Ed.	2
Other	

Student Body Demographics: Average Age 27, 57% female, 43% male
Percent Ethnic Minorities: Hispanic-American 1%, African-American 4%, Native-American 1%
Geographic Representation: Midwest 100%
Graduate Career Paths: K-12 Teaching 40%, School Counseling 5%, K-12 Special Ed 15%, School Administration 40%
Tuition: 165/hr (in state), 165/hr (out of state)
Financial Aid Recipients: 10%
Average Annual Housing Cost: N/A
Application Deadline: N/A
Number of: applicants annually 260; applicants accepted annually 250; students enrolled annually 240

Tests Required	Preferred/Min Score
Graduate Record Exam	
National Teachers Exam	
Praxis II Exam	

Maryville University School of Education

Gander Hall, 13550 Conway Road, St. Louis, MO 63141-7299
Admissions: (PH)314 529-9542, (FAX)314 529-9921
Dean: (PH)314 529-9466
Total Enrollment: 1,000–5,000
Grad Enrollment: Off campus 100%
Program Membership: N/A
Academic Programs Available: MASTERS: Art Ed., Early Childhood Ed., Elementary Ed., Mid Level Ed., Sec. Ed.,

DOCTORATE: Art Ed., Early Childhood Ed., Elementary Ed., Mid Level Ed., Sec. Ed.

Library: Maryville University Library, 252,000 volumes

Computer Resources: Macintosh, Dual Platform, PCs, CD-ROM, Videodisc

Research Areas	#Faculty
Adult Education	
Art Education	1
Bilingual Education	
Counselor Education	
Early Childhood Ed.	2
Ed. Admin	
Ed. Tech.	
Elementary Ed.	
Foreign Lang. Ed.	
Higher Ed.	
Math Ed.	2
Mid. Lev. Ed.	2
Multicultural Ed.	
Music Ed.	
Physical Ed.	
Read/Lang. Arts Ed.	1
School Counseling	
Science Ed.	
Secondary Ed.	
Soc. Studies Ed.	
Special Ed.	
Other	

Student Body Demographics: Average Age 35, 85% female, 15% male

Percent Ethnic Minorities: Asian-American 1%, African-American 12%

Geographic Representation: Midwest 100%

Graduate Career Paths: K-12 Teaching 95%

Tuition: 295/hr (in state), 295/hr (out of state)

Financial Aid Recipients: N/A

Average Annual Housing Cost: N/A

Application Deadline: rolling

Number of: applicants annually 120; applicants accepted annually 115; students enrolled annually 110

Tests Required	Preferred/Min Score
Graduate Record Exam	
National Teachers Exam	
Praxis II Exam	

Southwest Missouri State University
College of Education

901 South National, Springfield, MO 65804

Admissions: (PH)417 836-5517, (FAX)417 836-6334

Dean: (PH)417 836-5254, (FAX)417 836-4884

Total Enrollment: 10,000–20,000

Grad Enrollment: FTM 9, PTM 194, On campus 1%, Off campus 99%

Program Membership: N/A

Academic Programs Available: MASTERS: Art Ed., Counselor Ed., Early Childhood Ed., Ed. Admin, Ed. Psych., Ed. Tech., Elementary Ed., Foreign Lang. Ed., Math Ed., Mid Level Ed., Music Ed., Physical Ed., Read/Lang Arts Ed., School Cons., Sci. Ed., Sec. Ed., Soc. Ed., Spec. Ed.
DOCTORATE: Art Ed., Counselor Ed., Early Childhood Ed., Ed. Admin, Ed. Psych., Ed. Tech., Elementary Ed., Foreign Lang. Ed., Math Ed., Mid Level Ed., Music Ed., Physical Ed., Read/Lang Arts Ed., School Cons., Sci. Ed., Sec. Ed., Soc. Ed., Spec. Ed.

Library: N/A

Computer Resources: Macintosh, Dual Platform, PCs, CD-ROM, Videodisc

Research Areas	#Faculty
Adult Education	
Art Education	1
Bilingual Education	
Counselor Education	3
Early Childhood Ed.	2
Ed. Admin	4
Ed. Tech.	2
Elementary Ed.	5
Foreign Lang. Ed.	2
Higher Ed.	
Math Ed.	4
Mid. Lev. Ed.	3
Multicultural Ed.	2
Music Ed.	1
Physical Ed.	5
Read/Lang. Arts Ed.	3
School Counseling	3
Science Ed.	3
Secondary Ed.	3
Soc. Studies Ed.	4
Special Ed.	3
Other	

Research Institutes/Centers: Center for Psycho-Educational Research

Student Body Demographics: Average Age 37, 59% female, 41% male

Percent Ethnic Minorities: Hispanic-American 2%, Asian-American 1%, African-American 2%, Native-American 1%

Geographic Representation: Midwest 95%, Southwest 1%, West 1%, Southeast 1%

Graduate Career Paths: K-12 Teaching 52%, Higher Ed Teaching 1%, School Counseling 15%, K-12 Special Ed 5%, School Administration 18%, Higher Ed Administration 1%

Tuition: 112/hr (in state), 208/hr (out of state)

Financial Aid Recipients: 5%

Average Annual Housing Cost: 3,000

Application Deadline: 5/1; 6/15; 12/1

Number of: applicants annually 100; applicants accepted annually 80; students enrolled annually N/A

Tests Required	Preferred/Min Score
Graduate Record Exam	900–1,000
National Teachers Exam	
Praxis II Exam	

University of Missouri-St. Louis
School of Education

144 Woods Hall, St. Louis, MO 63121

Admissions: (PH)314 516-5459, (FAX)314 516-5310

Dean: (PH)314 516-5483, (FAX)314 516-5227, (EMAIL)c1812@umslvma.umsl.edu

Total Enrollment: 10,000–20,000

Grad Enrollment: FTM 438, PTM 737, FTD 23, PTD 38, Off campus 100%

Program Membership: Holmes Partnership

Academic Programs Available: MASTERS: Adult Ed., Counselor Ed., Early Childhood Ed., Ed. Admin, Elementary Ed., Foreign Lang. Ed., Higher Ed., Math Ed., Music Ed., Physical Ed., Read/Lang Arts Ed., School Cons., Sci. Ed., Sec. Ed., Soc. Ed., Spec. Ed. DOCTORATE: Adult Ed., Counselor Ed., Early Childhood Ed., Ed. Admin, Elementary Ed., Foreign Lang. Ed., Higher Ed., Math Ed., Music Ed., Physical Ed., Read/Lang Arts Ed., School Cons., Sci. Ed., Sec. Ed., Soc. Ed., Spec. Ed.

Library: Ward Barnes Education Library, 55,000 volumes

Computer Resources: Macintosh, Dual Platform, PCs, CD-ROM, Videodisc

Research Areas	#Faculty
Adult Education	1
Art Education	
Bilingual Education	
Counselor Education	10
Early Childhood Ed.	1
Ed. Admin	3
Ed. Tech.	1
Elementary Ed.	8
Foreign Lang. Ed.	1
Higher Ed.	
Math Ed.	3
Mid. Lev. Ed.	1
Multicultural Ed.	
Music Ed.	1
Physical Ed.	4
Read/Lang. Arts Ed.	4
School Counseling	
Science Ed.	3
Secondary Ed.	3
Soc. Studies Ed.	2
Special Ed.	4
Other	

Research Institutes/Centers: Center for Excellence in Urban Education, Regional Institute for the Advancement of Science Education, Citizenship Education Clearninghouse

Student Body Demographics: Average Age N/A, 75% female, 25% male

Percent Ethnic Minorities: Hispanic-American 1%, Asian-American 1%, African-American 16%, Native-American 1%

Geographic Representation: Midwest 98%

Graduate Career Paths: K-12 Teaching 43%, Higher Ed Teaching 1%, School Counseling 20%, K-12 School Administration 20%, Community Counseling 16%

Tuition: 140/hr (in state), 416/hr (out of state)

Financial Aid Recipients: 18%

Average Annual Housing Cost: 2,600

Application Deadline: 7/1; 12/1; 5/1

Number of: applicants annually N/A; applicants accepted annually 565; students enrolled annually N/A

Tests Required	Preferred/Min Score
Graduate Record Exam	1,000–1,100
National Teachers Exam	
Praxis II Exam	

MONTANA

Montana State University-Bozeman College of Education, Health and Human Development

112 Reid Hall, Bozeman, MT 59717

Admissions: (PH)406 994-6786, (FAX)406 994-1854, (EMAIL)aedit@msu.oscs.montana.edu

Dean: (PH)406 994-6752, (FAX)406 994-1854, (EMAIL)addpc@msu.oscs.montana.edu

Total Enrollment: 10,000–20,000

Program Membership: Holmes Partnership

Academic Programs Available: MASTERS: Adult Ed., Counselor Ed., Ed. Admin, Higher Ed., Math Ed., Physical Ed., School Cons., DOCTORATE: Adult Ed., Counselor Ed., Ed. Admin, Higher Ed., Math Ed., Physical Ed., School Cons.

Library: Renne Library

Computer Resources: Macintosh, Dual Platform, PCs, CD-ROM, Videodisc

Research Areas	#Faculty
Adult Education	3
Art Education	
Bilingual Education	
Counselor Education	3
Early Childhood Ed.	6
Ed. Admin	5
Ed. Tech.	2
Elementary Ed.	2
Foreign Lang. Ed.	
Higher Ed.	2
Math Ed.	4
Mid. Lev. Ed.	
Multicultural Ed.	2
Music Ed.	1
Physical Ed.	
Read/Lang. Arts Ed.	3
School Counseling	1
Science Ed.	4
Secondary Ed.	4
Soc. Studies Ed.	1
Special Ed.	
Other	

Research Institutes/Centers: Center for Bilingual/Multicultural Studies, Center for School/Community Development, Center for Adult and Higher Education

Student Body Demographics: Average Age 35, 41% female, 59% male

Percent Ethnic Minorities: Hispanic-American 0.5%, Asian-American 0.5%, African-American 0.5%, Native-American 3.5%

Geographic Representation: Northwest 85%

Graduate Career Paths: K-12 Higher Ed Teaching 20%, K-12 School Administration 30%, Higher Ed Administration 10%

Tuition: 1,244 (in state), 2,665 (out of state)

Financial Aid Recipients: 10%

Average Annual Housing Cost: 5,000

Application Deadline: 9/30; 5/30; 3/30

Number of: applicants annually 120; applicants accepted annually 116; students enrolled annually 80

Tests Required	Preferred/Min Score
Graduate Record Exam	850–1000
National Teachers Exam	
Praxis II Exam	
TOEFL	550–580

Montana State University-Northern

Department of Graduate Programs, P.O. Box 7751, Havre, MT 59501
Admissions: (PH)406 265-3704, (FAX)406 265-3777
Dean: (PH)406 265-3738, (FAX)406 265-3777
Total Enrollment: 1,000–5,000
Grad Enrollment: On campus 1%, Off campus 99%
Program Membership: N/A
Academic Programs Available: MASTERS: Counselor Ed., Elementary Ed., Sci. Ed., DOCTORATE: Counselor Ed., Elementary Ed., Sci. Ed.
Library: Vande Bogart Library
Computer Resources: Macintosh, Dual Platform, PCs, CD-ROM, Videodisc

Research Areas	#Faculty
Adult Education	
Art Education	
Bilingual Education	
Counselor Education	
Early Childhood Ed.	
Ed. Admin	
Ed. Tech.	
Elementary Ed.	
Foreign Lang. Ed.	
Higher Ed.	
Math Ed.	
Mid. Lev. Ed.	
Multicultural Ed.	
Music Ed.	
Physical Ed.	
Read/Lang. Arts Ed.	
School Counseling	
Science Ed.	
Secondary Ed.	
Soc. Studies Ed.	
Special Ed.	
Other	

Student Body Demographics: Average Age 39, 65% female, 35% male
Percent Ethnic Minorities: Native-American 2%
Geographic Representation: Northwest 99%
Graduate Career Paths: K-12 Teaching 30%, Higher Ed Teaching 3%, School Counseling 60%, K-12 Higher Ed Counseling 5%, Community Counseling 2%
Tuition: N/A (in state), N/A (out of state)
Financial Aid Recipients: N/A
Average Annual Housing Cost: N/A
Number of: applicants annually 200; applicants accepted annually 175; students enrolled annually N/A

Tests Required	Preferred/Min Score
Graduate Record Exam	

National Teachers Exam
Praxis II Exam

University of Montana School of Education

Admissions & New Student Services, Missoula, MT 59807
Admissions: (PH)406 243-6266, (FAX)406 243-4087, (EMAIL)admiss@selway.umt.edu
Dean: (PH)406 243-4911, (FAX)406 243-4908, (EMAIL)robsond@selway.umt.edu
Total Enrollment: 10,000–20,000
Grad Enrollment: FTM 32, PTM 60, FTD 11, PTD 23, On campus 10%, Off campus 90%
Program Membership: Holmes Partnership
Academic Programs Available: MASTERS: Bilingual Ed., Counselor Ed., Ed. Admin, Ed. Psych., Ed. Tech., Elementary Ed., Higher Ed., Math Ed., Music Ed., Read/Lang Arts Ed., School Cons., Sci. Ed., Sec. Ed., Soc. Ed., Spec. Ed. DOCTORATE: Bilingual Ed., Counselor Ed., Ed. Admin, Ed. Psych., Ed. Tech., Elementary Ed., Higher Ed., Math Ed., Music Ed., Read/Lang Arts Ed., School Cons., Sci. Ed., Sec. Ed., Soc. Ed., Spec. Ed.
Library: Mansfield Library, 660,000 volumes
Computer Resources: Macintosh, Dual Platform, PCs, CD-ROM, Videodisc

Research Areas	#Faculty
Adult Education	
Art Education	
Bilingual Education	2
Counselor Education	3
Early Childhood Ed.	1
Ed. Admin	5
Ed. Tech.	3
Elementary Ed.	5
Foreign Lang. Ed.	
Higher Ed.	1
Math Ed.	2
Mid. Lev. Ed.	1
Multicultural Ed.	1
Music Ed.	
Physical Ed.	
Read/Lang. Arts Ed.	3
School Counseling	3
Science Ed.	2
Secondary Ed.	2
Soc. Studies Ed.	2
Special Ed.	3
Other	7

Research Institutes/Centers: Division of Educational Research & Service, Academy for Curriculum Leadership & Technology
Student Body Demographics: Average Age 40, 60% female, 40% male
Percent Ethnic Minorities: Hispanic-American 1%, Asian-American 3%, African-American 1%, Native-American 7%
Geographic Representation: New England 5%, Midwest 10%, Southwest 10%, West 20%, Northwest 50%
Graduate Career Paths: K-12 Teaching 25%, Higher Ed Teaching 10%, School Counseling 15%, K-12 School

Administration 25%, Higher Ed Administration 5%, Higher Ed Counseling 5%, Community Counseling 15%
Tuition: 110/hr (in state), 255/hr (out of state)
Financial Aid Recipients: 10%
Average Annual Housing Cost: 3,600
Application Deadline: 10/1; 3/1; 6/1
Number of: applicants annually 150-200; applicants accepted annually 150; students enrolled annually 105-110

Tests Required	Preferred/Min Score
Graduate Record Exam	900–1,100
National Teachers Exam	
Praxis II Exam	
TOEFL	580

NEBRASKA

Hastings College Department of Teacher Education

7th and Turner, Hurley-McDonald Hall, Hastings, NE 68902
Admissions: (PH)402 461-7316, (FAX)402 461-7480
Dean: (PH)402 461-7388, (FAX)402 461-7480
Total Enrollment: 1,000–5,000
Grad Enrollment: FTM 30, PTM 75, On campus 10%, Off campus 90%
Program Membership: N/A
Academic Programs Available: MASTERS: Art Ed., Elementary Ed., Foreign Lang. Ed., Math Ed., Music Ed., Physical Ed., Read/Lang Arts Ed., Sci. Ed., Soc. Ed., Spec. Ed. DOCTORATE: Art Ed., Elementary Ed., Foreign Lang. Ed., Math Ed., Music Ed., Physical Ed., Read/Lang Arts Ed., Sci. Ed., Soc. Ed., Spec. Ed.
Library: Perkins Library, 114,000 volumes
Computer Resources: Macintosh, Dual Platform, PCs, CD-ROM, Videodisc

Research Areas	#Faculty
Adult Education	
Art Education	
Bilingual Education	
Counselor Education	
Early Childhood Ed.	
Ed. Admin	
Ed. Tech.	
Elementary Ed.	1
Foreign Lang. Ed.	
Higher Ed.	
Math Ed.	
Mid. Lev. Ed.	
Multicultural Ed.	1
Music Ed.	
Physical Ed.	
Read/Lang. Arts Ed.	
School Counseling	
Science Ed.	
Secondary Ed.	

Soc. Studies Ed.
Special Ed.

Other	3

Student Body Demographics: Average Age 30, 60% female, 40% male
Percent Ethnic Minorities: Hispanic-American 2%, Asian-American 1%, African-American 6%
Geographic Representation: Midwest 75%, West 25%
Graduate Career Paths: K-12 Teaching 90%, Higher Ed Teaching 10%
Tuition: 141/hr (in state), 141/hr (out of state)
Financial Aid Recipients: N/A
Average Annual Housing Cost: 1,460
Application Deadline: 8/28; 1/30
Number of: applicants annually 20-25; applicants accepted annually 20; students enrolled annually 20

Tests Required	Preferred/Min Score
Graduate Record Exam	950
National Teachers Exam	
Praxis II Exam	

University of Nebraska-Lincoln Teachers College

Graduate College, 301 Administration Building, Lincoln, NE 68588-0434
Admissions: (PH)402 472-2878, (FAX)402 472-3834
Dean: (PH)402 472-5400, (FAX)402 472-0522, (EMAIL)pfogerty@unlinfo.unl.edu
Total Enrollment: 20,000
Grad Enrollment: FTM 142, PTM 259, FTD 114, PTD 292, CAS 23, On campus 5%, Off campus 95%
Program Membership: Holmes Partnership
Academic Programs Available: MASTERS: Adult Ed., Art Ed., Counselor Ed., Early Childhood Ed., Ed. Admin, Ed. Psych., Ed. Tech., Elementary Ed., Foreign Lang. Ed., Higher Ed., Math Ed., Mid Level Ed., Multicultural Ed., Music Ed., Physical Ed., Read/Lang Arts Ed., School Cons., Sci. Ed., Sec. Ed., Soc. Ed., Spec. Ed.
DOCTORATE: Adult Ed., Art Ed., Counselor Ed., Early Childhood Ed., Ed. Admin, Ed. Psych., Ed. Tech., Elementary Ed., Foreign Lang. Ed., Higher Ed., Math Ed., Mid Level Ed., Multicultural Ed., Music Ed., Physical Ed., Read/Lang Arts Ed., School Cons., Sci. Ed., Sec. Ed., Soc. Ed., Spec. Ed.
Library: Love Library, 2.1 million volumes
Computer Resources: Macintosh, Dual Platform, PCs, CD-ROM, Videodisc

Research Areas	#Faculty
Adult Education	3
Art Education	1
Bilingual Education	1
Counselor Education	5
Early Childhood Ed.	1
Ed. Admin	9
Ed. Tech.	3
Elementary Ed.	3
Foreign Lang. Ed.	1
Higher Ed.	2

Math Ed.	3
Mid. Lev. Ed.	2
Multicultural Ed.	4
Music Ed.	4
Physical Ed.	6
Read/Lang. Arts Ed.	5
School Counseling	3
Science Ed.	2
Secondary Ed.	2
Soc. Studies Ed.	2
Special Ed.	9
Other	

Research Institutes/Centers: Buros Institute of Mental Measurements, Center for Language, Cognition and Instruction
Student Body Demographics: Average Age 39, 70% female, 30% male
Percent Ethnic Minorities: Hispanic-American 1.6%, Asian-American 3.5%, African-American 3.4%, Native-American 0.5%
Geographic Representation: New England 2%, Midwest 88%, Mid Atlantic 2%, Southwest 2%, West 2%, Southeast 2%, Northwest 2%
Graduate Career Paths: K-12 Teaching 9%, Higher Ed Teaching 36%, School Counseling 3%, K-12 Special Ed 1%, School Administration 23%, Higher Ed Administration 7%, Higher Ed Counseling 0.5%, Community Counseling 6%
Tuition: 90/hr (in state), 224/hr (out of state)
Financial Aid Recipients: 22%
Average Annual Housing Cost: 3,145
Application Deadline: 1/15
Number of: applicants annually 570; applicants accepted annually 260; students enrolled annually 225

Tests Required	Preferred/Min Score
Graduate Record Exam	1,000–1,200
National Teachers Exam	
Praxis II Exam	
TOEFL	500

NEW HAMPSHIRE

Rivier College Education Department

School of Graduate Studies, 420 Main Street, Nashua, NH 03060
Admissions: (PH)603 888-1311 x8282, (FAX)603 888-4049
Dean: (PH)603 888-1311 x8235, (FAX)603 888-6447
Total Enrollment: 1,000
Grad Enrollment: FTM 17, PTM 234, Off campus 100%
Program Membership: N/A
Academic Programs Available: MASTERS: Adult Ed., Art Ed., Counselor Ed., Early Childhood Ed., Ed. Admin, Elementary Ed., Foreign Lang. Ed., Math Ed., Read/Lang Arts Ed., School Cons., Sci. Ed., Sec. Ed., Soc. Ed., Spec. Ed. DOCTORATE: Adult Ed., Art Ed., Counselor Ed., Early Childhood Ed., Ed. Admin, Elementary Ed., Foreign Lang.

Ed., Math Ed., Read/Lang Arts Ed., School Cons., Sci. Ed., Sec. Ed., Soc. Ed., Spec.
Library: Regina Library
Computer Resources: Macintosh, Dual Platform, PCs, CD-ROM, Videodisc

Research Areas	#Faculty
Adult Education	
Art Education	
Bilingual Education	
Counselor Education	2
Early Childhood Ed.	1
Ed. Admin	1
Ed. Tech.	
Elementary Ed.	1
Foreign Lang. Ed.	
Higher Ed.	
Math Ed.	
Mid. Lev. Ed.	
Multicultural Ed.	
Music Ed.	
Physical Ed.	
Read/Lang. Arts Ed.	
School Counseling	1
Science Ed.	
Secondary Ed.	
Soc. Studies Ed.	
Special Ed.	3
Other	

Research Institutes/Centers: Center for Collaborative Leadership
Student Body Demographics: Average Age 28, 68% female, 32% male
Percent Ethnic Minorities: Hispanic-American 1%, Asian-American 3%, African-American 1%, Native-American 1%
Geographic Representation: New England 100%
Graduate Career Paths: K-12 Teaching 40%, School Counseling 5%, K-12 Special Ed 35%, School Administration 5%, Community Counseling 10%
Tuition: 254/hr (in state), 254/hr (out of state)
Financial Aid Recipients: 22%
Average Annual Housing Cost: N/A
Application Deadline: rolling
Number of: applicants annually N/A; applicants accepted annually 348; students enrolled annually 322

Tests Required	Preferred/Min Score
Graduate Record Exam	
National Teachers Exam	
Praxis II Exam	

University of New Hampshire Department of Education

Durham, NH 03824
Admissions: (PH)603 862-2317
Grad Enrollment: 400 total
Program Membership: Holmes Partnership
Academic Programs Available: MASTERS: Counselor Ed., Early Childhood Ed., Ed. Admin, Elementary Ed., Read/Lang Arts Ed., Sec. Ed., Spec. Ed. DOCTORATE:

Counselor Ed., Early Childhood Ed., Ed. Admin, Elementary
Ed., Read/Lang Arts Ed., Sec. Ed., Spec. Ed.
Library: N/A

Research Areas	#Faculty
Adult Education	
Art Education	
Bilingual Education	
Counselor Education	
Early Childhood Ed.	
Ed. Admin	
Ed. Tech.	
Elementary Ed.	
Foreign Lang. Ed.	
Higher Ed.	
Math Ed.	
Mid. Lev. Ed.	
Multicultural Ed.	
Music Ed.	
Physical Ed.	
Read/Lang. Arts Ed.	
School Counseling	
Science Ed.	
Secondary Ed.	
Soc. Studies Ed.	
Special Ed.	
Other	

Student Body Demographics: N/A
Percent Ethnic Minorities: N/A
Geographic Representation: N/A
Tuition: 4,170 (in state), 12840 (out of state)
Financial Aid Recipients: N/A
Average Annual Housing Cost: N/A
Application Deadline: rolling
Number of: applicants annually 307; applicants accepted
annually 209; students enrolled annually N/A

Tests Required	Preferred/Min Score
Graduate Record Exam	
National Teachers Exam	
Praxis II Exam	

NEW JERSEY

Caldwell College Education Department

Graduate Program, 9 Ryerson Avenue, Caldwell, NJ 07006
Admissions: (PH)201 228-4424, (FAX)201 228-3851
Total Enrollment: 1,000–5,000
Grad Enrollment: PTM 134, Off campus 100%
Program Membership: N/A
Academic Programs Available: MASTERS: DOCTORATE:
Library: Jennings Library, 100,000 volumes
Computer Resources: Macintosh, Dual Platform, PCs,
CD-ROM, Videodisc

Research Areas	#Faculty
Adult Education	
Art Education	

Bilingual Education	
Counselor Education	
Early Childhood Ed.	
Ed. Admin	3
Ed. Tech.	
Elementary Ed.	
Foreign Lang. Ed.	
Higher Ed.	
Math Ed.	
Mid. Lev. Ed.	
Multicultural Ed.	
Music Ed.	
Physical Ed.	
Read/Lang. Arts Ed.	
School Counseling	
Science Ed.	
Secondary Ed.	
Soc. Studies Ed.	1
Special Ed.	1
Other	

Student Body Demographics: Average Age 43, 83% female,
17% male
Percent Ethnic Minorities: Hispanic-American 4%,
Asian-American 1%, African-American 20%,
Native-American 1%
Geographic Representation: Mid Atlantic 100%
Graduate Career Paths: K-12 Teaching 100%
Tuition: 300/hr (in state), 300/hr (out of state)
Financial Aid Recipients: N/A
Average Annual Housing Cost: N/A
Application Deadline: 10/15; 4/1; 5/1
Number of: applicants annually 150; applicants accepted
annually 100; students enrolled annually 75

Tests Required	Preferred/Min Score
Graduate Record Exam	950
National Teachers Exam	
Praxis II Exam	

College of Saint Elizabeth
Graduate Programs in Education

2 Covenant Road, Morristown, NJ 07960-6989
Admissions: (PH)201 292-6447, (FAX)201 292-6777
Dean: (PH)201 292-6793
Total Enrollment: 1,000–5,000
Grad Enrollment: FTM 6, PTM 62, Off campus 100%
Program Membership: N/A
Academic Programs Available: MASTERS: Ed. Tech.,
DOCTORATE: Ed. Tech.
Library: Mahoney Library, 187,000 volumes
Computer Resources: Macintosh, Dual Platform, PCs,
CD-ROM, Videodisc

Research Areas	#Faculty
Adult Education	1
Art Education	
Bilingual Education	
Counselor Education	
Early Childhood Ed.	4
Ed. Admin	
Ed. Tech.	4

Elementary Ed.	5
Foreign Lang. Ed.	
Higher Ed.	
Math Ed.	
Mid. Lev. Ed.	2
Multicultural Ed.	3
Music Ed.	
Physical Ed.	
Read/Lang. Arts Ed.	3
School Counseling	
Science Ed.	
Secondary Ed.	
Soc. Studies Ed.	3
Special Ed.	4
Other	

Student Body Demographics: Average Age N/A, 92% female, 8% male
Percent Ethnic Minorities: African-American 6%
Geographic Representation: Mid Atlantic 100%
Graduate Career Paths: K-12 Teaching 95%, K-12 Special Ed 5%
Tuition: 315/hr (in state), 315/hr (out of state)
Financial Aid Recipients: 15%
Average Annual Housing Cost: N/A
Application Deadline: 8/25; 1/10; 5/10
Number of: applicants annually 100; applicants accepted annually 85; students enrolled annually 85

Tests Required	Preferred/Min Score
Graduate Record Exam	
National Teachers Exam	
Praxis II Exam	
TOEFL	550

Jersey City State College

Graduate Studies, 2039 Kennedy Boulevard, H-206, Jersey City, NJ 07305
Admissions: (PH)201 200-3409
Total Enrollment: 5,000–10,000
Grad Enrollment: FTM 50, PTM 1212, Off campus 100%
Program Membership: N/A
Academic Programs Available: MASTERS: Art Ed., Bilingual Ed., Early Childhood Ed., Ed. Admin, Ed. Psych., Elementary Ed., Math Ed., Multicultural Ed., Music Ed., Read/Lang Arts Ed., School Cons., Spec. Ed. DOCTORATE: Art Ed., Bilingual Ed., Early Childhood Ed., Ed. Admin, Ed. Psych., Elementary Ed., Math Ed., Multicultural Ed., Music Ed., Read/Lang Arts Ed., School Cons., Spec. Ed.
Library: Forest A. Irwin Library, 228,000 volumes
Computer Resources: Macintosh, Dual Platform, PCs, CD-ROM, Videodisc

Research Areas	#Faculty
Adult Education	
Art Education	
Bilingual Education	
Counselor Education	
Early Childhood Ed.	
Ed. Admin	
Ed. Tech.	

Elementary Ed.	
Foreign Lang. Ed.	
Higher Ed.	
Math Ed.	
Mid. Lev. Ed.	
Multicultural Ed.	
Music Ed.	
Physical Ed.	
Read/Lang. Arts Ed.	
School Counseling	
Science Ed.	
Secondary Ed.	
Soc. Studies Ed.	
Special Ed.	
Other	

Research Institutes/Centers: Center for Media and Technology, International Studies Center, Center for Technology and Teaching
Student Body Demographics: Average Age 32, N/A female, N/A male
Percent Ethnic Minorities: N/A
Geographic Representation: N/A
Tuition: 153 (in state), 191 (out of state)
Financial Aid Recipients: N/A
Average Annual Housing Cost: N/A
Application Deadline: 8/1; 12/1; 5/1
Number of: applicants annually 920; applicants accepted annually 850; students enrolled annually N/A

Tests Required	Preferred/Min Score
Graduate Record Exam	900
National Teachers Exam	
Praxis II Exam	
TOEFL	550

Rowan College of New Jersey
School of Education

Memorial Hall, 201 Mullica Hill Road, Glassboro, NJ 08028-1701
Admissions: (PH)609 256-4050, (FAX)609 256-4436 (EMAIL)gilchrist@heroes.rowan.edu
Dean: (PH)609 256-4750, (FAX)609 256-4918, (EMAIL)kapel@heroes.rowan.edu
Total Enrollment: 5,000–10,000
Grad Enrollment: FTM 90, PTM 1162, Off campus 100%
Program Membership: N/A
Academic Programs Available: MASTERS: Art Ed., Counselor Ed., Ed. Admin, Elementary Ed., Higher Ed., Math Ed., Music Ed., Read/Lang Arts Ed., School Cons., Sci. Ed., Spec. Ed. DOCTORATE: Art Ed., Counselor Ed., Ed. Admin, Elementary Ed., Higher Ed., Math Ed., Music Ed., Read/Lang Arts Ed., School Cons., Sci. Ed., Spec. Ed.
Library: New Library, 322,000 volumes
Computer Resources: Macintosh, Dual Platform, PCs, CD-ROM, Videodisc

Research Areas	#Faculty
Adult Education	
Art Education	2
Bilingual Education	1

Counselor Education	1
Early Childhood Ed.	2
Ed. Admin	7
Ed. Tech.	3
Elementary Ed.	13
Foreign Lang. Ed.	1
Higher Ed.	1
Math Ed.	2
Mid. Lev. Ed.	
Multicultural Ed.	4
Music Ed.	2
Physical Ed.	13
Read/Lang. Arts Ed.	8
School Counseling	1
Science Ed.	2
Secondary Ed.	2
Soc. Studies Ed.	1
Special Ed.	10
Other	

Research Institutes/Centers: Education Institute, Curriculum Development Council
Student Body Demographics: Average Age N/A, 25% female, 75% male
Percent Ethnic Minorities: Hispanic-American 1%, Asian-American 1%, African-American 7%
Geographic Representation: Mid Atlantic 99%
Graduate Career Paths: K-12 Teaching 16%, Higher Ed Teaching 2%, School Counseling 10%, K-12 Special Ed 7%, School Administration 43%
Tuition: 176/hr (in state), 266/hr (out of state)
Financial Aid Recipients: 65%
Average Annual Housing Cost: N/A
Application Deadline: rolling
Number of: applicants annually 750; applicants accepted annually 615; students enrolled annually N/A

Tests Required	Preferred/Min Score
Graduate Record Exam	800–900
National Teachers Exam	
Praxis II Exam	
TOEFL	550

Rutgers Graduate School of Education

Van Nest Hall, Room 204, College Ave. Campus, New Brunswick, NJ 08903
Admissions: (PH)908 932-7712, (FAX)908 932-8231
Dean: (PH)908 932-7496 x117, (FAX)908 932-8206
Total Enrollment: 20,000
Grad Enrollment: Off campus 99%
Program Membership: Holmes Partnership
Academic Programs Available: MASTERS: Adult Ed., Bilingual Ed., Counselor Ed., Early Childhood Ed., Ed. Admin, Ed. Psych., Ed. Tech., Elementary Ed., Foreign Lang. Ed., Math Ed., Read/Lang Arts Ed., School Cons., Sci. Ed., Soc. DOCTORATE: Adult Ed., Bilingual Ed., Counselor Ed., Early Childhood Ed., Ed. Admin, Ed. Psych., Ed. Tech., Elementary Ed., Foreign Lang. Ed., Math Ed., Read/Lang Arts Ed., School Cons., Sci. Ed., Soc.

Library: Alexander Library, 2.3 million volumes
Computer Resources: Macintosh, Dual Platform, PCs, CD-ROM, Videodisc

Research Areas	#Faculty
Adult Education	2
Art Education	
Bilingual Education	2
Counselor Education	3
Early Childhood Ed.	3
Ed. Admin	4
Ed. Tech.	3
Elementary Ed.	3
Foreign Lang. Ed.	1
Higher Ed.	
Math Ed.	3
Mid. Lev. Ed.	
Multicultural Ed.	
Music Ed.	
Physical Ed.	
Read/Lang. Arts Ed.	2
School Counseling	3
Science Ed.	3
Secondary Ed.	3
Soc. Studies Ed.	4
Special Ed.	3
Other	2

Research Institutes/Centers: Center for Educational Policy Analysis, Center for Studies in Literacy Education, Center for Math, Science and Computer
Student Body Demographics: Average Age 32, 76% female, 24% male
Percent Ethnic Minorities: Hispanic-American 1%, Asian-American 3%, African-American 7%
Geographic Representation: Mid Atlantic 97%
Graduate Career Paths: K-12 Teaching 30%, Higher Ed Teaching 2%, School Counseling 14%, K-12 Special Ed 3%, School Administration 16%, Community Counseling 14%
Tuition: 5,874 (in state), 8,288 (out of state)
Financial Aid Recipients: 2%
Average Annual Housing Cost: 3,252
Application Deadline: 1/15; 3/1
Number of: applicants annually 1,037; applicants accepted annually 563; students enrolled annually 343

Tests Required	Preferred/Min Score
Graduate Record Exam	1,000–1,150
National Teachers Exam	
Praxis II Exam	
TOEFL	550

Seton Hall University College of Education and Human Services

South Orange, NJ 07090
Admissions: (PH)201 761-9668, (FAX)201 761-7642
Dean: (PH)201 761-9025
Total Enrollment: 5,000–10,000
Grad Enrollment: FTM 75, PTM 350, FTD 45, PTD 425, On campus 1%, Off campus 99%

Program Membership: N/A
Academic Programs Available: MASTERS: Bilingual Ed., Counselor Ed., Early Childhood Ed., Ed. Admin, Ed. Psych., Foreign Lang. Ed., Mid Level Ed., Physical Ed., School Cons., Sec. Ed., DOCTORATE: Bilingual Ed., Counselor Ed., Early Childhood Ed., Ed. Admin, Ed. Psych., Foreign Lang. Ed., Mid Level Ed., Physical Ed., School Cons., Sec. Ed.
Library: Walsh Library
Computer Resources: Macintosh, Dual Platform, PCs, CD-ROM, Videodisc

Research Areas	#Faculty
Adult Education	2
Art Education	
Bilingual Education	2
Counselor Education	
Early Childhood Ed.	3
Ed. Admin	5
Ed. Tech.	2
Elementary Ed.	5
Foreign Lang. Ed.	2
Higher Ed.	2
Math Ed.	
Mid. Lev. Ed.	2
Multicultural Ed.	3
Music Ed.	
Physical Ed.	2
Read/Lang. Arts Ed.	2
School Counseling	8
Science Ed.	
Secondary Ed.	
Soc. Studies Ed.	2
Special Ed.	3
Other	13

Student Body Demographics: Average Age 32, 52% female, 48% male
Percent Ethnic Minorities: Hispanic-American 10%, Asian-American 2%, African-American 12%
Geographic Representation: New England 5%, Mid Atlantic 90%, Southeast 5%
Graduate Career Paths: K-12 Teaching 8%, Higher Ed Teaching 2%, School Counseling 5%, K-12 Special Ed 10%, School Administration 20%, Higher Ed Administration 5%, Higher Ed Counseling 2%, Community Counseling 15%
Tuition: 413/hr (in state), 413/hr (out of state)
Financial Aid Recipients: N/A
Average Annual Housing Cost: N/A
Application Deadline: 5/1; 11/1
Number of: applicants annually 1,200; applicants accepted annually 140; students enrolled annually 135

Tests Required	Preferred/Min Score
Graduate Record Exam	
National Teachers Exam	
Praxis II Exam	

NEW MEXICO

College of Santa Fe Education Department

1600 St. Michael's Drive, Santa Fe, NM 87505
Admissions: (PH)805 473-6133, (FAX)805 473-6127
Dean: (PH)805 473-6292, (FAX)805 473-6127, (EMAIL)nmjim@nets.com
Total Enrollment: 1,000–5,000
Grad Enrollment: PTM 80, On campus 10%, Off campus 90%
Program Membership: N/A
Academic Programs Available: MASTERS: Bilingual Ed., Ed. Admin, School Cons., DOCTORATE: Bilingual Ed., Ed. Admin, School Cons.
Library: Fogelson Library, 4,000 volumes
Computer Resources: Macintosh, Dual Platform, PCs, CD-ROM, Videodisc

Research Areas	#Faculty
Adult Education	
Art Education	
Bilingual Education	
Counselor Education	
Early Childhood Ed.	
Ed. Admin	
Ed. Tech.	
Elementary Ed.	4
Foreign Lang. Ed.	
Higher Ed.	
Math Ed.	
Mid. Lev. Ed.	
Multicultural Ed.	2
Music Ed.	
Physical Ed.	
Read/Lang. Arts Ed.	
School Counseling	
Science Ed.	
Secondary Ed.	
Soc. Studies Ed.	
Special Ed.	2
Other	

Student Body Demographics: Average Age N/A, 84% female, 16% male
Percent Ethnic Minorities: Native-American 8%
Geographic Representation: Southeast 75%
Tuition: 1,508 (in state), 1,508 (out of state)
Financial Aid Recipients: 39%
Average Annual Housing Cost: 4,500
Application Deadline: N/A
Number of: applicants annually 60; applicants accepted annually 42; students enrolled annually N/A

Tests Required	Preferred/Min Score
Graduate Record Exam	
National Teachers Exam	
Praxis II Exam	

New Mexico State University
College of Education

The Graduate School, Box 30001, Dept. 36, Las Cruces, NM 88003-8001
Admissions: (PH)505 646-2736, (FAX)505 646-7721, (EMAIL)barvia@nmsu.edu
Dean: (PH)505 646-2736, (FAX)505 646-7721
Total Enrollment: 10,000–20,000
Grad Enrollment: FTM 450, PTM 250, FTD 45, PTD 70, On campus 20%, Off campus 80%
Program Membership: Holmes Partnership
Academic Programs Available: MASTERS: Bilingual Ed., Counselor Ed., Early Childhood Ed., Ed. Admin, Ed. Tech., Elementary Ed., Foreign Lang. Ed., Higher Ed., Math Ed., Multicultural Ed., Music Ed., Read/Lang Arts Ed., School Cons., Sci. Ed., Sec. Ed., Soc. Ed., Spec. Ed.
DOCTORATE: Bilingual Ed., Counselor Ed., Early Childhood Ed., Ed. Admin, Ed. Tech., Elementary Ed., Foreign Lang. Ed., Higher Ed., Math Ed., Multicultural Ed., Music Ed., Read/Lang Arts Ed., School Cons., Sci. Ed., Sec. Ed., Soc. Ed., Spec. Ed.
Library: University Library, 1.1 million volumes
Computer Resources: Macintosh, Dual Platform, PCs, CD-ROM, Videodisc

Research Areas	#Faculty
Adult Education	
Art Education	
Bilingual Education	3
Counselor Education	7
Early Childhood Ed.	3
Ed. Admin	7
Ed. Tech.	3
Elementary Ed.	4
Foreign Lang. Ed.	1
Higher Ed.	2
Math Ed.	2
Mid. Lev. Ed.	
Multicultural Ed.	7
Music Ed.	7
Physical Ed.	6
Read/Lang. Arts Ed.	7
School Counseling	7
Science Ed.	1
Secondary Ed.	1
Soc. Studies Ed.	1
Special Ed.	10
Other	

Student Body Demographics: Average Age 43, 60% female, 40% male
Percent Ethnic Minorities: Hispanic-American 24%, Asian-American 1%, African-American 1%, Native-American 1%
Geographic Representation: New England 3%, Midwest 5%, Mid Atlantic 2%, Southwest 80%, West 5%
Graduate Career Paths: K-12 Teaching 40%, Higher Ed Teaching 10%, School Counseling 5%, K-12 Special Ed 15%, School Administration 10%, Higher Ed Administration 3%, Higher Ed Counseling 2%, Community Counseling 3%
Tuition: 1,116 (in state), 3,483 (out of state)

Financial Aid Recipients: 35%
Average Annual Housing Cost: 4,500
Application Deadline: 7/1; 11/1; 4/1
Number of: applicants annually 1,000; applicants accepted annually 500; students enrolled annually 400

Tests Required	Preferred/Min Score
Graduate Record Exam	
National Teachers Exam	
Praxis II Exam	

University of New Mexico College of Education

Office of Graduate Studies, 107 Humanities Building, Albuquerque, NM 87131-1041
Admissions: (PH)505 277-2711, (FAX)505 277-7405
Dean: (PH)505 277-3638, (FAX)505 277-8427
Total Enrollment: 20,000
Grad Enrollment: FTM 260, PTM 171, FTD 179, PTD 115, CAS 54, On campus 1%, Off campus 99%
Program Membership: Holmes Partnership
Academic Programs Available: MASTERS: Art Ed., Bilingual Ed., Counselor Ed., Early Childhood Ed., Ed. Admin, Ed. Psych., Elementary Ed., Foreign Lang. Ed., Math Ed., Mid Level Ed., Multicultural Ed., Physical Ed., Read/Lang Arts Ed., School Cons., Sci. Ed., Sec. Ed., Spec. Ed.
DOCTORATE: Art Ed., Bilingual Ed., Counselor Ed., Early Childhood Ed., Ed. Admin, Ed. Psych., Elementary Ed., Foreign Lang. Ed., Math Ed., Mid Level Ed., Multicultural Ed., Physical Ed., Read/Lang Arts Ed., School Cons., Sci. Ed., Sec. Ed., Spec. Ed.
Library: Tireman Library
Computer Resources: Macintosh, Dual Platform, PCs, CD-ROM, Videodisc

Research Areas	#Faculty
Adult Education	7
Art Education	2
Bilingual Education	6
Counselor Education	
Early Childhood Ed.	5
Ed. Admin	5
Ed. Tech.	2
Elementary Ed.	7
Foreign Lang. Ed.	3
Higher Ed.	6
Math Ed.	3
Mid. Lev. Ed.	6
Multicultural Ed.	20
Music Ed.	
Physical Ed.	11
Read/Lang. Arts Ed.	12
School Counseling	2
Science Ed.	3
Secondary Ed.	3
Soc. Studies Ed.	3
Special Ed.	15
Other	10

Research Institutes/Centers: Center for Educational Policy, Bureau for Educational Planning and Development, Latin

American Programs in Education, Multicultural Education Center
Student Body Demographics: Average Age 29, 48% female, 52% male
Percent Ethnic Minorities: Hispanic-American 22%, Asian-American 2%, African-American 1%, Native-American 2%
Geographic Representation: New England 2%, Midwest 10%, Mid Atlantic 1%, Southwest 70%, West 6%, Southeast 6%, Northwest 3%
Graduate Career Paths: K-12 Teaching 27%, Higher Ed Teaching 23%, School Counseling 5%, K-12 Special Ed 14%, School Administration 5%, Higher Ed Administration 3%, Higher Ed Counseling 1%
Tuition: 91/hr (in state), 91/hr (out of state)
Financial Aid Recipients: 26%
Average Annual Housing Cost: 4,800
Application Deadline: varies
Number of: applicants annually 465; applicants accepted annually 212; students enrolled annually N/A

Tests Required	Preferred/Min Score
Graduate Record Exam	
National Teachers Exam	
Praxis II Exam	
TOEFL	550

NEW YORK

Adelphi University School of Education
South Ave., Levermore Hall, Garden City, NY 11530
Admissions: (PH)516 877-3050, (FAX)516 877-3039
Dean: (PH)516 877-4065, (FAX)516 877-4097
Total Enrollment: 5,000–10,000
Grad Enrollment: FTM 294, PTM 1,369, CAS 10
Program Membership: N/A
Academic Programs Available: MASTERS: Art Ed., Bilingual Ed., Early Childhood Ed., Elementary Ed., Math Ed., Physical Ed., Read/Lang Arts Ed., Sec. Ed., Soc. Ed., Spec. Ed. DOCTORATE: Art Ed., Bilingual Ed., Early Childhood Ed., Elementary Ed., Math Ed., Physical Ed., Read/Lang Arts Ed., Sec. Ed., Soc. Ed., Spec. Ed.
Library: Swirbol Library, 691,000 volumes
Computer Resources: Macintosh, Dual Platform, PCs, CD-ROM, Videodisc

Research Areas	#Faculty
Adult Education	
Art Education	2
Bilingual Education	4
Counselor Education	
Early Childhood Ed.	10
Ed. Admin	
Ed. Tech.	
Elementary Ed.	10
Foreign Lang. Ed.	4

Higher Ed.	
Math Ed.	3
Mid. Lev. Ed.	
Multicultural Ed.	4
Music Ed.	
Physical Ed.	8
Read/Lang. Arts Ed.	3
School Counseling	
Science Ed.	4
Secondary Ed.	4
Soc. Studies Ed.	3
Special Ed.	4
Other	12

Research Institutes/Centers: Child Activity Center, Hy Weinberg Center for Communication Disorders, Exercise Physiology Lab
Student Body Demographics: Average Age 29, 82% female, 18% male
Percent Ethnic Minorities: Hispanic-American 7%, Asian-American 27%, African-American 8%
Geographic Representation: Mid Atlantic 99%
Graduate Career Paths: K-12 Teaching 68%, K-12 Special Ed 23%
Tuition: 14,250 (in state), 14,250 (out of state)
Financial Aid Recipients: 65%
Average Annual Housing Cost: N/A
Application Deadline: rolling
Number of: applicants annually 1,154; applicants accepted annually 612; students enrolled annually 540

Tests Required	Preferred/Min Score
Graduate Record Exam	1,000
National Teachers Exam	
Praxis II Exam	

Bank Street Graduate School of Education
610 West 112 Street, New York, NY 10025
Admissions: (PH)212 875-4404, (FAX)212 875-4678, (EMAIL)grad.courses@bnk1.bnkst.edu
Dean: (PH)212 875-4469, (FAX)212 875-4753, (EMAIL)jlynch@bnk1.bnkst.edu
Total Enrollment: 1,000–5,000
Grad Enrollment: FTM 299, PTM 610
Program Membership: Holmes Partnership
Academic Programs Available: MASTERS: Bilingual Ed., Early Childhood Ed., Ed. Admin, Elementary Ed., Math Ed., Mid Level Ed., Read/Lang Arts Ed., Spec. Ed. DOCTORATE: Bilingual Ed., Early Childhood Ed., Ed. Admin, Elementary Ed., Math Ed., Mid Level Ed., Read/Lang Arts Ed., Spec. Ed.
Library: N/A
Computer Resources: Macintosh, Dual Platform, PCs, CD-ROM, Videodisc

Research Areas	#Faculty
Adult Education	
Art Education	
Bilingual Education	
Counselor Education	
Early Childhood Ed.	
Ed. Admin	
Ed. Tech.	

Elementary Ed.
Foreign Lang. Ed.
Higher Ed.
Math Ed.
Mid. Lev. Ed.
Multicultural Ed.
Music Ed.
Physical Ed.
Read/Lang. Arts Ed.
School Counseling
Science Ed.
Secondary Ed.
Soc. Studies Ed.
Special Ed.
Other

Student Body Demographics: Average Age 35, 88% female, 12% male

Percent Ethnic Minorities: Hispanic-American 8%, Asian-American 35%, African-American 12%, Native-American 0.5%

Geographic Representation: New England 12%, Midwest 2%, Mid Atlantic 74%, West 6%, Southeast 2%

Graduate Career Paths: K-12 Teaching 60%, K-12 Special Ed 15%, School Administration 19%

Tuition: 510 (in state), 510 (out of state)

Financial Aid Recipients: 56%

Average Annual Housing Cost: N/A

Application Deadline: varies

Number of: applicants annually 585; applicants accepted annually 392; students enrolled annually 366

Tests Required	Preferred/Min Score
Graduate Record Exam	
National Teachers Exam	
Praxis II Exam	
TOEFL	550

Binghamton University School of Education and Human Development

P.O. Box 6000, Binghamton, NY 13902-6000
Admissions: (PH)607 777-2727, (FAX)607 777-2501
Dean: (PH)607 777-2833, (FAX)607 777-6041
Total Enrollment: 10,000–20,000
Grad Enrollment: FTM 80, PTM 160, FTD 6, PTD 32, On campus 10%, Off campus 90%
Program Membership: N/A
Academic Programs Available: MASTERS: Elementary Ed., Foreign Lang. Ed., Math Ed., Read/Lang Arts Ed., Sci. Ed., Soc. Ed., Spec. DOCTORATE: Elementary Ed., Foreign Lang. Ed., Math Ed., Read/Lang Arts Ed., Sci. Ed., Soc. Ed.
Library: Glenn G. Bartle Library, 1.5 million volumes
Computer Resources: Macintosh, Dual Platform, PCs, CD-ROM, Videodisc

Research Areas	#Faculty
Adult Education	
Art Education	
Bilingual Education	
Counselor Education	
Early Childhood Ed.	1
Ed. Admin	

Ed. Tech.	1
Elementary Ed.	2
Foreign Lang. Ed.	1
Higher Ed.	
Math Ed.	1
Mid. Lev. Ed.	1
Multicultural Ed.	4
Music Ed.	
Physical Ed.	
Read/Lang. Arts Ed.	3
School Counseling	
Science Ed.	1
Secondary Ed.	1
Soc. Studies Ed.	2
Special Ed.	4
Other	9

Student Body Demographics: Average Age 28, 70% female, 30% male

Percent Ethnic Minorities: Hispanic-American 2%, Asian-American 1%, African-American 2%

Geographic Representation: New England 95%, Midwest 1%, Southwest 2%, Southeast 1%

Graduate Career Paths: K-12 Teaching 85%, Higher Ed Teaching 3%, K-12 Special Ed 10%, School Administration 2%

Tuition: 5,100 (in state), 8,416 (out of state)

Financial Aid Recipients: 7%

Average Annual Housing Cost: 3,710

Application Deadline: 2/15; 4/1; 11/1

Number of: applicants annually 160; applicants accepted annually 100; students enrolled annually 80

Tests Required	Preferred/Min Score
Graduate Record Exam	1,000–1,200
National Teachers Exam	
Praxis II Exam	

Canisius College School of Education and Human Services

2001 Main Street, Buffalo, NY 14208
Admissions: (PH)716 888-2545, (FAX)716 888-3290
Dean: (PH)716 888-2545, (FAX)716 888-3290
Total Enrollment: 1,000–5,000
Grad Enrollment: FTM 450, PTM 500, On campus 7%, Off campus 93%
Program Membership: N/A
Academic Programs Available: MASTERS: Counselor Ed., Ed. Admin, Elementary Ed., Foreign Lang. Ed., Higher Ed., Math Ed., Physical Ed., Read/Lang Arts Ed., Sci. Ed., Sec. Ed., Soc. Ed., Spec. Ed. DOCTORATE: Counselor Ed., Ed. Admin, Elementary Ed., Foreign Lang. Ed., Higher Ed., Math Ed., Physical Ed., Read/Lang Arts Ed., Sci. Ed., Sec. Ed., Soc. Ed., Spec. Ed.
Library: N/A
Computer Resources: Macintosh, Dual Platform, PCs, CD-ROM, Videodisc

Research Areas	#Faculty
Adult Education	
Art Education	
Bilingual Education	

Counselor Education
Early Childhood Ed.
Ed. Admin
Ed. Tech.
Elementary Ed.
Foreign Lang. Ed.
Higher Ed.
Math Ed.
Mid. Lev. Ed.
Multicultural Ed.
Music Ed.
Physical Ed.
Read/Lang. Arts Ed.
School Counseling
Science Ed.
Secondary Ed.
Soc. Studies Ed.
Special Ed.
Other

Student Body Demographics: Average Age 28, 60% female, 40% male

Percent Ethnic Minorities: N/A

Geographic Representation: Mid Atlantic 65%

Graduate Career Paths: K-12 Teaching 45%, School Counseling 15%, K-12 Special Ed 2%, School Administration 6%, Community Counseling 5%

Tuition: 358/hr (in state), 358/hr (out of state)

Financial Aid Recipients: N/A

Average Annual Housing Cost: 3,500

Application Deadline: rolling

Number of: applicants annually 1,100; applicants accepted annually 475; students enrolled annually N/A

Tests Required	Preferred/Min Score
Graduate Record Exam	
National Teachers Exam	
Praxis II Exam	

City University of New York/ Queens College School of Education

65-30 Kissena Blvd., Flushing, NY 11367

Admissions: (PH)718 997-5200, (FAX)718 997-5222, (EMAIL)mrc@queens.gadm

Dean: (PH)718 997-5220, (FAX)718 997-5222

Total Enrollment: 10,000–20,000

Program Membership: N/A

Academic Programs Available: MASTERS: Art Ed., Bilingual Ed., Counselor Ed., Early Childhood Ed., Ed. Admin, Elementary Ed., Foreign Lang. Ed., Math Ed., Physical Ed., Read/Lang Arts Ed., School Cons., Sci. Ed., Sec. Ed., DOCTORATE: Art Ed., Bilingual Ed., Counselor Ed., Early Childhood Ed., Ed. Admin, Elementary Ed., Foreign Lang. Ed., Math Ed., Physical Ed., Read/Lang Arts Ed., School Cons., Sci. Ed., Sec. Ed.

Library: Rosenthal Library

Computer Resources: Macintosh, Dual Platform, PCs, CD-ROM, Videodisc

Research Areas	#Faculty
Adult Education	

Art Education	1
Bilingual Education	1
Counselor Education	5
Early Childhood Ed.	3
Ed. Admin	5
Ed. Tech.	1
Elementary Ed.	20
Foreign Lang. Ed.	
Higher Ed.	
Math Ed.	2
Mid. Lev. Ed.	
Multicultural Ed.	
Music Ed.	
Physical Ed.	
Read/Lang. Arts Ed.	2
School Counseling	
Science Ed.	1
Secondary Ed.	1
Soc. Studies Ed.	1
Special Ed.	4
Other	6

Research Institutes/Centers: Center for the Improvement of Education, Center for Educational Technology

Student Body Demographics: Average Age N/A, female N/A, male N/A

Percent Ethnic Minorities: N/A

Geographic Representation: New England 2%, Mid Atlantic 98%

Graduate Career Paths: K-12 Teaching 70%, School Counseling 6%, K-12 Special Ed 10%, School Administration 8%

Tuition: 185/hr (in state), 225/hr (out of state)

Financial Aid Recipients: N/A

Average Annual Housing Cost: N/A

Application Deadline: 11/1; 4/1

Number of: applicants annually 1,500; applicants accepted annually 1,100; students enrolled annually 950

Tests Required	Preferred/Min Score
Graduate Record Exam	
National Teachers Exam	
Praxis II Exam	
TOEFL	600

College of Saint Rose School of Education

432 Western Ave., Albany, NY 12203-1250

Admissions: (PH)518 454-5136

Dean: (PH)518 454-5136

Total Enrollment: 1,000–5,000

Grad Enrollment: FTM 190, PTM 995, On campus 25%, Off campus 75%

Program Membership: N/A

Academic Programs Available: MASTERS: Art Ed., Counselor Ed., Early Childhood Ed., Ed. Admin, Ed. Psych., Elementary Ed., Music Ed., Read/Lang Arts Ed., School Cons., Sec. Ed., Spec. Ed. DOCTORATE: Art Ed., Counselor Ed., Early Childhood Ed., Ed. Admin, Ed. Psych., Elementary Ed., Music Ed., Read/Lang Arts Ed., School Cons., Sec. Ed., Spec. Ed.

Library: Neil Hellman Library, 195,000 volumes

Computer Resources: Macintosh, Dual Platform, PCs, CD-ROM, Videodisc

Research Areas	#Faculty
Adult Education	
Art Education	8
Bilingual Education	
Counselor Education	3
Early Childhood Ed.	2
Ed. Admin	2
Ed. Tech.	
Elementary Ed.	5
Foreign Lang. Ed.	
Higher Ed.	
Math Ed.	
Mid. Lev. Ed.	
Multicultural Ed.	1
Music Ed.	6
Physical Ed.	
Read/Lang. Arts Ed.	3
School Counseling	2
Science Ed.	
Secondary Ed.	
Soc. Studies Ed.	
Special Ed.	6
Other	7

Student Body Demographics: Average Age 32, 65% female, 35% male
Percent Ethnic Minorities: Hispanic-American 1%, Asian-American 0.5%, African-American 1%
Geographic Representation: New England 5%, Mid Atlantic 95%
Graduate Career Paths: K-12 School Counseling 5%, K-12 Special Ed 7%, School Administration 2%, Community Counseling 2%
Tuition: 364/hr (in state), 364/hr (out of state)
Financial Aid Recipients: 60%
Average Annual Housing Cost: 3,000
Application Deadline: 4/1; 10/1
Number of: applicants annually 1,200; applicants accepted annually 400; students enrolled annually 350

Tests Required	Preferred/Min Score
Graduate Record Exam	
National Teachers Exam	
Praxis II Exam	

College of Staten Island, CUNY Education Department

2800 Victory Blvd., Staten Island, NY 10314
Admissions: (PH)718 982-2010
Total Enrollment: 10,000–20,000
Grad Enrollment: Off campus 100%
Program Membership: Holmes Partnership
Academic Programs Available: MASTERS: Elementary Ed., Sec. Ed., Spec. Ed. DOCTORATE: Elementary Ed., Sec. Ed., Spec. Ed.
Library: 100,000 volumes
Computer Resources: Macintosh, Dual Platform, PCs, CD-ROM, Videodisc

Research Areas	#Faculty
Adult Education	
Art Education	
Bilingual Education	
Counselor Education	
Early Childhood Ed.	2
Ed. Admin	2
Ed. Tech.	
Elementary Ed.	
Foreign Lang. Ed.	
Higher Ed.	
Math Ed.	
Mid. Lev. Ed.	
Multicultural Ed.	
Music Ed.	
Physical Ed.	
Read/Lang. Arts Ed.	3
School Counseling	
Science Ed.	2
Secondary Ed.	2
Soc. Studies Ed.	
Special Ed.	3
Other	

Student Body Demographics: Average Age 27, 82% female, 18% male
Percent Ethnic Minorities: Hispanic-American 2%, Asian-American 2%, African-American 5%
Geographic Representation: Mid Atlantic 98%
Graduate Career Paths: K-12 Teaching 61%, K-12 Special Ed 29%, School Administration 9%
Tuition: 185/hr (in state), 320/hr (out of state)
Financial Aid Recipients: 42%
Average Annual Housing Cost: N/A
Application Deadline: rolling
Number of: applicants annually 500; applicants accepted annually 430; students enrolled annually 400

Tests Required	Preferred/Min Score
Graduate Record Exam	
National Teachers Exam	
Praxis II Exam	

Cornell University Field of Education

Sage Graduate Center, Ithaca, NY 14853
Admissions: (PH)607 255-4278, (EMAIL)cahll@cornell.edu
Total Enrollment: 20,000
Grad Enrollment: FTM 43, FTD 52
Program Membership: Holmes Partnership
Academic Programs Available: MASTERS: Adult Ed., Ed. Admin, Ed. Psych., Math Ed., Sci. Ed., DOCTORATE: Adult Ed., Ed. Admin, Ed. Psych., Math Ed., Sci. Ed.
Library: N/A
Computer Resources: Macintosh, Dual Platform, PCs, CD-ROM, Videodisc

Research Areas	#Faculty
Adult Education	3
Art Education	
Bilingual Education	
Counselor Education	2
Early Childhood Ed.	

Ed. Admin	3
Ed. Tech.	
Elementary Ed.	
Foreign Lang. Ed.	
Higher Ed.	
Math Ed.	2
Mid. Lev. Ed.	
Multicultural Ed.	
Music Ed.	
Physical Ed.	
Read/Lang. Arts Ed.	
School Counseling	
Science Ed.	3
Secondary Ed.	3
Soc. Studies Ed.	
Special Ed.	
Other	

Student Body Demographics: Average Age N/A, 60% female, 40% male
Percent Ethnic Minorities: Asian-American 5%, African-American 2%
Geographic Representation: N/A
Graduate Career Paths: K-12 Teaching 20%, Higher Ed Teaching 12%
Tuition: 10,000 (in state), 10,000 (out of state)
Financial Aid Recipients: 20%
Average Annual Housing Cost: N/A
Application Deadline: 3/15; 10/15
Number of: applicants annually 200; applicants accepted annually 100; students enrolled annually 50

Tests Required	Preferred/Min Score
Graduate Record Exam	940–1,200
National Teachers Exam	
Praxis II Exam	
TOEFL	550–600

D'Youville College Division of Education & Social Work

320 Porter Ave., Buffalo, NY 14201
Admissions: (PH)716 881-7676, (FAX)716 881-7790
Total Enrollment: 1,000–5,000
Program Membership: N/A
Academic Programs Available: MASTERS: Spec. Ed. DOCTORATE: Spec. Ed.
Library: N/A

Research Areas	#Faculty
Adult Education	
Art Education	
Bilingual Education	
Counselor Education	
Early Childhood Ed.	
Ed. Admin	
Ed. Tech.	
Elementary Ed.	
Foreign Lang. Ed.	
Higher Ed.	
Math Ed.	
Mid. Lev. Ed.	

Multicultural Ed.	
Music Ed.	
Physical Ed.	
Read/Lang. Arts Ed.	
School Counseling	
Science Ed.	
Secondary Ed.	
Soc. Studies Ed.	
Special Ed.	
Other	

Student Body Demographics: Average Age 30, 85% female, 15% male
Percent Ethnic Minorities: N/A
Geographic Representation: Mid Atlantic 100%
Tuition: 307/hr (in state), 307/hr (out of state)
Financial Aid Recipients: N/A
Average Annual Housing Cost: 4,470
Application Deadline: rolling
Number of: applicants annually N/A; applicants accepted annually N/A; students enrolled annually N/A

Tests Required	Preferred/Min Score
Graduate Record Exam	
National Teachers Exam	
Praxis II Exam	

Hofstra University School of Education

100 Hofstra University, Hempstead, NY 11550-1090
Admissions: (PH)516 463-6707, (FAX)516 560-7660, (EMAIL)hofstra@vaxc.hofstra.edu
Grad Enrollment: 1285 total
Program Membership: Holmes Partnership
Academic Programs Available: MASTERS: Art Ed., Bilingual Ed., Early Childhood Ed., Ed. Admin, Elementary Ed., Physical Ed., Read/Lang Arts Ed., School Cons., Sec. Ed., Spec. Ed. DOCTORATE: Bilingual Ed., Early Childhood Ed., Ed. Admin, Elementary Ed., Physical Ed., Read/Lang Arts Ed., School Cons., Sec. Ed., Spec. Ed.
Library: University Library, 1.4 million volumes

Research Areas	#Faculty
Adult Education	
Art Education	
Bilingual Education	
Counselor Education	
Early Childhood Ed.	
Ed. Admin	
Ed. Tech.	
Elementary Ed.	
Foreign Lang. Ed.	
Higher Ed.	
Math Ed.	
Mid. Lev. Ed.	
Multicultural Ed.	
Music Ed.	
Physical Ed.	
Read/Lang. Arts Ed.	
School Counseling	
Science Ed.	
Secondary Ed.	
Soc. Studies Ed.	

Special Ed.
Other
Student Body Demographics: N/A
Percent Ethnic Minorities: N/A
Geographic Representation: N/A
Tuition: 382/hr (in state), 382/hr (out of state)
Financial Aid Recipients: N/A
Average Annual Housing Cost: 4,000
Application Deadline: rolling
Number of: applicants annually 1,716; applicants accepted annually 532; students enrolled annually N/A

Tests Required	Preferred/Min Score
Graduate Record Exam	
National Teachers Exam	
Praxis II Exam	

Iona College Education Department

Office of Graduate Admissions, 715 North Avenue, New Rochelle, NY 10801
Admissions: (PH)914 633-2328, (FAX)914 633-2023
Dean: (PH)914 633-2328, (FAX)914 633-2023
Grad Enrollment: Off campus 100%
Program Membership: N/A
Academic Programs Available: MASTERS: Ed. Admin, Elementary Ed., Math Ed., Sec. Ed., DOCTORATE: Ed. Admin, Elementary Ed., Math Ed., Sec. Ed.
Library: Ryan Library, 250,000 volumes
Computer Resources: Macintosh, Dual Platform, PCs, CD-ROM, Videodisc

Research Areas	#Faculty
Adult Education	
Art Education	
Bilingual Education	
Counselor Education	
Early Childhood Ed.	
Ed. Admin	2
Ed. Tech.	
Elementary Ed.	15
Foreign Lang. Ed.	3
Higher Ed.	
Math Ed.	3
Mid. Lev. Ed.	
Multicultural Ed.	6
Music Ed.	
Physical Ed.	
Read/Lang. Arts Ed.	2
School Counseling	
Science Ed.	2
Secondary Ed.	2
Soc. Studies Ed.	5
Special Ed.	
Other	

Student Body Demographics: Average Age 30, 64% female, 36% male
Percent Ethnic Minorities: N/A
Geographic Representation: New England 25%, Mid Atlantic 75%
Graduate Career Paths: K-12 Teaching 90%, K-12 School Administration 10%

Tuition: 355/hr (in state), 355/hr (out of state)
Financial Aid Recipients: N/A
Average Annual Housing Cost: N/A
Application Deadline: rolling
Number of: applicants annually N/A; applicants accepted annually N/A; students enrolled annually N/A

Tests Required	Preferred/Min Score
Graduate Record Exam	
National Teachers Exam	
Praxis II Exam	

LeMoyne College Department of Education

Reilley Hall, Syracuse, NY 13214
Admissions: (PH)315 445-4376, (FAX)315 445-4540
Dean: (PH)315 445-4658, (FAX)315445-4540, (EMAIL)collins@maple.lemoyne.edu
Total Enrollment: 1,000–5,000
Grad Enrollment: FTM 100, PTM 240, Off campus 100%
Program Membership: N/A
Academic Programs Available: MASTERS: Elementary Ed., Sec. Ed., DOCTORATE: Elementary Ed., Sec. Ed.
Library: LeMoyne Library
Computer Resources: Macintosh, Dual Platform, PCs, CD-ROM, Videodisc

Research Areas	#Faculty
Adult Education	
Art Education	
Bilingual Education	
Counselor Education	
Early Childhood Ed.	
Ed. Admin	
Ed. Tech.	1
Elementary Ed.	2
Foreign Lang. Ed.	1
Higher Ed.	
Math Ed.	2
Mid. Lev. Ed.	2
Multicultural Ed.	3
Music Ed.	
Physical Ed.	
Read/Lang. Arts Ed.	3
School Counseling	
Science Ed.	2
Secondary Ed.	2
Soc. Studies Ed.	2
Special Ed.	2
Other	2

Research Institutes/Centers: Professional Development Council, Center for Economic Education
Student Body Demographics: Average Age 26, 90% female, 10% male
Percent Ethnic Minorities: Hispanic-American 3%, Asian-American 2%, African-American 4%, Native-American 2%
Geographic Representation: New England 5%, Mid Atlantic 95%
Graduate Career Paths: K-12 Teaching 95%
Tuition: 290/hr (in state), 290/hr (out of state)
Financial Aid Recipients: 60%

Average Annual Housing Cost: N/A
Number of: applicants annually N/A; applicants accepted annually N/A; students enrolled annually N/A

Tests Required	Preferred/Min Score
Graduate Record Exam	
National Teachers Exam	
Praxis II Exam	

Application Deadline: rolling
Number of: applicants annually 300; applicants accepted annually 250; students enrolled annually 250

Tests Required	Preferred/Min Score
Graduate Record Exam	
National Teachers Exam	
Praxis II Exam	

Long Island University-Brooklyn Campus School of Education

1 University Plaza, Brooklyn, NY 11201
Admissions: (PH)718 488-1011, (FAX)718 797-2399, (EMAIL)sullivan@ezra.livnet.edu
Dean: (PH)718 488-1055, (FAX)718 488-3472
Total Enrollment: 1,000–5,000
Grad Enrollment: FTM 200, PTM 1200, CAS 120
Program Membership: N/A
Academic Programs Available: MASTERS: Art Ed., Bilingual Ed., Counselor Ed., Ed. Psych., Ed. Tech., Elementary Ed., Math Ed., Read/Lang Arts Ed., School Cons., Sci. Ed., Sec. Ed., Soc. Ed., Spec. Ed. DOCTORATE: Art Ed., Bilingual Ed., Counselor Ed., Ed. Psych., Ed. Tech., Elementary Ed., Math Ed., Read/Lang Arts Ed., School Cons., Sci. Ed., Sec. Ed., Soc. Ed., Spec. Ed.
Library: LUI Library, 259,000 volumes
Computer Resources: Macintosh, Dual Platform, PCs, CD-ROM, Videodisc

Research Areas	#Faculty
Adult Education	
Art Education	5
Bilingual Education	5
Counselor Education	4
Early Childhood Ed.	
Ed. Admin	2
Ed. Tech.	1
Elementary Ed.	5
Foreign Lang. Ed.	
Higher Ed.	
Math Ed.	1
Mid. Lev. Ed.	1
Multicultural Ed.	5
Music Ed.	
Physical Ed.	1
Read/Lang. Arts Ed.	2
School Counseling	4
Science Ed.	1
Secondary Ed.	1
Soc. Studies Ed.	1
Special Ed.	4
Other	

Student Body Demographics: Average Age 32, 80% female, 20% male
Percent Ethnic Minorities: Hispanic-American 30%, Asian-American 10%, African-American 40%
Geographic Representation: N/A
Tuition: 405 (in state), N/A (out of state)
Financial Aid Recipients: 60%
Average Annual Housing Cost: N/A

New York University School of Education

32 Washington Place, 2nd Floor, New York, NY 10003
Admissions: (PH)212 998-5030, (FAX)212 995-4328
Total Enrollment: 20,000
Grad Enrollment: FTM 1,222, PTM 1,913, FTD 168, PTD 782, On campus 18%, Off campus 82%
Program Membership: Holmes Partnership
Academic Programs Available: MASTERS: Art Ed., Bilingual Ed., Counselor Ed., Early Childhood Ed., Ed. Admin, Ed. Psych., Ed. Tech., Elementary Ed., Foreign Lang. Ed., Higher Ed., Math Ed., Music Ed., Read/Lang Arts Ed., School Cons., Sci. Ed., Sec. Ed., Soc. Ed., Spec. Ed. DOCTORATE: Art Ed., Bilingual Ed., Counselor Ed., Early Childhood Ed., Ed. Admin, Ed. Psych., Ed. Tech., Elementary Ed., Foreign Lang. Ed., Higher Ed., Math Ed., Music Ed., Read/Lang Arts Ed., School Cons., Sci. Ed., Sec. Ed., Soc. Ed., Spec. Ed.
Library: Elmer Holmes Bobst Library, 2.5 million volumes
Computer Resources: Macintosh, Dual Platform, PCs, CD-ROM, Videodisc

Research Areas	#Faculty
Adult Education	
Art Education	
Bilingual Education	
Counselor Education	
Early Childhood Ed.	
Ed. Admin	
Ed. Tech.	
Elementary Ed.	
Foreign Lang. Ed.	
Higher Ed.	
Math Ed.	
Mid. Lev. Ed.	
Multicultural Ed.	
Music Ed.	
Physical Ed.	
Read/Lang. Arts Ed.	
School Counseling	
Science Ed.	
Secondary Ed.	
Soc. Studies Ed.	
Special Ed.	
Other	

Research Institutes/Centers: Center for the Study of American Culture and Education, Center for Urban Community College Leadership, Center for Women in Music, Metropolitan Center for Urban Education
Student Body Demographics: Average Age 28, 75% female, 25% male

Percent Ethnic Minorities: Hispanic-American 10%, Asian-American 14%, African-American 13%, Native-American 1%
Geographic Representation: New England 15%, Midwest 2%, Mid Atlantic 59%, Southwest 2%, West 5%, Southeast 2%, Northwest 2%
Tuition: 578/hr (in state), 578/hr (out of state)
Financial Aid Recipients: 40%
Average Annual Housing Cost: 6,000
Application Deadline: 2/1; 3/1
Number of: applicants annually 7,000; applicants accepted annually 3,100; students enrolled annually N/A

Tests Required	Preferred/Min Score
Graduate Record Exam	
National Teachers Exam	
Praxis II Exam	

Niagara University College of Education

O'Shea Hall, Room B-9, Niagara University, NY 14109
Admissions: (PH)716 286-8560, (FAX)(716) 286-8561
Dean: (PH)716 286-8560
Total Enrollment: 1,000
Grad Enrollment: FTM 180, PTM 250, Off campus 100%
Program Membership: N/A
Academic Programs Available: MASTERS: Counselor Ed., Ed. Admin, Elementary Ed., School Cons., Sec. Ed., DOCTORATE: Counselor Ed., Ed. Admin, Elementary Ed., School Cons., Sec. Ed.
Library: Niagara University Library, 290,000 volumes
Computer Resources: PCs, CD-ROM, Videodisc

Research Areas	#Faculty
Adult Education	
Art Education	
Bilingual Education	
Counselor Education	2
Early Childhood Ed.	
Ed. Admin	2
Ed. Tech.	
Elementary Ed.	3
Foreign Lang. Ed.	
Higher Ed.	
Math Ed.	
Mid. Lev. Ed.	2
Multicultural Ed.	
Music Ed.	
Physical Ed.	
Read/Lang. Arts Ed.	
School Counseling	
Science Ed.	
Secondary Ed.	
Soc. Studies Ed.	
Special Ed.	1
Other	

Research Institutes/Centers: Center for Excellence in Mental Health Counseling
Student Body Demographics: Average Age 30, 70% female, 30% male

Percent Ethnic Minorities: Hispanic-American 1%, Asian-American 2%, African-American 2%, Native-American 1%
Geographic Representation: Mid Atlantic 57%
Graduate Career Paths: K-12 Teaching 70%, School Counseling 10%, K-12 School Administration 10%, Community Counseling 10%
Tuition: 291/hr (in state), 291/hr (out of state)
Financial Aid Recipients: 5%
Average Annual Housing Cost: N/A
Application Deadline: rolling
Number of: applicants annually 600; applicants accepted annually 260; students enrolled annually 260

Tests Required	Preferred/Min Score
Graduate Record Exam	950
National Teachers Exam	
Praxis II Exam	

Queens College of the City of New York College of Education

Kissena Blvd., Flushing, NY 11367
Admissions: (PH)918 997-5200
Dean: (PH)718 997-5220, (FAX)718 997-5222, (EMAIL)slsqc@qcvaxa.acc.qc.edu
Total Enrollment: 10,000–20,000
Grad Enrollment: FTM 108, PTM 1,401, CAS 272, Off campus 100%
Program Membership: N/A
Academic Programs Available: MASTERS: Art Ed., Bilingual Ed., Counselor Ed., Early Childhood Ed., Elementary Ed., Foreign Lang. Ed., Math Ed., Music Ed., Physical Ed., Sci. Ed., Soc. Ed., Spec. Ed. DOCTORATE: Art Ed., Bilingual Ed., Counselor Ed., Early Childhood Ed., Elementary Ed., Foreign Lang. Ed., Math Ed., Music Ed., Physical Ed., Sci. Ed., Soc. Ed., Spec. Ed.
Library: Benjamin Rosenthal Library, 683,000 volumes
Computer Resources: Macintosh, Dual Platform, PCs, CD-ROM, Videodisc

Research Areas	#Faculty
Adult Education	
Art Education	
Bilingual Education	2
Counselor Education	4
Early Childhood Ed.	4
Ed. Admin	3
Ed. Tech.	2
Elementary Ed.	10
Foreign Lang. Ed.	1
Higher Ed.	
Math Ed.	2
Mid. Lev. Ed.	2
Multicultural Ed.	3
Music Ed.	2
Physical Ed.	3
Read/Lang. Arts Ed.	3
School Counseling	
Science Ed.	1
Secondary Ed.	1

Soc. Studies Ed.	2
Special Ed.	4
Other	

Student Body Demographics: Average Age 30, 65% female, 35% male
Percent Ethnic Minorities: Hispanic-American 4%, Asian-American 2%, African-American 7%
Geographic Representation: N/A
Graduate Career Paths: K-12 Teaching 40%, School Counseling 20%, K-12 Special Ed 20%, School Administration 5%, Community Counseling 5%
Tuition: 185/hr (in state), 320/hr (out of state)
Financial Aid Recipients: 60%
Average Annual Housing Cost: N/A
Application Deadline: 4/1; 11/1
Number of: applicants annually 1,500; applicants accepted annually 1,100; students enrolled annually 660

Tests Required	Preferred/Min Score
Graduate Record Exam	646–650
National Teachers Exam	
Praxis II Exam	
TOEFL	600

St. John's University School of Education and Human Services

8000 Utopia Parkway, Jamaica, NY 11439
Admissions: (PH)718 990-6107, (FAX)718 990-1677
Dean: (PH)718 990-1302, (FAX)718 990-6096
Total Enrollment: 10,000–20,000
Grad Enrollment: FTM 87, PTM 935, FTD 8, PTD 81, Off campus 100%
Program Membership: Holmes Partnership
Academic Programs Available: MASTERS: Bilingual Ed., Early Childhood Ed., Ed. Admin, Elementary Ed., Higher Ed., Read/Lang Arts Ed., School Cons., Spec. Ed. DOCTORATE: Bilingual Ed., Early Childhood Ed., Ed. Admin, Elementary Ed., Higher Ed., Read/Lang Arts Ed., School Cons., Spec. Ed.
Library: SJU Library, 20,000 volumes
Computer Resources: Macintosh, Dual Platform, PCs, CD-ROM, Videodisc

Research Areas	#Faculty
Adult Education	
Art Education	
Bilingual Education	1
Counselor Education	
Early Childhood Ed.	2
Ed. Admin	4
Ed. Tech.	3
Elementary Ed.	3
Foreign Lang. Ed.	
Higher Ed.	4
Math Ed.	2
Mid. Lev. Ed.	
Multicultural Ed.	1
Music Ed.	
Physical Ed.	
Read/Lang. Arts Ed.	3
School Counseling	2

Science Ed.	2
Secondary Ed.	2
Soc. Studies Ed.	
Special Ed.	2
Other	2

Student Body Demographics: Average Age 30, 82% female, 18% male
Percent Ethnic Minorities: Hispanic-American 7%, Asian-American 2%, African-American 7%, Native-American 0.2%
Geographic Representation: Mid Atlantic 98%
Tuition: 430/hr (in state), 430/hr (out of state)
Financial Aid Recipients: 39%
Average Annual Housing Cost: N/A
Application Deadline: N/A
Number of: applicants annually N/A; applicants accepted annually N/A; students enrolled annually N/A

Tests Required	Preferred/Min Score
Graduate Record Exam	1,050–1,100
National Teachers Exam	
Praxis II Exam	

St. Joseph's College Child Study Department

155 West Roe Blvd., Patchogue, NY 11772-2603
Admissions: (PH)516 447-3317, (FAX)516 447-1734
Dean: (PH)516 447-3242, (FAX)516 654-1782
Total Enrollment: 1,000–5,000
Grad Enrollment: PTM 30, Off campus 100%
Program Membership: N/A
Academic Programs Available: MASTERS: Spec. Ed. DOCTORATE: Spec. Ed.
Library: Callahan Library, 77,000 volumes
Computer Resources: Macintosh, Dual Platform, PCs, CD-ROM, Videodisc

Research Areas	#Faculty
Adult Education	
Art Education	
Bilingual Education	
Counselor Education	
Early Childhood Ed.	5
Ed. Admin	
Ed. Tech.	
Elementary Ed.	
Foreign Lang. Ed.	
Higher Ed.	
Math Ed.	
Mid. Lev. Ed.	
Multicultural Ed.	
Music Ed.	
Physical Ed.	
Read/Lang. Arts Ed.	
School Counseling	
Science Ed.	
Secondary Ed.	
Soc. Studies Ed.	1
Special Ed.	3
Other	3

Student Body Demographics: Average Age 27, 100% female, 0% male

Percent Ethnic Minorities: N/A
Geographic Representation: N/A
Tuition: 350/cr (in state), 350/cr (out of state)
Financial Aid Recipients: N/A
Average Annual Housing Cost: N/A
Application Deadline: varies
Number of: applicants annually N/A; applicants accepted annually N/A; students enrolled annually N/A

Tests Required	Preferred/Min Score
Graduate Record Exam	
National Teachers Exam	
Praxis II Exam	

SUNY at Buffalo Graduate School of Education

Buffalo, NY 14260-1000
Dean: (PH)716 645-2491, (FAX)716 645-2479
Total Enrollment: 20,000
Grad Enrollment: FTM 146, PTM 241, FTD 204, PTD 431, CAS 157
Program Membership: Holmes Partnership
Academic Programs Available: MASTERS: Ed. Admin, Ed. Psych., Elementary Ed., Foreign Lang. Ed., Math Ed., Read/Lang Arts Ed., School Cons., Sci. Ed., Soc. Ed., DOCTORATE: Counselor Ed., Ed. Admin, Ed. Psych., Elementary Ed., Foreign Lang. Ed., Math Ed., Read/Lang Arts Ed., Sci. Ed., Spec. Ed.
Library: Lockwood Library, 2.7 million volumes
Computer Resources: Macintosh, Dual Platform, PCs, CD-ROM, Videodisc

Research Areas	#Faculty
Adult Education	
Art Education	
Bilingual Education	
Counselor Education	1
Early Childhood Ed.	2
Ed. Admin	11
Ed. Tech.	4
Elementary Ed.	3
Foreign Lang. Ed.	3
Higher Ed.	1
Math Ed.	4
Mid. Lev. Ed.	1
Multicultural Ed.	
Music Ed.	
Physical Ed.	
Read/Lang. Arts Ed.	5
School Counseling	1
Science Ed.	3
Secondary Ed.	3
Soc. Studies Ed.	2
Special Ed.	2
Other	10

Research Institutes/Centers: Center for Educational Resources and Technologies, Center for Comparative and Global Studies in Education
Student Body Demographics: Average Age N/A, 72% female, 28% male

Percent Ethnic Minorities: N/A
Geographic Representation: N/A
Graduate Career Paths: K-12 Teaching 35%, Higher Ed Teaching 12%, School Counseling 9%, K-12 Special Ed 1%, School Administration 3%, Higher Ed Administration 6%, Higher Ed Counseling 3%, Community Counseling 6%
Tuition: 2,550 (in state), 4,208 (out of state)
Financial Aid Recipients: 9%
Average Annual Housing Cost: N/A
Application Deadline: 2/1; 10/15
Number of: applicants annually 950; applicants accepted annually 400; students enrolled annually N/A

Tests Required	Preferred/Min Score
Graduate Record Exam	
National Teachers Exam	
Praxis II Exam	
TOEFL	550

SUNY at New Paltz School of Education

HAB 804, School of Graduate Studies, New Paltz, NY 12561
Admissions: (PH)914 257-3285, (FAX)914 257-3284
Dean: (PH)914 257-2800, (FAX)914 257-2799, (EMAIL)schmidtp@snynewvm
Total Enrollment: 5,000–10,000
Grad Enrollment: FTM 70, PTM 1303, On campus 5%, Off campus 95%
Program Membership: N/A
Academic Programs Available: MASTERS: Bilingual Ed., Early Childhood Ed., Ed. Admin, Elementary Ed., Foreign Lang. Ed., Math Ed., Mid Level Ed., Read/Lang Arts Ed., Sci. Ed., Sec. Ed., Soc. Ed., Spec. Ed. DOCTORATE: Bilingual Ed., Early Childhood Ed., Ed. Admin, Elementary Ed., Foreign Lang. Ed., Math Ed., Mid Level Ed., Read/Lang Arts Ed., Sci. Ed., Sec. Ed., Soc. Ed., Spec. Ed.
Library: Sojourner Truth Library
Computer Resources: Macintosh, Dual Platform, PCs, CD-ROM, Videodisc

Research Areas	#Faculty
Adult Education	2
Art Education	3
Bilingual Education	2
Counselor Education	
Early Childhood Ed.	2
Ed. Admin	5
Ed. Tech.	2
Elementary Ed.	9
Foreign Lang. Ed.	2
Higher Ed.	2
Math Ed.	5
Mid. Lev. Ed.	3
Multicultural Ed.	5
Music Ed.	
Physical Ed.	
Read/Lang. Arts Ed.	4
School Counseling	
Science Ed.	2
Secondary Ed.	2
Soc. Studies Ed.	2

Special Ed.	5
Other	

Research Institutes/Centers: Institute for the Study of Postsecondary Education, Institute for Multicultural Education

Student Body Demographics: Average Age 37, 60% female, 40% male

Percent Ethnic Minorities: Hispanic-American 4%, Asian-American 3%, African-American 10%, Native-American 1%

Geographic Representation: N/A

Graduate Career Paths: K-12 Teaching 78%, Higher Ed Teaching 1%, K-12 Special Ed 10%, School Administration 5%, Higher Ed Administration 1%, Community Counseling 3%

Tuition: 168/cr (in state), 308/cr (out of state)

Financial Aid Recipients: 10%

Average Annual Housing Cost: 2,920

Application Deadline: N/A

Number of: applicants annually 2,000; applicants accepted annually 1,850; students enrolled annually 1,800

Tests Required	Preferred/Min Score
Graduate Record Exam	900
National Teachers Exam	
Praxis II Exam	

SUNY at Stony Brook School of Professional Development

SBS, N-223, SUNY Stony Brook, Stony Brook, NY 11794-4310
Admissions: (PH)516 632-7050, (FAX)516 9046
Dean: (PH)516 632-7055, (FAX)516 632-9046, (EMAIL)mglockner@sunysb.edu
Total Enrollment: 10,000–20,000
Grad Enrollment: FTM 50, PTM 250, On campus 3%, Off campus 97%
Program Membership: N/A
Academic Programs Available: MASTERS: Bilingual Ed., Ed. Tech., Foreign Lang. Ed., Math Ed., Sci. Ed., Soc. Ed., DOCTORATE: Bilingual Ed., Ed. Tech., Foreign Lang. Ed., Math Ed., Sci. Ed., Soc. Ed.
Library: Ward F. Melville Library, 1.6 million volumes
Computer Resources: Macintosh, Dual Platform, PCs, CD-ROM, Videodisc

Research Areas	#Faculty
Adult Education	
Art Education	
Bilingual Education	11
Counselor Education	
Early Childhood Ed.	
Ed. Admin	2
Ed. Tech.	9
Elementary Ed.	
Foreign Lang. Ed.	18
Higher Ed.	
Math Ed.	57
Mid. Lev. Ed.	
Multicultural Ed.	3
Music Ed.	
Physical Ed.	
Read/Lang. Arts Ed.	

School Counseling	
Science Ed.	79
Secondary Ed.	79
Soc. Studies Ed.	15
Special Ed.	
Other	

Research Institutes/Centers: Center for Excellence & Innovation in Education, Center for Science, Math & Technology Education, Mathematics Learning Center

Student Body Demographics: Average Age 28, 52% female, 48% male

Percent Ethnic Minorities: Hispanic-American 12%, Asian-American 9%, African-American 18%, Native-American 0.3%

Geographic Representation: New England 1%, Midwest 0.3%, Mid Atlantic 97%

Graduate Career Paths: K-12 Teaching 95%, K-12 School Administration 5%

Tuition: 213/cr (in state), 351 (out of state)

Financial Aid Recipients: N/A

Average Annual Housing Cost: N/A

Application Deadline: rolling

Number of: applicants annually 987; applicants accepted annually 800; students enrolled annually 750

Tests Required	Preferred/Min Score
Graduate Record Exam	1,000
National Teachers Exam	
Praxis II Exam	

SUNY College at Fredonia Division of Educational Studies

Fenner House, Fredonia, NY 14063
Admissions: (PH)716 673-3251, (FAX)716 673-3249, (EMAIL)bolton@fredonia.edu
Dean: (PH)716 673-3449, (FAX)716 673-3224, (EMAIL)maziarczyk@fredonia.edu
Total Enrollment: 1,000–5,000
Grad Enrollment: FTM 20, PTM 400, CAS 30, Off campus 100%
Program Membership: N/A
Academic Programs Available: MASTERS: Early Childhood Ed., Elementary Ed., Music Ed., Read/Lang Arts Ed., Sec. Ed., Soc. Ed., DOCTORATE: Early Childhood Ed., Elementary Ed., Music Ed., Read/Lang Arts Ed., Sec. Ed., Soc. Ed.
Library: Reed Library, 400,000 volumes
Computer Resources: Macintosh, Dual Platform, PCs, CD-ROM, Videodisc

Research Areas	#Faculty
Adult Education	
Art Education	
Bilingual Education	
Counselor Education	
Early Childhood Ed.	2
Ed. Admin	2
Ed. Tech.	1
Elementary Ed.	10
Foreign Lang. Ed.	
Higher Ed.	
Math Ed.	2

Mid. Lev. Ed.	1
Multicultural Ed.	1
Music Ed.	
Physical Ed.	
Read/Lang. Arts Ed.	4
School Counseling	
Science Ed.	2
Secondary Ed.	2
Soc. Studies Ed.	2
Special Ed.	4
Other	5

Research Institutes/Centers: Youngerman Center for Communication Disorders
Student Body Demographics: Average Age 25, 80% female, 20% male
Percent Ethnic Minorities: Hispanic-American 2%, Asian-American 1%, African-American 2%, Native-American 1%
Geographic Representation: Mid Atlantic 100%
Graduate Career Paths: K-12 Teaching 85%, K-12 School Administration 1%
Tuition: 2,200 (in state), 4,000 (out of state)
Financial Aid Recipients: 5%
Average Annual Housing Cost: N/A
Application Deadline: 11/1; 3/1; 6/1
Number of: applicants annually 150; applicants accepted annually 80; students enrolled annually 50

Tests Required	Preferred/Min Score
Graduate Record Exam	
National Teachers Exam	
Praxis II Exam	

SUNY College at Potsdam School of Education

Satterlee 115, 44 Pierrepont Ave., Potsdam, NY 13676
Admissions: (PH)315 267-2165, (FAX)315 267-4802, (EMAIL)murphysl@potsdam.edu
Dean: (PH)315 267-2165, (FAX)315 267-4802, (EMAIL)crawfolw@potsdam.edu
Total Enrollment: 1,000–5,000
Grad Enrollment: FTM 227, PTM 298, On campus 4%, Off campus 96%
Program Membership: N/A
Academic Programs Available: MASTERS: Ed. Tech., Elementary Ed., Math Ed., Music Ed., Read/Lang Arts Ed., Sci. Ed., Sec. Ed., Soc. Ed., Spec. Ed. DOCTORATE: Ed. Tech., Elementary Ed., Math Ed., Music Ed., Read/Lang Arts Ed., Sci. Ed., Sec. Ed., Soc. Ed., Spec. Ed.
Library: Frederick W. Crumb Library, 1 million volumes
Computer Resources: Macintosh, Dual Platform, PCs, CD-ROM, Videodisc

Research Areas	#Faculty
Adult Education	
Art Education	
Bilingual Education	
Counselor Education	
Early Childhood Ed.	
Ed. Admin	
Ed. Tech.	
Elementary Ed.	
Foreign Lang. Ed.	

Higher Ed.	
Math Ed.	
Mid. Lev. Ed.	
Multicultural Ed.	
Music Ed.	
Physical Ed.	
Read/Lang. Arts Ed.	
School Counseling	
Science Ed.	
Secondary Ed.	
Soc. Studies Ed.	
Special Ed.	
Other	

Student Body Demographics: Average Age 26, 64% female, 36% male
Percent Ethnic Minorities: Native-American 1%
Geographic Representation: N/A
Graduate Career Paths: K-12 Teaching 84%, K-12 Special Ed 6%
Tuition: 2,550 (in state), 4,208 (out of state)
Financial Aid Recipients: N/A
Average Annual Housing Cost: N/A
Application Deadline: rolling
Number of: applicants annually 400; applicants accepted annually 347; students enrolled annually 340

Tests Required	Preferred/Min Score
Graduate Record Exam	
National Teachers Exam	
Praxis II Exam	

SUNY Oswego School of Education

Culkin Hall, Oswego, NY 13126
Admissions: (PH)315 341-3152
Dean: (PH)315 341-3152
Total Enrollment: 5,000–10,000
Grad Enrollment: On campus 2%, Off campus 98%
Program Membership: N/A
Academic Programs Available: MASTERS: Counselor Ed., Ed. Admin, Elementary Ed., Read/Lang Arts Ed., School Cons., Sec. Ed., Spec. DOCTORATE: Counselor Ed., Ed. Admin, Elementary Ed., Read/Lang Arts Ed., School Cons., Sec. Ed., Spec. Ed.
Library: Penfield Library
Computer Resources: Macintosh, Dual Platform, PCs, CD-ROM, Videodisc

Research Areas	#Faculty
Adult Education	
Art Education	2
Bilingual Education	
Counselor Education	3
Early Childhood Ed.	2
Ed. Admin	3
Ed. Tech.	3
Elementary Ed.	6
Foreign Lang. Ed.	
Higher Ed.	
Math Ed.	1
Mid. Lev. Ed.	1
Multicultural Ed.	
Music Ed.	

Physical Ed.

Research Areas	#Faculty
Read/Lang. Arts Ed.	4
School Counseling	3
Science Ed.	1
Secondary Ed.	1
Soc. Studies Ed.	1
Special Ed.	3

Other

Student Body Demographics: N/A
Percent Ethnic Minorities: N/A
Geographic Representation: N/A
Tuition: 2,550 (in state), 4,208 (out of state)
Financial Aid Recipients: N/A
Application Deadline: 4/1; 7/1; 11/1
Number of: applicants annually 689; applicants accepted annually 599; students enrolled annually N/A

Tests Required	Preferred/Min Score
Graduate Record Exam	
National Teachers Exam	
Praxis II Exam	

Syracuse University School of Education

212 Archbold, Syracuse, NY 13244
Admissions: (PH)315 443-2505,
Dean: (PH)315 443-2506, (FAX)315 443-5732,
Total Enrollment: 10,000–20,000
Grad Enrollment: FTM 269, PTM 267, FTD 62, PTD 187, CAS 27
Program Membership: Holmes Partnership
Academic Programs Available: MASTERS: Art Ed., Counselor Ed., Early Childhood Ed., Ed. Admin, Ed. Tech., Foreign Lang. Ed., Higher Ed., Math Ed., Multicultural Ed., Music Ed., Physical Ed., Read/Lang Arts Ed., School Cons., Sci. Ed., Sec. Ed., Soc. Ed., Spec. Ed. DOCTORATE: Counselor Ed., Early Childhood Ed., Ed. Admin, Ed. Tech., Foreign Lang. Ed., Higher Ed., Math Ed., Multicultural Ed., Music Ed., Physical Ed., Read/Lang Arts Ed., School Cons., Sci. Ed., Sec. Ed., Soc. Ed., Spec. Ed.
Library: Bird Library, 5 million volumes
Computer Resources: Macintosh, PCs, CD-ROM, Videodisc

Research Areas	#Faculty
Adult Education	1
Art Education	1
Bilingual Education	
Counselor Education	1
Early Childhood Ed.	
Ed. Admin	1
Ed. Tech.	
Elementary Ed.	
Foreign Lang. Ed.	
Higher Ed.	1
Math Ed.	3
Mid. Lev. Ed.	
Multicultural Ed.	1
Music Ed.	1
Physical Ed.	
Read/Lang. Arts Ed.	1
School Counseling	1
Science Ed.	2
Secondary Ed.	2

Soc. Studies Ed.
Special Ed.
Other
Research Institutes/Centers: Center for Research on Aggression, Center on Human Policy
Student Body Demographics: Average Age N/A, 70% female, 30% male
Percent Ethnic Minorities: Hispanic-American 1%, Asian-American 1%, African-American 4%, Native-American 1%
Geographic Representation: N/A
Graduate Career Paths: K-12 Teaching 28%, Higher Ed Teaching 11%, School Counseling 6%, K-12 Special Ed 20%, School Administration 2%, Higher Ed Administration 4%
Tuition: 479/cr (in state), 479/cr (out of state)
Financial Aid Recipients: 33%
Average Annual Housing Cost: 550
Application Deadline: 2/1
Number of: applicants annually 650; applicants accepted annually 475; students enrolled annually N/A

Tests Required	Preferred/Min Score
Graduate Record Exam	1,000
National Teachers Exam	
Praxis II Exam	

Teachers College, Columbia University

Box 302, 525 W. 120th Street, New York, NY 10027
Admissions: (PH)212 678-3710, (FAX)212 678-4171, (EMAIL)admiss@cutcsq.tc.columbia.edu
Dean: (PH)212 678-3050, (FAX)212 678-4048
Grad Enrollment: FTM 773, PTM 1507, FTD 782, PTD 1054, CAS 800, On campus 15%, Off campus 85%
Program Membership: Holmes Partnership
Academic Programs Available: MASTERS: Adult Ed., Art Ed., Bilingual Ed., Counselor Ed., Early Childhood Ed., Ed. Admin, Ed. Psych., Ed. Tech., Elementary Ed., Foreign Lang. Ed., Higher Ed., Math Ed., Mid Level Ed., Music Ed., Physical Ed., Read/Lang Arts Ed., School Cons., Sci. Ed., Sec. Ed., Soc. Ed., Spec. Ed.
DOCTORATE: Adult Ed., Art Ed., Bilingual Ed., Counselor Ed., Early Childhood Ed., Ed. Admin, Ed. Psych., Ed. Tech., Elementary Ed., Foreign Lang. Ed., Higher Ed., Math Ed., Mid Level Ed., Music Ed., Physical Ed., Read/Lang Arts Ed., School Cons., Sci. Ed., Sec. Ed., Soc. Ed., Spec. Ed.
Library: Milbank Memorial Library, 1.8 million volumes
Computer Resources: Macintosh, Dual Platform, PCs, CD-ROM, Videodisc

Research Areas	#Faculty
Adult Education	3
Art Education	3
Bilingual Education	2
Counselor Education	7
Early Childhood Ed.	2
Ed. Admin	11
Ed. Tech.	5
Elementary Ed.	
Foreign Lang. Ed.	
Higher Ed.	4
Math Ed.	2
Mid. Lev. Ed.	

Multicultural Ed.
Music Ed. 3
Physical Ed. 1
Read/Lang. Arts Ed. 5
School Counseling 7
Science Ed. 3
Secondary Ed. 3
Soc. Studies Ed. 2
Special Ed. 8
Other
Research Institutes/Centers: Center for the Study &
Education of the Gifted, Institute for Learning Technologies
Student Body Demographics: Average Age 35, 72% female,
28% male
Percent Ethnic Minorities: Hispanic-American 6%,
Asian-American 6%, African-American 12%,
Native-American 1%
Geographic Representation: New England 20%,
Midwest 1%, Mid Atlantic 60%, Southwest 1%, West 4%,
Southeast 3%, Northwest 1%
Tuition: 550/point (in state), 550/point (out of state)
Financial Aid Recipients: 40%
Average Annual Housing Cost: 6,000
Application Deadline: 2/1
Number of: applicants annually 3,400; applicants accepted
annually 1,400; students enrolled annually 800
Tests Required   **Preferred/Min Score**

Union College Educational Studies Program

Lamont House, Schenectady, NY 12308
Admissions: (PH)518 388-6361, (FAX)518 388-6362,
(EMAIL)allep@gar.union.edu
Dean: (PH)518 388-6361, (FAX)518 388-6362,
(EMAIL)allenp@gar.union.edu
Total Enrollment: 1,000–5,000
Grad Enrollment: FTM 25, PTM 10, On campus 4%, Off
campus 96%
Program Membership: N/A
Academic Programs Available: MASTERS: Foreign Lang.
Ed., Math Ed., Sci. Ed., Soc. Ed., DOCTORATE: Foreign
Lang. Ed., Math Ed., Sci. Ed., Soc. Ed.
Library: Schaeffer Library
Computer Resources: Macintosh, Dual Platform

Research Areas	#Faculty
Adult Education	
Art Education	
Bilingual Education	
Counselor Education	
Early Childhood Ed.	
Ed. Admin	
Ed. Tech.	
Elementary Ed.	
Foreign Lang. Ed.	
Higher Ed.	
Math Ed.	
Mid. Lev. Ed.	
Multicultural Ed.	
Music Ed.	
Physical Ed.	

Read/Lang. Arts Ed.
School Counseling
Science Ed.
Secondary Ed.
Soc. Studies Ed.
Special Ed.
Other
Research Institutes/Centers: Teaching and Learning Center
Student Body Demographics: Average Age 26, 60% female,
40% male
Percent Ethnic Minorities: Hispanic-American 2%,
African-American 2%
Geographic Representation: N/A
Graduate Career Paths: K-12 Teaching 95%
Tuition: 995/cse (in state), 995/cse (out of state)
Financial Aid Recipients: 15%
Average Annual Housing Cost: 3,000
Application Deadline: 4/1
Number of: applicants annually 150; applicants accepted
annually 60; students enrolled annually 40
Tests Required   **Preferred/Min Score**
Graduate Record Exam
National Teachers Exam
Praxis II Exam

University at Albany-SUNY
School of Education

Administration Building, Room 112, Albany, NY 12222
Admissions: (PH)518 442-3980, (FAX)518 442-3922,
(EMAIL)graduate@cnsibm.albany.edu
Dean: (PH)518 442-4988, (FAX)518 442-4953,
(EMAIL)pv998@cnsibm.albany.edu
Total Enrollment: 10,000–20,000
Grad Enrollment: FTM 302, PTM 463, FTD 132, PTD 227,
CAS 45
Program Membership: N/A
Academic Programs Available: MASTERS: Bilingual Ed.,
Counselor Ed., Ed. Admin., Ed. Psych., Ed. Tech., Foreign
Lang. Ed., Higher Ed., Math Ed., Read/Lang Arts Ed.,
School Cons., Sci. Ed., Soc. Ed., Spec. Ed. DOCTORATE:
Bilingual Ed., Counselor Ed., Ed. Admin, Ed. Psych., Ed.
Tech., Foreign Lang. Ed., Higher Ed., Math Ed., Read/Lang
Arts Ed., School Cons., Sci. Ed., Soc. Ed., Spec. Ed.
Library: University at Albany Libraries, 1.8 million volumes
Computer Resources: Macintosh, Dual Platform, PCs,
CD-ROM, Videodisc

Research Areas	#Faculty
Adult Education	1
Art Education	
Bilingual Education	2
Counselor Education	5
Early Childhood Ed.	2
Ed. Admin	15
Ed. Tech.	4
Elementary Ed.	
Foreign Lang. Ed.	3
Higher Ed.	5
Math Ed.	2
Mid. Lev. Ed.	5

Multicultural Ed.	2
Music Ed.	
Physical Ed.	
Read/Lang. Arts Ed.	10
School Counseling	6
Science Ed.	3
Secondary Ed.	3
Soc. Studies Ed.	1
Special Ed.	3
Other	

Student Body Demographics: Average Age 33, 72% female, 28% male

Percent Ethnic Minorities: Hispanic-American 4%, Asian-American 1%, African-American 5%, Native-American 0.3%

Geographic Representation: Mid Atlantic 95%

Graduate Career Paths: K-12 Teaching 44%, Higher Ed Teaching 6%, School Counseling 14%, K-12 Special Ed 6%, School Administration 15%, Higher Ed Administration 7%, Higher Ed Counseling 2%, Community Counseling 6%

Tuition: 5,511 (in state), 8,827 (out of state)

Financial Aid Recipients: N/A

Average Annual Housing Cost: 4,836

Application Deadline: N/A

Number of: applicants annually 1,066; applicants accepted annually 723; students enrolled annually 381

Tests Required	Preferred/Min Score
Graduate Record Exam	
National Teachers Exam	
Praxis II Exam	

University of Rochester
Warner Graduate School of
Education and Human Development

Dewey Hall, 2-147, Rochester, NY 14627

Admissions: (PH)716 275-3950, (FAX)716 473-7598

Dean: (PH)716 275-0880, (FAX)716 473-7598

Grad Enrollment: FTM 54, PTM 99, FTD 45, PTD 112, On campus 20%, Off campus 80%

Program Membership: Holmes Partnership

Academic Programs Available: MASTERS: Bilingual Ed., Counselor Ed., Ed. Admin, Elementary Ed., Foreign Lang. Ed., Higher Ed., Math Ed., Mid Level Ed., School Cons., Sec. Ed., Soc. Ed., DOCTORATE: Bilingual Ed., Counselor Ed., Ed. Admin, Elementary Ed., Foreign Lang. Ed., Higher Ed., Math Ed., Mid Level Ed., School Cons., Sec. Ed., Soc. Ed.

Library: Rush Rhees Library, 2 million volumes

Computer Resources: Macintosh, Dual Platform, PCs, CD-ROM, Videodisc

Research Areas	#Faculty
Adult Education	
Art Education	
Bilingual Education	1
Counselor Education	5
Early Childhood Ed.	
Ed. Admin	4
Ed. Tech.	
Elementary Ed.	2
Foreign Lang. Ed.	1

Higher Ed.	6
Math Ed.	1
Mid. Lev. Ed.	6
Multicultural Ed.	1
Music Ed.	
Physical Ed.	
Read/Lang. Arts Ed.	
School Counseling	5
Science Ed.	1
Secondary Ed.	1
Soc. Studies Ed.	2
Special Ed.	1
Other	4

Student Body Demographics: Average Age 30, 70% female, 30% male

Percent Ethnic Minorities: Hispanic-American 2%, Asian-American 2%, African-American 5%, Native-American 1%

Geographic Representation: New England 5%, Midwest 3%, Mid Atlantic 80%, Southwest 2%, West 1%, Southeast 2%, Northwest 2%

Graduate Career Paths: K-12 Teaching 35%, Higher Ed Teaching 10%, School Counseling 35%, K-12 School Administration 5%, Higher Ed Administration 5%, Community Counseling 5%

Tuition: 585/hr (in state), 585/hr (out of state)

Financial Aid Recipients: 20%

Average Annual Housing Cost: N/A

Application Deadline: varies

Number of: applicants annually 225; applicants accepted annually 190; students enrolled annually 100

Tests Required	Preferred/Min Score
Graduate Record Exam	
National Teachers Exam	
Praxis II Exam	

Wagner College

Professional Programs, 631 Howard Avenue, Staten Island, NY 10301

Admissions: (PH)718 390-3411, (FAX)718 390-3105

Dean: (PH)718 390-3464, (FAX)718 390-3467

Total Enrollment: 1,000–5,000

Grad Enrollment: 34 total, On campus 33%, Off campus 67%

Program Membership: N/A

Academic Programs Available: MASTERS: Early Childhood Ed., Elementary Ed., Foreign Lang. Ed., Math Ed., Mid Level Ed., Read/Lang Arts Ed., Sec. Ed., Soc. Ed., Spec. Ed. DOCTORATE: Early Childhood Ed., Elementary Ed., Foreign Lang. Ed., Math Ed., Mid Level Ed., Read/Lang Arts Ed., Sec. Ed., Soc. Ed., Spec. Ed.

Library: Horrmann Library, 285,000 volumes

Computer Resources: Macintosh, Dual Platform, PCs, CD-ROM, Videodisc

Research Areas	#Faculty
Adult Education	
Art Education	
Bilingual Education	
Counselor Education	
Early Childhood Ed.	

Ed. Admin
Ed. Tech.
Elementary Ed.
Foreign Lang. Ed.
Higher Ed.
Math Ed.
Mid. Lev. Ed.
Multicultural Ed.
Music Ed.
Physical Ed.
Read/Lang. Arts Ed.
School Counseling
Science Ed.
Secondary Ed.
Soc. Studies Ed.
Special Ed.
Other
Student Body Demographics: Average Age 23, 76% female, 24% male
Percent Ethnic Minorities: Hispanic-American 4%, Asian-American 3%, African-American 6%, Native-American 2%
Geographic Representation: Mid Atlantic 93%
Graduate Career Paths: K-12 Teaching 75%, K-12 Special Ed 25%
Tuition: 490/cr (in state), 490/cr (out of state)
Financial Aid Recipients: N/A
Average Annual Housing Cost: 5,800
Application Deadline: N/A
Number of: applicants annually 43; applicants accepted annually 40; students enrolled annually N/A

Tests Required	Preferred/Min Score
Graduate Record Exam	
National Teachers Exam	
Praxis II Exam	

NORTH CAROLINA

Appalachian State University
Reich College of Education
Cratis D. Williams Graduate School, Boone, NC 28608
Admissions: (PH)704 262-2693
Dean: (PH)704 262-2234, (FAX)704 262-2128, (EMAIL)dukecr@appstate.edu
Total Enrollment: 10,000–20,000
Grad Enrollment: FTM 603, PTM 428, FTD 23, Off campus 100%
Program Membership: Holmes Partnership
Academic Programs Available: MASTERS: Counselor Ed., Ed. Admin, Ed. Tech., Elementary Ed., Foreign Lang. Ed., Higher Ed., Math Ed., Mid Level Ed., Music Ed., Read/Lang Arts Ed., School Cons., Soc. Ed., Spec. Ed. DOCTORATE: Counselor Ed., Ed. Admin, Ed. Tech., Elementary Ed., Foreign Lang. Ed., Higher Ed., Math Ed., Mid Level Ed.,

Music Ed., Read/Lang Arts Ed., School Cons., Soc. Ed., Spec. Ed.
Library: Belk Library, 500,000 volumes
Computer Resources: Macintosh, Dual Platform, PCs, CD-ROM, Videodisc

Research Areas	#Faculty
Adult Education	
Art Education	
Bilingual Education	
Counselor Education	
Early Childhood Ed.	
Ed. Admin	
Ed. Tech.	
Elementary Ed.	
Foreign Lang. Ed.	
Higher Ed.	
Math Ed.	
Mid. Lev. Ed.	
Multicultural Ed.	
Music Ed.	
Physical Ed.	
Read/Lang. Arts Ed.	
School Counseling	
Science Ed.	
Secondary Ed.	
Soc. Studies Ed.	
Special Ed.	
Other	

Research Institutes/Centers: Appalachian Consortium, Center for the Study of Environmental Change, Gerontology Institute
Student Body Demographics: Average Age 27, 62% female, 38% male
Percent Ethnic Minorities: African-American 4%
Geographic Representation: Mid Atlantic 5%, Southeast 90%
Tuition: 764 (in state), 7,248 (out of state)
Financial Aid Recipients: 34%
Average Annual Housing Cost: 2,300
Application Deadline: varies
Number of: applicants annually 1,200; applicants accepted annually 600–700; students enrolled annually 400

Tests Required	Preferred/Min Score
Graduate Record Exam	
National Teachers Exam	
Praxis II Exam	

Campbell University School of Education
P.O. Box 5466, Buies Creek, NC 27506
Admissions: (PH)910 893-1306, (FAX)910 893-1288
Dean: (PH)910 893-1631, (FAX)910 893-1999
Total Enrollment: 5,000–10,000
Program Membership: N/A
Academic Programs Available: MASTERS: Counselor Ed., Ed. Admin, Elementary Ed., Math Ed., Mid Level Ed., Physical Ed., School Cons., Sec. Ed., Soc. Ed., DOCTORATE: Counselor Ed., Ed. Admin, Elementary Ed., Math Ed., Mid Level Ed., Physical Ed., School Cons., Sec. Ed., Soc. Ed.
Library: Carrie Rich Library, 185,000 volumes

Computer Resources: Macintosh, Dual Platform, PCs, CD-ROM, Videodisc

Research Areas	#Faculty
Adult Education	
Art Education	
Bilingual Education	
Counselor Education	3
Early Childhood Ed.	
Ed. Admin	1
Ed. Tech.	
Elementary Ed.	2
Foreign Lang. Ed.	
Higher Ed.	
Math Ed.	
Mid. Lev. Ed.	
Multicultural Ed.	
Music Ed.	
Physical Ed.	2
Read/Lang. Arts Ed.	
School Counseling	3
Science Ed.	
Secondary Ed.	
Soc. Studies Ed.	
Special Ed.	
Other	

Student Body Demographics: Average Age 27, 70% female, 30% male

Percent Ethnic Minorities: African-American 15%, Native-American 1%

Geographic Representation: Southeast 99%

Graduate Career Paths: K-12 Teaching 45%, School Counseling 10%, K-12 School Administration 10%, Community Counseling 20%

Tuition: 150/cr (in state), 150/cr (out of state)

Financial Aid Recipients: N/A

Average Annual Housing Cost: N/A

Application Deadline: rolling

Number of: applicants annually 189; applicants accepted annually 111; students enrolled annually 65–70

Tests Required	Preferred/Min Score
Graduate Record Exam	
National Teachers Exam	
Praxis II Exam	

East Carolina University School of Education

Speigal 154, Greenville, NC 27858

Dean: (PH)919 328-4260, (FAX)919 328-4219

Total Enrollment: 10,000–20,000

Grad Enrollment: 65 total

Program Membership: Holmes Partnership

Academic Programs Available: MASTERS: Adult Ed., Counselor Ed., Ed. Admin, Ed. Tech., Elementary Ed., Math Ed., Mid Level Ed., Music Ed., Physical Ed., Read/Lang Arts Ed., School Cons., Sci. Ed., Sec. Ed., Soc. Ed., Spec. Ed. DOCTORATE: Adult Ed., Counselor Ed., Ed. Admin, Ed. Tech., Elementary Ed., Math Ed., Mid Level Ed., Music Ed., Physical Ed., Read/Lang Arts Ed., School Cons., Sci. Ed., Sec. Ed., Soc. Ed., Spec. Ed.

Library: J.Y. Joyner Library, 1 million volumes

Computer Resources: Macintosh, Dual Platform, PCs, CD-ROM, Videodisc

Research Areas	#Faculty
Adult Education	2
Art Education	3
Bilingual Education	
Counselor Education	5
Early Childhood Ed.	
Ed. Admin	8
Ed. Tech.	3
Elementary Ed.	9
Foreign Lang. Ed.	1
Higher Ed.	
Math Ed.	6
Mid. Lev. Ed.	3
Multicultural Ed.	
Music Ed.	3
Physical Ed.	6
Read/Lang. Arts Ed.	5
School Counseling	
Science Ed.	5
Secondary Ed.	5
Soc. Studies Ed.	1
Special Ed.	8
Other	11

Student Body Demographics: Average Age 36, 78% female, 22% male

Percent Ethnic Minorities: Hispanic-American 1%, Asian-American 1%, African-American 11%, Native-American 1%

Geographic Representation: New England 3%, Midwest 1%, Mid Atlantic 10%, Southeast 85%

Graduate Career Paths: K-12 Teaching 50%, Higher Ed Teaching 1%, School Counseling 5%, K-12 Special Ed 9%, School Administration 20%, Community Counseling 5%

Tuition: 810 (in state), 4,757 (out of state)

Financial Aid Recipients: N/A

Average Annual Housing Cost: 1,660

Application Deadline: 10/15; 3/15; 5/1

Number of: applicants annually 600; applicants accepted annually 500; students enrolled annually 275

Tests Required	Preferred/Min Score
Graduate Record Exam	1,000
National Teachers Exam	
Praxis II Exam	
TOEFL	550

Elon College Department of Education

2700 Campus Box, Elon College, NC 27244

Admissions: (FAX)910 538-3986

Dean: (PH)910 584-2355, (FAX)910 538-2609, (EMAIL)dillasha@vax1.elon.edu

Total Enrollment: 1,000–5,000

Grad Enrollment: FTM 2, PTM 49

Program Membership: N/A

Academic Programs Available: MASTERS: Elementary Ed., Spec. Ed. DOCTORATE: Elementary Ed., Spec. Ed.

Library: McEwen Library

Computer Resources: Macintosh, Dual Platform, PCs, CD-ROM, Videodisc

Research Areas	#Faculty
Adult Education	
Art Education	
Bilingual Education	
Counselor Education	
Early Childhood Ed.	
Ed. Admin	
Ed. Tech.	
Elementary Ed.	4
Foreign Lang. Ed.	
Higher Ed.	
Math Ed.	
Mid. Lev. Ed.	
Multicultural Ed.	
Music Ed.	
Physical Ed.	
Read/Lang. Arts Ed.	
School Counseling	
Science Ed.	
Secondary Ed.	
Soc. Studies Ed.	
Special Ed.	2
Other	

Student Body Demographics: Average Age 30, 95% female, 5% male
Percent Ethnic Minorities: African-American 4%
Geographic Representation: N/A
Tuition: 177/hr (in state), 177/hr (out of state)
Financial Aid Recipients: 10%
Average Annual Housing Cost: N/A
Application Deadline: rolling
Number of: applicants annually 70; applicants accepted annually 60; students enrolled annually 50

Tests Required	Preferred/Min Score
Graduate Record Exam	800
National Teachers Exam	
Praxis II Exam	

North Carolina State University College of Education and Psychology

Graduate School, Raleigh, NC 27695-7102
Admissions: (PH)919 515-2872, (FAX)919 515-2873, (EMAIL)debra_stewart@ncsu.edu
Dean: (PH)919 515-2231, (FAX)919 515-5836, (EMAIL)bruce@poe.coe.ncsu.edu
Total Enrollment: 20,000
Grad Enrollment: FTM 114, PTM 350, FTD 91, PTD 382, On campus 2%, Off campus 98%
Program Membership: N/A
Academic Programs Available: MASTERS: Adult Ed., Counselor Ed., Ed. Psych., Ed. Tech., Elementary Ed., Foreign Lang. Ed., Higher Ed., Math Ed., Mid Level Ed., Read/Lang Arts Ed., School Cons., Sci. Ed., Soc. Ed., Spec. Ed. DOCTORATE: Adult Ed., Counselor Ed., Ed. Psych., Ed. Tech., Elementary Ed., Foreign Lang. Ed., Higher Ed., Math Ed., Mid Level Ed., Read/Lang Arts Ed., School Cons., Sci. Ed., Soc. Ed., Spec. Ed.

Library: D. Hill Library, 1 million volumes
Computer Resources: Macintosh, Dual Platform, PCs, CD-ROM, Videodisc

Research Areas	#Faculty
Adult Education	15
Art Education	
Bilingual Education	
Counselor Education	6
Early Childhood Ed.	
Ed. Admin	
Ed. Tech.	3
Elementary Ed.	1
Foreign Lang. Ed.	2
Higher Ed.	2
Math Ed.	7
Mid. Lev. Ed.	2
Multicultural Ed.	
Music Ed.	
Physical Ed.	
Read/Lang. Arts Ed.	4
School Counseling	
Science Ed.	7
Secondary Ed.	7
Soc. Studies Ed.	2
Special Ed.	4
Other	

Research Institutes/Centers: National Institute for Leadership in Education, Center for Research in Mathematics and Science Education
Student Body Demographics: Average Age 35, 74% female, 26% male
Percent Ethnic Minorities: Hispanic-American 1%, Asian-American 1%, African-American 17%, Native-American 1%
Geographic Representation: New England 3%, Mid Atlantic 1%, Southeast 96%
Graduate Career Paths: K-12 Teaching 62%, Higher Ed Teaching 5%, School Counseling 5%, K-12 Special Ed 10%, School Administration 10%, Higher Ed Administration 5%, Higher Ed Counseling 3%
Tuition: 869 (in state), 4,927 (out of state)
Financial Aid Recipients: 12%
Average Annual Housing Cost: 7,200
Application Deadline: 11/25; 5/10; 6/25
Number of: applicants annually N/A; applicants accepted annually N/A; students enrolled annually N/A

Tests Required	Preferred/Min Score
Graduate Record Exam	
National Teachers Exam	
Praxis II Exam	
TOEFL	550

Salem College Education Department

Graduate Office, Winston-Salem, NC 27108
Admissions: (PH)910 721-2658, (FAX)910 721-2683
Dean: (PH)910 721-2656
Total Enrollment: 1,000
Grad Enrollment: FTM 16, PTM 92, Off campus 100%
Program Membership: N/A

Academic Programs Available: MASTERS: Early Childhood Ed., Elementary Ed., Read/Lang Arts Ed., DOCTORATE: Early Childhood Ed., Elementary Ed., Read/Lang Arts Ed.
Library: Gromley Library
Computer Resources: Macintosh, Dual Platform, PCs, CD-ROM, Videodisc

Research Areas	#Faculty
Adult Education	
Art Education	
Bilingual Education	
Counselor Education	
Early Childhood Ed.	1
Ed. Admin	
Ed. Tech.	
Elementary Ed.	
Foreign Lang. Ed.	
Higher Ed.	
Math Ed.	
Mid. Lev. Ed.	
Multicultural Ed.	
Music Ed.	
Physical Ed.	
Read/Lang. Arts Ed.	2
School Counseling	
Science Ed.	
Secondary Ed.	
Soc. Studies Ed.	
Special Ed.	1
Other	

Student Body Demographics: Average Age 30, 85% female, 15% male
Percent Ethnic Minorities: Asian-American 1%, African-American 4%, Native-American 1%
Geographic Representation: N/A
Graduate Career Paths: K-12 Teaching 100%
Tuition: 165/hr (in state), 165/hr (out of state)
Financial Aid Recipients: N/A
Average Annual Housing Cost: N/A
Application Deadline: rolling
Number of: applicants annually N/A; applicants accepted annually N/A; students enrolled annually N/A

Tests Required	Preferred/Min Score
Graduate Record Exam	
National Teachers Exam	
Praxis II Exam	

University of North Carolina at Chapel Hill
School of Education

Chapel Hill, NC 27599
Admissions: (PH)919 966-1346, (FAX)919 962-15533
Dean: (PH)919 966-7000, (EMAIL)djstedma@email.unc.edu
Grad Enrollment: 305 total
Program Membership: Holmes Partnership
Academic Programs Available: MASTERS: Early Childhood Ed., Ed. Admin, Ed. Psych., Ed. Tech., Foreign Lang. Ed., Math Ed., Mid Level Ed., Music Ed., Read/Lang Arts Ed., School Cons., Sci. Ed., Soc. Ed., Spec. Ed. DOCTORATE: Early Childhood Ed., Ed. Admin, Ed. Psych., Ed. Tech., Foreign Lang. Ed., Math Ed., Mid Level Ed., Music Ed., Read/Lang Arts Ed., School Cons., Sci. Ed., Soc. Ed., Spec. Ed.
Library: N/A

Research Areas	#Faculty
Adult Education	
Art Education	
Bilingual Education	
Counselor Education	
Early Childhood Ed.	
Ed. Admin	
Ed. Tech.	
Elementary Ed.	
Foreign Lang. Ed.	
Higher Ed.	
Math Ed.	
Mid. Lev. Ed.	
Multicultural Ed.	
Music Ed.	
Physical Ed.	
Read/Lang. Arts Ed.	
School Counseling	
Science Ed.	
Secondary Ed.	
Soc. Studies Ed.	
Special Ed.	
Other	

Student Body Demographics: N/A
Percent Ethnic Minorities: N/A
Geographic Representation: N/A
Tuition: 948 (in state), 9,046 (out of state)
Financial Aid Recipients: N/A
Average Annual Housing Cost: N/A
Application Deadline: rolling
Number of: applicants annually 593; applicants accepted annually 237; students enrolled annually N/A

Tests Required	Preferred/Min Score
Graduate Record Exam	1,000
National Teachers Exam	
Praxis II Exam	

University of North Carolina at Charlotte
College of Education and Allied Professions

Charlotte, NC 28223
Admissions: (PH)704 547-3366
Grad Enrollment: 557 total
Program Membership: N/A
Academic Programs Available: MASTERS: Counselor Ed., Ed. Admin, Ed. Tech., Elementary Ed., Mid Level Ed., Read/Lang Arts Ed., Sec. Ed., Spec. Ed. DOCTORATE: Counselor Ed., Ed. Admin, Ed. Tech., Elementary Ed., Mid Level Ed., Read/Lang Arts Ed., Sec. Ed., Spec. Ed.
Library: N/A

Research Areas	#Faculty
Adult Education	
Art Education	
Bilingual Education	
Counselor Education	
Early Childhood Ed.	

	#Faculty
Ed. Admin	
Ed. Tech.	
Elementary Ed.	
Foreign Lang. Ed.	
Higher Ed.	
Math Ed.	
Mid. Lev. Ed.	
Multicultural Ed.	
Music Ed.	
Physical Ed.	
Read/Lang. Arts Ed.	
School Counseling	
Science Ed.	
Secondary Ed.	
Soc. Studies Ed.	
Special Ed.	
Other	

Student Body Demographics: N/A
Percent Ethnic Minorities: N/A
Geographic Representation: N/A
Tuition: 1,568 (in state), 8,462 (out of state)
Financial Aid Recipients: N/A
Average Annual Housing Cost: N/A
Application Deadline: 7/1
Number of: applicants annually 264; applicants accepted annually 193; students enrolled annually N/A

Tests Required	Preferred/Min Score
Graduate Record Exam	
National Teachers Exam	
Praxis II Exam	

University of North Carolina at Greensboro School of Education

241 Mossman Building, Greensboro, NC 27412
Admissions: (PH)910 334-5596, (FAX)910 334-3009
Dean: (PH)910 334-3410, (FAX)910 334-4120, (EMAIL)knightt@dewey.uncg.edu
Total Enrollment: 10,000–20,000
Grad Enrollment: FTM 205, PTM 340, FTD 80, PTD 132, On campus 2%, Off campus 98%
Program Membership: N/A
Academic Programs Available: MASTERS: Art Ed., Counselor Ed., Early Childhood Ed., Ed. Admin, Ed. Tech., Elementary Ed., Foreign Lang. Ed., Higher Ed., Math Ed., Mid Level Ed., Music Ed., Physical Ed., Read/Lang Arts Ed., School Cons., Sci. Ed., Soc. Ed., Spec. Ed. DOCTORATE: Art Ed., Counselor Ed., Early Childhood Ed., Ed. Admin, Ed. Tech., Elementary Ed., Foreign Lang. Ed., Higher Ed., Math Ed., Mid Level Ed., Music Ed., Physical Ed., Read/Lang Arts Ed., School Cons., Sci. Ed., Soc. Ed., Spec. Ed.
Library: Jackson Library, 550,000 volumes
Computer Resources: Macintosh, Dual Platform, PCs, CD-ROM, Videodisc

Research Areas	#Faculty
Adult Education	1
Art Education	3
Bilingual Education	
Counselor Education	7
Early Childhood Ed.	

Ed. Admin	4
Ed. Tech.	
Elementary Ed.	10
Foreign Lang. Ed.	1
Higher Ed.	2
Math Ed.	2
Mid. Lev. Ed.	2
Multicultural Ed.	1
Music Ed.	6
Physical Ed.	4
Read/Lang. Arts Ed.	3
School Counseling	1
Science Ed.	2
Secondary Ed.	2
Soc. Studies Ed.	1
Special Ed.	3
Other	14

Research Institutes/Centers: Center for School Accountability, Center for Educational Research and Evaluation, Center for Educational Studies and Development
Student Body Demographics: Average Age 35, 73% female, 27% male
Percent Ethnic Minorities: African-American 9%
Geographic Representation: Southeast 95%
Tuition: 858/9 hours (in state), 4379 (out of state)
Financial Aid Recipients: N/A
Average Annual Housing Cost: N/A
Application Deadline: varies
Number of: applicants annually 574; applicants accepted annually 434; students enrolled annually N/A

Tests Required	Preferred/Min Score
Graduate Record Exam	800–1,000
National Teachers Exam	
Praxis II Exam	

NORTH DAKOTA

University of North Dakota Center for Teaching and Learning

Graduate School, Box 8178, Grand Forks, ND 58202
Admissions: (PH)701 777-2945, (FAX)701 777-3619
Dean: (PH)701 777-2674, (FAX)701 777-4393
Total Enrollment: 10,000–20,000
Grad Enrollment: FTM 18, PTM 106, FTD 20, PTD 64, CAS 5, On campus 10%, Off campus 90%
Program Membership: Holmes Partnership
Academic Programs Available: MASTERS: Counselor Ed., Early Childhood Ed., Ed. Admin, Elementary Ed., Physical Ed., Read/Lang Arts Ed., Sec. Ed., Spec. Ed. DOCTORATE: Counselor Ed., Early Childhood Ed., Ed. Admin, Elementary Ed., Physical Ed., Read/Lang Arts Ed., Sec. Ed., Spec. Ed.
Library: Chester Fritz Library, 819,000 volumes
Computer Resources: Macintosh, Dual Platform, PCs, CD-ROM, Videodisc

Research Areas	#Faculty
Adult Education	1
Art Education	
Bilingual Education	
Counselor Education	4
Early Childhood Ed.	2
Ed. Admin	3
Ed. Tech.	
Elementary Ed.	1
Foreign Lang. Ed.	
Higher Ed.	4
Math Ed.	1
Mid. Lev. Ed.	2
Multicultural Ed.	2
Music Ed.	
Physical Ed.	
Read/Lang. Arts Ed.	4
School Counseling	
Science Ed.	1
Secondary Ed.	1
Soc. Studies Ed.	2
Special Ed.	4
Other	3

Research Institutes/Centers: Bureau for Educational Services and Applied Research
Student Body Demographics: Average Age 40, 75% female, 25% male
Percent Ethnic Minorities: African-American 2%, Native-American 11%
Geographic Representation: New England 2%, Midwest 84%, Mid Atlantic 2%, Southwest 2%, West 4%, Southeast 2%, Northwest 4%
Graduate Career Paths: K-12 Teaching 25%, Higher Ed Teaching 25%, K-12 Special Ed 25%, School Administration 20%, Higher Ed Administration 3%, Higher Ed Counseling 2%
Tuition: 1,319 (in state), 3,256 (out of state)
Financial Aid Recipients: 16%
Average Annual Housing Cost: 5,000
Application Deadline: N/A
Number of: applicants annually 108; applicants accepted annually 91; students enrolled annually 70

Tests Required	Preferred/Min Score
Graduate Record Exam	
National Teachers Exam	
Praxis II Exam	

OHIO

Bowling Green State University
College of Education
Bowling Green, OH 43403
Admissions: (PH)419 372-7407
Grad Enrollment: 580 total

Program Membership: Holmes Partnership
Academic Programs Available: N/A
Library: N/A

Research Areas	#Faculty
Adult Education	
Art Education	
Bilingual Education	
Counselor Education	
Early Childhood Ed.	
Ed. Admin	
Ed. Tech.	
Elementary Ed.	
Foreign Lang. Ed.	
Higher Ed.	
Math Ed.	
Mid. Lev. Ed.	
Multicultural Ed.	
Music Ed.	
Physical Ed.	
Read/Lang. Arts Ed.	
School Counseling	
Science Ed.	
Secondary Ed.	
Soc. Studies Ed.	
Special Ed.	
Other	

Student Body Demographics: N/A
Percent Ethnic Minorities: N/A
Geographic Representation: N/A
Tuition: 5,117 (in state), 9,705 (out of state)
Financial Aid Recipients: %
Application Deadline: 2/15
Number of: applicants annually 563; applicants accepted annually 230; students enrolled annually N/A

Tests Required	Preferred/Min Score
Graduate Record Exam	
National Teachers Exam	
Praxis II Exam	

Cleveland State University
College of Education
Cleveland, OH 44115
Admissions: (PH)216 687-4625
Grad Enrollment: 800 total
Program Membership: N/A
Academic Programs Available: MASTERS: Adult Ed., Counselor Ed., Elementary Ed., Higher Ed., Sec. Ed
Library: N/A

Research Areas	#Faculty
Adult Education	
Art Education	
Bilingual Education	
Counselor Education	
Early Childhood Ed.	
Ed. Admin	
Ed. Tech.	
Elementary Ed.	
Foreign Lang. Ed.	

Higher Ed.
Math Ed.
Mid. Lev. Ed.
Multicultural Ed.
Music Ed.
Physical Ed.
Read/Lang. Arts Ed.
School Counseling
Science Ed.
Secondary Ed.
Soc. Studies Ed.
Special Ed.
Other
Student Body Demographics: N/A
Percent Ethnic Minorities: N/A
Geographic Representation: N/A
Tuition: 119 (in state), 238 (out of state)
Financial Aid Recipients: N/A
Number of: applicants annually 204; applicants accepted annually 112; students enrolled annually

Tests Required　　　　　**Preferred/Min Score**
Graduate Record Exam
National Teachers Exam
Praxis II Exam

Kent State University Graduate School of Education

Kent, OH 44242
Admissions: (PH)216 672-2536, (FAX)216 672-3549
Grad Enrollment: 1300 total
Program Membership: Holmes Partnership
Academic Programs Available: MASTERS: Counselor Ed., Ed. Admin, Ed. Psych., Ed. Tech., Elementary Ed., Higher Ed., Math Ed., Read/Lang Arts Ed., Sec. Ed., DOCTORATE: Counselor Ed., Ed. Admin, Ed. Psych., Ed. Tech., Elementary Ed., Higher Ed., Math Ed., Read/Lang Arts Ed., Sec. Ed.
Library: N/A

Research Areas　　　　　**#Faculty**
Adult Education
Art Education
Bilingual Education
Counselor Education
Early Childhood Ed.
Ed. Admin
Ed. Tech.
Elementary Ed.
Foreign Lang. Ed.
Higher Ed.
Math Ed.
Mid. Lev. Ed.
Multicultural Ed.
Music Ed.
Physical Ed.
Read/Lang. Arts Ed.
School Counseling
Science Ed.
Secondary Ed.
Soc. Studies Ed.

Special Ed.
Other
Student Body Demographics: N/A
Percent Ethnic Minorities: N/A
Geographic Representation: N/A
Tuition: 4,350 (in state), 8,434 (out of state)
Financial Aid Recipients: N/A
Application Deadline: 4/1
Number of: applicants annually 450; applicants accepted annually 338; students enrolled annually N/A
Tests Required　　　　　**Preferred/Min Score**
Graduate Record Exam
National Teachers Exam
Praxis II Exam

Malone College

515 25th Street N.W., Canton, OH 44709
Admissions: (PH)216 471-8210, (FAX)216 454-6977
Dean: (PH)216 471-8225
Total Enrollment: 1,000–5,000
Grad Enrollment: FTM 167, PTM 410
Program Membership: N/A
Academic Programs Available: MASTERS: Counselor Ed., Early Childhood Ed., Elementary Ed., Mid Level Ed., Physical Ed., Read/Lang Arts Ed., School Cons., Sec. Ed., Spec. Ed. DOCTORATE: Counselor Ed., Early Childhood Ed., Elementary Ed., Mid Level Ed., Physical Ed., Read/Lang Arts Ed., School Cons., Sec. Ed., Spec. Ed.
Library: Everett L. Cattell Library, 150,000 volumes
Computer Resources: PCs

Research Areas　　　　　**#Faculty**
Adult Education
Art Education
Bilingual Education
Counselor Education
Early Childhood Ed.
Ed. Admin
Ed. Tech.
Elementary Ed.
Foreign Lang. Ed.
Higher Ed.
Math Ed.
Mid. Lev. Ed.
Multicultural Ed.
Music Ed.
Physical Ed.
Read/Lang. Arts Ed.
School Counseling
Science Ed.
Secondary Ed.
Soc. Studies Ed.
Special Ed.
Other
Student Body Demographics: Average Age 37, 82% female, 18% male
Percent Ethnic Minorities: Hispanic-American 1%, African-American 3%
Geographic Representation: N/A

Graduate Career Paths: K-12 Teaching 4%, School Counseling 2%, K-12 Special Ed 15%, Community Counseling 18%
Tuition: 265/hr (in state), 265/hr (out of state)
Financial Aid Recipients: 14%
Average Annual Housing Cost: N/A
Application Deadline: 12/1; 4/1; 8/1
Number of: applicants annually N/A; applicants accepted annually N/A; students enrolled annually N/A

Tests Required	Preferred/Min Score
Graduate Record Exam	
National Teachers Exam	
Praxis II Exam	

Miami University School of Education and Allied Professions

102 Roudebush, Oxford, OH 45056
Admissions: (PH)513 529-4125, (FAX)513 529-3762, (EMAIL)johnson_bob_c.robmail@msmail.muohio.edu
Dean: (PH)513 529-6317, (FAX)513 529-7270
Total Enrollment: 10,000–20,000
Grad Enrollment: FTM 223, PTM 177, FTD 16, PTD 34
Program Membership: Holmes Partnership, NNER
Academic Programs Available: MASTERS: Art Ed., Ed. Admin, Ed. Psych., Elementary Ed., Math Ed., Read/Lang Arts Ed., Sci. Ed., Sec. Ed., Soc. Ed., Spec. Ed. DOCTORATE: Art Ed., Ed. Admin, Ed. Psych., Elementary Ed., Math Ed., Read/Lang Arts Ed., Sci. Ed., Sec. Ed., Soc. Ed., Spec. Ed.
Library: King Library, 1.8 million volumes
Computer Resources: Macintosh, Dual Platform, PCs, CD-ROM, Videodisc

Research Areas	#Faculty
Adult Education	
Art Education	
Bilingual Education	
Counselor Education	
Early Childhood Ed.	
Ed. Admin	
Ed. Tech.	
Elementary Ed.	
Foreign Lang. Ed.	
Higher Ed.	
Math Ed.	
Mid. Lev. Ed.	
Multicultural Ed.	
Music Ed.	
Physical Ed.	
Read/Lang. Arts Ed.	
School Counseling	
Science Ed.	
Secondary Ed.	
Soc. Studies Ed.	
Special Ed.	
Other	

Research Institutes/Centers: Center for Education and Cultural Studies, Center for Excellence in Mathematics and Science Education, Family and Child Studies Center, Heckert Center for Children's Reading and Writing

Student Body Demographics: Average Age N/A, 69% female, 31% male
Percent Ethnic Minorities: African-American 8%
Geographic Representation: N/A
Tuition: 2,555 (in state), 5,270 (out of state)
Financial Aid Recipients: 30%
Average Annual Housing Cost: 3,800
Application Deadline: varies
Number of: applicants annually N/A; applicants accepted annually N/A; students enrolled annually N/A

Tests Required	Preferred/Min Score
Graduate Record Exam	
National Teachers Exam	
Praxis II Exam	

Notre Dame College of Ohio

Graduate Studies, 4545 College Road, South Euclid, OH 44121
Admissions: (PH)216 381-1680, (FAX)216 381-3802
Dean: (PH)216 381-1680 x337
Total Enrollment: 1,000
Grad Enrollment: PTM 45, CAS 24, Off campus 100%
Program Membership: N/A
Academic Programs Available: N/A
Library: Clara Fritzsche Library, 100,000 volumes
Computer Resources: Macintosh, Dual Platform, PCs, CD-ROM, Videodisc

Research Areas	#Faculty
Adult Education	
Art Education	
Bilingual Education	
Counselor Education	
Early Childhood Ed.	
Ed. Admin	
Ed. Tech.	
Elementary Ed.	
Foreign Lang. Ed.	
Higher Ed.	
Math Ed.	
Mid. Lev. Ed.	
Multicultural Ed.	
Music Ed.	
Physical Ed.	
Read/Lang. Arts Ed.	1
School Counseling	
Science Ed.	
Secondary Ed.	
Soc. Studies Ed.	
Special Ed.	1
Other	2

Student Body Demographics: Average Age 35, 99% female, 1% male
Percent Ethnic Minorities: African-American 10%
Geographic Representation: Midwest 100%
Graduate Career Paths: K-12 Teaching 90%, K-12 Special Ed 8%
Tuition: 300/hr (in state), 300/hr (out of state)
Financial Aid Recipients: 4%
Average Annual Housing Cost: N/A

Application Deadline: N/A
Number of: applicants annually 12; applicants accepted annually 12; students enrolled annually 11

Tests Required	Preferred/Min Score
Graduate Record Exam	800
National Teachers Exam	
Praxis II Exam	

Ohio State University College of Education

110 Arps Hall, 1945 N. High Street, Columbus,
OH 43210-1172
Admissions: (PH)614 292-2581, (FAX)614 292-4547,
(EMAIL)bryant.l@osu.edu
Dean: (PH)614 292-2461, (FAX)614 292-8052
Total Enrollment: 20,000
Grad Enrollment: FTM 672, PTM 1,007, FTD 465, PTD 659,
On campus 10%, Off campus 90%
Program Membership: N/A
Academic Programs Available: MASTERS: Adult Ed.,
Art Ed., Counselor Ed., Early Childhood Ed., Ed.
Admin, Ed. Psych., Ed. Tech., Elementary Ed., Foreign
Lang. Ed., Higher Ed., Math Ed., Multicultural Ed.,
Music Ed., Physical Ed., Read/Lang Arts Ed.,
School Cons., Sci. Ed., Sec. Ed., Soc. Ed., Spec. Ed.
DOCTORATE: Adult Ed., Art Ed., Counselor Ed.,
Early Childhood Ed., Ed. Admin, Ed. Psych.,
Ed. Tech., Elementary Ed., Foreign Lang. Ed.,
Higher Ed., Math Ed., Multicultural Ed., Music
Ed., Physical Ed., School Cons., Sci. Ed., Sec. Ed.,
Soc. Ed., Spec. Ed.
Library: N/A
Computer Resources: Macintosh, Dual Platform, PCs,
CD-ROM, Videodisc

Research Areas	#Faculty
Adult Education	
Art Education	
Bilingual Education	
Counselor Education	
Early Childhood Ed.	
Ed. Admin	
Ed. Tech.	
Elementary Ed.	
Foreign Lang. Ed.	
Higher Ed.	
Math Ed.	
Mid. Lev. Ed.	
Multicultural Ed.	
Music Ed.	
Physical Ed.	
Read/Lang. Arts Ed.	
School Counseling	
Science Ed.	
Secondary Ed.	
Soc. Studies Ed.	
Special Ed.	
Other	

Research Institutes/Centers: Center for Education &
Training in Education, Center for Special Needs Populations,
Eisenhower Center for Math and Science

Student Body Demographics: Average Age 31, 75% female,
25% male
Percent Ethnic Minorities: Hispanic-American 1%,
Asian-American 1%, African-American 1%
Geographic Representation: N/A
Tuition: 4,707 (in state), 12,222 (out of state)
Financial Aid Recipients: N/A
Average Annual Housing Cost: 4,755
Application Deadline: rolling
Number of: applicants annually 1,277; applicants accepted
annually 584; students enrolled annually 391

Tests Required	Preferred/Min Score
Graduate Record Exam	
National Teachers Exam	
Praxis II Exam	
TOEFL	500

Ohio University College of Education

124 McCracken Hall, Athens, OH 45701
Admissions: (PH)614 593-4413
Total Enrollment: 10,000–20,000
Grad Enrollment: 550 total
Program Membership: Holmes Partnership
Academic Programs Available: MASTERS: Counselor Ed.,
Ed. Admin, Ed. Tech., Elementary Ed., Higher Ed., Math Ed.,
Mid Level Ed., Read/Lang Arts Ed., Sec. Ed., Spec. Ed.
DOCTORATE: Counselor Ed., Ed. Admin, Ed. Tech.,
Elementary Ed., Higher Ed., Math Ed., Mid Level Ed.,
Read/Lang Arts Ed., Sec. Ed., Spec. Ed.
Library: Alden Library, 1.1 million volumes

Research Areas	#Faculty
Adult Education	
Art Education	
Bilingual Education	
Counselor Education	
Early Childhood Ed.	
Ed. Admin	
Ed. Tech.	
Elementary Ed.	
Foreign Lang. Ed.	
Higher Ed.	
Math Ed.	
Mid. Lev. Ed.	
Multicultural Ed.	
Music Ed.	
Physical Ed.	
Read/Lang. Arts Ed.	
School Counseling	
Science Ed.	
Secondary Ed.	
Soc. Studies Ed.	
Special Ed.	
Other	

Student Body Demographics: N/A
Percent Ethnic Minorities: N/A
Geographic Representation: N/A
Tuition: 178 (in state), 347 (out of state)
Financial Aid Recipients: N/A
Average Annual Housing Cost: 3,500

Application Deadline: 4/1
Number of: applicants annually 352; applicants accepted annually 235; students enrolled annually

Tests Required	Preferred/Min Score
Graduate Record Exam	
National Teachers Exam	
Praxis II Exam	

University of Cincinnati College of Education

Cincinnati, OH 45221
Admissions: (PH)513 556-4430
Grad Enrollment: 979 total
Program Membership: Holmes Partnership
Academic Programs Available: MASTERS: Counselor Ed., Ed. Admin, Ed. Psych., Elementary Ed., Sec. Ed., Spec. Ed. DOCTORATE: Counselor Ed., Ed. Admin, Ed. Psych., Elementary Ed., Sec. Ed., Spec. Ed.
Library: Langsam Library, 3 million volumes

Research Areas	#Faculty
Adult Education	
Art Education	
Bilingual Education	
Counselor Education	6
Early Childhood Ed.	5
Ed. Admin	5
Ed. Tech.	5
Elementary Ed.	10
Foreign Lang. Ed.	
Higher Ed.	1
Math Ed.	4
Mid. Lev. Ed.	
Multicultural Ed.	2
Music Ed.	
Physical Ed.	
Read/Lang. Arts Ed.	8
School Counseling	6
Science Ed.	3
Secondary Ed.	3
Soc. Studies Ed.	3
Special Ed.	10
Other	

Research Institutes/Centers: Curriculum Resource Center
Student Body Demographics: N/A
Percent Ethnic Minorities: N/A
Geographic Representation: N/A
Tuition: 2,047 (in state), 4,017 (out of state)
Financial Aid Recipients: N/A
Application Deadline: 2/15
Number of: applicants annually 623; applicants accepted annually 415; students enrolled annually

Tests Required	Preferred/Min Score
Graduate Record Exam	
National Teachers Exam	
Praxis II Exam	

University of Dayton School of Education

Dayton, OH 45469
Admissions: (PH)513 229-3146

Grad Enrollment: 2400 total
Program Membership: N/A
Academic Programs Available: MASTERS: Counselor Ed., Ed. Admin, Ed. Psych., Elementary Ed., Music Ed., Physical Ed., Sec. Ed., DOCTORATE: Counselor Ed., Ed. Admin, Ed. Psych., Elementary Ed., Music Ed., Physical Ed., Sec. Ed.
Library: N/A

Research Areas	#Faculty
Adult Education	
Art Education	
Bilingual Education	
Counselor Education	
Early Childhood Ed.	
Ed. Admin	
Ed. Tech.	
Elementary Ed.	
Foreign Lang. Ed.	
Higher Ed.	
Math Ed.	
Mid. Lev. Ed.	
Multicultural Ed.	
Music Ed.	
Physical Ed.	
Read/Lang. Arts Ed.	
School Counseling	
Science Ed.	
Secondary Ed.	
Soc. Studies Ed.	
Special Ed.	
Other	

Student Body Demographics: Average Age 67% female, 33% male
Percent Ethnic Minorities: N/A
Geographic Representation: N/A
Tuition: 1,548 (in state), 1,548 (out of state)
Financial Aid Recipients: N/A
Average Annual Housing Cost: N/A
Application Deadline: rolling
Number of: applicants annually 408; applicants accepted annually 375; students enrolled annually N/A

Tests Required	Preferred/Min Score
Graduate Record Exam	
National Teachers Exam	
Praxis II Exam	

University of Rio Grande Graduate Education

Roberts House, 218 N. College Ave., Rio Grande, OH 45674
Admissions: (PH)614 245-7208, (FAX)614 245-7260
Dean: (PH)614 245-7328, (FAX)614 245-7110
Total Enrollment: 1,000–5,000
Grad Enrollment: PTM 90, Off campus 100%
Program Membership: N/A
Academic Programs Available: MASTERS: Art Ed., Math Ed., Read/Lang Arts Ed., Spec. Ed. DOCTORATE: Art Ed., Math Ed., Read/Lang Arts Ed., Spec. Ed.
Library: Jeanette A. Davis Library, 230,000 volumes
Computer Resources: Macintosh, Dual Platform, PCs, CD-ROM, Videodisc

Research Areas	#Faculty
Adult Education	
Art Education	4
Bilingual Education	
Counselor Education	
Early Childhood Ed.	
Ed. Admin	
Ed. Tech.	
Elementary Ed.	
Foreign Lang. Ed.	
Higher Ed.	
Math Ed.	1
Mid. Lev. Ed.	
Multicultural Ed.	
Music Ed.	1
Physical Ed.	
Read/Lang. Arts Ed.	2
School Counseling	
Science Ed.	
Secondary Ed.	
Soc. Studies Ed.	
Special Ed.	2
Other	

Student Body Demographics: Average Age 38, 83% female, 17% male
Percent Ethnic Minorities: N/A
Geographic Representation: N/A
Graduate Career Paths: K-12 Teaching 100%
Tuition: 148/hr (in state), 148/hr (out of state)
Financial Aid Recipients: 1%
Average Annual Housing Cost: N/A
Application Deadline: rolling
Number of: applicants annually 150; applicants accepted annually 123; students enrolled annually 75

Tests Required	Preferred/Min Score
Graduate Record Exam	
National Teachers Exam	
Praxis II Exam	

University of Toledo College of Education & Allied Professions

2801 W. Bancroft St., Admissions Office, Toledo, OH 43606
Admissions: (PH)419 530-2696, (FAX)419 530-4504
Dean: (PH)419 530-2925, (FAX)419 530-7719, (EMAIL)jmaynard@utnet.utoledo.edu
Total Enrollment: 20,000
Grad Enrollment: FTM 50, PTM 463, FTD 40, PTD 163, On campus 1%, Off campus 99%
Program Membership: Holmes Partnership
Academic Programs Available: MASTERS: Art Ed., Counselor Ed., Early Childhood Ed., Ed. Admin, Ed. Psych., Ed. Tech., Elementary Ed., Higher Ed., Math Ed., Mid Level Ed., Multicultural Ed., Music Ed., Physical Ed., Read/Lang Arts Ed., School Cons., Sci. Ed., Sec. Ed., Soc. Ed., Spec. Ed. DOCTORATE: Art Ed., Counselor Ed., Early Childhood Ed., Ed. Admin, Ed. Psych., Ed. Tech., Elementary Ed., Higher Ed., Math Ed., Mid Level Ed., Multicultural Ed., Music Ed., Physical Ed., Read/Lang Arts Ed., School Cons., Sci. Ed., Sec. Ed., Soc. Ed., Spec. Ed.

Library: Carlson Library, 3.3 million volumes
Computer Resources: Macintosh, Dual Platform, PCs, CD-ROM, Videodisc

Research Areas	#Faculty
Adult Education	
Art Education	6
Bilingual Education	
Counselor Education	5
Early Childhood Ed.	5
Ed. Admin	6
Ed. Tech.	4
Elementary Ed.	11
Foreign Lang. Ed.	1
Higher Ed.	4
Math Ed.	3
Mid. Lev. Ed.	6
Multicultural Ed.	5
Music Ed.	2
Physical Ed.	16
Read/Lang. Arts Ed.	5
School Counseling	5
Science Ed.	2
Secondary Ed.	2
Soc. Studies Ed.	2
Special Ed.	7
Other	14

Research Institutes/Centers: Ada D. Stephens Early Childhood Demonstration & Research Center, Center for Educational Development, Educational Improvement Center
Student Body Demographics: Average Age 34, 55% female, 45% male
Percent Ethnic Minorities: Hispanic-American 2%, Asian-American 2%, African-American 11%
Geographic Representation: New England 1%, Midwest 90%, Mid Atlantic 1%, Southwest 1%, Northwest 1%
Tuition: 1,686 (in state), 3,356 (out of state)
Financial Aid Recipients: N/A
Average Annual Housing Cost: 5,560
Application Deadline: rolling
Number of: applicants annually 975; applicants accepted annually 771; students enrolled annually 720

Tests Required	Preferred/Min Score
Graduate Record Exam	800–1,200
National Teachers Exam	
Praxis II Exam	
TOEFL	500–550

OKLAHOMA

Northwestern Oklahoma State University School of Education, Psychology and HPE

709 Oklahome Road, Alva, OK 73717
Admissions: (PH)405 327-1700, (FAX)405 327-1881
Dean: (PH)405 327-8455, (EMAIL)(405) 327-1881

Total Enrollment: 1,000–5,000
Grad Enrollment: On campus 2%, Off campus 98%
Program Membership: N/A
Academic Programs Available: MASTERS: Counselor Ed., Early Childhood Ed., Ed. Admin, Elementary Ed., Read/Lang Arts Ed., School Cons., Sec. Ed., DOCTORATE: Counselor Ed., Early Childhood Ed., Ed. Admin, Elementary Ed., Read/Lang Arts Ed., School Cons., Sec. Ed.
Library: J. W. Martin Library, 785,000 volumes
Computer Resources: Macintosh, Dual Platform, PCs, CD-ROM, Videodisc

Research Areas	#Faculty
Adult Education	
Art Education	
Bilingual Education	
Counselor Education	2
Early Childhood Ed.	2
Ed. Admin	1
Ed. Tech.	1
Elementary Ed.	
Foreign Lang. Ed.	
Higher Ed.	
Math Ed.	
Mid. Lev. Ed.	
Multicultural Ed.	
Music Ed.	
Physical Ed.	
Read/Lang. Arts Ed.	
School Counseling	2
Science Ed.	
Secondary Ed.	
Soc. Studies Ed.	
Special Ed.	
Other	

Student Body Demographics: Average Age 37, 72% female, 28% male
Percent Ethnic Minorities: N/A
Geographic Representation: New England 2%, Midwest 80%, Mid Atlantic 1%, Southwest 10%, West 1%, Southeast 5%, Northwest 1%
Graduate Career Paths: K-12 Teaching 60%, Higher Ed Teaching 10%, School Counseling 15%, K-12 School Administration 10%
Tuition: 65/hr (in state), 155/hr (out of state)
Financial Aid Recipients: N/A
Average Annual Housing Cost: 1,100
Application Deadline: N/A
Number of: applicants annually N/A; applicants accepted annually N/A; students enrolled annually N/A

Tests Required	Preferred/Min Score
Graduate Record Exam	900
National Teachers Exam	
Praxis II Exam	
TOEFL	550

Oklahoma State University
College of Education

Graduate College, 202 Whitehurst, Stillwater, OK 74078
Admissions: (PH)405 744-6501, (FAX)405 744-6244, (EMAIL)grad-l@okway.okstate.edu
Dean: (PH)405 744-9463, (FAX)405 744-6399
Total Enrollment: 10,000–20,000
Grad Enrollment: FTM 88, PTM 202, FTD 34, PTD 209, On campus 5%, Off campus 95%
Program Membership: Holmes Partnership
Academic Programs Available: MASTERS: Adult Ed., Art Ed., Counselor Ed., Early Childhood Ed., Ed. Admin, Ed. Psych., Ed. Tech., Elementary Ed., Higher Ed., Math Ed., Physical Ed., Read/Lang Arts Ed., School Cons., Sci. Ed., Sec. Ed., Soc. Ed., Spec. Ed. DOCTORATE: Adult Ed., Art Ed., Counselor Ed., Early Childhood Ed., Ed. Admin, Ed. Psych., Ed. Tech., Elementary Ed., Higher Ed., Math Ed., Physical Ed., Read/Lang Arts Ed., School Cons., Sci. Ed., Sec. Ed., Soc. Ed., Spec. Ed.
Library: Edmon Low Library, 5.5 million volumes
Computer Resources: Macintosh, Dual Platform, PCs, CD-ROM, Videodisc

Research Areas	#Faculty
Adult Education	5
Art Education	1
Bilingual Education	
Counselor Education	2
Early Childhood Ed.	3
Ed. Admin	10
Ed. Tech.	1
Elementary Ed.	10
Foreign Lang. Ed.	
Higher Ed.	3
Math Ed.	3
Mid. Lev. Ed.	3
Multicultural Ed.	7
Music Ed.	
Physical Ed.	4
Read/Lang. Arts Ed.	3
School Counseling	4
Science Ed.	2
Secondary Ed.	2
Soc. Studies Ed.	2
Special Ed.	6
Other	21

Student Body Demographics: Average Age 32, 60% female, 40% male
Percent Ethnic Minorities: Hispanic-American 2%, Asian-American 3%, African-American 3%, Native-American 4%
Geographic Representation: New England 5%, Midwest 35%, Mid Atlantic 5%, Southwest 35%, West 3%, Southeast 10%, Northwest 2%
Graduate Career Paths: K-12 Teaching 10%, Higher Ed Teaching 35%, School Counseling 1%, K-12 Special Ed 3%, School Administration 10%, Higher Ed Administration 5%, Higher Ed Counseling 5%, Community Counseling 12%
Tuition: 80/sch (in state), 228/sch (out of state)
Financial Aid Recipients: 50%

Average Annual Housing Cost: 3,000
Application Deadline: 10/1; 2/1; 4/15
Number of: applicants annually 350; applicants accepted annually 198; students enrolled annually N/A

Tests Required	Preferred/Min Score
Graduate Record Exam	950
National Teachers Exam	
Praxis II Exam	
TOEFL	550

Oral Roberts University School of Education

7777 S. Lewis Avenue, Tulsa, OK 74171
Admissions: (PH)918 495-6665, (FAX)918 495-6050
Dean: (PH)918 495-7084, (FAX)918 495-6050
Total Enrollment: 5,000–10,000
Grad Enrollment: FTM 52, PTM 85, On campus 2%, Off campus 98%
Program Membership: N/A
Academic Programs Available: MASTERS: Art Ed., Early Childhood Ed., Ed. Admin, Elementary Ed., Math Ed., Music Ed., Physical Ed., Sci. Ed., Sec. Ed., Soc. Ed., DOCTORATE: Art Ed., Early Childhood Ed., Ed. Admin, Elementary Ed., Math Ed., Music Ed., Physical Ed., Sci. Ed., Sec. Ed., Soc. Ed.
Library: Oral Roberts University Library, 750,000 volumes
Computer Resources: Macintosh, Dual Platform, PCs, CD-ROM, Videodisc

Research Areas	#Faculty
Adult Education	
Art Education	
Bilingual Education	
Counselor Education	
Early Childhood Ed.	1
Ed. Admin	3
Ed. Tech.	
Elementary Ed.	
Foreign Lang. Ed.	
Higher Ed.	
Math Ed.	
Mid. Lev. Ed.	
Multicultural Ed.	
Music Ed.	
Physical Ed.	
Read/Lang. Arts Ed.	
School Counseling	
Science Ed.	
Secondary Ed.	
Soc. Studies Ed.	
Special Ed.	
Other	

Student Body Demographics: Average Age 32, 74% female, 26% male
Percent Ethnic Minorities: Hispanic-American 1%, Asian-American 1%, African-American 13%, Native-American 1%
Geographic Representation: New England 1%, Midwest 45%, Mid Atlantic 1%, Southwest 50%, West 1%, Southeast 1%, Northwest 1%
Graduate Career Paths: K-12 Teaching 65%, K-12 School Administration 20%

Tuition: 215/hr (in state), 215/hr (out of state)
Financial Aid Recipients: 90%
Average Annual Housing Cost: 4,475
Application Deadline: 8/1; 1/1; 5/1
Number of: applicants annually 140; applicants accepted annually 130; students enrolled annually N/A

Tests Required	Preferred/Min Score
Graduate Record Exam	1,000
National Teachers Exam	
Praxis II Exam	
TOEFL	550

Southern Nazarene University School of Education

6729 N.W. 39th Expressway, Bethany, OK 73008
Admissions: (PH)405 491-6316, (FAX)405 491-6302
Dean: (PH)405 491-6316
Total Enrollment: 1,000–5,000
Program Membership: N/A
Academic Programs Available: MASTERS: Early Childhood Ed., Elementary Ed., Read/Lang Arts Ed., DOCTORATE: Early Childhood Ed., Elementary Ed., Read/Lang Arts Ed.
Library: 168,000 volumes

Research Areas	#Faculty
Adult Education	
Art Education	
Bilingual Education	
Counselor Education	
Early Childhood Ed.	1
Ed. Admin	
Ed. Tech.	
Elementary Ed.	
Foreign Lang. Ed.	
Higher Ed.	1
Math Ed.	
Mid. Lev. Ed.	
Multicultural Ed.	
Music Ed.	
Physical Ed.	
Read/Lang. Arts Ed.	2
School Counseling	
Science Ed.	
Secondary Ed.	
Soc. Studies Ed.	
Special Ed.	1
Other	1

Research Institutes/Centers: Northwest Regional Lab
Student Body Demographics: Average Age 27, female N/A, male N/A
Percent Ethnic Minorities: N/A
Geographic Representation: N/A
Tuition: 244/cr (in state), 244/cr (out of state)
Financial Aid Recipients: N/A
Average Annual Housing Cost: N/A
Number of: applicants annually N/A; applicants accepted annually N/A; students enrolled annually N/A

Tests Required	Preferred/Min Score
Graduate Record Exam	
National Teachers Exam	
Praxis II Exam	
TOEFL	550

OREGON

George Fox College Education Department
414 N. Meridian, Newberg, OR 97132
Admissions: (PH)503 538-8383
Dean: (PH)503 538-8383
Total Enrollment: 1,000–5,000
Grad Enrollment: FTM 45, PTM 53, Off campus 100%
Program Membership: N/A
Academic Programs Available: MASTERS: Elementary Ed., Math Ed., Music Ed., Physical Ed., Sci. Ed., Sec. Ed., Soc. Ed., DOCTORATE: Elementary Ed., Math Ed., Music Ed., Physical Ed., Sci. Ed., Sec. Ed., Soc. Ed.
Library: MJ Murdock Learning Resource Center, 110,000 volumes
Computer Resources: Macintosh, Dual Platform, PCs, CD-ROM, Videodisc

Research Areas	#Faculty
Adult Education	
Art Education	
Bilingual Education	
Counselor Education	
Early Childhood Ed.	
Ed. Admin	
Ed. Tech.	2
Elementary Ed.	4
Foreign Lang. Ed.	
Higher Ed.	
Math Ed.	
Mid. Lev. Ed.	
Multicultural Ed.	
Music Ed.	
Physical Ed.	
Read/Lang. Arts Ed.	2
School Counseling	
Science Ed.	
Secondary Ed.	
Soc. Studies Ed.	
Special Ed.	
Other	

Student Body Demographics: Average Age 28, 75% female, 25% male
Percent Ethnic Minorities: Hispanic-American 1%, Native-American 1%
Geographic Representation: Midwest 4%, West 6%, Northwest 90%
Graduate Career Paths: K-12 Teaching 90%
Tuition: N/A (in state), N/A (out of state)

Financial Aid Recipients: N/A
Average Annual Housing Cost: N/A
Application Deadline: varies
Number of: applicants annually 100; applicants accepted annually 45; students enrolled annually 45

Tests Required	Preferred/Min Score
Graduate Record Exam	
National Teachers Exam	
Praxis II Exam	

Oregon State University School of Education
Office of Admission, Corvallis, OR 97331
Dean: (PH)503 737-5960, (FAX)503 737-2040
Total Enrollment: 10,000–20,000
Grad Enrollment: FTM 130, PTM 170, FTD 20, PTD 12, On campus 5%, Off campus 95%
Program Membership: Holmes Partnership
Academic Programs Available: MASTERS: Adult Ed., Counselor Ed., Ed. Tech., Elementary Ed., Math Ed., Mid Level Ed., Music Ed., Physical Ed., Read/Lang Arts Ed., Sci. Ed., DOCTORATE: Adult Ed., Counselor Ed., Ed. Tech., Elementary Ed., Math Ed., Mid Level Ed., Music Ed., Physical Ed., Read/Lang Arts Ed., Sci. Ed.
Library: Kerr Library
Computer Resources: Macintosh, Dual Platform, PCs, CD-ROM, Videodisc

Research Areas	#Faculty
Adult Education	9
Art Education	
Bilingual Education	
Counselor Education	
Early Childhood Ed.	
Ed. Admin	
Ed. Tech.	2
Elementary Ed.	4
Foreign Lang. Ed.	
Higher Ed.	
Math Ed.	3
Mid. Lev. Ed.	2
Multicultural Ed.	
Music Ed.	1
Physical Ed.	2
Read/Lang. Arts Ed.	2
School Counseling	5
Science Ed.	3
Secondary Ed.	3
Soc. Studies Ed.	
Special Ed.	
Other	2

Student Body Demographics: Average Age 29, 70% female, 30% male
Percent Ethnic Minorities: Hispanic-American 2%, Asian-American 5%, African-American 2%, Native-American 1%
Geographic Representation: Northwest 95%
Graduate Career Paths: K-12 Teaching 50%, Higher Ed Teaching 15%, School Counseling 20%, K-12 Higher Ed Administration 15%
Tuition: 1,635 (in state), 3,026 (out of state)

Financial Aid Recipients: N/A
Average Annual Housing Cost: N/A
Application Deadline: varies
Number of: applicants annually 400; applicants accepted annually 200; students enrolled annually 190

Tests Required	Preferred/Min Score
Graduate Record Exam	
National Teachers Exam	
Praxis II Exam	
TOEFL	550–575

University of Oregon College of Education

Eugene, OR 97403
Admissions: (PH)503 346-3527
Grad Enrollment: 520 total
Program Membership: Holmes Partnership
Academic Programs Available: MASTERS: Counselor Ed., Ed. Admin, Ed. Psych., Ed. Tech., Spec. Ed. DOCTORATE: Counselor Ed., Ed. Admin, Ed. Psych., Ed. Tech., Spec. Ed.
Library: N/A

Research Areas	#Faculty
Adult Education	
Art Education	
Bilingual Education	
Counselor Education	
Early Childhood Ed.	
Ed. Admin	
Ed. Tech.	
Elementary Ed.	
Foreign Lang. Ed.	
Higher Ed.	
Math Ed.	
Mid. Lev. Ed.	
Multicultural Ed.	
Music Ed.	
Physical Ed.	
Read/Lang. Arts Ed.	
School Counseling	
Science Ed.	
Secondary Ed.	
Soc. Studies Ed.	
Special Ed.	
Other	

Student Body Demographics: N/A
Percent Ethnic Minorities: N/A
Geographic Representation: N/A
Tuition: 5,376 (in state), 8,877 (out of state)
Financial Aid Recipients: N/A
Average Annual Housing Cost: N/A
Number of: applicants annually 444; applicants accepted annually 177; students enrolled annually N/A

Tests Required	Preferred/Min Score
Graduate Record Exam	
National Teachers Exam	
Praxis II Exam	

PENNSYLVANIA

Drexel University Teacher Education

32nd and Chestnut Streets, Philadelphia, PA 19104
Admissions: (PH)215 895-2400, (FAX)215 895-5939, (EMAIL)johnsomm@duvm.ocs.drexel.edu
Dean: (PH)215 895-6770, (FAX)215 895-4999, (EMAIL)reismafk@duvm.ocs.drexel.edu
Total Enrollment: 10,000–20,000
Grad Enrollment: FTM 2, PTM 75, Off campus 100%
Program Membership: N/A
Academic Programs Available: MASTERS: Elementary Ed., Math Ed., Sec. Ed., DOCTORATE: Elementary Ed., Math Ed., Sec. Ed.
Library: Haggerty Library, 493,000 volumes
Computer Resources: Macintosh, Dual Platform, PCs, CD-ROM, Videodisc

Research Areas	#Faculty
Adult Education	
Art Education	
Bilingual Education	
Counselor Education	
Early Childhood Ed.	
Ed. Admin	
Ed. Tech.	
Elementary Ed.	1
Foreign Lang. Ed.	
Higher Ed.	
Math Ed.	1
Mid. Lev. Ed.	
Multicultural Ed.	
Music Ed.	
Physical Ed.	
Read/Lang. Arts Ed.	1
School Counseling	1
Science Ed.	
Secondary Ed.	
Soc. Studies Ed.	
Special Ed.	
Other	

Research Institutes/Centers: Drexel Diagnostic Mathematics Learning Lab
Student Body Demographics: Average Age 43, 50% female, 50% male
Percent Ethnic Minorities: Hispanic-American 5%, Asian-American 10%, African-American 10%
Geographic Representation: N/A
Graduate Career Paths: K-12 Teaching 100%
Tuition: 502 (in state), 502 (out of state)
Financial Aid Recipients: 90%
Average Annual Housing Cost: N/A
Application Deadline: rolling
Number of: applicants annually 150; applicants accepted annually 75; students enrolled annually N/A

Tests Required	Preferred/Min Score
Graduate Record Exam	
National Teachers Exam	
Praxis II Exam	

Duquesne University School of Education

214 Canevin Hall, Pittsburgh, PA 15282
Admissions: (PH)412 396-6091, (FAX)412 396-5585
Dean: (PH)412 396-6093, (FAX)412 396-5585
Total Enrollment: 5,000–10,000
Grad Enrollment: FTM 217, PTM 621, FTD 34, On campus 1%, Off campus 99%
Program Membership: N/A
Academic Programs Available: MASTERS: Counselor Ed., Ed. Admin, Ed. Psych., Elementary Ed., Foreign Lang. Ed., Math Ed., Mid Level Ed., Music Ed., Read/Lang Arts Ed., School Cons., Sci. Ed., Sec. Ed., Soc. Ed., Spec. Ed. DOCTORATE: Counselor Ed., Ed. Admin, Ed. Psych., Elementary Ed., Foreign Lang. Ed., Math Ed., Mid Level Ed., Music Ed., Read/Lang Arts Ed., School Cons., Sci. Ed., Sec. Ed., Soc. Ed., Spec. Ed.
Library: Gumberg Library, 649,000 volumes
Computer Resources: Macintosh, Dual Platform, PCs, CD-ROM, Videodisc

Research Areas	#Faculty
Adult Education	
Art Education	
Bilingual Education	
Counselor Education	5
Early Childhood Ed.	
Ed. Admin	3
Ed. Tech.	
Elementary Ed.	3
Foreign Lang. Ed.	2
Higher Ed.	
Math Ed.	2
Mid. Lev. Ed.	
Multicultural Ed.	2
Music Ed.	
Physical Ed.	
Read/Lang. Arts Ed.	3
School Counseling	
Science Ed.	2
Secondary Ed.	2
Soc. Studies Ed.	1
Special Ed.	3
Other	

Student Body Demographics: Average Age 31, 75% female, 25% male
Percent Ethnic Minorities: N/A
Geographic Representation: Mid Atlantic 98%
Graduate Career Paths: K-12 Teaching 17%, School Counseling 8%, K-12 Special Ed 8%, School Administration 10%, Higher Ed Counseling 0.5%, Community Counseling 7%
Tuition: 444/cr (in state), 444/cr (out of state)
Financial Aid Recipients: 0.2%
Average Annual Housing Cost: 5,580
Application Deadline: 5/1; 8/1; 12/1
Number of: applicants annually 750-800; applicants accepted annually 475-550; students enrolled annually N/A

Tests Required	Preferred/Min Score
Graduate Record Exam	
National Teachers Exam	
Praxis II Exam	
TOEFL	550

Eastern College Education Department

10 Fairview Drive, St. Davids, PA 19087-3696
Admissions: (PH)610 341-5972, (FAX)610 341-1466
Dean: (PH)610 341-5947, (FAX)610 341-1466
Total Enrollment: 1,000–5,000
Grad Enrollment: FTM 61, PTM 211, On campus 1%, Off campus 99%
Program Membership: N/A
Academic Programs Available: MASTERS: Adult Ed., Bilingual Ed., Counselor Ed., Early Childhood Ed., Elementary Ed., Foreign Lang. Ed., Math Ed., Multicultural Ed., Physical Ed., Read/Lang Arts Ed., School Cons., Sci. Ed., Sec. Ed., Soc. Ed., Spec. Ed. DOCTORATE: Adult Ed., Bilingual Ed., Counselor Ed., Early Childhood Ed., Elementary Ed., Foreign Lang. Ed., Math Ed., Multicultural Ed., Physical Ed., Read/Lang Arts Ed., School Cons., Sci. Ed., Sec. Ed., Soc. Ed., Spec. Ed.
Library: Warner Library
Computer Resources: Macintosh, Dual Platform, PCs, CD-ROM, Videodisc

Research Areas	#Faculty
Adult Education	
Art Education	
Bilingual Education	1
Counselor Education	2
Early Childhood Ed.	1
Ed. Admin	
Ed. Tech.	
Elementary Ed.	1
Foreign Lang. Ed.	3
Higher Ed.	
Math Ed.	1
Mid. Lev. Ed.	
Multicultural Ed.	5
Music Ed.	
Physical Ed.	
Read/Lang. Arts Ed.	1
School Counseling	2
Science Ed.	1
Secondary Ed.	1
Soc. Studies Ed.	1
Special Ed.	1
Other	

Student Body Demographics: Average Age N/A, 64% female, 36% male
Percent Ethnic Minorities: Hispanic-American 1%, Asian-American 2%, African-American 15%, Native-American 1%
Geographic Representation: New England 15%, Midwest 4%, Mid Atlantic 75%, Southwest 1%, West 3%, Southeast 2%
Tuition: 325/cr (in state), 325/cr (out of state)
Financial Aid Recipients: N/A
Average Annual Housing Cost: 4,300
Application Deadline: rolling

Number of: applicants annually 181; applicants accepted annually 162; students enrolled annually N/A

Tests Required	Preferred/Min Score
Graduate Record Exam	
National Teachers Exam	
Praxis II Exam	

Gwynedd Mercy College
Graduate Education Division

118 Connelly Faculty Center, Gwynedd Valley, PA 19437
Admissions: (PH)215 641-5561, (EMAIL)vurdien@hslc.org
Dean: (PH)215 641-5525
Total Enrollment: 1,000–5,000
Grad Enrollment: PTM 225, Off campus 100%
Program Membership: N/A
Academic Programs Available: MASTERS: Counselor Ed., Ed. Admin, Read/Lang Arts Ed., School Cons., DOCTORATE: Counselor Ed., Ed. Admin, Read/Lang Arts Ed., School Cons.
Library: Lourdes Library

Research Areas	#Faculty
Adult Education	
Art Education	
Bilingual Education	
Counselor Education	
Early Childhood Ed.	
Ed. Admin	
Ed. Tech.	
Elementary Ed.	
Foreign Lang. Ed.	
Higher Ed.	
Math Ed.	
Mid. Lev. Ed.	
Multicultural Ed.	
Music Ed.	
Physical Ed.	
Read/Lang. Arts Ed.	1
School Counseling	
Science Ed.	
Secondary Ed.	
Soc. Studies Ed.	
Special Ed.	
Other	

Student Body Demographics: Average Age 33, 98% female, 2% male
Percent Ethnic Minorities: N/A
Geographic Representation: N/A
Graduate Career Paths: K-12 Teaching 50%
Tuition: 280 (in state), 280 (out of state)
Financial Aid Recipients: N/A
Average Annual Housing Cost: N/A
Application Deadline: rolling
Number of: applicants annually 100; applicants accepted annually 95; students enrolled annually 90

Tests Required	Preferred/Min Score
Graduate Record Exam	
National Teachers Exam	
Praxis II Exam	

Immaculata College Educational Leadership and Administration

Graduate Division, Immaculata, PA 19345-0500
Admissions: (PH)610 647-4400 x3211, (FAX)610 251-1668
Total Enrollment: 1,000
Grad Enrollment: On campus 1%, Off campus 99%
Program Membership: N/A
Academic Programs Available: MASTERS: Bilingual Ed., Counselor Ed., Ed. Admin, Elementary Ed., Higher Ed., Multicultural Ed., Music Ed., School Cons., DOCTORATE: Bilingual Ed., Counselor Ed., Ed. Admin, Elementary Ed., Higher Ed., Multicultural Ed., Music Ed., School Cons.
Library: Gabriele Library, 130,000 volumes
Computer Resources: Macintosh, Dual Platform, PCs, CD-ROM, Videodisc

Research Areas	#Faculty
Adult Education	
Art Education	
Bilingual Education	
Counselor Education	
Early Childhood Ed.	
Ed. Admin	
Ed. Tech.	
Elementary Ed.	
Foreign Lang. Ed.	
Higher Ed.	
Math Ed.	
Mid. Lev. Ed.	
Multicultural Ed.	
Music Ed.	
Physical Ed.	
Read/Lang. Arts Ed.	
School Counseling	
Science Ed.	
Secondary Ed.	
Soc. Studies Ed.	
Special Ed.	
Other	

Student Body Demographics: Average Age 33, 52% female, 48% male
Percent Ethnic Minorities: N/A
Geographic Representation: Mid Atlantic 98%
Tuition: 330/hr (in state), 330/hr (out of state)
Financial Aid Recipients: 85%
Average Annual Housing Cost: 512
Application Deadline: rolling
Number of: applicants annually 470; applicants accepted annually 420; students enrolled annually 215

Tests Required	Preferred/Min Score
Graduate Record Exam	1,000
National Teachers Exam	
Praxis II Exam	
TOEFL	550

Indiana University of Pennsylvania College of Education

101 Stright Hall, Indiana, PA 15705
Admissions: (PH)412 357-2222, (FAX)412 357-4862, (EMAIL)cvaneman@grove.iup.edu
Dean: (PH)412 357-2480, (FAX)412 357-5595, (EMAIL)jwbutzow@grove.iup.edu
Total Enrollment: 10,000–20,000
Grad Enrollment: FTM 366, PTM 168, FTD 123, PTD 161, CAS 14, Off campus 100%
Program Membership: N/A
Academic Programs Available: MASTERS: Adult Ed., Counselor Ed., Early Childhood Ed., Ed. Admin, Ed. Psych., Elementary Ed., Higher Ed., Math Ed., Mid Level Ed., Read/Lang Arts Ed., School Cons., Spec. Ed. DOCTORATE: Adult Ed., Counselor Ed., Early Childhood Ed., Ed. Admin, Ed. Psych., Elementary Ed., Higher Ed., Math Ed., Mid Level Ed., Read/Lang Arts Ed., School Cons., Spec. Ed.
Library: Stapleton Library
Computer Resources: Macintosh, Dual Platform, PCs, CD-ROM, Videodisc

Research Areas	#Faculty
Adult Education	2
Art Education	
Bilingual Education	
Counselor Education	3
Early Childhood Ed.	4
Ed. Admin	2
Ed. Tech.	5
Elementary Ed.	20
Foreign Lang. Ed.	
Higher Ed.	3
Math Ed.	5
Mid. Lev. Ed.	
Multicultural Ed.	2
Music Ed.	
Physical Ed.	
Read/Lang. Arts Ed.	4
School Counseling	3
Science Ed.	3
Secondary Ed.	3
Soc. Studies Ed.	2
Special Ed.	15
Other	

Student Body Demographics: Average Age N/A, 79% female, 21% male
Percent Ethnic Minorities: Hispanic-American 10%, Asian-American 1%, African-American 5%, Native-American 1%
Geographic Representation: Mid Atlantic 95%
Graduate Career Paths: K-12 Teaching 42%, Higher Ed Teaching 1%, School Counseling 7%, K-12 Special Ed 3%, School Administration 6%, Higher Ed Administration 13%, Community Counseling 9%
Tuition: 1,612 (in state), 2,897 (out of state)
Financial Aid Recipients: N/A
Average Annual Housing Cost: 2,000
Application Deadline: rolling

Number of: applicants annually 460; applicants accepted annually 329; students enrolled annually N/A

Tests Required	Preferred/Min Score
Graduate Record Exam	
National Teachers Exam	
Praxis II Exam	
TOEFL	500

Kutztown University College of Graduate Studies and Extended Learning

Graduate Centre, Kutztown, PA 19530
Admissions: (PH)610 683-4200
Dean: (PH)610 683-4200, (FAX)610 683-1393, (EMAIL)ezell@kutztown.edu
Total Enrollment: 5,000–10,000
Grad Enrollment: FTM 20, PTM 610, Off campus 100%
Program Membership: N/A
Academic Programs Available: MASTERS: Art Ed., Counselor Ed., Elementary Ed., Higher Ed., Math Ed., School Cons., Sci. Ed., Sec. Ed., Soc. Ed., DOCTORATE: Art Ed., Counselor Ed., Elementary Ed., Higher Ed., Math Ed., School Cons., Sci. Ed., Sec. Ed., Soc. Ed.
Library: Rohrbach Library, 350,000 volumes
Computer Resources: Macintosh, Dual Platform, PCs, CD-ROM, Videodisc

Research Areas	#Faculty
Adult Education	
Art Education	15
Bilingual Education	
Counselor Education	12
Early Childhood Ed.	
Ed. Admin	
Ed. Tech.	
Elementary Ed.	16
Foreign Lang. Ed.	
Higher Ed.	
Math Ed.	18
Mid. Lev. Ed.	
Multicultural Ed.	
Music Ed.	
Physical Ed.	
Read/Lang. Arts Ed.	5
School Counseling	7
Science Ed.	10
Secondary Ed.	10
Soc. Studies Ed.	5
Special Ed.	2
Other	

Student Body Demographics: Average Age 33, 70% female, 30% male
Percent Ethnic Minorities: N/A
Geographic Representation: N/A
Tuition: 1,905 (in state), 3,190 (out of state)
Financial Aid Recipients: 10%
Average Annual Housing Cost: N/A
Application Deadline: 3/1; 7/1
Number of: applicants annually N/A; applicants accepted annually N/A; students enrolled annually 800

Tests Required   Preferred/Min Score
Graduate Record Exam
National Teachers Exam
Praxis II Exam

La Salle University Graduate Programs in Education

1900 West Olney Avenue, Philadelphia, PA 19141
Admissions: (PH)215 951-1593, (FAX)215 951-1843
Dean: (PH)215 951-1593, (FAX)215 951-1843
Total Enrollment: 5,000–10,000
Grad Enrollment: FTM 75, PTM 88, On campus 2%, Off campus 98%
Program Membership: N/A
Academic Programs Available: MASTERS: Bilingual Ed., Elementary Ed., Foreign Lang. Ed., Math Ed., Sci. Ed., Sec. Ed., Soc. Ed., DOCTORATE: Bilingual Ed., Elementary Ed., Foreign Lang. Ed., Math Ed., Sci. Ed., Sec. Ed., Soc. Ed.
Library: Connelly Library, 280,000 volumes
Computer Resources: Macintosh, Dual Platform, PCs, CD-ROM, Videodisc

Research Areas	#Faculty
Adult Education	
Art Education	
Bilingual Education	
Counselor Education	
Early Childhood Ed.	
Ed. Admin	
Ed. Tech.	
Elementary Ed.	
Foreign Lang. Ed.	
Higher Ed.	
Math Ed.	
Mid. Lev. Ed.	
Multicultural Ed.	
Music Ed.	
Physical Ed.	
Read/Lang. Arts Ed.	
School Counseling	
Science Ed.	
Secondary Ed.	
Soc. Studies Ed.	
Special Ed.	
Other	

Student Body Demographics: Average Age 34, 63% female, 37% male
Percent Ethnic Minorities: N/A
Geographic Representation: N/A
Graduate Career Paths: K-12 Teaching 69%
Tuition: 395/cr (in state), 395/cr (out of state)
Financial Aid Recipients: 35%
Average Annual Housing Cost: 3,400
Application Deadline: N/A
Number of: applicants annually 100; applicants accepted annually 58; students enrolled annually 55

Tests Required   Preferred/Min Score
Graduate Record Exam
National Teachers Exam
Praxis II Exam

Lehigh University College of Education

111 Research Drive, Bethlehem, PA 18015
Admissions: (PH)610 758-3221
Dean: (PH)610 758-3221
Total Enrollment: 5,000–10,000
Grad Enrollment: 500 total, Off campus 99%
Program Membership: Holmes Partnership
Academic Programs Available: MASTERS: Counselor Ed., Ed. Admin, Ed. Tech., Elementary Ed., Multicultural Ed., Read/Lang Arts Ed., School Cons., Sec. Ed., Spec. Ed. DOCTORATE: Counselor Ed., Ed. Admin, Ed. Tech., Elementary Ed., Multicultural Ed., Read/Lang Arts Ed., School Cons., Sec. Ed., Spec. Ed.
Library: 900,000 volumes
Computer Resources: Macintosh, PCs

Research Areas	#Faculty
Adult Education	1
Art Education	
Bilingual Education	
Counselor Education	3
Early Childhood Ed.	1
Ed. Admin	2
Ed. Tech.	5
Elementary Ed.	2
Foreign Lang. Ed.	
Higher Ed.	
Math Ed.	1
Mid. Lev. Ed.	1
Multicultural Ed.	1
Music Ed.	
Physical Ed.	
Read/Lang. Arts Ed.	6
School Counseling	1
Science Ed.	2
Secondary Ed.	2
Soc. Studies Ed.	
Special Ed.	4
Other	

Student Body Demographics: N/A
Percent Ethnic Minorities: N/A
Geographic Representation: N/A
Tuition: 430 (in state), 430 (out of state)
Financial Aid Recipients: N/A
Average Annual Housing Cost: 4,050
Application Deadline: 2/1
Number of: applicants annually N/A; applicants accepted annually N/A; students enrolled annually N/A

Tests Required   Preferred/Min Score
Graduate Record Exam
National Teachers Exam
Praxis II Exam

Marywood College Graduate Education Department

Graduate School of Arts and Sciences Admissions Office, Scranton, PA 18509
Admissions: (PH)717 348-6211 x2393, (FAX)717 961-4745
Dean: (PH)717 348-6230, (FAX)717 961-4745
Total Enrollment: 1,000–5,000
Grad Enrollment: FTM 37, PTM 153, On campus 3%, Off campus 97%
Program Membership: N/A
Academic Programs Available: MASTERS: Art Ed., Counselor Ed., Early Childhood Ed., Ed. Admin, Ed. Tech., Elementary Ed., Music Ed., Read/Lang Arts Ed., School Cons., Spec. Ed. DOCTORATE: Art Ed., Counselor Ed., Early Childhood Ed., Ed. Admin, Ed. Tech., Elementary Ed., Music Ed., Read/Lang Arts Ed., School Cons., Spec. Ed.
Library: Learning Resource Center, 202,000 volumes
Computer Resources: Macintosh, Dual Platform, PCs, CD-ROM, Videodisc

Research Areas	#Faculty
Adult Education	
Art Education	
Bilingual Education	
Counselor Education	3
Early Childhood Ed.	
Ed. Admin	3
Ed. Tech.	
Elementary Ed.	
Foreign Lang. Ed.	
Higher Ed.	
Math Ed.	
Mid. Lev. Ed.	
Multicultural Ed.	
Music Ed.	
Physical Ed.	
Read/Lang. Arts Ed.	1
School Counseling	
Science Ed.	
Secondary Ed.	
Soc. Studies Ed.	
Special Ed.	2
Other	

Research Institutes/Centers: Military Family Institute
Student Body Demographics: Average Age 32, 88% female, 12% male
Percent Ethnic Minorities: N/A
Geographic Representation: Mid Atlantic 100%
Graduate Career Paths: K-12 Teaching 51%, School Counseling 23%, K-12 Special Ed 17%, School Administration 9%
Tuition: 6,890 (in state), 6,890 (out of state)
Financial Aid Recipients: 40%
Average Annual Housing Cost: 4,800
Application Deadline: 7/15; 12/1
Number of: applicants annually 68; applicants accepted annually 56; students enrolled annually 35

Tests Required	Preferred/Min Score
Graduate Record Exam	
National Teachers Exam	
Praxis II Exam	

Pennsylvania State University at Harrisburg Division of Behavioral Sciences and Education

Middletown, PA 17057
Admissions: (PH)717 948-6250, (FAX)tis1@psuvm.adm, (EMAIL)(717) 948-6325
Dean: (PH)717 948-6205, (FAX)717 948-6209, (EMAIL)wah1@oas.psu.edu
Total Enrollment: 1,000–5,000
Grad Enrollment: PTD 46
Program Membership: N/A
Academic Programs Available: MASTERS: Adult Ed., DOCTORATE: Adult Ed.
Library: Heindel Library
Computer Resources: Macintosh, Dual Platform, PCs, CD-ROM, Videodisc

Research Areas	#Faculty
Adult Education	1
Art Education	1
Bilingual Education	
Counselor Education	
Early Childhood Ed.	2
Ed. Admin	2
Ed. Tech.	1
Elementary Ed.	12
Foreign Lang. Ed.	
Higher Ed.	
Math Ed.	2
Mid. Lev. Ed.	
Multicultural Ed.	
Music Ed.	1
Physical Ed.	
Read/Lang. Arts Ed.	4
School Counseling	
Science Ed.	1
Secondary Ed.	1
Soc. Studies Ed.	1
Special Ed.	
Other	

Research Institutes/Centers: Center for Interdisciplinary Education, Center for Economic Education
Student Body Demographics: Average Age 29, 75% female, 25% male
Percent Ethnic Minorities: N/A
Geographic Representation: N/A
Graduate Career Paths: K-12 Teaching 96%, Higher Ed Teaching 2%, K-12 School Administration 2%
Tuition: 234/cl (in state), 473/cl (out of state)
Financial Aid Recipients: N/A
Average Annual Housing Cost: N/A
Application Deadline: N/A
Number of: applicants annually N/A; applicants accepted annually N/A; students enrolled annually N/A

Tests Required	Preferred/Min Score
Graduate Record Exam	850
National Teachers Exam	
Praxis II Exam	

Pennsylvania State University
College of Education

201 Kern Building, University Park, PA 16802
Admissions: (PH)814 865-1795, (FAX)814 863-4627
Dean: (PH)814 865-2526, (FAX)814 865-0555,
(EMAIL)slmi@psuadmin
Total Enrollment: 20,000
Grad Enrollment: FTM 151, PTM 279, FTD 274, PTD 333, On campus 30%, Off campus 70%
Program Membership: Holmes Partnership
Academic Programs Available: MASTERS: Adult Ed., Counselor Ed., Ed. Admin, Ed. Psych., Ed. Tech., Elementary Ed., Higher Ed., Math Ed., Read/Lang Arts Ed., School Cons., Sci. Ed., Sec. Ed., Soc. Ed., Spec. Ed. DOCTORATE: Adult Ed., Counselor Ed., Ed. Admin, Ed. Psych., Ed. Tech., Elementary Ed., Higher Ed., Math Ed., Read/Lang Arts Ed., School Cons., Sci. Ed., Sec. Ed., Soc. Ed., Spec. Ed.
Library: Pattee Library
Computer Resources: Macintosh, Dual Platform, PCs, CD-ROM, Videodisc

Research Areas	#Faculty
Adult Education	4
Art Education	
Bilingual Education	2
Counselor Education	5
Early Childhood Ed.	3
Ed. Admin	6
Ed. Tech.	6
Elementary Ed.	7
Foreign Lang. Ed.	1
Higher Ed.	6
Math Ed.	4
Mid. Lev. Ed.	2
Multicultural Ed.	3
Music Ed.	
Physical Ed.	
Read/Lang. Arts Ed.	5
School Counseling	2
Science Ed.	4
Secondary Ed.	4
Soc. Studies Ed.	3
Special Ed.	8
Other	

Research Institutes/Centers: Institute for the Study of Adult Literacy, Center for Total Quality Management of Schools
Student Body Demographics: Average Age 32, 60% female, 40% male
Percent Ethnic Minorities: Hispanic-American 1%, Asian-American 1%, African-American 8%, Native-American 0.5%
Geographic Representation: New England 5%, Midwest 10%, Mid Atlantic 60%, Southwest 5%, West 5%, Southeast 10%, Northwest 5%
Graduate Career Paths: K-12 Teaching 4%, Higher Ed Teaching 48%, School Counseling 5%, K-12 Special Ed 2%, School Administration 11%, Higher Ed Administration 8%, Higher Ed Counseling 4%, Community Counseling 1%
Tuition: 5,316 (in state), 10632 (out of state)

Financial Aid Recipients: 25%
Average Annual Housing Cost: N/A
Number of: applicants annually 600–700; applicants accepted annually 130-150; students enrolled annually N/A

Tests Required	Preferred/Min Score
Graduate Record Exam	
National Teachers Exam	
Praxis II Exam	
TOEFL	550–600

Robert Morris College Education Department

Admissions Office, Coraopolis, PA 15108
Admissions: (PH)412 262-8304, (FAX)412 262-8619, (EMAIL)zimmer@robert-morris.edu
Dean: (PH)412 262-8279, (FAX)412 262-8494, (EMAIL)shank@robert-morris.edu
Total Enrollment: 5,000–10,000
Grad Enrollment: FTM 2, PTM 45, Off campus 100%
Program Membership: N/A
Academic Programs Available: N/A
Library: Patrick Henry Library, 122,000 volumes
Computer Resources: Macintosh, Dual Platform, PCs, CD-ROM, Videodisc

Research Areas	#Faculty
Adult Education	
Art Education	
Bilingual Education	
Counselor Education	
Early Childhood Ed.	
Ed. Admin	
Ed. Tech.	
Elementary Ed.	
Foreign Lang. Ed.	
Higher Ed.	
Math Ed.	1
Mid. Lev. Ed.	
Multicultural Ed.	
Music Ed.	
Physical Ed.	
Read/Lang. Arts Ed.	
School Counseling	
Science Ed.	
Secondary Ed.	
Soc. Studies Ed.	
Special Ed.	
Other	7

Student Body Demographics: Average Age 32, 95% female, 5% male
Percent Ethnic Minorities: N/A
Geographic Representation: Mid Atlantic 100%
Graduate Career Paths: K-12 Teaching 70%, Higher Ed Teaching 15%
Tuition: 263/cr (in state), 263/cr (out of state)
Financial Aid Recipients: N/A
Average Annual Housing Cost: 4,448
Application Deadline: 12/1; 6/1; 8/1
Number of: applicants annually 52; applicants accepted annually 52; students enrolled annually 44

Tests Required   **Preferred/Min Score**
Graduate Record Exam
National Teachers Exam
Praxis II Exam

Seton Hill College

Greensburg, PA 15601-1599
Admissions: (PH)412 838-4250, (FAX)412 830-4611
Dean: (PH)412 838-4216, (FAX)412 2752
Total Enrollment: 1,000
Grad Enrollment: FTM 25, Off campus 100%
Program Membership: N/A
Academic Programs Available: MASTERS: Elementary Ed., DOCTORATE: Elementary Ed.
Library: Reeves Memorial Library, 113,000 volumes
Computer Resources: Macintosh, Dual Platform, PCs, CD-ROM, Videodisc

Research Areas	#Faculty
Adult Education	
Art Education	
Bilingual Education	
Counselor Education	
Early Childhood Ed.	
Ed. Admin	
Ed. Tech.	1
Elementary Ed.	1
Foreign Lang. Ed.	1
Higher Ed.	
Math Ed.	
Mid. Lev. Ed.	
Multicultural Ed.	
Music Ed.	1
Physical Ed.	
Read/Lang. Arts Ed.	1
School Counseling	
Science Ed.	
Secondary Ed.	
Soc. Studies Ed.	1
Special Ed.	1
Other	

Student Body Demographics: Average Age 30, 90% female, 10% male
Percent Ethnic Minorities: N/A
Geographic Representation: N/A
Graduate Career Paths: K-12 Teaching 100%
Tuition: 540/cr (in state), 540/cr (out of state)
Financial Aid Recipients: N/A
Average Annual Housing Cost: N/A
Application Deadline: 6/1; 8/1; 1/1
Number of: applicants annually 35; applicants accepted annually 30; students enrolled annually 23

Tests Required	Preferred/Min Score
Graduate Record Exam	960–1,140
National Teachers Exam	
Praxis II Exam	

Shippensburg University of Pennsylvania Teacher Education Department

Graduate Office, 1871 Old Main Drive, Shippensburg, PA 17257
Admissions: (PH)717 532-1213, (FAX)717 532-1273, (EMAIL)gradschool@ark.ship.edu
Dean: (PH)717 532-1213, (FAX)717 532-1273
Total Enrollment: 1,000–5,000
Grad Enrollment: FTM 17, PTM 36, Off campus 100%
Program Membership: N/A
Academic Programs Available: MASTERS: Counselor Ed., Ed. Admin, Ed. Tech., Elementary Ed., Math Ed., Mid Level Ed., Read/Lang Arts Ed., School Cons., Sec. Ed., Spec. Ed. DOCTORATE: Counselor Ed., Ed. Admin, Ed. Tech., Elementary Ed., Math Ed., Mid Level Ed., Read/Lang Arts Ed., School Cons., Sec. Ed., Spec. Ed.
Library: Ezra Lehman Memorial Library, 425,000 volumes
Computer Resources: Macintosh, Dual Platform, PCs, CD-ROM, Videodisc

Research Areas	#Faculty
Adult Education	
Art Education	
Bilingual Education	
Counselor Education	
Early Childhood Ed.	
Ed. Admin	
Ed. Tech.	
Elementary Ed.	
Foreign Lang. Ed.	
Higher Ed.	
Math Ed.	
Mid. Lev. Ed.	
Multicultural Ed.	
Music Ed.	
Physical Ed.	
Read/Lang. Arts Ed.	
School Counseling	
Science Ed.	
Secondary Ed.	
Soc. Studies Ed.	
Special Ed.	
Other	

Student Body Demographics: Average Age 27, 57% female, 43% male
Percent Ethnic Minorities: Hispanic-American 8%, Asian-American 5%, African-American 3.4%, Native-American 2%
Geographic Representation: N/A
Tuition: 171/cr (in state), 289/cr (out of state)
Financial Aid Recipients: 40%
Average Annual Housing Cost: 400
Application Deadline: varies
Number of: applicants annually 903; applicants accepted annually 854; students enrolled annually 535

Tests Required	Preferred/Min Score
Graduate Record Exam	1,000
National Teachers Exam	
Praxis II Exam	
TOEFL	560

St. Joseph's University

Education and Health Services, Admissions Office,
Philadelphia, PA 19131
Admissions: (PH)610 660-1289, (FAX)610 660-1264
Dean: (PH)610 660-1289, (FAX)610 660-1264
Total Enrollment: 5,000–10,000
Grad Enrollment: FTM 48, PTM 410, Off campus 100%
Program Membership: N/A
Academic Programs Available: MASTERS: Ed. Admin,
Elementary Ed., Math Ed., Read/Lang Arts Ed., Sec. Ed.,
DOCTORATE: Ed. Admin, Elementary Ed., Math Ed.,
Read/Lang Arts Ed., Sec. Ed.
Library: Drexel Library
Computer Resources: Macintosh, Dual Platform, PCs,
CD-ROM, Videodisc

Research Areas	#Faculty
Adult Education	
Art Education	
Bilingual Education	
Counselor Education	
Early Childhood Ed.	
Ed. Admin	1
Ed. Tech.	
Elementary Ed.	4
Foreign Lang. Ed.	1
Higher Ed.	
Math Ed.	
Mid. Lev. Ed.	
Multicultural Ed.	
Music Ed.	
Physical Ed.	
Read/Lang. Arts Ed.	3
School Counseling	
Science Ed.	1
Secondary Ed.	1
Soc. Studies Ed.	
Special Ed.	
Other	

Student Body Demographics: Average Age 30, 75% female,
25% male
Percent Ethnic Minorities: Hispanic-American 3%,
Asian-American 3%, African-American 25%
Geographic Representation: N/A
Graduate Career Paths: K-12 Teaching 90%, K-12 School
Administration 10%
Tuition: 693/cse (in state), 693/cse (out of state)
Financial Aid Recipients: 90%
Average Annual Housing Cost: N/A
Application Deadline: rolling
Number of: applicants annually 300; applicants accepted
annually 150; students enrolled annually 150

Tests Required	Preferred/Min Score
Graduate Record Exam	1,000
National Teachers Exam	
Praxis II Exam	
TOEFL	500

Temple University College of Education

Philadelphia, PA 19122
Admissions: (PH)215 204-8011, (FAX)215 204-5622
Total Enrollment: 20,000
Grad Enrollment: 1396 total
Program Membership: Holmes Partnership
Academic Programs Available: MASTERS: Adult Ed., Art
Ed., Ed. Admin, Ed. Psych., Ed. Tech., Elementary Ed., Math
Ed., Read/Lang Arts Ed., Sci. Ed., Sec. Ed., DOCTORATE:
Adult Ed., Art Ed., Ed. Admin, Ed. Psych., Ed. Tech.,
Elementary Ed., Math Ed., Read/Lang Arts Ed., Sci. Ed., Sec.
Ed.
Library: N/A

Research Areas	#Faculty
Adult Education	
Art Education	
Bilingual Education	
Counselor Education	
Early Childhood Ed.	
Ed. Admin	
Ed. Tech.	
Elementary Ed.	
Foreign Lang. Ed.	
Higher Ed.	
Math Ed.	
Mid. Lev. Ed.	
Multicultural Ed.	
Music Ed.	
Physical Ed.	
Read/Lang. Arts Ed.	
School Counseling	
Science Ed.	
Secondary Ed.	
Soc. Studies Ed.	
Special Ed.	
Other	

Student Body Demographics: N/A
Percent Ethnic Minorities: N/A
Geographic Representation: N/A
Tuition: 269 (in state), 382 (out of state)
Financial Aid Recipients: N/A
Average Annual Housing Cost: N/A
Number of: applicants annually 1,172; applicants accepted
annually 586; students enrolled annually N/A

Tests Required	Preferred/Min Score
Graduate Record Exam	
National Teachers Exam	
Praxis II Exam	

University of Pennsylvania Graduate School of Education

3700 Walnut Street, Philadelphia, PA 19104-6216
Admissions: (PH)215 898-6455, (FAX)215 573-2166,
(EMAIL)admissions@nwfs.gse.upenn.edu
Dean: (PH)215 898-7014
Total Enrollment: 20,000
Grad Enrollment: FTM 210, PTM 100, FTD 64, PTD 108,
CAS 311

Program Membership: Holmes Partnership
Academic Programs Available: MASTERS: Bilingual Ed., Counselor Ed., Early Childhood Ed., Ed. Admin, Ed. Psych., Elementary Ed., Foreign Lang. Ed., Higher Ed., Math Ed., Mid Level Ed., Read/Lang Arts Ed., School Cons., Sec. Ed., DOCTORATE: Bilingual Ed., Counselor Ed., Early Childhood Ed., Ed. Admin, Ed. Psych., Elementary Ed., Foreign Lang. Ed., Higher Ed., Math Ed., Mid Level Ed., Read/Lang Arts Ed., School Cons., Sec. Ed.
Library: Van Pelt Library, 4 million volumes
Computer Resources: Macintosh, Dual Platform, PCs, CD-ROM, Videodisc

Research Areas	#Faculty
Adult Education	2
Art Education	
Bilingual Education	3
Counselor Education	1
Early Childhood Ed.	1
Ed. Admin	1
Ed. Tech.	1
Elementary Ed.	1
Foreign Lang. Ed.	1
Higher Ed.	2
Math Ed.	2
Mid. Lev. Ed.	1
Multicultural Ed.	4
Music Ed.	
Physical Ed.	
Read/Lang. Arts Ed.	4
School Counseling	1
Science Ed.	1
Secondary Ed.	1
Soc. Studies Ed.	1
Special Ed.	1
Other	

Research Institutes/Centers: Center for Research and Evaluation in Social Policy, Center for School Study Councils, Center for Urban Ethnography, Institute for Research on Higher Education
Student Body Demographics: Average Age 25, 75% female, 25% male
Percent Ethnic Minorities: Hispanic-American 1%, Asian-American 2%, African-American 12%, Native-American 1%
Geographic Representation: Mid Atlantic 65%
Tuition: 2,478/cse (in state), 2,478/cse (out of state)
Financial Aid Recipients: 60%
Average Annual Housing Cost: 3,600
Application Deadline: varies
Number of: applicants annually 1,072; applicants accepted annually 691; students enrolled annually 374

Tests Required	Preferred/Min Score
Graduate Record Exam	
National Teachers Exam	
Praxis II Exam	
TOEFL	550

University of Pittsburgh School of Education

5L Forbes Quadrangle, Pittsburgh, PA 15260
Admissions: (PH)412 648-2230, (FAX)412 648-1899
Dean: (PH)412 648-1769, (FAX)412 648-1825
Total Enrollment: 20,000
Grad Enrollment: FTM 656, PTM 458, FTD 216, PTD 434
Program Membership: Holmes Partnership
Academic Programs Available: MASTERS: Art Ed., Bilingual Ed., Early Childhood Ed., Ed. Admin, Ed. Psych., Ed. Tech., Elementary Ed., Foreign Lang. Ed., Higher Ed., Math Ed., Physical Ed., Read/Lang Arts Ed., School Cons., Sci. Ed., Soc. Ed., Spec. Ed. DOCTORATE: Art Ed., Bilingual Ed., Early Childhood Ed., Ed. Admin, Ed. Psych., Ed. Tech., Elementary Ed., Foreign Lang. Ed., Higher Ed., Math Ed., Physical Ed., Read/Lang Arts Ed., School Cons., Sci. Ed., Soc. Ed., Spec. Ed.
Library: Hillman Library, 1.2 million volumes
Computer Resources: Macintosh, Dual Platform, PCs, CD-ROM, Videodisc

Research Areas	#Faculty
Adult Education	
Art Education	1
Bilingual Education	1
Counselor Education	
Early Childhood Ed.	2
Ed. Admin	9
Ed. Tech.	3
Elementary Ed.	6
Foreign Lang. Ed.	1
Higher Ed.	4
Math Ed.	4
Mid. Lev. Ed.	
Multicultural Ed.	3
Music Ed.	
Physical Ed.	18
Read/Lang. Arts Ed.	5
School Counseling	4
Science Ed.	3
Secondary Ed.	3
Soc. Studies Ed.	2
Special Ed.	8
Other	

Research Institutes/Centers: International Institute for Studies in Education, Institute for Practice and Research in Education
Student Body Demographics: Average Age N/A, 67% female, 33% male
Percent Ethnic Minorities: Hispanic-American 1%, Asian-American 6%, African-American 8%
Geographic Representation: N/A
Tuition: 3,727 (in state), 7,396 (out of state)
Financial Aid Recipients: 30%
Average Annual Housing Cost: N/A
Application Deadline: 2/1; 11/15
Number of: applicants annually 2,200; applicants accepted annually 1,650; students enrolled annually 600

Tests Required	Preferred/Min Score
Graduate Record Exam	
National Teachers Exam	

Praxis II Exam
TOEFL 550–650

University of Scranton Education Department

The Graduate School, Scranton, PA 18510
Admissions: (PH)717 941-7540, (FAX)717 941-4252
Dean: (PH)717 941-7600, (FAX)717 941-4252
Total Enrollment: 5,000–10,000
Grad Enrollment: Off campus 100%
Program Membership: N/A
Academic Programs Available: MASTERS: Counselor Ed., Early Childhood Ed., Ed. Admin, Elementary Ed., School Cons., Sec. Ed., DOCTORATE: Counselor Ed., Early Childhood Ed., Ed. Admin, Elementary Ed., School Cons., Sec. Ed.
Library: Weinberg Memorial Library, 310,000 volumes
Computer Resources: Macintosh, Dual Platform, PCs, CD-ROM, Videodisc

Research Areas	#Faculty
Adult Education	
Art Education	
Bilingual Education	
Counselor Education	
Early Childhood Ed.	
Ed. Admin	2
Ed. Tech.	
Elementary Ed.	2
Foreign Lang. Ed.	1
Higher Ed.	
Math Ed.	
Mid. Lev. Ed.	
Multicultural Ed.	
Music Ed.	
Physical Ed.	
Read/Lang. Arts Ed.	3
School Counseling	
Science Ed.	1
Secondary Ed.	1
Soc. Studies Ed.	1
Special Ed.	
Other	

Student Body Demographics: Average Age 31, 66% female, 34% male
Percent Ethnic Minorities: Native-American 6%
Geographic Representation: New England 20%, Mid Atlantic 80%
Graduate Career Paths: K-12 Teaching 78%, School Counseling 10%, K-12 School Administration 12%
Tuition: 391/cr (in state), 391/cr (out of state)
Financial Aid Recipients: N/A
Average Annual Housing Cost: 400
Application Deadline: 3/1; 11/1
Number of: applicants annually 106; applicants accepted annually 97; students enrolled annually N/A

Tests Required	Preferred/Min Score
Graduate Record Exam	
National Teachers Exam	
Praxis II Exam	
TOEFL	550

RHODE ISLAND

Rhode Island College School of Education and Human Development

Providence, RI 02908-1991
Total Enrollment: 10,000–20,000
Grad Enrollment: FTM 118, PTM 344, PTD 15, CAS 54
Off campus 100%
Program Membership: N/A
Academic Programs Available: MASTERS: Art Ed., Bilingual Ed., Counselor Ed., Early Childhood Ed., Ed. Admin, Ed. Psych., Elementary Ed., Math Ed., Music Ed., Read/Lang Arts Ed., Sci. Ed., Sec. Ed., Spec. Ed. DOCTORATE: Art Ed., Bilingual Ed., Counselor Ed., Early Childhood Ed., Ed. Admin, Ed. Psych., Elementary Ed., Math Ed., Music Ed., Read/Lang Arts Ed., Sci. Ed., Sec. Ed., Spec. Ed.
Library: Adams Library, 373,000 volumes
Computer Resources: Macintosh, Dual Platform, PCs, CD-ROM, Videodisc

Research Areas	#Faculty
Adult Education	
Art Education	1
Bilingual Education	2
Counselor Education	2
Early Childhood Ed.	2
Ed. Admin	2
Ed. Tech.	2
Elementary Ed.	6
Foreign Lang. Ed.	1
Higher Ed.	
Math Ed.	4
Mid. Lev. Ed.	1
Multicultural Ed.	3
Music Ed.	1
Physical Ed.	3
Read/Lang. Arts Ed.	3
School Counseling	2
Science Ed.	3
Secondary Ed.	3
Soc. Studies Ed.	2
Special Ed.	7
Other	

Research Institutes/Centers: Center for Evaluation and Research
Student Body Demographics: Average Age 31, 75% female, 25% male
Percent Ethnic Minorities: Hispanic-American 3%, Asian-American 2%, African-American 3%
Geographic Representation: New England 98%
Tuition: 150/cr (in state), 292/cr (out of state)
Financial Aid Recipients: 10%
Average Annual Housing Cost: 2,583
Application Deadline: 4/1; 11/1
Number of: applicants annually 500; applicants accepted annually 450; students enrolled annually 430

Tests Required	Preferred/Min Score
Graduate Record Exam	900
National Teachers Exam	
Praxis II Exam	

Salve Regina University Graduate Education Program

Ochre Point Avenue, Newport, RI 2840
Admissions: (PH)401 847-6650
Total Enrollment: 1,000–5,000
Grad Enrollment: On campus 3%, Off campus 97%
Program Membership: N/A
Academic Programs Available: MASTERS: Early Childhood Ed., Elementary Ed., Spec. Ed. DOCTORATE: Early Childhood Ed., Elementary Ed., Spec. Ed.
Library: McKillok Library
Computer Resources: Macintosh, Dual Platform, PCs, CD-ROM, Videodisc

Research Areas	#Faculty
Adult Education	
Art Education	
Bilingual Education	
Counselor Education	
Early Childhood Ed.	2
Ed. Admin	
Ed. Tech.	
Elementary Ed.	6
Foreign Lang. Ed.	
Higher Ed.	
Math Ed.	1
Mid. Lev. Ed.	
Multicultural Ed.	
Music Ed.	
Physical Ed.	
Read/Lang. Arts Ed.	3
School Counseling	
Science Ed.	3
Secondary Ed.	3
Soc. Studies Ed.	1
Special Ed.	4
Other	

Student Body Demographics: Average Age 34, 80% female, 20% male
Percent Ethnic Minorities: Hispanic-American 5%, Asian-American 5%, African-American 5%
Geographic Representation: New England 85%, Midwest 5%, Mid Atlantic 10%
Graduate Career Paths: K-12 Teaching 70%, K-12 Special Ed 30%
Tuition: 150/cr (in state), 150/cr (out of state)
Financial Aid Recipients: 8%
Average Annual Housing Cost: N/A
Application Deadline: 8/3; 1/2; 5/1
Number of: applicants annually 50; applicants accepted annually 45; students enrolled annually 40

Tests Required	Preferred/Min Score
Graduate Record Exam	
National Teachers Exam	
Praxis II Exam	

University of Rhode Island College of Human Science and Services

Kingston, RI 2881
Admissions: (PH)401 792-2244
Total Enrollment: 10,000–20,000
Grad Enrollment: 300 total
Program Membership: Holmes Partnership
Academic Programs Available: MASTERS: Adult Ed., Counselor Ed., Elementary Ed., Physical Ed., Read/Lang Arts Ed., Sec. Ed., DOCTORATE: Adult Ed., Counselor Ed., Elementary Ed., Physical Ed., Read/Lang Arts Ed., Sec. Ed.
Library: N/A

Research Areas	#Faculty
Adult Education	
Art Education	
Bilingual Education	
Counselor Education	
Early Childhood Ed.	
Ed. Admin	
Ed. Tech.	
Elementary Ed.	
Foreign Lang. Ed.	
Higher Ed.	
Math Ed.	
Mid. Lev. Ed.	
Multicultural Ed.	
Music Ed.	
Physical Ed.	
Read/Lang. Arts Ed.	
School Counseling	
Science Ed.	
Secondary Ed.	
Soc. Studies Ed.	
Special Ed.	
Other	

Student Body Demographics: N/A
Percent Ethnic Minorities: N/A
Geographic Representation: N/A
Tuition: 3,312 (in state), 8,136 (out of state)
Financial Aid Recipients: N/A
Average Annual Housing Cost: 4,500
Application Deadline: 4/15
Number of: applicants annually N/A; applicants accepted annually N/A; studentsN/A

Tests Required	Preferred/Min Score
Graduate Record Exam	
National Teachers Exam	
Praxis II Exam	
TOEFL	600

SOUTH CAROLINA

Clemson University College of Education

Clemson, SC 29634
Admissions: (PH)803 656-3485
Grad Enrollment: 800 total
Program Membership: Holmes Partnership
Academic Programs Available: MASTERS: Counselor Ed.,
Ed. Admin, Elementary Ed., Read/Lang Arts Ed., Sec. Ed.,
Spec. Ed. DOCTORATE: Counselor Ed., Ed. Admin,
Elementary Ed., Read/Lang Arts Ed., Sec. Ed., Spec. Ed.
Library: N/A

Research Areas	#Faculty
Adult Education	
Art Education	
Bilingual Education	
Counselor Education	
Early Childhood Ed.	
Ed. Admin	
Ed. Tech.	
Elementary Ed.	
Foreign Lang. Ed.	
Higher Ed.	
Math Ed.	
Mid. Lev. Ed.	
Multicultural Ed.	
Music Ed.	
Physical Ed.	
Read/Lang. Arts Ed.	
School Counseling	
Science Ed.	
Secondary Ed.	
Soc. Studies Ed.	
Special Ed.	
Other	

Student Body Demographics: N/A
Percent Ethnic Minorities: N/A
Geographic Representation: N/A
Tuition: 2,922 (in state), 5,844 (out of state)
Financial Aid Recipients: N/A
Application Deadline: 6/1
Number of: applicants annually 346; applicants accepted
annually 260; students enrolled annually

Tests Required	Preferred/Min Score
Graduate Record Exam	
National Teachers Exam	
Praxis II Exam	

Coastal Carolina University School of Education and Graduate Studies

P.O. Box 1954, Conway, SC 29526
Admissions: (PH)803 349-2026, (FAX)803 349-2127,
(EMAIL)tim@coastal.edu
Dean: (PH)803 349-2600, (FAX)803 349-2940,
(EMAIL)dennis@coastal.edu

Grad Enrollment: FTM 2, PTM 309, Off campus 100%
Program Membership: N/A
Academic Programs Available: MASTERS: Early
Childhood Ed., Elementary Ed., Sec. Ed., DOCTORATE:
Early Childhood Ed., Elementary Ed., Sec. Ed.
Library: Kimbel Library, 202,000 volumes
Computer Resources: Macintosh, Dual Platform, PCs,
CD-ROM, Videodisc

Research Areas	#Faculty
Adult Education	
Art Education	
Bilingual Education	
Counselor Education	
Early Childhood Ed.	4
Ed. Admin	
Ed. Tech.	
Elementary Ed.	4
Foreign Lang. Ed.	
Higher Ed.	
Math Ed.	8
Mid. Lev. Ed.	3
Multicultural Ed.	
Music Ed.	
Physical Ed.	
Read/Lang. Arts Ed.	
School Counseling	
Science Ed.	1
Secondary Ed.	1
Soc. Studies Ed.	2
Special Ed.	
Other	

Research Institutes/Centers: Center for Education and
Community, Center of Excellence in Middle Level
Education, Center of Excellence in Composition
Student Body Demographics: N/A
Percent Ethnic Minorities: N/A
Geographic Representation: Southeast 100%
Graduate Career Paths: K-12 Teaching 100%
Tuition: 513 (in state), 1,044 (out of state)
Financial Aid Recipients: N/A
Average Annual Housing Cost: N/A
Application Deadline: 8/15
Number of: applicants annually N/A; applicants accepted
annually N/A; students enrolled annually N/A

Tests Required	Preferred/Min Score
Graduate Record Exam	800
National Teachers Exam	
Praxis II Exam	

Columbia International University

7435 Monticello Road, P.O. Box 3122, Columbia,
SC 29230-3122
Admissions: (PH)800 777-2227 x3024, (FAX)803 786-4209,
(EMAIL)cavs63b@prodigy.com
Dean: (PH)800 777-2227 x3130
Total Enrollment: 1,000
Program Membership: N/A

Academic Programs Available: MASTERS: Early Childhood Ed., Elementary Ed., DOCTORATE: Early Childhood Ed., Elementary Ed.
Library: C. Allen Fleeco Library, 102,000 volumes
Computer Resources: Macintosh, Dual Platform, PCs, CD-ROM, Videodisc

Research Areas	#Faculty
Adult Education	
Art Education	
Bilingual Education	
Counselor Education	
Early Childhood Ed.	
Ed. Admin	
Ed. Tech.	
Elementary Ed.	
Foreign Lang. Ed.	
Higher Ed.	
Math Ed.	
Mid. Lev. Ed.	
Multicultural Ed.	
Music Ed.	
Physical Ed.	
Read/Lang. Arts Ed.	
School Counseling	
Science Ed.	
Secondary Ed.	
Soc. Studies Ed.	
Special Ed.	
Other	

Student Body Demographics: Average Age N/A, 60% female, 40% male
Percent Ethnic Minorities: N/A
Geographic Representation: N/A
Tuition: 7,690 (in state), 7,690 (out of state)
Financial Aid Recipients: N/A
Average Annual Housing Cost: 3,830
Application Deadline: N/A
Number of: applicants annually N/A; applicants accepted annually N/A; students enrolled annually 4,045

Tests Required	Preferred/Min Score
Graduate Record Exam	
National Teachers Exam	
Praxis II Exam	

The Citadel Department of Education

171 Moultrie Street, Charleston, SC 2,9409
Admissions: (PH)803 953-5188, (FAX)803 953-7084, (EMAIL)ezellp@citadel.edu
Dean: (PH)803953-5097, (FAX)803 953-7084, (EMAIL)templetonr@citadel.edu
Total Enrollment: 1,000–5,000
Grad Enrollment: FTM 88, PTM 430, Off campus 100%
Program Membership: N/A
Academic Programs Available: MASTERS: Counselor Ed., Ed. Admin, Math Ed., Physical Ed., Read/Lang Arts Ed., School Cons., Soc. Ed., Spec. Ed. DOCTORATE: Counselor Ed., Ed. Admin, Math Ed., Physical Ed., Read/Lang Arts Ed., School Cons., Soc. Ed., Spec. Ed.
Library: Daniel Library, 250,000 volumes

Computer Resources: Macintosh, Dual Platform, PCs, CD-ROM, Videodisc

Research Areas	#Faculty
Adult Education	
Art Education	
Bilingual Education	
Counselor Education	
Early Childhood Ed.	
Ed. Admin	
Ed. Tech.	
Elementary Ed.	
Foreign Lang. Ed.	
Higher Ed.	
Math Ed.	
Mid. Lev. Ed.	
Multicultural Ed.	
Music Ed.	
Physical Ed.	
Read/Lang. Arts Ed.	
School Counseling	
Science Ed.	
Secondary Ed.	
Soc. Studies Ed.	
Special Ed.	
Other	

Student Body Demographics: Average Age 38, 75% female, 25% male
Percent Ethnic Minorities: Hispanic-American 1%, African-American 8%
Geographic Representation: Southeast 95%
Graduate Career Paths: K-12 Teaching 65%, School Counseling 15%, K-12 School Administration 15%
Tuition: 130/hr (in state), 130/hr (out of state)
Financial Aid Recipients: N/A
Average Annual Housing Cost: N/A
Application Deadline: rolling
Number of: applicants annually 250; applicants accepted annually 210; students enrolled annually 150

Tests Required	Preferred/Min Score
Graduate Record Exam	900
National Teachers Exam	
Praxis II Exam	

University of South Carolina Wardlaw College of Education

Student Affairs, Columbia, SC 29208
Admissions: (PH)803 777-6732, (FAX)803 777-3068
Dean: (PH)803 777-3075, (FAX)803 777-3035
Total Enrollment: 20,000
Program Membership: Holmes Partnership
Academic Programs Available: MASTERS: Adult Ed., Art Ed., Counselor Ed., Early Childhood Ed., Ed. Admin, Ed. Tech., Elementary Ed., Foreign Lang. Ed., Higher Ed., Math Ed., Physical Ed., Read/Lang Arts Ed., School Cons., Sci. Ed., Sec. Ed., Soc. Ed., Spec. Ed. DOCTORATE: Adult Ed., Art Ed., Counselor Ed., Early Childhood Ed., Ed. Admin, Ed. Tech., Elementary Ed., Foreign Lang. Ed., Higher Ed., Math Ed., Physical Ed., Read/Lang Arts Ed., School Cons., Sci. Ed., Sec. Ed., Soc. Ed., Spec. Ed.

Library: N/A
Computer Resources: Macintosh, Dual Platform, PCs, CD-ROM, Videodisc

Research Areas	#Faculty
Adult Education	
Art Education	
Bilingual Education	
Counselor Education	
Early Childhood Ed.	
Ed. Admin	
Ed. Tech.	
Elementary Ed.	
Foreign Lang. Ed.	
Higher Ed.	
Math Ed.	
Mid. Lev. Ed.	
Multicultural Ed.	
Music Ed.	
Physical Ed.	
Read/Lang. Arts Ed.	
School Counseling	
Science Ed.	
Secondary Ed.	
Soc. Studies Ed.	
Special Ed.	
Other	

Research Institutes/Centers: Career Development Training Institute, Center for Excellence in Special Education Technology, Writing Improvement Network
Student Body Demographics: Average Age N/A, female N/A, male N/A
Percent Ethnic Minorities: N/A
Geographic Representation: N/A
Tuition: N/A (in state), N/A (out of state)
Financial Aid Recipients: N/A
Average Annual Housing Cost: N/A
Application Deadline: N/A
Number of: applicants annually N/A; applicants accepted annually N/A; students enrolled annually N/A

Tests Required	Preferred/Min Score
Graduate Record Exam	800–1,000
National Teachers Exam	
Praxis II Exam	

University of South Carolina-Aiken
School of Education

204 B&E Building, 171 University Parkway, Aiken, SC 29801
Admissions: (PH)803 641-3489, (FAX)803 641-3698
Dean: (PH)803 641-3483, (FAX)803 641-3698
Total Enrollment: 1,000
Grad Enrollment: Off campus 100%
Program Membership: N/A
Academic Programs Available: MASTERS: Elementary Ed., DOCTORATE: Elementary Ed.
Library: Gregg-Graniteville Library
Computer Resources: Macintosh, Dual Platform, PCs, CD-ROM, Videodisc

Research Areas	#Faculty
Adult Education	

Research Areas (cont.)	#Faculty
Art Education	
Bilingual Education	
Counselor Education	
Early Childhood Ed.	2
Ed. Admin	
Ed. Tech.	1
Elementary Ed.	1
Foreign Lang. Ed.	
Higher Ed.	
Math Ed.	
Mid. Lev. Ed.	1
Multicultural Ed.	
Music Ed.	
Physical Ed.	
Read/Lang. Arts Ed.	2
School Counseling	
Science Ed.	1
Secondary Ed.	1
Soc. Studies Ed.	
Special Ed.	
Other	

Research Institutes/Centers: Learning Styles Network Center
Student Body Demographics: N/A
Percent Ethnic Minorities: N/A
Geographic Representation: Southeast 100%
Graduate Career Paths: K-12 Teaching 100%
Tuition: 134/cr (in state)
Financial Aid Recipients: N/A
Average Annual Housing Cost: N/A
Application Deadline: N/A
Number of: applicants annually 35; applicants accepted annually 25; students enrolled annually 18

Tests Required	Preferred/Min Score
Graduate Record Exam	800
National Teachers Exam	
Praxis II Exam	

SOUTH DAKOTA

Northern State University Graduate Studies

1200 South Jay Street, Aberdeen, SD 57401
Admissions: (PH)605 626-2558, (FAX)605 626-2542
Dean: (PH)605 626-7788, (FAX)605 626-2542, (EMAIL)fullerd@wolf.northern.edu
Total Enrollment: 1,000–5,000
Grad Enrollment: FTM 68, PTM 223, On campus 2%, Off campus 98%
Program Membership: N/A
Academic Programs Available: MASTERS: Art Ed., Counselor Ed., Ed. Admin, Elementary Ed., Math Ed., Physical Ed., School Cons., Sci. Ed., Sec. Ed., Soc. Ed., DOCTORATE: Art Ed., Counselor Ed., Ed. Admin, Elementary Ed., Math Ed., Physical Ed., School Cons., Sci. Ed., Sec. Ed., Soc. Ed.

Library: Beulah Williams Library, 193,000 volumes
Computer Resources: Macintosh, Dual Platform, PCs, CD-ROM, Videodisc

Research Areas	#Faculty
Adult Education	
Art Education	
Bilingual Education	
Counselor Education	
Early Childhood Ed.	
Ed. Admin	
Ed. Tech.	
Elementary Ed.	
Foreign Lang. Ed.	
Higher Ed.	
Math Ed.	
Mid. Lev. Ed.	
Multicultural Ed.	
Music Ed.	
Physical Ed.	
Read/Lang. Arts Ed.	
School Counseling	
Science Ed.	
Secondary Ed.	
Soc. Studies Ed.	
Special Ed.	
Other	

Student Body Demographics: Average Age 23, 67% female, 33% male
Percent Ethnic Minorities: Hispanic-American 0.5%, Asian-American 1%, African-American 0.8%, Native-American 2%
Geographic Representation: Midwest 99%, Mid Atlantic 1%
Tuition: 96/hr (in state), 201/hr (out of state)
Financial Aid Recipients: 23%
Average Annual Housing Cost: 585
Application Deadline: varies
Number of: applicants annually 250; applicants accepted annually 200; students enrolled annually N/A

Tests Required	Preferred/Min Score
Graduate Record Exam	1,200
National Teachers Exam	
Praxis II Exam	
TOEFL	550

University of South Dakota
School of Education

414 E. Clark Street, Vermillion, SD 57069
Admissions: (PH)605 677-6498
Dean: (PH)605 677-5437, (FAX)605 677-5438, (EMAIL)lbright@charlie.usd.edu
Total Enrollment: 5,000–10,000
Grad Enrollment: FTM 228, FTD 131
Program Membership: Holmes Partnership
Academic Programs Available: MASTERS: Adult Ed., Counselor Ed., Ed. Admin, Ed. Psych., Elementary Ed., Higher Ed., Physical Ed., School Cons., Sec. Ed., Spec. Ed. DOCTORATE: Adult Ed., Counselor Ed., Ed. Admin, Ed.

Psych., Elementary Ed., Higher Ed., Physical Ed., School Cons., Sec. Ed., Spec. Ed.
Library: I.D. Weeks Library, 1.2 million volumes
Computer Resources: Macintosh, Dual Platform, PCs, CD-ROM, Videodisc

Research Areas	#Faculty
Adult Education	4
Art Education	
Bilingual Education	
Counselor Education	5
Early Childhood Ed.	2
Ed. Admin	9
Ed. Tech.	10
Elementary Ed.	6
Foreign Lang. Ed.	
Higher Ed.	4
Math Ed.	2
Mid. Lev. Ed.	3
Multicultural Ed.	3
Music Ed.	
Physical Ed.	5
Read/Lang. Arts Ed.	3
School Counseling	8
Science Ed.	2
Secondary Ed.	2
Soc. Studies Ed.	2
Special Ed.	8
Other	11

Research Institutes/Centers: Educational Research and Service Center
Student Body Demographics: Average Age N/A, 55% female, 45% male
Percent Ethnic Minorities: Native-American 2%
Geographic Representation: N/A
Graduate Career Paths: K-12 Teaching 20%, Higher Ed Teaching 7%, School Counseling 12%, K-12 Special Ed 7%, School Administration 31%, Higher Ed Administration 2%, Community Counseling 21%
Tuition: 115/cr (in state), 207/cr (out of state)
Financial Aid Recipients: 15%
Average Annual Housing Cost: 1,836
Application Deadline: N/A
Number of: applicants annually 265; applicants accepted annually N/A; students enrolled annually N/A

Tests Required	Preferred/Min Score
Graduate Record Exam	700–900
National Teachers Exam	
Praxis II Exam	
TOEFL	550

TENNESSEE

Union University School of Education and Human Studies

Jackson, TN 38305
Admissions: (PH)901 661-5000
Dean: (PH)901 661-5372
Total Enrollment: 1,000–5,000
Grad Enrollment: FTM 10, PTM 100, Off campus 100%
Program Membership: N/A
Academic Programs Available: MASTERS: Art Ed., Early Childhood Ed., Elementary Ed., Foreign Lang. Ed., Math Ed., Music Ed., Physical Ed., Sci. Ed., Soc. Ed., Spec. Ed. DOCTORATE: Art Ed., Early Childhood Ed., Elementary Ed., Foreign Lang. Ed., Math Ed., Music Ed., Physical Ed., Sci. Ed., Soc. Ed., Spec. Ed.
Library: N/A
Computer Resources: Macintosh, Dual Platform, PCs, CD-ROM, Videodisc

Research Areas	#Faculty
Adult Education	
Art Education	
Bilingual Education	
Counselor Education	
Early Childhood Ed.	3
Ed. Admin	
Ed. Tech.	1
Elementary Ed.	2
Foreign Lang. Ed.	
Higher Ed.	1
Math Ed.	
Mid. Lev. Ed.	
Multicultural Ed.	
Music Ed.	
Physical Ed.	2
Read/Lang. Arts Ed.	3
School Counseling	
Science Ed.	
Secondary Ed.	
Soc. Studies Ed.	1
Special Ed.	1
Other	2

Student Body Demographics: Average Age 30, 90% female, 10% male
Percent Ethnic Minorities: Hispanic-American 1%, African-American 12%
Geographic Representation: Midwest 10%, Southeast 90%
Graduate Career Paths: K-12 Teaching 80%, Higher Ed Teaching 3%, K-12 Special Ed 10%
Tuition: 145/hr (in state), 145/hr (out of state)
Financial Aid Recipients: N/A
Average Annual Housing Cost: N/A
Application Deadline: N/A
Number of: applicants annually 30; applicants accepted annually 25; students enrolled annually 25

Tests Required	Preferred/Min Score
Graduate Record Exam	
National Teachers Exam	

Praxis II Exam

University of Tennessee College of Education

Graduate School, Knoxville, TN 37996
Admissions: (PH)423 974-1345, (FAX)423 974-6541, (EMAIL)kaplon@utkumi.tuk.edu
Dean: (FAX)423 974-2805, (EMAIL)cwminkel@utrux.utk.edu
Total Enrollment: 20,000
Grad Enrollment: 1122 total
Program Membership: Holmes Partnership
Academic Programs Available: MASTERS: Adult Ed., Art Ed., Bilingual Ed., Counselor Ed., Early Childhood Ed., Ed. Admin, Ed. Psych., Ed. Tech., Elementary Ed., Foreign Lang. Ed., Higher Ed., Math Ed., Multicultural Ed., Music Ed., Physical Ed., Read/Lang Arts Ed., School Cons., Sci. Ed., Soc. Ed., Spec. Ed. DOCTORATE: Adult Ed., Art Ed., Bilingual Ed., Counselor Ed., Early Childhood Ed., Ed. Admin, Ed. Psych., Ed. Tech., Elementary Ed., Foreign Lang. Ed., Higher Ed., Math Ed., Multicultural Ed., Music Ed., Physical Ed., Read/Lang Arts Ed., School Cons., Sci. Ed., Soc. Ed., Spec. Ed.
Library: Hodges Library, 2 million volumes
Computer Resources: Macintosh, Dual Platform, PCs, CD-ROM, Videodisc

Research Areas	#Faculty
Adult Education	3
Art Education	2
Bilingual Education	1
Counselor Education	5
Early Childhood Ed.	4
Ed. Admin	4
Ed. Tech.	3
Elementary Ed.	6
Foreign Lang. Ed.	1
Higher Ed.	3
Math Ed.	2
Mid. Lev. Ed.	
Multicultural Ed.	5
Music Ed.	4
Physical Ed.	
Read/Lang. Arts Ed.	6
School Counseling	5
Science Ed.	2
Secondary Ed.	2
Soc. Studies Ed.	1
Special Ed.	6
Other	

Research Institutes/Centers: Institute for Educational Innovation
Student Body Demographics: Average Age 30, 67% female, 33% male
Percent Ethnic Minorities: Hispanic-American 1%, Asian-American 1%, African-American 5%, Native-American 1%
Geographic Representation: Midwest 5%, Mid Atlantic 5%, Southeast 85%
Tuition: 1,139 (in state), 3106 (out of state)
Financial Aid Recipients: 10%
Average Annual Housing Cost: 4,000

Application Deadline: varies
Number of: applicants annually N/A; applicants accepted annually N/A; students enrolled annually N/A

Tests Required	Preferred/Min Score
Graduate Record Exam	
National Teachers Exam	
Praxis II Exam	

Vanderbilt University Peabody College
P.O. Box 327, Nashville, TN 37202
Admissions: (PH)615 322-8410, (FAX)615 322-8401, (EMAIL)johnstbj@ctrvax.vanderbilt.edu
Dean: (PH)615 322-8407, (FAX)615 322-8501
Total Enrollment: 5,000–10,000
Grad Enrollment: FTM 185, PTM 142, FTD 253, PTD 80
Program Membership: Holmes Partnership
Academic Programs Available: MASTERS: Counselor Ed., Early Childhood Ed., Ed. Admin, Ed. Psych., Ed. Tech., Elementary Ed., Higher Ed., Math Ed., Read/Lang Arts Ed., School Cons., Sci. Ed., Sec. Ed., Soc. Ed., Spec. Ed. DOCTORATE: Counselor Ed., Early Childhood Ed., Ed. Admin, Ed. Psych., Ed. Tech., Elementary Ed., Higher Ed., Math Ed., Read/Lang Arts Ed., School Cons., Sci. Ed., Sec. Ed., Soc. Ed., Spec. Ed.
Library: Peabody College Education Library
Computer Resources: Macintosh, Dual Platform, PCs, CD-ROM, Videodisc

Research Areas	#Faculty
Adult Education	
Art Education	
Bilingual Education	
Counselor Education	
Early Childhood Ed.	
Ed. Admin	
Ed. Tech.	
Elementary Ed.	
Foreign Lang. Ed.	
Higher Ed.	
Math Ed.	
Mid. Lev. Ed.	
Multicultural Ed.	
Music Ed.	
Physical Ed.	
Read/Lang. Arts Ed.	
School Counseling	
Science Ed.	
Secondary Ed.	
Soc. Studies Ed.	
Special Ed.	
Other	

Student Body Demographics: Average Age 30, 70% female, 30% male
Percent Ethnic Minorities: Hispanic-American 2%, Asian-American 2%, African-American 12%, Native-American 2%
Geographic Representation: N/A
Tuition: 560-786 (in state), N/A (out of state)
Financial Aid Recipients: N/A
Average Annual Housing Cost: 6,905

Application Deadline: 1/15; 3/1
Number of: applicants annually 800; applicants accepted annually 350; students enrolled annually 200

Tests Required	Preferred/Min Score
Graduate Record Exam	950
National Teachers Exam	
Praxis II Exam	
TOEFL	550

TEXAS

Baylor University School of Education
Waco, TX 76798
Admissions: (PH)817 755-3111
Grad Enrollment: 253 total
Program Membership: Holmes Partnership
Academic Programs Available: N/A
Library: N/A

Research Areas	#Faculty
Adult Education	
Art Education	
Bilingual Education	
Counselor Education	
Early Childhood Ed.	
Ed. Admin	
Ed. Tech.	
Elementary Ed.	
Foreign Lang. Ed.	
Higher Ed.	
Math Ed.	
Mid. Lev. Ed.	
Multicultural Ed.	
Music Ed.	
Physical Ed.	
Read/Lang. Arts Ed.	
School Counseling	
Science Ed.	
Secondary Ed.	
Soc. Studies Ed.	
Special Ed.	
Other	

Student Body Demographics: N/A
Percent Ethnic Minorities: N/A
Geographic Representation: N/A
Tuition: 6,192 (in state), 6,192 (out of state)
Financial Aid Recipients: N/A
Application Deadline: rolling
Number of: applicants annually N/A; applicants accepted annually N/A; students enrolled annually N/A

Tests Required	Preferred/Min Score
Graduate Record Exam	
National Teachers Exam	
Praxis II Exam	

East Texas State University
College of Education

ET Station, Commerce, TX 75429
Admissions: (PH)903 886-5081, (FAX)903 886-5888,
(EMAIL)sw5101@etsuadmn.etsu.edu
Dean: (PH)903 886-5180, (FAX)903 886-5156,
(EMAIL)don_coker@etsu.edu
Total Enrollment: 5,000–10,000
Grad Enrollment: FTM 551, PTM 1670, PTD 372
Program Membership: Holmes Partnership
Academic Programs Available: MASTERS: Counselor Ed.,
Early Childhood Ed., Ed. Admin, Ed. Psych., Ed. Tech.,
Elementary Ed., Higher Ed., Physical Ed., Read/Lang Arts
Ed., School Cons., Sec. Ed., Spec. Ed. DOCTORATE:
Counselor Ed., Early Childhood Ed., Ed. Admin, Ed. Psych.,
Ed. Tech., Elementary Ed., Higher Ed., Physical Ed.,
Read/Lang Arts Ed., School Cons., Sec. Ed., Spec. Ed.
Library: James Gilliam Gee Library, 1.5 million volumes
Computer Resources: Macintosh, Dual Platform, PCs,
CD-ROM, Videodisc

Research Areas	#Faculty
Adult Education	
Art Education	
Bilingual Education	
Counselor Education	5
Early Childhood Ed.	
Ed. Admin	
Ed. Tech.	7
Elementary Ed.	
Foreign Lang. Ed.	
Higher Ed.	2
Math Ed.	1
Mid. Lev. Ed.	1
Multicultural Ed.	1
Music Ed.	
Physical Ed.	8
Read/Lang. Arts Ed.	
School Counseling	4
Science Ed.	1
Secondary Ed.	1
Soc. Studies Ed.	1
Special Ed.	3
Other	6

Student Body Demographics: Average Age 36, 61% female,
39% male
Percent Ethnic Minorities: Hispanic-American 3.5%,
Asian-American 1.3%, African-American 11%,
Native-American 2%
Geographic Representation: Midwest 5%, Mid Atlantic 5%,
Southwest 40%, West 5%, Southeast 40%, Northwest 5%
Graduate Career Paths: K-12 Teaching 8%, Higher Ed
Teaching 12%, School Counseling 14%, K-12 Special Ed 7%,
School Administration 17%, Higher Ed Administration 20%,
Community Counseling 13%
Tuition: 4,606 (in state), 13186 (out of state)
Financial Aid Recipients: N/A
Average Annual Housing Cost: 4,510
Application Deadline: varies

Number of: applicants annually N/A; applicants accepted
annually N/A; students enrolled annually N/A

Tests Required	Preferred/Min Score
Graduate Record Exam	600–850
National Teachers Exam	
Praxis II Exam	
TOEFL	500

Texas A&M University College of Education

Office of Graduate Admissions, College Station, TX 77843
Admissions: (PH)409 845-1044
Dean: (PH)409 845-5311, (FAX)409 845-6129,
(EMAIL)bcarr@tamu.edu
Total Enrollment: 20,000
Grad Enrollment: FTM 161, PTM 147, FTD 204, PTD 397,
Off campus 100%
Program Membership: Holmes Partnership, NNER
Academic Programs Available: MASTERS: Adult Ed.,
Bilingual Ed., Ed. Admin, Ed. Psych., Ed. Tech., Higher Ed.,
Physical Ed., DOCTORATE: Adult Ed., Bilingual Ed., Ed.
Admin, Ed. Psych., Ed. Tech., Higher Ed., Physical Ed.,
School Cons.
Library: Evans Library, 2.2 million volumes
Computer Resources: Macintosh, Dual Platform, PCs,
CD-ROM, Videodisc

Research Areas	#Faculty
Adult Education	3
Art Education	
Bilingual Education	7
Counselor Education	7
Early Childhood Ed.	4
Ed. Admin	14
Ed. Tech.	8
Elementary Ed.	
Foreign Lang. Ed.	
Higher Ed.	3
Math Ed.	7
Mid. Lev. Ed.	
Multicultural Ed.	
Music Ed.	
Physical Ed.	2
Read/Lang. Arts Ed.	9
School Counseling	7
Science Ed.	
Secondary Ed.	
Soc. Studies Ed.	1
Special Ed.	9
Other	16

Research Institutes/Centers: The Principals' Center, Center
for Community Education, Institute for Gifted and Talented
Students, Center for Distance Learning Research
Student Body Demographics: Average Age N/A,
63% female, 37% male
Percent Ethnic Minorities: Hispanic-American 8.5%,
Asian-American 1.3%, African-American 5.1%,
Native-American 0.1%
Geographic Representation: N/A
Tuition: 1,004 (in state), 2,732 (out of state)
Financial Aid Recipients: 38%

Average Annual Housing Cost: N/A
Application Deadline: 1/1; 9/1
Number of: applicants annually 568; applicants accepted annually 285; students enrolled annually 195

Tests Required	Preferred/Min Score
Graduate Record Exam	
National Teachers Exam	
Praxis II Exam	
TOEFL	550

Texas Tech University College of Education

Lubbock, TX 79409
Admissions: (PH)806 742-2377
Grad Enrollment: 800 total
Program Membership: Holmes Partnership
Academic Programs Available: MASTERS: Ed. Admin, Ed. Psych., Ed. Tech., Elementary Ed., Higher Ed., Read/Lang Arts Ed., Sec. Ed., Spec. Ed. DOCTORATE: Ed. Admin, Ed. Psych., Ed. Tech., Elementary Ed., Higher Ed., Read/Lang Arts Ed., Sec. Ed., Spec. Ed.
Library: N/A

Research Areas	#Faculty
Adult Education	
Art Education	
Bilingual Education	
Counselor Education	
Early Childhood Ed.	
Ed. Admin	
Ed. Tech.	
Elementary Ed.	
Foreign Lang. Ed.	
Higher Ed.	
Math Ed.	
Mid. Lev. Ed.	
Multicultural Ed.	
Music Ed.	
Physical Ed.	
Read/Lang. Arts Ed.	
School Counseling	
Science Ed.	
Secondary Ed.	
Soc. Studies Ed.	
Special Ed.	
Other	

Student Body Demographics: N/A
Percent Ethnic Minorities: N/A
Geographic Representation: N/A
Tuition: 58/hr (in state), 204/hr (out of state)
Financial Aid Recipients: N/A
Average Annual Housing Cost: N/A
Application Deadline: 4/15
Number of: applicants annually 1,019; applicants accepted annually 540; students enrolled annually N/A

Tests Required	Preferred/Min Score
Graduate Record Exam	985
National Teachers Exam	
Praxis II Exam	

Texas Wesleyan University
School of Education

1201 Wesleyan Street, Fort Worth, TX 76105
Admissions: (PH)817 531-4218, (FAX)817 531-4425
Dean: (PH)817 531-4945, (FAX)817 531-4814
Total Enrollment: 1,000–5,000
Grad Enrollment: FTM 67, PTM 205, Off campus 100%
Program Membership: N/A
Academic Programs Available: MASTERS: Bilingual Ed., Early Childhood Ed., Elementary Ed., Read/Lang Arts Ed., Sci. Ed., Soc. Ed., DOCTORATE: Bilingual Ed., Early Childhood Ed., Elementary Ed., Read/Lang Arts Ed., Sci. Ed., Soc.
Library: Eunice and James West Library, 193,000 volumes
Computer Resources: Macintosh, Dual Platform, PCs, CD-ROM, Videodisc

Research Areas	#Faculty
Adult Education	
Art Education	
Bilingual Education	2
Counselor Education	
Early Childhood Ed.	2
Ed. Admin	
Ed. Tech.	
Elementary Ed.	4
Foreign Lang. Ed.	
Higher Ed.	
Math Ed.	1
Mid. Lev. Ed.	
Multicultural Ed.	
Music Ed.	1
Physical Ed.	
Read/Lang. Arts Ed.	2
School Counseling	
Science Ed.	1
Secondary Ed.	1
Soc. Studies Ed.	2
Special Ed.	
Other	

Research Institutes/Centers: Center for Creative and Analytical Thinking
Student Body Demographics: Average Age 33, 73% female, 27% male
Percent Ethnic Minorities: Hispanic-American 13%, African-American 11%
Geographic Representation: N/A
Graduate Career Paths: K-12 Teaching 100%
Tuition: 230/hr (in state), 230/hr (out of state)
Financial Aid Recipients: 80%
Average Annual Housing Cost: N/A
Application Deadline: rolling
Number of: applicants annually 283; applicants accepted annually 179; students enrolled annually N/A

Tests Required	Preferred/Min Score
Graduate Record Exam	
National Teachers Exam	
Praxis II Exam	

Texas Woman's University College of Education and Human Ecology

P.O. Box 425589, Denton, TX 76204
Admissions: (PH)817 898-3000, (FAX)817 898-3198
Dean: (PH)817 898-2204, (FAX)817 898-2209
Total Enrollment: 5,000–10,000
Grad Enrollment: FTM 126, PTM 1089, FTD 46, PTD 113, On campus 4%, Off campus 96%
Program Membership: N/A
Academic Programs Available: MASTERS: Art Ed., Bilingual Ed., Counselor Ed., Early Childhood Ed., Ed. Admin, Ed. Psych., Elementary Ed., Math Ed., Multicultural Ed., Music Ed., Physical Ed., Read/Lang Arts Ed., School DOCTORATE: Art Ed., Bilingual Ed., Counselor Ed., Early Childhood Ed., Ed. Admin, Ed. Psych., Elementary Ed., Math Ed., Multicultural Ed., Music Ed., Physical Ed., Read/Lang Arts Ed., School
Library: Blagg-Huey Library, 775,000 volumes
Computer Resources: Macintosh, Dual Platform, PCs, CD-ROM, Videodisc

Research Areas	#Faculty
Adult Education	1
Art Education	2
Bilingual Education	3
Counselor Education	5
Early Childhood Ed.	4
Ed. Admin	4
Ed. Tech.	
Elementary Ed.	5
Foreign Lang. Ed.	
Higher Ed.	
Math Ed.	2
Mid. Lev. Ed.	
Multicultural Ed.	3
Music Ed.	
Physical Ed.	
Read/Lang. Arts Ed.	6
School Counseling	5
Science Ed.	2
Secondary Ed.	2
Soc. Studies Ed.	1
Special Ed.	
Other	

Research Institutes/Centers: Center for Applied Research
Student Body Demographics: Average Age 27, 96% female, 4% male
Percent Ethnic Minorities: Hispanic-American 77%, Asian-American 8%, African-American 12%, Native-American 2%
Geographic Representation: Southwest 97%
Graduate Career Paths: K-12 Teaching 44%, Higher Ed Teaching 2%, School Counseling 5%, K-12 Special Ed 11%, School Administration 36%
Tuition: 700 (in state), 1,800 (out of state)
Financial Aid Recipients: 10%
Average Annual Housing Cost: 2,200
Application Deadline: N/A
Number of: applicants annually 1,000; applicants accepted annually 800; students enrolled annually N/A

Tests Required	Preferred/Min Score
Graduate Record Exam	
National Teachers Exam	700–1,000
Praxis II Exam	

University of Houston-Clear Lake School of Education

2700 Bay Area Blvd., Houston, TX 77056
Admissions: (PH)713 283-2525
Dean: (PH)713 283-3500, (EMAIL)spuck@cl.uh.edu
Total Enrollment: 5,000–10,000
Grad Enrollment: FTM 191, PTM 791, Off campus 100%
Program Membership: Holmes Partnership
Academic Programs Available: MASTERS: Counselor Ed., Early Childhood Ed., Ed. Admin, Ed. Tech., Elementary Ed., Multicultural Ed., Read/Lang Arts Ed., School Cons., Sec. Ed., DOCTORATE: Counselor Ed., Early Childhood Ed., Ed. Admin, Ed. Tech., Elementary Ed., Multicultural Ed., Read/Lang Arts Ed., School Cons., Sec. Ed.
Library: Alfred R. Neumann Library, 650,000 volumes
Computer Resources: Macintosh, Dual Platform, PCs, CD-ROM, Videodisc

Research Areas	#Faculty
Adult Education	
Art Education	
Bilingual Education	3
Counselor Education	1
Early Childhood Ed.	1
Ed. Admin	1
Ed. Tech.	3
Elementary Ed.	4
Foreign Lang. Ed.	
Higher Ed.	
Math Ed.	1
Mid. Lev. Ed.	1
Multicultural Ed.	3
Music Ed.	
Physical Ed.	
Read/Lang. Arts Ed.	5
School Counseling	1
Science Ed.	2
Secondary Ed.	2
Soc. Studies Ed.	1
Special Ed.	2
Other	

Research Institutes/Centers: Research Center for Language and Culture, Center for Professional Development and Technology, Center for Educational Programs
Student Body Demographics: Average Age 32, 80% female, 20% male
Percent Ethnic Minorities: Hispanic-American 6%, Asian-American 1%, African-American 7%
Geographic Representation: N/A
Graduate Career Paths: K-12 Teaching 30%, School Counseling 20%, K-12 Special Ed 7%, School Administration 30%
Tuition: 52/hr (in state), 171/hr (out of state)
Financial Aid Recipients: N/A

Average Annual Housing Cost: N/A
Application Deadline: varies
Number of: applicants annually N/A; applicants accepted annually N/A; students enrolled annually N/A
Tests Required   **Preferred/Min Score**
Graduate Record Exam
National Teachers Exam
Praxis II Exam

University of Mary Hardin-Baylor
School of Education

Box 8004, UMHB Station, Belton, TX 76513
Admissions: (PH)817 939-4522, (FAX)817 939-4535
Dean: (PH)817 939-4572, (FAX)817 933-4480, (EMAIL)ham@tenet.edu
Total Enrollment: 1,000–5,000
Grad Enrollment: PTM 150, Off campus 100%
Program Membership: N/A
Academic Programs Available: MASTERS: Counselor Ed., Early Childhood Ed., Ed. Admin, Ed. Psych., Read/Lang Arts Ed., School Cons., Spec. Ed. DOCTORATE: Counselor Ed., Early Childhood Ed., Ed. Admin, Ed. Psych., Read/Lang Arts Ed., School Cons., Spec. Ed.
Library: Townsend Memorial Library
Computer Resources: Macintosh, Dual Platform, PCs, CD-ROM, Videodisc

Research Areas	#Faculty
Adult Education	
Art Education	
Bilingual Education	
Counselor Education	
Early Childhood Ed.	
Ed. Admin	
Ed. Tech.	
Elementary Ed.	
Foreign Lang. Ed.	
Higher Ed.	
Math Ed.	
Mid. Lev. Ed.	
Multicultural Ed.	
Music Ed.	
Physical Ed.	1
Read/Lang. Arts Ed.	
School Counseling	
Science Ed.	
Secondary Ed.	
Soc. Studies Ed.	
Special Ed.	
Other	

Student Body Demographics: Average Age 33, 70% female, 30% male
Percent Ethnic Minorities: N/A
Geographic Representation: Southwest 95%
Graduate Career Paths: K-12 Teaching 40%, School Counseling 10%, K-12 School Administration 50%
Tuition: 205 (in state), 205 (out of state)
Financial Aid Recipients: N/A
Average Annual Housing Cost: N/A

Number of: applicants annually 100; applicants accepted annually 75; students enrolled annually 75
Tests Required   **Preferred/Min Score**
Graduate Record Exam   850–950
National Teachers Exam
Praxis II Exam

University of North Texas
College of Education

Toulouse School of Graduate Studies, P.O. Box 5446, Denton, TX 76203
Admissions: (PH)817 565-2383, (FAX)817 565-2141, (EMAIL)gradsch@abn.unt.edu
Dean: (PH)817 565-2383, (FAX)817 565-2141
Total Enrollment: 20,000
Grad Enrollment: FTM 241, PTM 890, FTD 103, PTD 318, On campus 3%, Off campus 97%
Program Membership: Holmes Partnership
Academic Programs Available: MASTERS: Counselor Ed., Early Childhood Ed., Ed. Admin, Ed. Tech., Elementary Ed., Higher Ed., Physical Ed., School Cons., Sec. Ed., Spec. Ed. DOCTORATE: Counselor Ed., Early Childhood Ed., Ed. Admin, Ed. Tech., Elementary Ed., Higher Ed., Physical Ed., School Cons., Sec. Ed., Spec. Ed.
Library: Willis Library, 2 million volumes
Computer Resources: Macintosh, Dual Platform, PCs, CD-ROM, Videodisc

Research Areas	#Faculty
Adult Education	2
Art Education	
Bilingual Education	
Counselor Education	17
Early Childhood Ed.	6
Ed. Admin	5
Ed. Tech.	
Elementary Ed.	12
Foreign Lang. Ed.	
Higher Ed.	8
Math Ed.	
Mid. Lev. Ed.	
Multicultural Ed.	3
Music Ed.	
Physical Ed.	15
Read/Lang. Arts Ed.	6
School Counseling	
Science Ed.	
Secondary Ed.	
Soc. Studies Ed.	
Special Ed.	6
Other	23

Research Institutes/Centers: Center for Higher Education, Center for Parent Education, Center for School-to-Work Transition, Center for Study of Educational Reform
Student Body Demographics: Average Age 35, 72% female, 28% male
Percent Ethnic Minorities: Hispanic-American 4%, Asian-American 3%, African-American 4%, Native-American 1%

Geographic Representation: Southwest 97%
Graduate Career Paths: K-12 Teaching 5%, Higher Ed
Teaching 19%, School Counseling 9%, K-12 Special Ed 6%,
School Administration 21%, Higher Ed Administration 21%,
Higher Ed Counseling 3%, Community Counseling 14%
Tuition: 56/hr (in state), 171/hr (out of state)
Financial Aid Recipients: 23%
Average Annual Housing Cost: 2,700
Application Deadline: 6/15; 12/1
Number of: applicants annually 1,019; applicants accepted
annually 790; students enrolled annually 669

Tests Required	Preferred/Min Score
Graduate Record Exam	900–1,200
National Teachers Exam	
Praxis II Exam	

University of Texas at Austin
College of Education

Austin, TX 78712
Admissions: (PH)512 471-7255
Total Enrollment: 20,000
Grad Enrollment: 1526 total
Program Membership: Holmes Partnership
Academic Programs Available: MASTERS: Ed. Admin, Ed.
Psych., Foreign Lang. Ed., Math Ed., Sci. Ed., Spec. Ed.
DOCTORATE: Ed. Admin, Ed. Psych., Foreign Lang. Ed.,
Math Ed., Sci. Ed., Spec. Ed.
Library: N/A

Research Areas	#Faculty
Adult Education	
Art Education	
Bilingual Education	
Counselor Education	
Early Childhood Ed.	
Ed. Admin	
Ed. Tech.	
Elementary Ed.	
Foreign Lang. Ed.	
Higher Ed.	
Math Ed.	
Mid. Lev. Ed.	
Multicultural Ed.	
Music Ed.	
Physical Ed.	
Read/Lang. Arts Ed.	
School Counseling	
Science Ed.	
Secondary Ed.	
Soc. Studies Ed.	
Special Ed.	
Other	

Student Body Demographics: N/A
Percent Ethnic Minorities: N/A
Geographic Representation: N/A
Tuition: 1,140 (in state), 6,048 (out of state)
Financial Aid Recipients: N/A
Average Annual Housing Cost: N/A
Application Deadline: 2/1

Number of: applicants annually 737; applicants accepted
annually 317; students enrolled annually N/A

Tests Required	Preferred/Min Score
Graduate Record Exam	
National Teachers Exam	
Praxis II Exam	

University of Texas at El Paso
College of Education

500 West University Avenue, El Paso, TX 79968
Admissions: (PH)915 747-5491, (FAX)915 747-6474
Grad Enrollment:
Program Membership: Holmes Partnership, NNER
Academic Programs Available: MASTERS: Bilingual Ed.,
Counselor Ed., Ed. Admin., Ed. Psych., Elementary Ed., Math
Ed., Physical Ed., Read/Lang Arts Ed., Sci. Ed., Sec. Ed.,
Spec. Ed. DOCTORATE: Bilingual Ed., Counselor Ed., Ed.
Admin, Ed. Psych., Elementary Ed., Math Ed., Physical Ed.,
Read/Lang Arts Ed., Sci. Ed., Sec. Ed., Spec. Ed.
Library: N/A

Research Areas	#Faculty
Adult Education	
Art Education	
Bilingual Education	
Counselor Education	
Early Childhood Ed.	
Ed. Admin	
Ed. Tech.	
Elementary Ed.	
Foreign Lang. Ed.	
Higher Ed.	
Math Ed.	
Mid. Lev. Ed.	
Multicultural Ed.	
Music Ed.	
Physical Ed.	
Read/Lang. Arts Ed.	
School Counseling	
Science Ed.	
Secondary Ed.	
Soc. Studies Ed.	
Special Ed.	
Other	

Student Body Demographics: N/A
Percent Ethnic Minorities: N/A
Geographic Representation: N/A
Tuition: 1,606 (in state), 6,214 (out of state)
Financial Aid Recipients: N/A
Average Annual Housing Cost: N/A
Application Deadline: 2/1
Number of: applicants annually 157; applicants accepted
annually 114; students enrolled annually N/A

Tests Required	Preferred/Min Score
Graduate Record Exam	940
National Teachers Exam	
Praxis II Exam	

University of Texas at San Antonio
Division of Education

Office of Admissions and Registrar, San Antonio, TX 78249
Admissions: (PH)210 691-4530
Dean: (PH)210 691-4370, (FAX)210 691-4487
Total Enrollment: 10,000–20,000
Grad Enrollment: FTM 50, PTM 1,200, Off campus 100%
Program Membership: N/A
Academic Programs Available: MASTERS: Adult Ed., Bilingual Ed., Counselor Ed., Early Childhood Ed., Ed. Admin, Ed. Psych., Elementary Ed., Higher Ed., Music Ed., Read/Lang Arts Ed., School Cons., Spec. Ed. DOCTORATE: Adult Ed., Bilingual Ed., Counselor Ed., Early Childhood Ed., Ed. Admin, Ed. Psych., Elementary Ed., Higher Ed., Music Ed., Read/Lang Arts Ed., School Cons., Spec. Ed.
Library: N/A
Computer Resources: Macintosh, Dual Platform, PCs, CD-ROM, Videodisc

Research Areas	#Faculty
Adult Education	2
Art Education	
Bilingual Education	2
Counselor Education	3
Early Childhood Ed.	4
Ed. Admin	5
Ed. Tech.	2
Elementary Ed.	4
Foreign Lang. Ed.	1
Higher Ed.	2
Math Ed.	2
Mid. Lev. Ed.	
Multicultural Ed.	2
Music Ed.	2
Physical Ed.	4
Read/Lang. Arts Ed.	4
School Counseling	3
Science Ed.	
Secondary Ed.	
Soc. Studies Ed.	
Special Ed.	3
Other	

Student Body Demographics: Average Age 35, 80% female, 20% male
Percent Ethnic Minorities: Hispanic-American 40%, Asian-American 2%, African-American 5%
Geographic Representation: Southwest 90%
Graduate Career Paths: K-12 Teaching 10%, Higher Ed Teaching 5%, School Counseling 20%, K-12 Special Ed 10%, School Administration 10%, Community Counseling 30%
Tuition: 145/hr (in state), 265/hr (out of state)
Financial Aid Recipients: 10%
Average Annual Housing Cost: N/A
Application Deadline: 7/1; 12/1; 5/1
Number of: applicants annually 900; applicants accepted annually 800–850; students enrolled annually 700

Tests Required	Preferred/Min Score
Graduate Record Exam	
National Teachers Exam	
Praxis II Exam	

University of Texas at Tyler School
of Education and Psychology

3900 University Blvd., Tyler, TX 75799
Admissions: (PH)903 566-7202, (FAX)903 566-8368
Dean: (PH)903 566-7050, (FAX)903 566-8368, (EMAIL)mac_moseley.ut_tyler.edu
Total Enrollment: 1,000–5,000
Program Membership: N/A
Academic Programs Available: MASTERS: Counselor Ed., Early Childhood Ed., Ed. Admin, Ed. Psych., Ed. Tech., Physical Ed., Read/Lang Arts Ed., School Cons., Spec. Ed. DOCTORATE: Counselor Ed., Early Childhood Ed., Ed. Admin, Ed. Psych., Ed. Tech., Physical Ed., Read/Lang Arts Ed., School Cons., Spec. Ed.
Library: R.L. Muntz Library
Computer Resources: Macintosh, Dual Platform, PCs, CD-ROM, Videodisc

Research Areas	#Faculty
Adult Education	
Art Education	
Bilingual Education	
Counselor Education	2
Early Childhood Ed.	2
Ed. Admin	2
Ed. Tech.	3
Elementary Ed.	2
Foreign Lang. Ed.	
Higher Ed.	1
Math Ed.	
Mid. Lev. Ed.	
Multicultural Ed.	
Music Ed.	
Physical Ed.	4
Read/Lang. Arts Ed.	5
School Counseling	2
Science Ed.	
Secondary Ed.	
Soc. Studies Ed.	
Special Ed.	3
Other	

Research Institutes/Centers: Learning Development Center, Human Development Center, Neuropsychology Center
Student Body Demographics: Average Age 30, 85% female, 15% male
Percent Ethnic Minorities: N/A
Geographic Representation: N/A
Tuition: N/A (in state), N/A (out of state)
Financial Aid Recipients: N/A
Average Annual Housing Cost: N/A
Application Deadline: N/A
Number of: applicants annually N/A; applicants accepted annually N/A; students enrolled annually N/A

Tests Required	Preferred/Min Score
Graduate Record Exam	
National Teachers Exam	
Praxis II Exam	

UTAH

Graduate Record Exam
National Teachers Exam
Praxis II Exam

Brigham Young University
College of Education

University Hill, Provo, UT 84602
Admissions: (PH)801 378-4091, (FAX)801 378-5238, (EMAIL)erlend_peterson@byu.edu
Dean: (PH)801 378-3695, (FAX)801 378-4017, (EMAIL)robert_patterson@byu.edu
Total Enrollment: 20,000
Grad Enrollment: FTM 95, PTM 73, FTD 26, PTD 98
Program Membership: N/A
Academic Programs Available: MASTERS: Art Ed., Ed. Admin, Ed. Psych., Elementary Ed., Foreign Lang. Ed., Math Ed., Music Ed., School Cons., Soc. Ed., Spec. Ed. DOCTORATE: Art Ed., Counselor Ed., Ed. Admin, Ed. Psych., Elementary Ed., Foreign Lang. Ed., Math Ed., Music Ed., Read/Lang Arts Ed., School Cons., Soc. Ed., Spec. Ed.
Library: Harold B. Lee Library
Computer Resources: Macintosh, Dual Platform, PCs, CD-ROM, Videodisc

Research Areas	#Faculty
Adult Education	
Art Education	
Bilingual Education	
Counselor Education	
Early Childhood Ed.	
Ed. Admin	
Ed. Tech.	
Elementary Ed.	
Foreign Lang. Ed.	
Higher Ed.	
Math Ed.	
Mid. Lev. Ed.	
Multicultural Ed.	
Music Ed.	
Physical Ed.	
Read/Lang. Arts Ed.	
School Counseling	
Science Ed.	
Secondary Ed.	
Soc. Studies Ed.	
Special Ed.	
Other	

Research Institutes/Centers: Teacher Education Research Group, Science Education Research Group
Student Body Demographics: Average Age 34, 53% female, 47% male
Percent Ethnic Minorities: Hispanic-American 3%, Asian-American 10%, Native-American 1%
Geographic Representation: N/A
Tuition: N/A
Financial Aid Recipients: 36%
Average Annual Housing Cost: 6,000
Application Deadline: 1/15
Number of: applicants annually 286; applicants accepted annually 166; students enrolled annually N/A

University of Utah Graduate
School of Education

250 Student Services Building, Salt Lake City, UT 84112
Admissions: (PH)801 581-7283, (FAX)801 585-3034
Dean: (PH)801 581-8221, (FAX)801 581-5223, (EMAIL)kennedy@gse.utah.edu
Total Enrollment: 20,000
Grad Enrollment: FTM 125, PTM 210, FTD 108, PTD 49, On campus 4%, Off campus 96%
Program Membership: Holmes Partnership, NNER
Academic Programs Available: MASTERS: Ed. Admin, Ed. Psych., Read/Lang Arts Ed., School Cons., Soc. Ed., DOCTORATE: Ed. Admin, Ed. Psych., Read/Lang Arts Ed., School Cons., Soc. Ed.
Library: Marriott Library, 2.5 million volumes
Computer Resources: Macintosh, Dual Platform, PCs, CD-ROM, Videodisc

Research Areas	#Faculty
Adult Education	1
Art Education	
Bilingual Education	
Counselor Education	
Early Childhood Ed.	2
Ed. Admin	13
Ed. Tech.	14
Elementary Ed.	4
Foreign Lang. Ed.	
Higher Ed.	4
Math Ed.	1
Mid. Lev. Ed.	
Multicultural Ed.	5
Music Ed.	
Physical Ed.	
Read/Lang. Arts Ed.	6
School Counseling	8
Science Ed.	2
Secondary Ed.	2
Soc. Studies Ed.	
Special Ed.	38
Other	36

Research Institutes/Centers: Center for the Advancement of Technology in Education, Education Policy Center
Student Body Demographics: Average Age 36, 67% female, 33% male
Percent Ethnic Minorities: Hispanic-American 2%, Asian-American 4%, African-American 1%, Native-American 1%
Geographic Representation: New England 1.8%, Midwest 3.5%, Mid Atlantic 2.6%, Southwest 2.2%, West 81.7%, Southeast 1%, Northwest 3.7%
Graduate Career Paths: K-12 Teaching 46%, K-12 Special Ed 18%, School Administration 20%, Higher Ed Administration 8%
Tuition: 631 (in state), 1,908 (out of state)

Financial Aid Recipients: 72%
Average Annual Housing Cost: 5,500
Application Deadline: 7/1; 11/15; 2/15
Number of: applicants annually 493; applicants accepted annually 186; students enrolled annually 181

Tests Required	Preferred/Min Score
Graduate Record Exam	900–1,200
National Teachers Exam	
Praxis II Exam	

Utah State University College of Education

Logan, UT 84322
Admissions: (PH)801 797-1437
Grad Enrollment: 650 total
Program Membership: N/A
Academic Programs Available: MASTERS: Art Ed., Ed. Tech., Elementary Ed., Math Ed., Music Ed., Physical Ed., Read/Lang Arts Ed., Sci. Ed., Soc. Ed., Spec. Ed. DOCTORATE: Art Ed., Ed. Tech., Elementary Ed., Math Ed., Music Ed., Physical Ed., Read/Lang Arts Ed., Sci. Ed., Soc. Ed., Spec. Ed.
Library: N/A

Research Areas	#Faculty
Adult Education	
Art Education	
Bilingual Education	
Counselor Education	
Early Childhood Ed.	
Ed. Admin	
Ed. Tech.	
Elementary Ed.	
Foreign Lang. Ed.	
Higher Ed.	
Math Ed.	
Mid. Lev. Ed.	
Multicultural Ed.	
Music Ed.	
Physical Ed.	
Read/Lang. Arts Ed.	
School Counseling	
Science Ed.	
Secondary Ed.	
Soc. Studies Ed.	
Special Ed.	
Other	

Student Body Demographics: N/A
Percent Ethnic Minorities: N/A
Geographic Representation: N/A
Tuition: 2,036 (in state), 6,180 (out of state)
Financial Aid Recipients: N/A
Average Annual Housing Cost: N/A
Number of: applicants annually 568; applicants accepted annually 227; students enrolled annually N/A

Tests Required	Preferred/Min Score
Graduate Record Exam	
National Teachers Exam	
Praxis II Exam	
TOEFL	550

VERMONT

College of St. Joseph Division of Education

71 Clement Road, Rutland, VT 05701
Admissions: (PH)802 773-5905
Dean: (PH)802 773-5900
Total Enrollment: 1,000
Grad Enrollment: FTM 3, PTM 75, Off campus 100%
Program Membership: N/A
Academic Programs Available: MASTERS: Elementary Ed., Read/Lang Arts Ed., Spec. Ed. DOCTORATE: Elementary Ed., Read/Lang Arts Ed., Spec. Ed.
Library: 48,000 volumes
Computer Resources: PCs, CD-ROM

Research Areas	#Faculty
Adult Education	
Art Education	
Bilingual Education	
Counselor Education	
Early Childhood Ed.	
Ed. Admin	
Ed. Tech.	
Elementary Ed.	
Foreign Lang. Ed.	
Higher Ed.	
Math Ed.	
Mid. Lev. Ed.	
Multicultural Ed.	
Music Ed.	
Physical Ed.	
Read/Lang. Arts Ed.	
School Counseling	
Science Ed.	
Secondary Ed.	
Soc. Studies Ed.	
Special Ed.	
Other	

Student Body Demographics: Average Age 27, 75% female, 25% male
Percent Ethnic Minorities: N/A
Geographic Representation: New England 100%
Graduate Career Paths: K-12 Teaching 50%, K-12 Special Ed 50%
Tuition: 190 (in state), 190 (out of state)
Financial Aid Recipients: 50%
Average Annual Housing Cost: 2,500
Application Deadline: rolling
Number of: applicants annually 50; applicants accepted annually 45; students enrolled annually N/A

Tests Required	Preferred/Min Score
Graduate Record Exam	
National Teachers Exam	
Praxis II Exam	

University of Vermont College of Education

335 Waterman Building, Burlington, VT 05403
Admissions: (PH)802 656-2699, (FAX)802 656-8429,
(EMAIL)ddurham@moose.uvm.edu
Dean: (PH)802 656-3160
Total Enrollment: 5,000–10,000
Grad Enrollment: 330 total, On campus 25%, Off campus 75%
Program Membership: Holmes Partnership
Academic Programs Available: MASTERS: Art Ed., Counselor Ed., Early Childhood Ed., Ed. Admin, Elementary Ed., Higher Ed., Math Ed., Music Ed., Physical Ed., Read/Lang Arts Ed., School Cons., Sci. Ed., Sec. Ed., Soc. Ed., Spec. DOCTORATE: Art Ed., Counselor Ed., Early Childhood Ed., Ed. Admin, Elementary Ed., Higher Ed., Math Ed., Music Ed., Physical Ed., Read/Lang Arts Ed., School Cons., Sci. Ed., Sec. Ed., Soc. Ed., Spec.
Library: Bailey Howe Library
Computer Resources: Macintosh, Dual Platform, PCs, CD-ROM, Videodisc

Research Areas	#Faculty
Adult Education	
Art Education	
Bilingual Education	
Counselor Education	
Early Childhood Ed.	
Ed. Admin	
Ed. Tech.	
Elementary Ed.	
Foreign Lang. Ed.	
Higher Ed.	
Math Ed.	
Mid. Lev. Ed.	
Multicultural Ed.	
Music Ed.	
Physical Ed.	
Read/Lang. Arts Ed.	
School Counseling	
Science Ed.	
Secondary Ed.	
Soc. Studies Ed.	
Special Ed.	
Other	

Research Institutes/Centers: University Affiliated Facility for Research on Disabilities
Student Body Demographics: Average Age 40, 65% female, 35% male
Percent Ethnic Minorities: Hispanic-American 1%, Asian-American 3%, African-American 1%, Native-American 1%
Geographic Representation: New England 90%, Midwest 1%, Mid Atlantic 5%, Southwest 1%, West 1%, Southeast 1%, Northwest 1%
Graduate Career Paths: K-12 Teaching 40%, School Counseling 5%, K-12 Special Ed 10%, School Administration 20%, Higher Ed Administration 20%, Community Counseling 5%
Tuition: 3,105 (in state), 7758 (out of state)
Financial Aid Recipients: 90%

Average Annual Housing Cost: 372
Application Deadline: 4/1; 6/1
Number of: applicants annually 454; applicants accepted annually 239; students enrolled annually 200

Tests Required	Preferred/Min Score
Graduate Record Exam	
National Teachers Exam	
Praxis II Exam	

VIRGINIA

Christopher Newport University Department of Education

50 Shoe Lane, Newport News, VA 23606
Admissions: (PH)804 594-7015, (FAX)804 594-7713
Dean: (PH)804 594-7380, (FAX)804 594-7862
Total Enrollment: 1,000–5,000
Grad Enrollment: FTM 15, PTM 29, Off campus 100%
Program Membership: N/A
Academic Programs Available: MASTERS: Math Ed., Read/Lang Arts Ed., Sci. Ed., DOCTORATE: Math Ed., Read/Lang Arts Ed., Sci. Ed.
Library: Captain John Smith Library, 308,000 volumes
Computer Resources: Macintosh, Dual Platform, PCs, CD-ROM, Videodisc

Research Areas	#Faculty
Adult Education	
Art Education	
Bilingual Education	
Counselor Education	
Early Childhood Ed.	
Ed. Admin	
Ed. Tech.	
Elementary Ed.	2
Foreign Lang. Ed.	
Higher Ed.	
Math Ed.	2
Mid. Lev. Ed.	1
Multicultural Ed.	2
Music Ed.	
Physical Ed.	
Read/Lang. Arts Ed.	6
School Counseling	
Science Ed.	
Secondary Ed.	
Soc. Studies Ed.	
Special Ed.	
Other	

Student Body Demographics: Average Age 30, 75% female, 25% male
Percent Ethnic Minorities: African-American 15%
Geographic Representation: Southeast 100%
Graduate Career Paths: K-12 Teaching 100%
Tuition: 134/hr (in state), 134/hr (out of state)

Financial Aid Recipients: N/A
Average Annual Housing Cost: N/A
Application Deadline: rolling
Number of: applicants annually 20; applicants accepted annually N/A; students enrolled annually N/A

Tests Required	Preferred/Min Score
Graduate Record Exam	
National Teachers Exam	
Praxis II Exam	

College of William and Mary
School of Education

Room 100, Hugh Jones Hall, Williamsburg, VA 23187
Admissions: (PH)804 221-2317, (FAX)804 221-2988, (EMAIL)gepear@facstaff.wm.edu
Dean: (PH)804 221-2314, (FAX)804 221-2988, (EMAIL)vamcla@facstaff.wm.edu
Total Enrollment: 5,000–10,000
Grad Enrollment: FTM 199, PTM 467, FTD 39, PTD 91, On campus 15%, Off campus 85%
Program Membership: N/A
Academic Programs Available: MASTERS: Counselor Ed., Ed. Admin, Elementary Ed., Foreign Lang. Ed., Higher Ed., Math Ed., Read/Lang Arts Ed., School Cons., Sci. Ed., Sec. Ed., Soc. Ed., Spec. Ed. DOCTORATE: Counselor Ed., Ed. Admin, Elementary Ed., Foreign Lang. Ed., Higher Ed., Math Ed., Read/Lang Arts Ed., School Cons., Sci. Ed., Sec. Ed., Soc. Ed., Spec. Ed.
Library: Swem Library, 935,000 volumes
Computer Resources: Macintosh, Dual Platform, PCs, CD-ROM, Videodisc

Research Areas	#Faculty
Adult Education	
Art Education	
Bilingual Education	
Counselor Education	
Early Childhood Ed.	2
Ed. Admin	4
Ed. Tech.	
Elementary Ed.	6
Foreign Lang. Ed.	1
Higher Ed.	3
Math Ed.	3
Mid. Lev. Ed.	
Multicultural Ed.	3
Music Ed.	
Physical Ed.	
Read/Lang. Arts Ed.	2
School Counseling	4
Science Ed.	1
Secondary Ed.	1
Soc. Studies Ed.	2
Special Ed.	6
Other	8

Research Institutes/Centers: Center for Gifted Education, Project Reclaim, Eastern Virginia Writing Project Program
Student Body Demographics: Average Age 38, 65% female, 35% male

Percent Ethnic Minorities: Hispanic-American 7%, Asian-American 9%, African-American 12%, Native-American 1%
Geographic Representation: New England 6%, Midwest 3%, Mid Atlantic 80%, Southwest 2%, West 2%, Southeast 4%, Northwest 1%
Graduate Career Paths: K-12 Teaching 14.8%, Higher Ed Teaching 7%, School Counseling 5%, K-12 Higher Ed Administration 19%, Community Counseling 27%
Tuition: 2,369 (in state), 7,214 (out of state)
Financial Aid Recipients: 12.5%
Average Annual Housing Cost: 1,195
Application Deadline: 10/1; 3/1
Number of: applicants annually 595; applicants accepted annually 357; students enrolled annually 254

Tests Required	Preferred/Min Score
Graduate Record Exam	1,000–1,250
National Teachers Exam	
Praxis II Exam	

George Mason University
Graduate School of Education

Admissions Office, 4400 University Drive, Fairfax, VA 22030
Admissions: (PH)703 993-2402, (FAX)703 993-2392
Dean: (PH)703 993-2004, (FAX)703 993-2001
Total Enrollment: 20,000
Grad Enrollment: 1,599 total, Off campus 100%
Program Membership: Holmes Partnership
Academic Programs Available: MASTERS: Bilingual Ed., Counselor Ed., Early Childhood Ed., Ed. Admin, Ed. Psych., Ed. Tech., Elementary Ed., Foreign Lang. Ed., Higher Ed., Math Ed., Mid Level Ed., Multicultural Ed., Music Ed., Physical Ed., Read/Lang Arts Ed., School Cons., Sci. Ed., Sec. Ed., Soc. Ed., Spec. Ed. DOCTORATE: Bilingual Ed., Counselor Ed., Early Childhood Ed., Ed. Admin, Ed. Psych., Ed. Tech., Elementary Ed., Foreign Lang. Ed., Higher Ed., Math Ed., Mid Level Ed., Multicultural Ed., Music Ed., Physical Ed., Read/Lang Arts Ed., School Cons., Sci. Ed., Sec. Ed., Soc. Ed., Spec. Ed.
Library: Fenwick Library, 450,000 volumes
Computer Resources: Macintosh, Dual Platform, PCs, CD-ROM, Videodisc

Research Areas	#Faculty
Adult Education	1
Art Education	
Bilingual Education	4
Counselor Education	4
Early Childhood Ed.	4
Ed. Admin	5
Ed. Tech.	
Elementary Ed.	2
Foreign Lang. Ed.	1
Higher Ed.	3
Math Ed.	1
Mid. Lev. Ed.	2
Multicultural Ed.	4
Music Ed.	
Physical Ed.	
Read/Lang. Arts Ed.	2

School Counseling	2
Science Ed.	1
Secondary Ed.	1
Soc. Studies Ed.	2
Special Ed.	7
Other	7

Research Institutes/Centers: Center for Human Disabilities, The Leadership Academy, The National Center for Community College Education
Student Body Demographics: Average Age 32, 80% female, 20% male
Percent Ethnic Minorities: Hispanic-American 2.7%, Asian-American 2.7%, African-American 5.6%, Native-American 0.2%
Geographic Representation: New England 2%, Midwest 1%, Mid Atlantic 82%, Southwest 1%, West 1%, Southeast 2%, Northwest 1%
Graduate Career Paths: K-12 Teaching 51%, Higher Ed Teaching 7%, K-12 Special Ed 18%, School Administration 9%
Tuition: 175/hr (in state), 483/hr (out of state)
Financial Aid Recipients: N/A
Average Annual Housing Cost: 4,500
Application Deadline: 5/1; 11/1; 3/1
Number of: applicants annually 1,662; applicants accepted annually 1,257; students enrolled annually 914

Tests Required	Preferred/Min Score
Graduate Record Exam	1,000
National Teachers Exam	
Praxis II Exam	
TOEFL	600

Hollins College Education Department

P.O. Box 9683, Roanoke, VA 24020
Admissions: (PH)703 362-6575, (FAX)703 362-6642
Dean: (PH)703 362-6664
Total Enrollment: 1,000–5,000
Grad Enrollment: PTM 14
Program Membership: N/A
Academic Programs Available: N/A
Library: Fishburn Library
Computer Resources: Macintosh, Dual Platform, PCs, CD-ROM, Videodisc

Research Areas	#Faculty
Adult Education	
Art Education	
Bilingual Education	
Counselor Education	
Early Childhood Ed.	
Ed. Admin	
Ed. Tech.	
Elementary Ed.	
Foreign Lang. Ed.	
Higher Ed.	
Math Ed.	
Mid. Lev. Ed.	
Multicultural Ed.	
Music Ed.	
Physical Ed.	

Read/Lang. Arts Ed.	
School Counseling	
Science Ed.	
Secondary Ed.	
Soc. Studies Ed.	
Special Ed.	
Other	

Student Body Demographics: Average Age 37, 100% female, 0% male
Percent Ethnic Minorities: African-American 20%
Geographic Representation: Southeast 100%
Graduate Career Paths: K-12 Teaching 100%
Tuition: 195/cr (in state), 195/cr (out of state)
Financial Aid Recipients: N/A
Average Annual Housing Cost: N/A
Application Deadline: 1/11
Number of: applicants annually 25; applicants accepted annually 18; students enrolled annually 14

Tests Required	Preferred/Min Score
Graduate Record Exam	
National Teachers Exam	
Praxis II Exam	

James Madison University College of Education and Psychology

Graduate School Office, Wilson Hall, Harrisonburg, VA 22807
Admissions: (PH)540 568-6131, (FAX)540 568-6266
Dean: (PH)540 568-6572, (FAX)540 568-3342
Total Enrollment: 10,000–20,000
Grad Enrollment: Off campus 100%
Program Membership: N/A
Academic Programs Available: MASTERS: Art Ed., Counselor Ed., Early Childhood Ed., Ed. Admin, Ed. Psych., Ed. Tech., Mid Level Ed., Music Ed., Physical Ed., Read/Lang Arts Ed., School Cons., Sec. Ed., Spec. Ed. DOCTORATE: Art Ed., Counselor Ed., Early Childhood Ed., Ed. Admin, Ed. Psych., Ed. Tech., Mid Level Ed., Music Ed., Physical Ed., Read/Lang Arts Ed., School Cons., Sec. Ed., Spec. Ed.
Library: Carrier Library
Computer Resources: Macintosh, Dual Platform, PCs, CD-ROM, Videodisc

Research Areas	#Faculty
Adult Education	1
Art Education	
Bilingual Education	
Counselor Education	2
Early Childhood Ed.	4
Ed. Admin	2
Ed. Tech.	4
Elementary Ed.	
Foreign Lang. Ed.	
Higher Ed.	
Math Ed.	1
Mid. Lev. Ed.	1
Multicultural Ed.	1
Music Ed.	

Physical Ed.	4
Read/Lang. Arts Ed.	3
School Counseling	2
Science Ed.	1
Secondary Ed.	1
Soc. Studies Ed.	1
Special Ed.	6
Other	12

Research Institutes/Centers: Human Development Center
Student Body Demographics: Average Age 26, 70% female, 30% male
Percent Ethnic Minorities: Hispanic-American 2%, African-American 2%
Geographic Representation: New England 30%, Mid Atlantic 40%, Southeast 30%
Tuition: 131/hr (in state), 363/hr (out of state)
Financial Aid Recipients: N/A
Average Annual Housing Cost: N/A
Application Deadline: 7/1; 11/1; 4/1
Number of: applicants annually N/A; applicants accepted annually N/A; students enrolled annually N/A

Tests Required	Preferred/Min Score
Graduate Record Exam	
National Teachers Exam	
Praxis II Exam	

Liberty University School of Education

Box 2,0000, Lynchburg, VA 24506
Admissions: (PH)804 582-2158
Dean: (PH)804 582-2314
Total Enrollment: 5,000–10,000
Grad Enrollment: PTM 25, Off campus 100%
Program Membership: N/A
Academic Programs Available: MASTERS: Ed. Admin, Elementary Ed., Read/Lang Arts Ed., Sec. Ed., DOCTORATE: Ed. Admin, Elementary Ed., Read/Lang Arts Ed., Sec. Ed.
Library: Liberty University Library, 278,000 volumes
Computer Resources: Macintosh, Dual Platform, PCs, CD-ROM, Videodisc

Research Areas	#Faculty
Adult Education	
Art Education	
Bilingual Education	
Counselor Education	
Early Childhood Ed.	
Ed. Admin	
Ed. Tech.	
Elementary Ed.	
Foreign Lang. Ed.	
Higher Ed.	
Math Ed.	
Mid. Lev. Ed.	
Multicultural Ed.	
Music Ed.	
Physical Ed.	
Read/Lang. Arts Ed.	
School Counseling	
Science Ed.	

Secondary Ed.	
Soc. Studies Ed.	
Special Ed.	
Other	

Student Body Demographics: Average Age N/A, 60% female, 40% male
Percent Ethnic Minorities: N/A
Geographic Representation: Mid Atlantic 100%
Graduate Career Paths: K-12 Teaching 50%, K-12 School Administration 50%
Tuition: 215/hr (in state), 215/hr (out of state)
Financial Aid Recipients: 5%
Average Annual Housing Cost: N/A
Application Deadline: N/A
Number of: applicants annually 30; applicants accepted annually 25; students enrolled annually 25

Tests Required	Preferred/Min Score
Graduate Record Exam	900
National Teachers Exam	
Praxis II Exam	

Lynchburg College School of Education and Human Development

1501 Lakeside Drive, Lynchburg, VA 24501
Admissions: (PH)804 544-8300, (FAX)804 544-8381
Dean: (PH)804 544-8483, (FAX)804 544-8483, (EMAIL)polloway@lopwood.lynchburg.edu
Total Enrollment: 1,000–5,000
Grad Enrollment: FTM 103, PTM 200, On campus 5%, Off campus 95%
Program Membership: N/A
Academic Programs Available: MASTERS: Counselor Ed., Early Childhood Ed., Ed. Admin, Mid Level Ed., School Cons., Sec. Ed., Spec. DOCTORATE: Counselor Ed., Early Childhood Ed., Ed. Admin, Mid Level Ed., School Cons., Sec. Ed.
Library: Knight-Capron Library
Computer Resources: Macintosh, Dual Platform, PCs, CD-ROM, Videodisc

Research Areas	#Faculty
Adult Education	
Art Education	
Bilingual Education	
Counselor Education	4
Early Childhood Ed.	4
Ed. Admin	2
Ed. Tech.	
Elementary Ed.	
Foreign Lang. Ed.	
Higher Ed.	
Math Ed.	1
Mid. Lev. Ed.	2
Multicultural Ed.	
Music Ed.	
Physical Ed.	
Read/Lang. Arts Ed.	
School Counseling	4
Science Ed.	1

Secondary Ed.	1
Soc. Studies Ed.	1
Special Ed.	5
Other	1

Research Institutes/Centers: Technical Assistance Center
Student Body Demographics: Average Age 28, 70% female, 30% male
Percent Ethnic Minorities: Hispanic-American 2%, Asian-American 2%, African-American 10%
Geographic Representation: Mid Atlantic 20%, Southeast 80%
Graduate Career Paths: K-12 Teaching 30%, School Counseling 15%, K-12 Special Ed 20%, School Administration 5%, Community Counseling 20%
Tuition: 200/cr (in state), 200/cr (out of state)
Financial Aid Recipients: N/A
Average Annual Housing Cost: N/A
Application Deadline: 11/15; 4/15; 7/15
Number of: applicants annually N/A; applicants accepted annually N/A; students enrolled annually 300

Tests Required	Preferred/Min Score
Graduate Record Exam	
National Teachers Exam	
Praxis II Exam	

Radford University College of Education and Human Development

Radford, VA 24142
Admissions: (PH)703 831-5439
Grad Enrollment: 316 total
Program Membership: N/A
Academic Programs Available: MASTERS: Counselor Ed., Ed. Admin, Ed. Tech., Physical Ed., Read/Lang Arts Ed., Spec. Ed. DOCTORATE: Counselor Ed., Ed. Admin, Ed. Tech., Physical Ed., Read/Lang Arts Ed., Spec. Ed.
Library: N/A

Research Areas	#Faculty
Adult Education	
Art Education	
Bilingual Education	
Counselor Education	
Early Childhood Ed.	
Ed. Admin	
Ed. Tech.	
Elementary Ed.	
Foreign Lang. Ed.	
Higher Ed.	
Math Ed.	
Mid. Lev. Ed.	
Multicultural Ed.	
Music Ed.	
Physical Ed.	
Read/Lang. Arts Ed.	
School Counseling	
Science Ed.	
Secondary Ed.	
Soc. Studies Ed.	
Special Ed.	

Other
Student Body Demographics: N/A
Percent Ethnic Minorities: N/A
Geographic Representation: N/A
Tuition: 3,272 (in state), 6,456 (out of state)
Financial Aid Recipients: N/A
Average Annual Housing Cost: N/A
Application Deadline: 3/1
Number of: applicants annually 216; applicants accepted annually 142; students enrolled annually N/A

Tests Required	Preferred/Min Score
Graduate Record Exam	
National Teachers Exam	
Praxis II Exam	

University of Virginia Curry School of Education

104 Ruffner Hall, 305 Emmet Street, Charlottesville, VA 22903
Admissions: (PH)804 924-3334, (FAX)804 924-0747, (EMAIL)curry@virginia.edu
Dean: (PH)804 924-3332, (FAX)804 924-0888, (EMAIL)rkb3b@virginia.edu
Total Enrollment: 10,000–20,000
Grad Enrollment: FTM 394, PTM 74, FTD 269, PTD 84, On campus 18%, Off campus 82%
Program Membership: Holmes Partnership
Academic Programs Available: MASTERS: Counselor Ed., Early Childhood Ed., Ed. Admin, Ed. Psych., Ed. Tech., Elementary Ed., Foreign Lang. Ed., Higher Ed., Math Ed., Mid Level Ed., Physical Ed., Read/Lang Arts Ed., School Cons., Sci. Ed., Soc. Ed., Spec. Ed. DOCTORATE: Counselor Ed., Early Childhood Ed., Ed. Admin, Ed. Psych., Ed. Tech., Elementary Ed., Foreign Lang. Ed., Higher Ed., Math Ed., Mid Level Ed., Physical Ed., Read/Lang Arts Ed., School Cons., Sci. Ed., Soc. Ed., Spec. Ed.
Library: Alderman Library, 4 million volumes
Computer Resources: Macintosh, Dual Platform, PCs, CD-ROM, Videodisc

Research Areas	#Faculty
Adult Education	3
Art Education	
Bilingual Education	1
Counselor Education	7
Early Childhood Ed.	4
Ed. Admin	6
Ed. Tech.	5
Elementary Ed.	6
Foreign Lang. Ed.	2
Higher Ed.	4
Math Ed.	2
Mid. Lev. Ed.	11
Multicultural Ed.	3
Music Ed.	
Physical Ed.	13
Read/Lang. Arts Ed.	5
School Counseling	7

Science Ed.	2
Secondary Ed.	2
Soc. Studies Ed.	2
Special Ed.	9
Other	

Research Institutes/Centers: Center for the Study of Higher Education, National Research Center on the Gifted and Talented, McGuffy Reading Center

Student Body Demographics: Average Age 29, 69% female, 31% male

Percent Ethnic Minorities: Hispanic-American 1%, Asian-American 2%, African-American 5%, Native-American 1%

Geographic Representation: N/A

Graduate Career Paths: K-12 Teaching 23%, Higher Ed Teaching 16%, School Counseling 11%, K-12 Special Ed 9%, School Administration 8%, Higher Ed Administration 3%, Higher Ed Counseling 1%, Community Counseling 3%

Tuition: 4,586 (in state), 13978 (out of state)

Financial Aid Recipients: 40%

Average Annual Housing Cost: 2,100

Application Deadline: 3/1

Number of: applicants annually 1,443; applicants accepted annually 683; students enrolled annually 501

Tests Required	Preferred/Min Score
Graduate Record Exam	900–1,200
National Teachers Exam	
Praxis II Exam	
TOEFL	600

Virginia Commonwealth University School of Education

P.O. Box 842526, 821 W. Franklin St., Richmond, VA 23284-2526

Admissions: (PH)804 828-1222, (FAX)804 828-1899

Dean: (PH)804 828-3382, (FAX)804 828-1323, (EMAIL)joehler@felix.vcu.edu

Total Enrollment: 20,000

Grad Enrollment: FTM 339, PTM 370, FTD 5, PTD 78, On campus 8%, Off campus 92%

Program Membership: Holmes Partnership

Academic Programs Available: MASTERS: Adult Ed., Art Ed., Counselor Ed., Early Childhood Ed., Ed. Admin, Ed. Tech., Elementary Ed., Foreign Lang. Ed., Math Ed., Mid Level Ed., Music Ed., Physical Ed., Read/Lang Arts Ed., School Cons., Sci. Ed., Sec. Ed., Soc. Ed., Spec. Ed. DOCTORATE: Adult Ed., Art Ed., Counselor Ed., Early Childhood Ed., Ed. Admin, Ed. Tech., Elementary Ed., Foreign Lang. Ed., Math Ed., Mid Level Ed., Music Ed., Physical Ed., Read/Lang Arts Ed., School Cons., Sci. Ed., Sec. Ed., Soc. Ed., Spec. Ed.

Library: James Branch Cabell Library, 787,000 volumes

Computer Resources: Macintosh, Dual Platform, PCs, CD-ROM, Videodisc

Research Areas	#Faculty
Adult Education	2
Art Education	
Bilingual Education	

Counselor Education	3
Early Childhood Ed.	3
Ed. Admin	4
Ed. Tech.	2
Elementary Ed.	2
Foreign Lang. Ed.	
Higher Ed.	2
Math Ed.	2
Mid. Lev. Ed.	2
Multicultural Ed.	2
Music Ed.	
Physical Ed.	1
Read/Lang. Arts Ed.	3
School Counseling	3
Science Ed.	1
Secondary Ed.	1
Soc. Studies Ed.	1
Special Ed.	7
Other	8

Research Institutes/Centers: Virginia Institute for Developmental Disabilities, Rehabilitation Research and Training Center, Metropolitan Educational Research Consortium

Student Body Demographics: Average Age 32, 67% female, 33% male

Percent Ethnic Minorities: Hispanic-American 1%, Asian-American 3%, African-American 9%, Native-American 1%

Geographic Representation: Mid Atlantic 98%, Southeast 2%

Graduate Career Paths: K-12 Teaching 68%, Higher Ed Teaching 1%, School Counseling 10%, K-12 Special Ed 13%, School Administration 8%

Tuition: 4,273 (in state), 10291 (out of state)

Financial Aid Recipients: 36%

Average Annual Housing Cost: 2,800

Application Deadline: 7/1; 11/1; 5/1

Number of: applicants annually 700; applicants accepted annually 600; students enrolled annually N/A

Tests Required	Preferred/Min Score
Graduate Record Exam	
National Teachers Exam	
Praxis II Exam	

Virginia Polytechnic Institute and State University College of Education

Blacksburg, VA 24061

Admissions: (PH)703 231-6426

Grad Enrollment: 452 total

Program Membership: Holmes Partnership

Academic Programs Available: MASTERS: Adult Ed., Counselor Ed., Ed. Admin, Ed. Psych., Ed. Tech., Elementary Ed., Higher Ed., Sec. Ed., Spec. Ed. DOCTORATE: Adult Ed., Counselor Ed., Ed. Admin, Ed. Psych., Ed. Tech., Elementary Ed., Higher Ed., Sec. Ed., Spec. Ed.

Library: N/A

Research Areas	#Faculty
Adult Education	

Art Education
Bilingual Education
Counselor Education
Early Childhood Ed.
Ed. Admin
Ed. Tech.
Elementary Ed.
Foreign Lang. Ed.
Higher Ed.
Math Ed.
Mid. Lev. Ed.
Multicultural Ed.
Music Ed.
Physical Ed.
Read/Lang. Arts Ed.
School Counseling
Science Ed.
Secondary Ed.
Soc. Studies Ed.
Special Ed.
Other

Student Body Demographics: N/A
Percent Ethnic Minorities: N/A
Geographic Representation: N/A
Tuition: 4,709 (in state), 6,941 (out of state)
Financial Aid Recipients: N/A
Average Annual Housing Cost: N/A
Application Deadline: 2/15
Number of: applicants annually 335; applicants accepted annually 231; students enrolled annually N/A

Tests Required	Preferred/Min Score
Graduate Record Exam	
National Teachers Exam	
Praxis II Exam	

WASHINGTON

Gonzaga University School of Education

E. 502 Boone, AD Box 102, Spokane, WA 99258
Admissions: (PH)509 328-4220, (FAX)509 324-5718, (EMAIL)almanza@gu.gonzaga.edu
Dean: (PH)509 328-4220 x3505, (FAX)509 324-5812, (EMAIL)pcriden@soe.gonzaga.edu
Total Enrollment: 1,000–5,000
Grad Enrollment: FTM 5,890, PTM 320,530, FTD 1,530, PTD 1,020, On campus 5%, Off campus 95%
Program Membership: N/A
Academic Programs Available: MASTERS: Art Ed., Counselor Ed., Early Childhood Ed., Ed. Admin, Ed. Tech., Elementary Ed., Math Ed., Music Ed., Physical Ed., School Cons., Sec. Ed., Soc. Ed., Spec. Ed. DOCTORATE: Art Ed., Counselor Ed., Early Childhood Ed., Ed. Admin, Ed. Tech., Elementary Ed., Math Ed., Music Ed., Physical Ed., School Cons., Sec. Ed., Soc. Ed., Spec. Ed.

Library: Foley Center, 400,000 volumes
Computer Resources: Macintosh, Dual Platform, PCs, CD-ROM, Videodisc

Research Areas	#Faculty
Adult Education	
Art Education	1
Bilingual Education	
Counselor Education	4
Early Childhood Ed.	3
Ed. Admin	10
Ed. Tech.	3
Elementary Ed.	4
Foreign Lang. Ed.	
Higher Ed.	4
Math Ed.	1
Mid. Lev. Ed.	
Multicultural Ed.	3
Music Ed.	1
Physical Ed.	5
Read/Lang. Arts Ed.	2
School Counseling	3
Science Ed.	
Secondary Ed.	
Soc. Studies Ed.	1
Special Ed.	5
Other	

Research Institutes/Centers: Academy for Educational Studies, Institute for Educational Innovation & Reform, Institute for Education and Art
Student Body Demographics: Average Age 34, 50% female, 50% male
Percent Ethnic Minorities: Hispanic-American 2%, Asian-American 1%, African-American 1%, Native-American 4%
Geographic Representation: Northwest 100%
Graduate Career Paths: K-12 Teaching 45%, Higher Ed Teaching 5%, School Counseling 2%, K-12 Special Ed 5%, School Administration 26%, Higher Ed Administration 5%, Community Counseling 12%
Tuition: 255/cr (in state), 255/cr (out of state)
Financial Aid Recipients: 42%
Average Annual Housing Cost: N/A
Application Deadline: varies
Number of: applicants annually 609; applicants accepted annually 369; students enrolled annually 303

Tests Required	Preferred/Min Score
Graduate Record Exam	
National Teachers Exam	
Praxis II Exam	

University of Washington
College of Education

206 Miller, Box 353600, Seattle, WA 98195-3600
Admissions: (PH)206 543-7833, (FAX)206 543-8439, (EMAIL)edinfo@u.washington.edu
Dean: (PH)206 616-4805
Total Enrollment: 20,000
Grad Enrollment: FTM 311, PTM 76, FTD 109, PTD 120

Program Membership: Holmes Partnership, NNER
Academic Programs Available: MASTERS: Counselor Ed., Early Childhood Ed., Ed. Admin, Ed. Psych., Ed. Tech., Elementary Ed., Foreign Lang. Ed., Higher Ed., Math Ed., Mid Level Ed., Multicultural Ed., Read/Lang Arts Ed., School Cons., Sci. Ed., Sec. Ed., Soc. Ed., Spec. Ed. DOCTORATE: Counselor Ed., Early Childhood Ed., Ed. Admin, Ed. Psych., Ed. Tech., Elementary Ed., Foreign Lang. Ed., Higher Ed., Math Ed., Mid Level Ed., Multicultural Ed., Read/Lang Arts Ed., School Cons., Sci. Ed., Sec. Ed., Soc. Ed., Spec. Ed.
Library: University of Washington Libraries, 5.4 million volumes
Computer Resources: Macintosh, Dual Platform, PCs, CD-ROM, Videodisc

Research Areas	#Faculty
Adult Education	
Art Education	
Bilingual Education	2
Counselor Education	3
Early Childhood Ed.	2
Ed. Admin	14
Ed. Tech.	2
Elementary Ed.	4
Foreign Lang. Ed.	
Higher Ed.	3
Math Ed.	2
Mid. Lev. Ed.	3
Multicultural Ed.	3
Music Ed.	
Physical Ed.	
Read/Lang. Arts Ed.	4
School Counseling	3
Science Ed.	3
Secondary Ed.	3
Soc. Studies Ed.	4
Special Ed.	10
Other	

Research Institutes/Centers: Center for Multicultural Education, Center for Eucational Renewal, Center for Students At-Risk
Student Body Demographics: Average Age 35, 68% female, 32% male
Percent Ethnic Minorities: Hispanic-American 4%, Asian-American 7%, African-American 3%, Native-American 2%
Geographic Representation: Northwest 84%
Tuition: 1,582 (in state), 3,963 (out of state)
Financial Aid Recipients: N/A
Average Annual Housing Cost: 7,000
Application Deadline: varies
Number of: applicants annually 700; applicants accepted annually 385; students enrolled annually 350

Tests Required	Preferred/Min Score
Graduate Record Exam	
National Teachers Exam	
Praxis II Exam	
TOEFL	580

Washington State University
College of Education

Pullman, WA 99164-2114
Dean: (PH)509 335-7091, (FAX)509 335-9172
Total Enrollment: 10,000–20,000
Grad Enrollment: 405 total, On campus 1%, Off campus 99%
Program Membership: Holmes Partnership
Academic Programs Available: MASTERS: Bilingual Ed., Counselor Ed., Ed. Admin, Ed. Psych., Elementary Ed., Higher Ed., Math Ed., Physical Ed., Read/Lang Arts Ed., School Cons., Sec. Ed., DOCTORATE: Bilingual Ed., Counselor Ed., Ed. Admin, Ed. Psych., Elementary Ed., Higher Ed., Math Ed., Physical Ed., Read/Lang Arts Ed., School Cons., Sec. Ed.
Library: Holland Library, 1.7 million volumes
Computer Resources: Macintosh, Dual Platform, PCs, CD-ROM, Videodisc

Research Areas	#Faculty
Adult Education	
Art Education	
Bilingual Education	1
Counselor Education	5
Early Childhood Ed.	
Ed. Admin	7
Ed. Tech.	
Elementary Ed.	4
Foreign Lang. Ed.	
Higher Ed.	2
Math Ed.	2
Mid. Lev. Ed.	1
Multicultural Ed.	1
Music Ed.	
Physical Ed.	2
Read/Lang. Arts Ed.	7
School Counseling	3
Science Ed.	2
Secondary Ed.	2
Soc. Studies Ed.	
Special Ed.	4
Other	

Student Body Demographics: Average Age 34, 67% female, 33% male
Percent Ethnic Minorities: Hispanic-American 5%, Asian-American 3%, African-American 4%, Native-American 1%
Geographic Representation: New England 1%, Mid Atlantic 1%, West 5%, Southeast 1%, Northwest 89%
Graduate Career Paths: K-12 Teaching 51%, Higher Ed Teaching 2%, K-12 School Administration 12%, Higher Ed Administration 2%
Tuition: 4,748 (in state), 11,892 (out of state)
Financial Aid Recipients: N/A
Average Annual Housing Cost: 5,000
Application Deadline: 2/1
Number of: applicants annually N/A; applicants accepted annually N/A; students enrolled annually N/A

Tests Required	Preferred/Min Score
Graduate Record Exam	

National Teachers Exam
Praxis II Exam

WEST VIRGINIA

Marshall University College of Education

400 Hal Greer Blvd., 125 Old Main, Huntington, WV 25755
Admissions: (PH)800 642-3463, (FAX)304 696-3135
Dean: (PH)304 696-3132, (FAX)304 696-6221,
(EMAIL)ded004@marshall.wvnet.edu
Total Enrollment: 10,000–20,000
Grad Enrollment: FTM 175, PTM 467, FTD 3, PTD 9, On
campus 1%, Off campus 99%
Program Membership: N/A
Academic Programs Available: MASTERS: Adult Ed., Art
Ed., Counselor Ed., Early Childhood Ed., Ed. Admin,
Elementary Ed., Foreign Lang. Ed., Higher Ed., Math Ed.,
Mid Level Ed., Music Ed., Physical Ed., Read/Lang Arts Ed.,
School Cons., Sci. Ed., Sec. Ed., Soc. Ed., Spec. Ed.
DOCTORATE: Adult Ed., Art Ed., Counselor Ed., Early
Childhood Ed., Ed. Admin, Elementary Ed., Foreign Lang.
Ed., Higher Ed., Math Ed., Mid Level Ed., Music Ed.,
Physical Ed., Read/Lang Arts Ed., School Cons., Sci. Ed.,
Sec. Ed., Soc. Ed., Spec. Ed.
Library: James E. Morrow Library
Computer Resources: Macintosh, Dual Platform, PCs,
CD-ROM, Videodisc

Research Areas	#Faculty
Adult Education	3
Art Education	2
Bilingual Education	
Counselor Education	8
Early Childhood Ed.	2
Ed. Admin	4
Ed. Tech.	
Elementary Ed.	8
Foreign Lang. Ed.	
Higher Ed.	2
Math Ed.	3
Mid. Lev. Ed.	2
Multicultural Ed.	
Music Ed.	2
Physical Ed.	13
Read/Lang. Arts Ed.	3
School Counseling	8
Science Ed.	2
Secondary Ed.	2
Soc. Studies Ed.	2
Special Ed.	6
Other	6

Student Body Demographics: Average Age 34, 80% female,
20% male

Percent Ethnic Minorities: Hispanic-American 1%,
Asian-American 3%, African-American 2%,
Native-American 0.5%
Geographic Representation: Midwest 1%, Mid
Atlantic 98%, Southeast 1%
Graduate Career Paths: K-12 Teaching 60%, Higher Ed
Teaching 10%, School Counseling 3%, K-12 Special Ed 7%,
School Administration 8%, Higher Ed Administration 5%,
Higher Ed Counseling 1%, Community Counseling 3%
Tuition: 1,100 (in state), 2,800 (out of state)
Financial Aid Recipients: 30%
Average Annual Housing Cost: N/A
Application Deadline: varies
Number of: applicants annually 671; applicants accepted
annually 615; students enrolled annually 382

Tests Required	Preferred/Min Score
Graduate Record Exam	800–900
National Teachers Exam	
Praxis II Exam	
TOEFL	525

WISCONSIN

Cardinal Stritch College
Teacher Education Division

6801 N. Yates Road, Milwaukee, WI 53217
Admissions: (PH)414 352-5400 x212, (FAX)414 357-7516
Dean: (PH)414 352-5400 x472
Total Enrollment: 5,000–10,000
Grad Enrollment: FTM 66, PTM 530, On campus 1%, Off
campus 99%
Program Membership: N/A
Academic Programs Available: MASTERS: Bilingual Ed.,
Early Childhood Ed., Ed. Admin, Ed. Tech., Read/Lang Arts
Ed., Spec. Ed. DOCTORATE: Bilingual Ed., Early Childhood
Ed., Ed. Admin, Ed. Tech., Read/Lang Arts Ed., Spec. Ed.
Library: College Library, 113,000 volumes
Computer Resources: Macintosh, Dual Platform, PCs,
CD-ROM, Videodisc

Research Areas	#Faculty
Adult Education	
Art Education	
Bilingual Education	2
Counselor Education	
Early Childhood Ed.	1
Ed. Admin	2
Ed. Tech.	3
Elementary Ed.	2
Foreign Lang. Ed.	
Higher Ed.	
Math Ed.	
Mid. Lev. Ed.	1
Multicultural Ed.	
Music Ed.	

Physical Ed.	
Read/Lang. Arts Ed.	4
School Counseling	
Science Ed.	
Secondary Ed.	
Soc. Studies Ed.	
Special Ed.	4
Other	

Research Institutes/Centers: Reading/Learning Center
Student Body Demographics: Average Age N/A, 76% female, 24% male
Percent Ethnic Minorities: Hispanic-American 1%, Asian-American 1%, African-American 6%, Native-American 0.5%
Geographic Representation: Midwest 100%
Graduate Career Paths: K-12 Teaching 18%, K-12 Special Ed 36%, School Administration 18%
Tuition: 270/cr (in state), 270/cr (out of state)
Financial Aid Recipients: 50%
Average Annual Housing Cost: 7,800
Application Deadline: rolling
Number of: applicants annually 300; applicants accepted annually 275; students enrolled annually 250

Tests Required	Preferred/Min Score
Graduate Record Exam	
National Teachers Exam	
Praxis II Exam	
TOEFL	600

Carroll College Graduate Program in Education

100 N. East Avenue, Waukesha, WI 53186
Admissions: (PH)800 227-7655, (FAX)414 524-7139, (EMAIL)cdaniels@ccadmin.cc.edu
Dean: (PH)414 524-7214, (FAX)414 524-7139, (EMAIL)vblack@carroll1.cc.edu
Total Enrollment: 1,000–5,000
Grad Enrollment: Off campus 100%
Program Membership: N/A
Academic Programs Available: MASTERS: Adult Ed., Elementary Ed., Multicultural Ed., Read/Lang Arts Ed., Sci. Ed., Sec. Ed., Soc. DOCTORATE: Adult Ed., Elementary Ed., Multicultural Ed., Read/Lang Arts Ed., Sci. Ed., Sec. Ed., Soc.
Library: Carrier Library, 250,000 volumes
Computer Resources: Macintosh, Dual Platform, PCs, CD-ROM, Videodisc

Research Areas	#Faculty
Adult Education	1
Art Education	
Bilingual Education	
Counselor Education	
Early Childhood Ed.	3
Ed. Admin	
Ed. Tech.	
Elementary Ed.	2
Foreign Lang. Ed.	
Higher Ed.	

Math Ed.	1
Mid. Lev. Ed.	2
Multicultural Ed.	3
Music Ed.	
Physical Ed.	
Read/Lang. Arts Ed.	1
School Counseling	
Science Ed.	1
Secondary Ed.	1
Soc. Studies Ed.	2
Special Ed.	
Other	

Research Institutes/Centers: Milwaukee Writing Project
Student Body Demographics: Average Age 35, 75% female, 25% male
Percent Ethnic Minorities: Hispanic-American 5%, African-American 7%, Native-American 2%
Geographic Representation: Midwest 100%
Graduate Career Paths: K-12 Teaching 70%, Higher Ed Teaching 10%
Tuition: 215 (in state), 215 (out of state)
Financial Aid Recipients: N/A
Average Annual Housing Cost: N/A
Application Deadline: rolling
Number of: applicants annually 25; applicants accepted annually 25; students enrolled annually 25

Tests Required	Preferred/Min Score
Graduate Record Exam	
National Teachers Exam	
Praxis II Exam	

Carthage College Graduate Program

2001 Alford Park Drive, Kenosha, WI 53140
Admissions: (PH)414 551-5924
Dean: (PH)414 551-5876, (FAX)414 551-5704
Total Enrollment: 1,000–5,000
Grad Enrollment: PTM 130
Program Membership: N/A
Academic Programs Available: MASTERS: Foreign Lang. Ed., Read/Lang Arts Ed., Sci. Ed., Soc. Ed., DOCTORATE: Foreign Lang. Ed., Read/Lang Arts Ed., Sci. Ed., Soc. Ed.
Library: John M. Ruthrauff Library, 208,000 volumes
Computer Resources: Macintosh, Dual Platform, PCs, CD-ROM, Videodisc

Research Areas	#Faculty
Adult Education	
Art Education	
Bilingual Education	
Counselor Education	
Early Childhood Ed.	
Ed. Admin	
Ed. Tech.	
Elementary Ed.	1
Foreign Lang. Ed.	2
Higher Ed.	
Math Ed.	1
Mid. Lev. Ed.	1
Multicultural Ed.	
Music Ed.	

Physical Ed.	
Read/Lang. Arts Ed.	1
School Counseling	1
Science Ed.	
Secondary Ed.	
Soc. Studies Ed.	1
Special Ed.	2
Other	

Student Body Demographics: Average Age 35, 70% female, 30% male
Percent Ethnic Minorities: Hispanic-American 5%, Asian-American 2%, African-American 5%
Geographic Representation: N/A
Graduate Career Paths: K-12 Teaching 100%
Tuition: 205 (in state), 205 (out of state)
Financial Aid Recipients: 10%
Average Annual Housing Cost: N/A
Application Deadline: rolling
Number of: applicants annually 25; applicants accepted annually 25; students enrolled annually

Tests Required	Preferred/Min Score
Graduate Record Exam	
National Teachers Exam	
Praxis II Exam	

Concordia University Wisconsin
Graduate School

12800 N. Lakeshore Drive, Mequon, WI 53097
Admissions: (PH)414 243-5700
Dean: (PH)414 243-4248, (FAX)414 243-4459, (EMAIL)jwalther@martin.cuw.edu
Total Enrollment: 1,000–5,000
Grad Enrollment: FTM 4, PTM 300, On campus 2%, Off campus 98%
Program Membership: N/A
Academic Programs Available: MASTERS: Early Childhood Ed., Ed. Admin, Elementary Ed., Read/Lang Arts Ed., DOCTORATE: Early Childhood Ed., Ed. Admin, Elementary Ed., Read/Lang Arts Ed.
Library: Rincker Library, 125,000 volumes
Computer Resources: Macintosh, Dual Platform, PCs, CD-ROM, Videodisc

Research Areas	#Faculty
Adult Education	
Art Education	
Bilingual Education	
Counselor Education	
Early Childhood Ed.	2
Ed. Admin	6
Ed. Tech.	
Elementary Ed.	3
Foreign Lang. Ed.	
Higher Ed.	
Math Ed.	
Mid. Lev. Ed.	
Multicultural Ed.	
Music Ed.	
Physical Ed.	

Read/Lang. Arts Ed.	1
School Counseling	
Science Ed.	
Secondary Ed.	
Soc. Studies Ed.	
Special Ed.	
Other	

Student Body Demographics: Average Age 27, 58% female, 42% male
Percent Ethnic Minorities: Asian-American 4%, African-American 5%
Geographic Representation: Midwest 95%, West 5%
Graduate Career Paths: K-12 Teaching 85%, K-12 School Administration 15%
Tuition: 200/hr (in state), 200/hr (out of state)
Financial Aid Recipients: 20%
Average Annual Housing Cost: 4,000
Application Deadline: 3/1; 7/1; 11/1
Number of: applicants annually 150; applicants accepted annually 130; students enrolled annually 130

Tests Required	Preferred/Min Score
Graduate Record Exam	
National Teachers Exam	
Praxis II Exam	

Mount Mary College Education Department

2900 North Menomonee River Parkway, Milwaukee, WI 53222-4597
Total Enrollment: 1,000–5,000
Grad Enrollment: PTM 125, Off campus 100%
Program Membership: N/A
Academic Programs Available: N/A
Library: Haggerty Library
Computer Resources: Macintosh, Dual Platform, PCs, CD-ROM, Videodisc

Research Areas	#Faculty
Adult Education	
Art Education	
Bilingual Education	
Counselor Education	1
Early Childhood Ed.	1
Ed. Admin	
Ed. Tech.	
Elementary Ed.	2
Foreign Lang. Ed.	
Higher Ed.	
Math Ed.	1
Mid. Lev. Ed.	
Multicultural Ed.	1
Music Ed.	
Physical Ed.	
Read/Lang. Arts Ed.	2
School Counseling	
Science Ed.	
Secondary Ed.	
Soc. Studies Ed.	
Special Ed.	
Other	

Student Body Demographics: Average Age 36, 95% female, 5% male

Percent Ethnic Minorities: Hispanic-American 2%, Asian-American 5%, African-American 5%, Native-American 2%

Geographic Representation: Midwest 100%

Tuition: 320/cr (in state), 320/cr (out of state)

Financial Aid Recipients: 2%

Average Annual Housing Cost: N/A

Application Deadline: rolling

Number of: applicants annually 30-40; applicants accepted annually 30-40; students enrolled annually N/A

Tests Required	Preferred/Min Score
Graduate Record Exam	
National Teachers Exam	
Praxis II Exam	

University of Wisconsin-Madison
School of Education

111 Education Building, 1000 Bascom Mall, Madison, WI 63706-1398

Admissions: (PH)608 262-0458, (FAX)608 265-2512, (EMAIL)jhay@macc.wisc.edu

Dean: (PH)608 262-6137, (FAX)608 265-2512, (EMAIL)hackler@macc.wisc.edu

Total Enrollment: 20,000

Grad Enrollment: FTM 338, PTM 336, FTD 492, PTD 230

Program Membership: Holmes Partnership

Academic Programs Available: MASTERS: Adult Ed., Art Ed., Bilingual Ed., Counselor Ed., Early Childhood Ed., Ed. Admin, Ed. Psych., Ed. Tech., Elementary Ed., Foreign Lang. Ed., Higher Ed., Math Ed., Mid Level Ed., Multicultural Ed., Music Ed., Physical Ed., Read/Lang Arts Ed., School Cons., Sci. Ed., Sec. Ed., DOCTORATE: Adult Ed., Art Ed., Bilingual Ed., Counselor Ed., Early Childhood Ed., Ed. Admin, Ed. Psych., Ed. Tech., Elementary Ed., Foreign Lang. Ed., Higher Ed., Math Ed., Mid Level Ed., Multicultural Ed., Music Ed., Physical Ed., Read/Lang Arts Ed., School Cons., Sci. Ed., Sec. Ed.

Library: Instructional Materials, 55,000 volumes

Computer Resources: Macintosh, Dual Platform, PCs, CD-ROM, Videodisc

Research Areas	#Faculty
Adult Education	12
Art Education	1
Bilingual Education	5
Counselor Education	12
Early Childhood Ed.	6
Ed. Admin	13
Ed. Tech.	3
Elementary Ed.	18
Foreign Lang. Ed.	4
Higher Ed.	3
Math Ed.	7
Mid. Lev. Ed.	2
Multicultural Ed.	10
Music Ed.	3
Physical Ed.	16

Read/Lang. Arts Ed.	8
School Counseling	12
Science Ed.	4
Secondary Ed.	4
Soc. Studies Ed.	6
Special Ed.	8
Other	41

Research Institutes/Centers: Wisconsin Center for Education Research, Center on Education and Work

Student Body Demographics: Average Age 30, 68% female, 32% male

Percent Ethnic Minorities: Hispanic-American 4%, Asian-American 2%, African-American 3%, Native-American 1%

Geographic Representation: Midwest 68%

Graduate Career Paths: K-12 Teaching 5.6%, Higher Ed Teaching 44.6%, School Counseling 5.6%, K-12 Special Ed 1%, School Administration 24%, Higher Ed Administration 1%, Higher Ed Counseling 1%, Community Counseling 8.5%

Tuition: 3,858 (in state), 11704 (out of state)

Financial Aid Recipients: 30%

Average Annual Housing Cost: 5,400

Application Deadline: varies

Number of: applicants annually 1,520; applicants accepted annually 417; students enrolled annually N/A

Tests Required	Preferred/Min Score
Graduate Record Exam	
National Teachers Exam	
Praxis II Exam	
TOEFL	580

University of Wisconsin-Milwaukee
School of Education

Graduate School, 3203 N. Downer Ave., Milwaukee, WI 53211

Admissions: (FAX)414 229-6967

Dean: (PH)414 229-4181, (FAX)414 229-6548

Total Enrollment: 20,000

Grad Enrollment: FTM 113, PTM 503, FTD 38, PTD 116

Program Membership: Holmes Partnership

Academic Programs Available: MASTERS: Adult Ed., Art Ed., Bilingual Ed., Counselor Ed., Early Childhood Ed., Ed. Admin, Ed. Psych., Elementary Ed., Foreign Lang. Ed., Math Ed., Mid Level Ed., Multicultural Ed., Read/Lang Arts Ed., School Cons., Sci. Ed., Sec. Ed., Soc. Ed., Spec. Ed. DOCTORATE: Adult Ed., Art Ed., Bilingual Ed., Counselor Ed., Early Childhood Ed., Ed. Admin, Ed. Psych., Elementary Ed., Foreign Lang. Ed., Math Ed., Mid Level Ed., Multicultural Ed., Read/Lang Arts Ed., School Cons., Sci. Ed., Sec. Ed., Soc. Ed., Spec. Ed.

Library: Golda Meir Library, 3.7 million volumes

Computer Resources: Macintosh, Dual Platform, PCs, CD-ROM, Videodisc

Research Areas	#Faculty
Adult Education	
Art Education	
Bilingual Education	

Counselor Education
Early Childhood Ed.
Ed. Admin
Ed. Tech.
Elementary Ed.
Foreign Lang. Ed.
Higher Ed.
Math Ed.
Mid. Lev. Ed.
Multicultural Ed.
Music Ed.
Physical Ed.
Read/Lang. Arts Ed.
School Counseling
Science Ed.
Secondary Ed.
Soc. Studies Ed.
Special Ed.
Other

Research Institutes/Centers: Center for Great Lakes Studies, Center for Latin America, Center for Twentieth Century Studies

Student Body Demographics: Average Age 36, 72% female, 28% male

Percent Ethnic Minorities: Hispanic-American 25%, Asian-American 4%, African-American 65%

Geographic Representation: N/A

Tuition: 2,070 (in state), 6,172 (out of state)

Financial Aid Recipients: N/A

Average Annual Housing Cost: 2,345

Application Deadline: 1/1; 9/1

Number of: applicants annually N/A; applicants accepted annually N/A; students enrolled annually N/A

Tests Required	Preferred/Min Score
Graduate Record Exam	
National Teachers Exam	
Praxis II Exam	
TOEFL	550

University of Wisconsin-Stevens Point School of Education

Graduate Advising, Rm 438, CPS Building, Stevens Point, WI 54481

Admissions: (PH)715 346-4403, (FAX)715 346-4846, (EMAIL)d1smith@uwspmail.uwsp.edu

Dean: (PH)715 346-4430, (FAX)715 346-4846

Total Enrollment: 5,000–10,000

Grad Enrollment: PTM 1,000, Off campus 100%

Program Membership: N/A

Academic Programs Available: MASTERS: Bilingual Ed., Counselor Ed., Early Childhood Ed., Ed. Admin, Elementary Ed., Foreign Lang. Ed., Math Ed., Mid Level Ed., Music Ed., Physical Ed., Read/Lang Arts Ed., School Cons., Sci. Ed., DOCTORATE: Bilingual Ed., Counselor Ed., Early Childhood Ed., Ed. Admin, Elementary Ed., Foreign Lang. Ed., Math Ed., Mid Level Ed., Music Ed., Physical Ed., Read/Lang Arts Ed., School Cons., Sci.

Library: Albertson Learning Resources Center, 351,000 volumes

Computer Resources: Macintosh, Dual Platform, PCs, CD-ROM, Videodisc

Research Areas	#Faculty
Adult Education	
Art Education	5
Bilingual Education	4
Counselor Education	6
Early Childhood Ed.	2
Ed. Admin	
Ed. Tech.	
Elementary Ed.	6
Foreign Lang. Ed.	4
Higher Ed.	
Math Ed.	3
Mid. Lev. Ed.	1
Multicultural Ed.	
Music Ed.	10
Physical Ed.	6
Read/Lang. Arts Ed.	3
School Counseling	6
Science Ed.	1
Secondary Ed.	1
Soc. Studies Ed.	1
Special Ed.	4
Other	15

Student Body Demographics: Average Age 26, 65% female, 35% male

Percent Ethnic Minorities: African-American 1%, Native-American 1%

Geographic Representation: Midwest 99%

Graduate Career Paths: K-12 Teaching 67%, School Counseling 1%, K-12 Special Ed 25%, School Administration 1%

Tuition: 172/hr (in state), 498/hr (out of state)

Financial Aid Recipients: N/A

Average Annual Housing Cost: N/A

Application Deadline: 3/15; 10/15; 7/15

Number of: applicants annually 100; applicants accepted annually 95; students enrolled annually N/A

Tests Required	Preferred/Min Score
Graduate Record Exam	
National Teachers Exam	
Praxis II Exam	

WYOMING

University of Wyoming College of Education

The Graduate School, P.O. Box 3108, Laramie, WY 32071

Admissions: (PH)307 766-2287, (FAX)307 766-4042, (EMAIL)cmendoza@uwyo.edu

Dean: (PH)307 766-3145, (FAX)307 766-6668, (EMAIL)jlebsack@uwyo.edu

Total Enrollment: 10,000–20,000
Grad Enrollment: FTM 20, PTM 120, FTD 35, PTD 35, On campus 90%, Off campus 10%
Program Membership: Holmes Partnership, NNER
Academic Programs Available: MASTERS: Adult Ed., Counselor Ed., Early Childhood Ed., Ed. Admin, Ed. Tech., Elementary Ed., Math Ed., Mid Level Ed., Multicultural Ed., School Cons., Sci. Ed., Sec. Ed., Soc. Ed., DOCTORATE: Adult Ed., Counselor Ed., Early Childhood Ed., Ed. Admin, Ed. Tech., Elementary Ed., Math Ed., Mid Level Ed., Multicultural Ed., School Cons., Sci. Ed., Sec. Ed., Soc. Ed.
Library: Coe Library, 1.1 million volumes
Computer Resources: Macintosh, Dual Platform, PCs, CD-ROM, Videodisc

Research Areas	#Faculty
Adult Education	5
Art Education	
Bilingual Education	
Counselor Education	5
Early Childhood Ed.	2
Ed. Admin	4
Ed. Tech.	4
Elementary Ed.	18
Foreign Lang. Ed.	
Higher Ed.	
Math Ed.	2
Mid. Lev. Ed.	2
Multicultural Ed.	2
Music Ed.	
Physical Ed.	
Read/Lang. Arts Ed.	4
School Counseling	
Science Ed.	2
Secondary Ed.	2
Soc. Studies Ed.	2
Special Ed.	5
Other	

Student Body Demographics: Average Age 36, 44% female, 56% male
Percent Ethnic Minorities: Hispanic-American 3%, Asian-American 1%, Native-American 0.5%
Geographic Representation: Midwest 5%, West 94%
Graduate Career Paths: K-12 Teaching 50%, School Counseling 5%, K-12 Special Ed 10%, School Administration 25%, Community Counseling 10%
Tuition: 1,212 (in state), 3,408 (out of state)
Financial Aid Recipients: 20%
Average Annual Housing Cost: 2,300
Application Deadline: 4/1; 6/1; 10/1
Number of: applicants annually 200; applicants accepted annually 150; students enrolled annually 125

Tests Required	Preferred/Min Score
Graduate Record Exam	9000–1,000
National Teachers Exam	
Praxis II Exam	
TOEFL	525

ADDRESSES FOR STATE OFFICES OF CERTIFICATION

Alabama
Certification Office
State Department of Education
P. O. Box 302101
Montgomery, AL 36130-2101
(205) 242-9977

Alaska
Certification Analyst
Department of Education
801 West 10th Street, Suite 200
Juneau, AK 99801-1894
(907) 465-2831

Arizona
Teacher Certification Unit-016
P. O. Box 25609
1535 West Jefferson
Phoenix, AZ 85002
(602) 542-4368

Arkansas
Teacher Education & Licensure
State Department of Education
4 State Capitol Mall
Little Rock, AR 72201-1071
(501) 682-4342

California
Commission on Teacher Credentialing
Box 944270
Sacramento, CA 94244-7000
(916) 445-7254

Colorado
Teacher Certification
State Department of Education
201 East Colfax Avenue
Denver, CO 80203
(303) 866-6628

Connecticut
Bureau of Certification and Professional Development
State Department of Education
Box 2219
Hartford, CT 06145-2219
(203) 566-5201

Delaware
Teacher Certification
Department of Public Instruction
P. O. Box
1402 Dover, DE 19903
(302) 739-4688

District of Columbia
Teacher Education and Certification Branch
Logan Administration Building
215 G Street, N. E.
Room 101A
Washington, D.C. 20002
(202) 724-4246

Florida
Bureau of Teacher Certification
Florida Education Center
325 W. Gaines, Room 201
Tallahassee, FL 32399
(904) 488-2317

Georgia
Professional Standards Commission
Certification Section
1452 Twin Towers East
Atlanta, GA 30334
(404) 657-9000

Hawaii
State of Hawaii
Department of Education
Office of Personnel Services
P. O. Box 2360
Honolulu, HI 96804
(808) 586-3420

Idaho
Certification Division
State Department of Education
L. B. Jordan Office Building
Boise, ID 83720-3650
(208) 334-3475

Illinois
Illinois State Board of Education
Certification & Placement Section
100 N. First Street
Springfield, IL 62777
(217) 782-4321

Indiana
Indiana Professional Standards Board
Teacher Licensing
251 East Ohio Street, Suite 201
Indianapolis, IN 46204-2133
(317) 232-9010

Iowa
Board of Educational Examiners
Grimes State Office Building
Des Moines, IA 50319-0147
(515) 281-3245

Kansas
Certification Specialist
Kansas State Department of Education
Kansas State Education Building
120 East 10th Street
Topeka, KS 66612-1182
(913) 296-2288

Kentucky
Kentucky Department of Education
Division of Certification
18th Floor-Capital Plaza Tower
500 Mero Street
Frankfort, KY 40601
(502)564-4606

Louisiana
Louisiana Department of Education
P. O. Box 94064
Baton Rouge, LA 70804-9064
(504) 342-3490

Maine
Division of Certification and Placement
Department of Education
State House Station 23
Augusta, ME 04333
(207) 287-5944

Maryland
Department of Certification 18100
State Department of Education
200 West Baltimore Street
Baltimore, MD 21201
(301) 333-2142

Massachusetts
Massachusetts Department of Education
Office of Teacher Certification and Credentialing
350 Main Street
Malden, MA 02148
(617) 388-3380

Michigan
Teacher Preparation & Certification
Michigan Department of Education
P. O. Box 30008
Lansing, MI 48909
(517) 373-3310

Minnesota
Teacher Licensing
State Department of Education
616 Capitol Square Building
St. Paul, MN 55101
(612) 296-2046

Mississippi
Teacher Certification
State Department of Education
Box 771
Jackson, MS 39205-0771
(601) 359-3483

Missouri
Teacher Certification
Department of Elementary and Secondary Education
P. O. Box 480
Jefferson City, MO 65102
(314) 751-3847

Montana
Teacher Certification
Office of Public Instruction
P. O. Box 202501
Helena, MT 59620-2501
(406) 444-3150

Nebraska
Teacher Certification
State Department of Education
301 Centennial Mall South
Box 94987
Lincoln, NE 68509-4987
(800) 371-4642

Nevada
Nevada Department of Education
State Mail Room
1850 E. Sahara, Suite 200
Las Vegas, NV 89158
(702) 386-5401

New Hampshire
Bureau of Credentialing
State Department of Education
101 Pleasant Street
Concord, NH 03301
(603) 271-2407

New Jersey
Office of Licensing and Academic Credentials
CN 503
Trenton, NJ 08625-0503
(609) 292-2070

New Mexico
Director
Professional Licensure Unit
Education Building
300 Don Gaspar
Santa Fe, NM 87501-2786
(505) 827-6587

New York
Office of Teaching
University of the State of New York
State Education Department
Albany, NY 12230
(518) 474-3901

Buffalo Board of Education
City Hall
65 Niagara Square
Buffalo, NY 14202
(716) 842-4646

North Carolina
Licensure Section
State Department of Public Instruction
Raleigh, NC 27601-2825
(919) 733-4125

North Dakota
Director of Certification
State Department of Public Instruction
Bismarck, ND 58505-0440
(701) 328-2264

Ohio
Teacher Education and Certification
State Department of Education
65 South Front Street
Room 416
Columbus, OH 43215-4183
(614) 466-3593

Oklahoma
Professional Standards
State Department of Education
2500 N. Lincoln Blvd.
Room 211
Oklahoma City, OK 73105-4599
(405) 521-3337

Oregon
Teacher Standards and Practices Commission
255 Capitol Street, N. E.
Suite 105
Salem, OR 97310-13332
(503) 378-3586

Pennsylvania
Bureau of Certification
Department of Education
333 Market Street
Harrisburg, PA 17126-0333
(717) 787-2967

Rhode Island
Office of Teacher Certification
State Department of Education
22 Hayes Street
Providence, RI 02908
(401) 277-2675

South Carolina
Office of Education Professions
Teacher Certification Section
1015 Rutledge Building
Columbia, SC 29201
(803) 774-8466

South Dakota
Teacher Education and Certification
Department of Education
700 Governors Drive
Pierre, SD 57501-2291
(605) 773-3553

Tennessee
Office of Teacher Education and Accreditation
6th Floor, Gateway Plaza
710 Robertson Parkway
Nashville, TN 37243-0375
(615) 741-1644

Texas
Texas Education Agency
1701 North Congress Ave.
Austin, TX 78701-1494
(512) 463-8976

Utah
Certification and Personnel Development Section
State Board of Education
250 East 500 South Street
Salt Lake City, UT 84111
(801)538-7740

Vermont
Licensing Office
Department of Education
120 State Street
Montpelier, VT 05602-2703
(802) 828-2445

Virginia
Office of Professional Licensure
Department of Education
P. O. Box 2120
Richmond, VA 23216-2120
(804) 225-2022

Washington
Professional Education and Certification
Superintendent of Public Instruction
Old Capitol Building
P. O. Box 47200
Olympia, WA 98504-7200
(206) 753-6773

West Virginia
State Department of Education
Building 6, Room 337
1900 Kanawha Blvd., East
Charleston, WV 25305-0330
(800) 982-2378

Wisconsin
Teacher Education, Licensing and Placement
Box 7841
Madison, WI 53707-7841
(608) 266-1027

Wyoming
Professional Teaching Standards Board
2300 Capitol Avenue
Hathaway Building, 2nd Floor
Cheyenne, WY 82002
(307) 777-7291

MASTER INDEX

University of Pittsburgh, 123
University of Rio Grande, 109
University of South Alabama, 9
University of South Carolina, 127
University of South Florida, 31
University of Southern Mississippi, 72
University of Tennessee, 130
University of Toledo, 110
University of Vermont, 140
University of Wisconsin (Madison), 151
University of Wisconsin (Milwaukee), 151
Utah State University, 139
Virginia Commonwealth University, 145
Wayne State University, 69

Bilingual Education

Adelphi University, 85
Arizona State University, 10
Bank Street College, 85
Boise State University, 36
Boston University, 59
California State University, San Bernardino, 13
California State Polytechnic University, Pomona, 14
California State University, Stanislaus, 14
California State University, Sacramento, 15
California State University, Dominguez Hills, 15
Cardinal Stritch College, 148
College of Santa Fe, 83
Concordia University, 37
Eastern College, 115
George Mason University, 141
Hofstra University, 89
Immaculata College, 116
Jersey City State College, 81
LaSalle University, 118
Long Island University-Brooklyn, 91
National-Louis University, 40
New Mexico State University, 84
New York University, 91
Point Loma Nazarene College, 18
Rhode Island College, 124
Rutgers University, 82
San Jose State University, 18
Seton Hall University, 82
St. Cloud State University, 70
Stanford University, 19
State University of New York at New Paltz, 94
State University of New York at Stony Brook, 95

Teachers College, Columbia University, 97
Texas A&M University, 132
Texas Wesleyan University, 133
Texas Woman's University, 134
University at Albany, SUNY, 98
University of Alabama, 8
University of Arizona, 11
University of California, Los Angeles, 20
University of California, Riverside, 21
University of Colorado (Boulder), 23
University of Colorado (Denver), 24
University of Connecticut, 26
University of Kansas, 51
University of Maryland, Baltimore County, 56
University of Miami, 31
University of Mississippi, 72
University of Montana, 77
University of New Mexico, 84
University of Pennsylvania, 122
University of Pittsburgh, 123
University of Rochester, 99
University of San Diego, 22
University of Southern Mississippi, 72
University of Tennessee, 130
University of Texas (El Paso), 136
University of Texas (San Antonio), 137
University of Wisconsin (Madison), 151
University of Wisconsin (Milwaukee), 151
University of Wisconsin (Stevens Point), 152
Washington State University, 147
Wayne State University, 69

Counselor Education

Andrews University, 64
Appalachian State University, 100
Arizona State University, 10
Arkansas State University, 11
Auburn University, 7
Boston College, 58
Boston University, 59
Bridgewater State College, 59
Brigham Young University, 138
Butler University, 44
California State University, San Bernardino, 13
California State University, Sacramento, 15
California State University, Dominguez Hills, 15
Campbell University, 100
Canisius College, 86
Central Michigan University, 65
Central Missouri State University, 73

The Citadel, 127
Clemson University, 126
Cleveland State University, 105
College of St. Rose, 87
College of William and Mary, 141
Concordia University, 37
Duquesne University, 115
East Carolina University, 101
East Texas State University, 132
Eastern College, 115
Eastern Illinois University, 38
Eastern Michigan University, 65
Emporia State University, 50
Florida Atlantic University, 29
Florida State University, 29
Fort Hays State University, 51
George Mason University, 141
Georgia Southern University, 34
Georgia State University, 34
Gonzaga University, 146
Gwynedd Mercy College, 116
Immaculata College, 116
Indiana University of Pennsylvania, 117
Indiana University (South Bend), 45
Indiana University-Purdue University, 45
Indiana University (Southeast), 46
Iowa State University, 49
Jackson State University, 71
James Madison University, 142
Kent State University, 106
Kutztown University, 117
Lehigh University, 118
Lesley College, 61
Lindenwood College, 74
Long Island University-Brooklyn, 91
Loyola College, 55
Loyola University, 39
Lynchburg College, 143
Malone College, 106
Marshall University, 148
Marywood University, 119
Michigan State University, 66
Mississippi State University, 71
Montana State University, 76
Montana State University, Northern, 77
New Mexico State University, 84
New York University, 91
Niagara University, 92
North Carolina State University, 102
Northeast Louisiana University, 53
Northern Illinois University, 40
Northern State University, 128
Northwestern Oklahoma State University, 110
Ohio State University, 108
Ohio University, 108
Oklahoma State University, 111
Oregon State University, 113
Pennsylvania State University, 120

Early Childhood Education

Educational Administration

Educational Psychology

Educational Technology

Vanderbilt University, 131
Virginia Commonwealth University, 145
Virginia Polytechnic Institute & State University, 145
Wayne State University, 69

Elementary Education

Adelphi University, 85
American International College, 57
Anderson University, 43
Andrews University, 64
Anna Maria College, 58
Appalachian State University, 100
Arizona State University, 10
Arizona State University-West, 10
Arkansas State University, 11
Auburn University, 7
Bank Street College, 85
Binghamton University, 86
Boston College, 58
Boston University, 59
Bridgewater State College, 59
Brigham Young University, 138
Butler University, 44
California State University, San Bernardino, 13
California State University, Stanislaus, 14
Campbell University, 100
Canisius College, 86
Carroll College, 149
Catholic University of America, 27
Central Michigan University, 65
Central Missouri State University, 73
Christopher Newport University, 140
The Citadel, 127
Clemson University, 126
Cleveland State University, 105
Coastal Carolina University, 126
Coe College, 47
College of St. Rose, 87
College of St. Joseph, 139
College of Staten Island, 88
College of William and Mary, 141
Columbia International University, 126
Concordia University (Wisconsin), 150
Dominican College, 16
Drake University, 48
Drexel University, 114
Duquesne University, 115
East Carolina University, 101
East Texas State University, 132
Eastern College, 115
Eastern Illinois University, 38
Eastern Michigan University, 65
Elon College, 101
Fitchburg State College, 60

Florida Atlantic University, 29
Florida State University, 29
Fort Hays State University, 51
George Fox College, 113
George Mason University, 141
George Washington University, 28
Gonzaga University, 146
Hastings College, 78
Henderson State University, 12
Hofstra University, 89
Immaculata College, 116
Indiana University of Pennsylvania, 117
Indiana University (South Bend), 45
Indiana University-Purdue University, 45
Indiana University (Southeast), 46
Iona College, 90
Iowa State University, 49
Jackson State University, 71
Jersey City State College, 81
Kent State University, 106
Kutztown University, 117
LaSalle University, 118
Lehigh University, 118
Lemoyne College, 90
Lesley College, 61
Liberty University, 143
Lindenwood College, 74
Long Island University-Brooklyn, 91
Loyola College, 55
Malone College, 106
Marshall University, 148
Maryville University, 74
Marywood University, 119
Miami University, 107
Mississippi State University, 71
Montana State University, Northern, 77
Morehead State University, 52
National-Louis University, 40
New Mexico State University, 84
New York University, 91
Niagara University, 92
North Carolina State University, 102
Northeast Louisiana University, 53
Northeastern University, 61
Northern Illinois University, 40
Northern State University, 128
Northwestern Oklahoma State University, 110
Northwestern University, 41
Oakland University, 67
Oglethorpe University, 35
Ohio State University, 108
Ohio University, 108
Oklahoma State University, 111
Oral Roberts University, 112
Oregon State University, 113
Pennsylvania State University, 120
Pepperdine University, 17
Point Loma Nazarene College, 18

Purdue University, 46
Rhode Island College, 124
Rivier College, 79
Roosevelt University, 42
Rowan College, 81
Rutgers University, 82
Salem College, 102
Salve Regina University, 125
San Francisco State University, 18
San Jose State University, 18
Seton Hill College, 121
Shippensburg University, 121
Simmons College, 62
Southeastern Louisiana University, 54
Southern Connecticut State University, 25
Southern Nazarene College, 112
Southwest Missouri State University, 75
Southwest State University, 69
Springfield College, 62
St. Cloud State University, 70
St. John's University, 93
St. Joseph's University, 122
State University of New York at Buffalo, 94
State University of New York at New Paltz, 94
State University of New York at Fredonia, 95
State University of New York at Potsdam, 96
State University of New York at Oswego, 96
Teachers College, Columbia University, 97
Temple University, 122
Texas Tech University, 133
Texas Wesleyan University, 133
Texas Woman's University, 134
Trinity College, 28
Tufts University, 63
Union University, 130
University of Alabama, 8
University of Arizona, 11
University of Arkansas, 12
University of California, Berkeley, 21
University of California, Los Angeles, 20
University of California, Santa Barbara, 22
University of Central Arkansas, 13
University of Central Florida, 30
University of Cincinnati, 109
University of Colorado (Boulder), 23
University of Colorado (Denver), 24
University of Connecticut, 26
University of Dayton, 109
University of Detroit-Mercy, 67
University of Florida, 30
University of Georgia, 36

Foreign Language Education

Higher Education

Mathematics Education

Middle Level Education

Multicultural Education

Reading and Language Arts

School Counseling

Secondary Education

Social Studies Education

Special Education